Introduction to Cognition and Communication

Introduction to Cognition and Communication

Keith Stenning, Alex Lascarides, and Jo Calder

A Bradford Book

The MIT Press
Cambridge, Massachusetts
London, England

MIT Press books may be purchased at special quantity discounts for business or sales promotional use. For information, please email special_sales@mitpress.mit.edu or write to Special Sales Department, The MIT Press, 55 Hayward Street, Cambridge, MA 02142.

This book was set in Times by the author using the LATEX document preparation system and was printed and bound in the United States of America.

Library of Congress Cataloging-in-Publication Data

Stenning, Keith
Introduction to cognition and communication / Keith Stenning, Alex Lascarides, and Jo Calder.
  p. cm.
"A Bradford Book."
Includes bibliographical references and index.
ISBN 0-262-19538-0 (alk. paper)
1. Communication. 2. Cognitive science. I. Lascarides, Alex. II. Calder, Jo. III. Title.

P91.S736 2006
302.2—dc22
                                                            2005049126

10 9 8 7 6 5 4 3 2 1

Contents

Preface

This book grew out of a course, and the course grew out of a very particular set of intellectual and institutional needs. The Centre for Cognitive Science was a department founded in 1969 (with the name, later changed, of "Epistemics") and that department initially taught only graduate-level courses in the interdisciplinary study of cognition. In 1994, we sought to extend the Centre's teaching into the undergraduate syllabus. It would have been possible to "start at the end" and teach final-year undergraduates a specialized course. Instead we decided to teach an introductory "service" course open to students from any department in the university.

We did this because the disciplines involved (linguistics, logic, AI, philosophy, and psychology) are all subjects that are not much taught in high school, and we wanted to put on a course that would give students from any background a grounding in how these disciplines combined to provide interdisciplinary theories of human communication.

This goal meant that surveying the various literatures was not really an option. Instead, we would have to isolate only a few topics for study, chosen on the basis that they brought several disciplines to bear on a single phenomena involving human communication. Our intention was to explore these few topics in some depth from several disciplinary angles.

We were assured by some that this would not work—how can students learn to put together several disciplines before they have been inducted into any discipline? Our view is that students start out with an interest in certain problems, and are often baffled by the way that different disciplines slice these problems up. In Edinburgh, the various relevant disciplines (Psychology, Philosophy, Artificial Intelligence, Computer Science, and Linguistics) are housed in departments with some miles between them. These kinds of distances between departments in the humanities and the sciences are not unusual in any university, even campus-based ones. And students bouncing between departments sometimes find a radical translation problem between the languages spoken on the different sides.

We felt that a "service" course that examined the difference in perspectives was what was needed. How much easier for the student if we started with target problems and tried to show how the various disciplines developed their distinctive views, and how those views relate, or fail to relate. This can serve two kinds of student: ones who would never pursue any of these disciplines any further, at least giving them an insight into some of the concepts underlying modern scientific treatments of human mental processes, and the technology that is all around them; and another group who might actually discover that one or more of these disciplines could be what they wanted to pursue. They would then have a rational basis for selecting their direction.

The course can, with different surrounding environments, be taught at a number of different levels. Certainly first year nonspecialist students have demonstrated that they can come to grips with this material. For them we have kept intratext references to a minimum and listed further readings at the end of each chapter. We have included some suggestions about how to go about studying this material. There is a website with multiple choice questions intended mainly as a study aid for such students (see `http://www.inf.ed.ac.uk/teaching/classes/hc1h` for a number of teaching resources that accompany this book, including slides). But it would not be difficult for lecturers to supplement this book with readings that would take any of the topics covered here into as much depth as desired (again, some leads in this direction are supplied at the end of each chapter). We have taught large parts of this course at the masters level to interdisciplinary classes of students, many of whom already know their own discipline's treatments of these topics. None have complained that the duplication has been mere redundancy, and some have commented that hearing the other perspectives on the same topic can be a source of ideas for their own research.

The course was a team effort from the start, and the book even more so. The author order is reverse alphabetical. Although the first author started the whole process off, each of the authors is an equal contributor to the text. We of course owe huge debts: first and foremost to the several years of students who have taken the course. Their feedback has substantially reshaped the end product. We also owe a debt of gratitude to our colleagues who supported the course, without which the book would not have happened, particularly to Jon Oberlander and John Lee who have taught the course in our periodical absences and to the many tutors (too numerous to mention individually)—their suggestions and feedback have greatly influenced the way this book is written. We would like to thank the reviewers for MIT Press, especially Georgia Green, whose detailed comments significantly improved the quality of the text. We are also indebted to the several editors and copy editors at MIT Press who made this book possible. And we apologize for delivering the final manuscript four years late! Last, but definitely not least, we would like to thank all staff at the Human Communication Research Centre at the University of Edinburgh for their support and encouragement over the years and for providing such a collegial and stimulating environment in which to do teaching and research.

We end with some remarks about the form of this book:

Conventions We use the following conventions in these notes. When we use a word or words as an example, we will write them like this: *Two dogs barked*. That style of typeface is also used to *emphasize* words in the text. A '?' preceeding a sentence indicates that that sentence is judged to sound odd. We will introduce technical terms in the following way: SYSTEMATICITY.

Exercises At a number of places below, we include exercises. Attempting the exercises may help you to improve your understanding. If you don't have time to complete the exercises, just making sure that you understand what each exercise is asking will be of benefit to you.

Experiments and intuitions Often we want you to reflect on your opinion on a particular claim, or to try a small psychological experiment on yourself. In some cases, reading ahead without thinking about the problem or doing the experiment may spoil the intuition you have about a problem, or may mean that you know what the "correct" result is.

Citations and References As we mentioned above, we have kept citations in the running text to an absolute minimum. Instead, at the end of each chapter, we have included a section entitled *Further Reading*, where we give details of not only the original references where content presented in the chapter first appeared, but also details of how one can follow up certain topics in more depth.

Glossary and Index An integrated glossary and index is supplied as appendix C. This is intended to help those readers who don't read the book from cover to cover to come to grips with the jargon. The glossary gives the page reference where the term in question was first introduced and defined; on occasion, the glossary itself will also include a short definition of the term in question. The index supplements this glossary with the page references where the various topics are discussed.

I PEOPLE COMMUNICATING—EXAMPLES

1 Communication and Cognitive Science

Human communication labels a rather wide range of phenomena: conversation, correspondence, lectures, theater, music, literature, painting, sculpture, maps, mass-media, advertising, propaganda, design, therapy, teaching/learning, fashion, dancing, decorating, religious rituals . . . . Communication is involved in all of these things and many more. There is not much in the way of human doings that does not involve communication, or cannot be construed as communication—very little that can be understood *without* understanding some communication. One consequence is that this book is a case of its own subject matter, a fact that will surface at various points.

In order to begin narrowing down the perspective we are going to take, two metaphors or analogies for communication are useful. Metaphors can help us abstract across this wide range of phenomena. These two contrasting metaphors help to understand two perspectives on communication: PHATIC and IDEATIONAL.

The first concentrates on communication as establishment of COMMUNITY—how communication defines group identities. The second concentrates on the transfer of ideas. These two major perspectives dominate sociological and cognitive approaches to communication respectively. Although this book emphasizes the latter perspective, don't forget the other.

Some would claim that the findings of these two approaches to communication are incompatible—that computational models of mind are inconsistent with the construction of social realities by intentional human beings. We would absolutely reject those claims of inconsistency. There are many interesting issues about how the two kinds of theory fit together in accounting for communication, but we can only scratch the surface of those issues at a few points in this book. However, it is still worth beginning with a warning that expecting cognitive science to give sociological answers can lead to unnecessary confusion.

Although we will only establish a few links to sociological issues in this book, cognitive science is an *interdisciplinary* approach which has ingredients from several disciplines. Understanding something about academic disciplines and the history of their breeding helps to understand this book's model of communication.

1.1   The Transport of Ideas vs. Resonance—Two Metaphors for Communication

One analogy for communication, probably the overwhelmingly dominant analogy in cognitive science, is to think of communication and the transfer of information as the transfer of physical things from person to person. In fact this analogy is so compelling that we need to pause to see that it is at best obliquely true. Sometimes communication involves the transfer of physical objects such as letters in envelopes from person to person, but more often it does not. We speak by disturbing the pressure of the air, and sound waves travel from speaker to hearer. But when communication has been achieved, the hearer does not *have* the waves in the way that the receiver of the letter has the letter.

Nevertheless, energy has to pass from sender to receiver (the light energy involved in reading and writing, the sound energy in speaking and hearing, and the amazing array of energies involved in complex modern communication technologies). Only telepathy is unlike telegraphy in involving no energy in information transmission. Perhaps because of this flow of energy, we tend to reinterpret our transmission analogy for communication at a more abstract level. If we cannot make too much sense out of thinking about what physical thing or energy speech transfers, then we reinterpret our analogy at the level of ideas. The speaker has an idea and disturbs the air in certain ways that are decoded by the hearer so that now the hearer has the same idea—the idea is what travels from head to head when the hearer "gets it."

We will see this analogy repeatedly in what follows. Like most analogies, it contains much truth, and it is probably essential to our understanding, but like most analogies, it is capable of overinterpretation. Analogies, by definition, are relations between phenomena that are like in some respects and unlike in others. Electric current is like water flowing in a pipe *in some respects*. So close is the analogy in these respects that familiar hydraulics can be used to teach unfamiliar relations between volts, amps, and ohms. But equally, water flowing in a pipe is quite unlike electricity. Electricity cannot be dirty; it has no weight; it does not rumble due to turbulence. The value of the analogy is also that water is *not* like electricity. If it were exactly like electricity it would be as unfamiliar and incomprehensible, and would be useless for teaching about electricity. It is generally unclear where analogies leave off. When it is exactly clear in what aspects one phenomenon resembles the other, then the relation can be mathematized and becomes a precise theory rather than analogy. Scientific theories start as undefined analogies and gradually become precise.

So when we catch ourselves thinking of communication as physical transfer, and ideas as a sort of abstract stuff transferred, then we need to think hard about which parts of this analogy fit and which are misleading. Communicating ideas is not just like transferring envelopes. Anyone can transfer an envelope to anyone else who will have it. Physical transfer places no restriction on the shared knowledge that is required for communication. If the recipient does not speak the language of the letter, or cannot read, or is in a place and time that they cannot relate to the place and time of the letter's sending, or they misunderstand the writer's intentions, or have an entirely different set of cultural beliefs, communication will not succeed even when the post office has done its job. The transfer metaphor tends to focus on the physical signal (sound, light, ...) at the expense of the required shared knowledge.

Our second common analogy for communication is a valuable antidote to the misunderstandings that result from thinking in terms of transporting idea-stuff. It is perhaps less prominent in our talk of communication, or perhaps it is just less prominent in cognitive scientists' thinking about communication. This is the analogy of RESONANCE. Physical systems vibrate with a natural resonant frequency, and transfer energy to other systems that happen to share the same natural resonant frequency, causing them to vibrate too. The soprano who shatters the glass is merely overdoing it a bit.

This analogy is as incomplete as any other analogy—perhaps more than most—but it captures just the aspect of communication that the transport-of-information analogy leaves out. Senders and receivers have to share a great deal in common before communication will work. And the result of communication is the establishment of a community of people who share something—in this analogy not a parcel of information but a common resonance. One reason why the analogy of resonance is so useful an antidote to the ruling communication-as-transport idea is that there are so many paradigm cases of communication for which it is far from clear just what the idea is that is shared after communication has taken place.

The anthropologist Malinowskiwriting in the 1920s coined the term

PHATIC communication as distinct from what he called IDEATIONAL communication to describe this kind of communication that functions to establish community but is not easily explained in terms of the transfer of information. The paradigm cases of phatic communication are ritual and fashion. Hem lines rise and fall, and with them the fortunes of an international industry. People are ostracized, or worse, from some groups because the distance of the hem to the knee is wrong. Wearing this as opposed to that communicates. Headscarves can indicate religious affiliations.

But why? We might try to reanalyze this phenomenon in terms of ideational communication by incorporating the apparatus of symbolism. Perhaps rising hemlines symbolise the PROPOSITION that the wearer is sexually available. Such an analysis may or may not bear some grain of truth, but it has caused many problems, both practical and theoretical. In fact the alternative symbolic analysis that rising hemlines in the population means that the wearer is less sexually available, for a given degree of exposure, might be a better fit to the data. But there seems something quite intellectually simplistic as well as distasteful about trying to turn this communication into these propositions.

The problem is not that fashion dispenses with the transmission of information. We have to see the hemline to get the message. There is the same requirement for energy transmission as in the more obviously ideational cases we have considered so far. Not even the 21st century post-modernist fashion industry has managed to sell clothes that remain unseen in the wardrobe. But if we analyze the information that is transmitted literally as "his cuffs are N inches above the ankle" we are left with the puzzle about why this is significant. After all, he could take out a classified newspaper ad reading: "My cuffs are N inches above the ankle." This would express the same proposition, but we would not (at least yet) regard this advertising as either fashionable or unfashionable behavior. It seems we can communicate the same proposition without communicating the desired phatic result.

The information that is transmitted by fashion is, most fundamentally, information about membership of community. Wearing this hemline communicates that the wearer is or aspires to be a member of the community that currently wears this hemline *as a fashion*. The last qualification is important. The absent minded lecturer who falls into fashion by failing to change his clothes since last they were in fashion is not a member of this community, though he might just be mistaken for a member. Although a sentence about cuffs does not achieve the same communication as wearing the cuffs, there is still an important element of arbitrariness in fashion. This arbitrariness is crucial to the signal's functioning as a phatic signal. If polar explorers have to have low cuffs because of frostbite problems, then it cannot be a fashion signal amongst polar explorers. Hemline is merely *functional* for this group. Phatic communication is about *choosing* to belong where we could have chosen not to.

Of course, there is an immensely complicated web of weak functional constraints that influence fashion but allow enough arbitrariness to let in the phatic. This indirect but nevertheless ever-present background is what people tend to appeal to when they analyze fashion symbolically as in the example above. Coverage and exposure are not unrelated to sexual availability, or wealth, or age in our culture. The cost of fashion is an important nonarbitrary aspect that imposes constraints that give symbolic meaning, quite capable of complex inversions at several removes. Fashion is about group membership, particularly in so far as that group membership is a matter of choice, and a matter of change.

In ritual there is less of a temporal dimension. The point of ritual is that it is a timeless reflection of the culture and community to which we belong. But we still see the importance of arbitrariness. Jonathan Swift could lampoon his culture's religious bigotry with his allegory of the culture that fought wars about which end of the boiled egg should be eaten first. The significance of such arbitrary symbols is a phatic significance and to understand it we have to understand how the symbols function in a society or subgroup.

Fashion and ritual are paradigmatic examples of phatic communication. Fashion and ritual are extreme examples, convenient for explaining the concept because they are so recalcitrant to ideational analysis. But phatic and ideational communication are not in general neatly separable. Communication always incorporates both aspects, though one may overshadow the other. For example, academic lectures might, on the face of it, appear to be pure ideational communication, with precious little phatic aspect to them. But to fall for this appearance would be a mistake. Undergraduate degrees are elaborate rituals of induction into academic communities. Students are learning what it is to be, say, a psychologist, just as much as learning the propositions that psychologists know.

Look at what is going on in this bit of this book in this part of your degree. An author is explaining to you the twin concepts of phatic and ideational communication. And what does that activity consist of? It is not as if you have no grasp of these concepts before reading this chapter. You know about hemlines and rituals—if you didn't you could not be a member of this culture or learn to make the distinction explicit. One aspect of what is going on is adding to your vocabulary two probably new words *phatic* and *ideational*. So if this book succeeds you will be equipped with two probably new words associated with two newly explicit concepts, hopefully useful for thinking about communication. You will be part of a community that can use these words, thus communicating your intellectual background to anyone equipped to understand. Phatic and ideational communication are not separable processes, even if we have to adopt one perspective on communication at any given time.

Cognitive science does not generally have much explicitly to say about phatic communication. The analogy of resonance is an important antidote to thinking that communication is merely about the transport of ideas. The analogy helps us get over the tendency to think of these as two modes of communication with two kinds of things communicated—ideas on the one hand and feelings of membership on the other. Once ideational communication becomes possible, the possibility of establishing communities of knowers arises. This applies not only to communities defined by the knowing of codes, but even to communities defined by knowledge of particular facts—being "in the know" is being a member of a community. From this perspective it is not that the arrival of ideational communication ousts the primitive phatic communication of animal groups, but rather that ideational communication hugely increases the space of phatic possibilities.

1.2 Narrowing Down to a Cognitive Science Approach

The historical setting of cognitive science

If phatic communication is what cognitive science mostly leaves to sociological approaches, what *does* cognitive science deal with? To understand this, a little history is useful. Cognitive science is an interdisciplinary field which began to be recognizable after World War II as a set of interactions between logic, psychology, linguistics, anthropology, electronic engineering, and computer science. Both the "cognitive" and the "science" are important to this historical breeding. So also are the technological changes that were accelerated by the war.

Electronics and computer science hardly existed before WWII. Computer science particularly grew out of logic, mathematics, and electronics during WWII. In 1936, Alan Turing published a mathematical theorem that proved that a particular research program to "mechanize mathematics" was impossible. The same Alan Turing spent the war designing the deciphering machines that cracked the German high command's code for controlling U-boats, and contributed to turning the course of war in the Atlantic. The deciphering machines were still electromechanical devices, but after the war, the new understanding of the abstractions met the electronics that had been accelerated by the development of radio and radar. The digital computer was born. The rest is history ... but also the topic of this book.

But what has all this military technology to do with social sciences and humanities such as psychology, linguistics, and philosophy? The mathematics that spawned the new technologies focused attention on a level of description of diverse phenomena in terms of INFORMATION in a peculiarly abstract way, which made certain commonalities between these subjects suddenly apparent. Before the war, Shannon and Weaver, workingat Bell telephone laboratories, had already asked themselves how to measure this curious abstract quantity information. In the early 1950s, Noam Chomsky at MIT saw that a new branch of mathematics, known as "automata theory", coming out of logic and the fledgling computer science, could be used to analyze natural language grammar—the patterns of our everyday language. Richard Montague, working at UCLA, challenged linguists to see natural languages as formal logical languages at the level of their meaning. We will see something of these logical languages later—for the moment think of them as artificial computer languages.

These mathematical (but not numerical) languages had been designed by philosophers such as Gottlob Frege and Russell at the turn of the 20th century precisely to get away from what they thought were the incurable ambiguities of natural languages like English. Chomsky and Montague completed the circle by turning the formalisms of logic and computer science back onto the analysis of natural language. George Miller, also working at Harvard, showed that these same mathematical theories of the structure of information were essential if we were to understand even the simplest feats of human memory, of perception, or of linguistic communication.

Before the war, the social sciences such as linguistics and psychology had been through a prolonged period in which their major goal was to establish the possibility of being objective in the pursuit of sciences of the subjective. BEHAVIORISM was a movement in psychology, echoed under various labels in linguistics, philosophy, and other disciplines, which wanted to replace subjective talk of mental experience by talk of objectively observed regularities in behavior.

Behaviorism was itself a reaction to some naive 19th century attempts to INTUIT the structure of the mind. Some early German psychologists supposed that intuition could provide direct explanations of the nature of mental life. Sitting in their armchairs they could, for example, intuit whether they inevitably experienced images when they solved problems. The behaviorists argued that such intuitions just have to be treated as another kind of data by psychologists, with the usual problems of indirectness and interpretation. They are not a direct window on the mind. This reaction led initially to a positive empirical interest in observations of peoples' doings, but by the 1950s, behaviorism had itself become an extravagant exercise by theorists at tying as many limbs as possible behind their backs while just leaving enough hand movement to write papers.

Skepticism about evidence had led to skepticism about existence. The mind did not exist—only behavior. And that could be studied as a ball on a pin table transitioning between "states" like the billiard balls of Newton's physics. What the new mathematical studies of information provided was ways of demonstrating the necessity of mental structure and describing it without giving up the demand for objective evidence. The aridity which late behaviorism had fallen into gave way to cognitivism, and topics in psychology and linguistics opened up again, topics that had been out-of-bounds for a generation or more. Behaviorism itself laid important groundwork for the appreciation of the informational level in psychological and linguistic understanding, and continues to have lessons for cognitivism when it strays too far from its evidence. But behaviorism's real legacy lives on in the experimental techniques that cognitive psychology still employs. More recently there has been a turning back of attention onto the issue of how to extract knowledge by statistical treatment of the data of experience. This movement has some of the interests of behaviorism, but is now far more a technical and less an ideological approach.

Disciplinary perspectives on communication

The interdisciplinary composition of cognitive science results from a conviction that though it was perhaps essential to differentiate the disciplinary approaches during the 19th century, solving the scientific problems about the mind that face us now requires all of these approaches simultaneously, and that usually means that teams of researchers work together. Their methods can usefully be classified into those that understand by analyzing and those that understand by synthesizing.

Ways of understanding an X:

- Analytical approaches:
    —observe an X in contexts
    —take an X to bits
- Synthetic approaches:
    —build an X
    —deduce the properties any possible X must have

Of the predominantly analytic approaches, linguistics and psychology adopt stances toward language and communication, which work by observation of people communicating. Observation here includes observation when the environment is systematically manipulated by the scientist experimenting. Linguistics focuses on the external representations of language: speech sounds, written sentences, characterizing and explaining their structure, and focusing on what is going on publicly. Psychology focuses on how language functions, and how the structures are processed, focusing on relations between what is going on outside and inside. Cognitive psychology's stance is sometimes called "black-box" methodology—figuring out what must be going on inside by observing how the organism responds, but "without taking the lid off." Neuroscience takes the analytic more literally and does take the lid off.

Of the predominantly synthetic approaches, ARTIFICIAL INTELLI-

GENCE (AI) is the name for the approach of building systems that share some of the properties of the mind. Of the approaches from the *a priori* mathematics and logic, both invent systems and prove that all systems of some kind *must* have certain properties. Philosophy is primarily concerned with constructing and evaluating arguments about how the world or the mind must be. Because philosophical arguments are generally about abstract properties, philosophy has a strong flavor of the *a priori*, though its methods are rather broad, as befits the ancestor of all these disciplines.

All of these methods make important contributions to cognitive science. Historically, most special sciences (physics, chemistry, biology, . . .) tend to have "spun out" from philosophy. Most of the constituents of cognitive science were not differentiated from philosophy until the late 19th century when psychology and logic became subjects in their own right. Psychologists collected data on actual language use. Logicians studied properties of all possible languages. Psychology developed a close affinity with some parts of biology, and logic with mathematics. Linguistics differentiated from the study of literature and the interpretation of texts both sacred and profane, with strong inputs from anthropology and sociology. In some ways, one can view cognitive science as a response to the need for reassembling the insights of these disciplines which divorced a century and a half ago.

An important distinction within philosophy has always been between the NORMATIVE and the DESCRIPTIVE stance towards a subject matter. One can study politics as a normative subject about how governments *ought* to govern, or as a descriptive subject about how governments *do* actually behave. Philosophers distinguish *moral* philosophy, which is normative, from *natural* philosophy, which characterises the natural world (and is now pretty much identified with natural science).

In fact, it is harder to separate these two stances in our subject area than it may at first seem. For most of the topics of cognitive science, this distinction runs right through them. We can ask how we *ought* to communicate (for optimum effect), or how we *do* communicate under the conditions we normally find, with all our limitations of expertise; or how we *ought* to reason, or how we *do* reason with all the systematic errors that we make. We can ask how people ought to speak or write (according to some notion of "correctness" in a local culture) or we can observe how they do actually speak or write.

The descriptive stance is the one we start from because this is science. But because this is social science, the related normative questions and approaches are not separable. Even if we take morality as our topic, we can adopt a descriptive stance toward it and analyze what kinds of moralities occur in what kinds of human societies (as an anthropologist might). The normative and the descriptive are bound to be inseparable in psychology since people have normative theories about their own behavior that have effects on how we act, and so even a descriptive account may have to incorporate some reference to the normative stance people adopt.

Even if we think of human beings as organisms that evolved by natural selection, which are "creations of nature" and are therefore only to be studied by describing what they actually *do*, we still find the blind processes of evolution OPTIMIZING systems for performing functions and we encounter a need to compare what the system does with what it *should* optimally do. We cannot throw away the distinction between descriptive and normative explanations. We have to acknowledge that neither is ever very far away. We will see this inseparability come to the fore even in the laboratory study of reasoning.

Another important feature of scientific method that sometimes seems quite illegitimate when science moves onto human territory is what is called IDEALIZATION. Sciences have to focus on some phenomena and systematically ignore others. Some of the most striking advances come from an insightful choice of what to ignore. One of Galileo's great insights was that ignoring friction (and minimizing it in experiments) allowed the development of general theories of motion. There is something outrageous about this. Friction is one of the main determinants of how objects move. How could it be reasonable to ignore friction?

Linguistics and psychology make all sorts of idealizations of their data. As you will see, when linguists describe the rules of English grammar they do not include all the patterns that are mistakes made by people who are tired, distracted, or intoxicated. When psychologists describe their data they may well throw out the data from the people who didn't follow the instructions, or made too many errors. Data is "cleaned up" in accordance with sometimes quite sweeping idealizations.

At different scales of inquiry, different idealizations turn out to be appropriate. One linguist's idealization (to ignore speech errors, perhaps) turn out to be another linguist's data (in analyzing the mechanisms of speech production). The logician may reject patterns of reasoning that people frequently appear to use, while the psychologist may take these logical "errors" as the main phenomenon to be explained. At some points in scientific development, there are major arguments about whether an idealization is a good one—as we shall see, for example, when we discuss logical analyses of human reasoning.

In the end, idealizations are justified by their fruitfulness. With work in progress one has to rely on one's own judgments about future usefulness. That is a good thing to keep in mind throughout this book. Just remember that one sometimes has to leave out what appears at first sight to be the main ingredient that should go in. Backgrounding phatic communication in favor of ideational is just one of the idealizations we made to get started, to which we will eventually return.

1.3   Book Summary

Communication is a broad range of phenomena and we focus on part of that range. Two metaphors for communication—transport and resonance—focus attention on the public message and the knowledge required to understand it respectively. Distinguishing phatic and ideational communication helps us to remember what we are leaving out as we narrow our approach. Cognitive science arose from a historical confluence of some highly abstract mathematical thinking and some very specific technological innovations. It welds together analytic and synthetic disciplinary approaches which have become highly differentiated since the 19th century. Sciences generally take a descriptive stance, as opposed to a normative one. But in studying communication these two kinds of phenomena are intertwined. Sciences define their subject matter partly through the idealizations they make about their data. Understanding the different idealizations made by the component disciplines of cognitive science helps us to understand how their accounts fit together.

The plan of the book is as follows. The remainder of part I introduces some example phenomena of human communication that are selected to illustrate cognitive science's approach to understanding the mind. We choose our particular illustrations because they are suited to demonstrating to the reader that the phenomena we go on to analyze actually apply to the reader's own mind. We also choose the particular illustrations because they allow us to examine how various formal frameworks for analyzing communication apply to the data generated by these demonstrations. This beginning allows us to illustrate how cognitive science is very different from longer established sciences like physics and biology. The interpretation of the phenomena we illustrate and analyze is still highly controversial. Even in an introductory book like this we would be irresponsible if we did not convey this controversial nature. Some readers may find controversy disappointing—they want the answers and now. Others may find it exciting. In this subject it is still possible for beginners to understand the important unsettled controversies that will determine the development of future understanding, and to understand how arguments have to be constructed from all the different disciplines and methods that can contribute.

Part II gives a brief introduction to some of the theoretical issues that arise in pursuing a cognitive science approach to the mind. A very brief introduction to a logical system allows us to draw out some of the points that arose in looking at the previous part's examples. We go on to describe some relations between logic and computation, and how these make the concept of representation central to cognitive science accounts of the mind. We then discuss the problem of how we can investigate the mind's representations by observing peoples' behavior.

Part III goes into the details of developing a model of natural language structure and just what is involved in "decoding" natural language communications. We attempt to show in as simple a way as possible how the process of constructing the meaning of a linguistic message from that message's structure can be mechanized. We also describe the various kinds of ambiguities that are exhibited by natural languages such as English, and how pervasive such ambiguities are. Resolving ambiguity is arguably *the* major challenge in computational linguistics—that is, the study of how one gets a machine to produce and interpret natural language utterances. We discuss briefly some simple approaches to machines processing language, and also report on experiments that reveal how humans do it.

Part IV describes how users of languages structured in the ways introduced in Part III, augment the semantic content of an utterance that's revealed by such structure with further information about semantic content. This content is based on *nonlinguistic* information such as world knowledge and the cognitive states—the beliefs and goals—of the participants who are having the conversation. We explore again how some of these phenomena concerning the link between an utterance and its meaning can be described in a formal way, on the basis of recent advances in AI research on logics for common sense reasoning.

Part V looks at communication employing graphical messages in order to draw out the similarities and differences between language and diagrams, and to look at how these similarities and differences impact on their users' communications.

Part VI stands back from the details of particular communication systems and looks at some general philosophical critiques of computational models of mind.

In the next chapter we look at a highly simplified and abstracted model of communication which originated in engineering—the Shannon and Weaver model which was developed for measuring quantities of information. The model is important not just because of its positive contributions, but also because its explicitness makes it easier to see its inadequacies.

1.4   Further Reading

• Goffman, E. (1969). *The Presentation of Self in Everyday Life*. London: Allen and Lane.
A classic from the sociological perspective on communication.
• Gardener, H. (1985). *The Mind's New Science: A History of the Cognitive Revolution*. New York: Basic Books.
A historical introduction which gives insight to how the disciplines contribute.

Exercises

Exercise 1.1: Think of your own examples to illustrate the distinction between phatic and ideational communication. Choose phenomena other than fashion or religious ritual. Write brief notes on why they are good examples of these concepts.

Exercise 1.2: Describe an episode involving some communication from your own experience this week. Describes the ideational and phatic aspects of this episode. How do they interact?

2 A (Too?) Simple Model of Communication

2.1 The Shannon and Weaver Model

The model of communication we discuss in this chapter is perhaps the simplest possible model of communication, but is nevertheless enough to have served for the development of a lot of mathematics/engineering. Its usefulness is both positive and negative—positively, it serves to help grasp the essentially abstract nature of information. Negatively, it is a useful framework for exploring what it leaves out.

The model proposes a sender, a receiver, a channel, and a set of signals, which can be thought of as states into that the sender can put the channel. The sender sets the channel into some state and this is transmitted through the channel to the receiver. States correspond to messages—meanings that the sender can convey to the receiver. These might be states of the sender's world—"there is a fire in my office," or "sell Ford!," or "I'm hungry."

The important conditions that are placed on the set of signals and on their corresponding messages are that each member of the set is mutually exclusive, and the set is exhaustive of the possibilities. For example, the channel might be a wire and might be at +1 volt, or at 0 volts, but it cannot be at both. Although the voltage varies continuously (in the jargon it is an ANALOGUE quantity) in reality, as far as the model is concerned, it is DIGITIZED so that voltages are thresholded into discrete categories. The same goes for the messages. The members of the set are each mutually exclusive, and severally exhaustive.

The digitization of communication signals is commonplace nowadays—CDs are digital representations of sound. But "digitization" is not just a feature of engineered systems. It has been shown that speech sounds such as the VOICING that distinguishes the first sounds of *pan* and *ban* is perceived in our brain in a digital fashion. A continuum of acoustic sounds (very much more complexly structured than the voltage example) is *not* heard as sounds starting like *p* and getting gradually more *b*-like, but rather as two discrete categories of sound. If a group of people hear a sound exactly on the borderline, half will hear a perfectly good *p* and half a perfectly good *b*. Making continuous dimensions into discrete categories is sometimes called QUANTIZATION.

In this simple model of communication, time is also considered to come in discrete periods. In each period the channel is deemed to be in a single state. It is most natural to think of the messages as carrying information about a changing world, where their arrival time at the receiver's end of the channel bears some fixed relation to the time that their corresponding state refers to. There is no reason why this mapping of time of the signal to the time referred to by its message has to be simple. But it is hard to avoid some temporal mapping, if a *sequence* of mutually exclusive signals is to carry information about mutually exclusive states.

This model of communication, only slightly augmented by information about the probability of states, and after some mathematical development, sufficed as a foundation of much of what we have come to know as communication technology. This body of mathematical theory is known simply as INFORMATION THEORY. Shannon and Weaver worked for Bell Telephone, and this mathematics was developed with the practical goal of measuring *how much* information was being transmitted to aid in designing optimal telephone systems. As befits the telephone company, the theory is pretty well silent about *what* is transmitted, focusing attention merely on the quantity.

The remaining idea that is required to base a measure of information on this conceptualization of information is that rare signals are more informative than common ones. If there is only a single state of the world and a single signal, no information is transmitted—the receiver can "guess" the message with unfailing accuracy. As soon as there is a range of possibility, the best strategy for guessing is to guess the most frequent signal, which is therefore less informative than its rarer counterparts. BIT is the name we give to the amount of information carried by one equiprobable binary pair of signals.

A nice natural illustration of this point is the predictability of vowels and consonants. With semitic languages like Hebrew and Arabic, just the consonants are written and the vowels omitted. The vowels, drawn from a smaller set, are sufficiently uninformative to be guessed from their consonantal context. The demonstration works reasonably well in English. Taking out the vowels does dramatically less damage than taking out the consonants. The vowels carry less information because there are less possibilities. Compare:

nc llstrtn f ths pnt s th prdctblt of vwls and cnsnnts. Smtc lnggs r wrttn wth jst cnsnnts nd th vwls mmttd ...

a ie iuaio o i oi i e eiaiiy o oe ooa. eii auae ae ie i u ooa a w oe oie ...

Although natural languages display some REDUNDANCY that is crucial to communication through NOISE, their "design" also exhibits many efficiencies of coding that information theory would predict. Zipf showed that natural languages obey an efficient coding scheme in information theoretic terms. He showed that frequent words (as evidenced by counting large samples of language) tend to be short and rare words to be longer. This was one of the first, if rather limited, applications of information theory to understanding natural human communication as opposed to engineered systems.

With just this rather minimal conceptual apparatus it is possible to show that the most effective way of transmitting information about a set of equiprobable possibilities is by means of binary signals that divide the set of possibilities successively into halves, and halves of halves, and so on. Each choice point is assigned to a binary signal. Anyone who has played twenty questions will have an intuitive grasp of the strategy. Asking whether "it" is an ocelot, before asking whether "it" is animal, vegetable, or a mineral, is not question-efficient. If there are 2^n possibilities, then at least n binary signals are required to discriminate them all.

This scheme of successive binary division has already smuggled in implicitly an interesting idea. We can expand the number of possibilities discriminable even if we are still stuck with a physical channel that is only binary, by transmitting a sequence of signals and interpreting the *sequence* as a "word." If we have 256 possibilities, we can assign eight-bit codes ($2^8 = 256$) in such a way that each is uniquely labeled. These codes range from 00000000 through 01100001 to 11111111. But notice that signals are now structured into "levels." In order to interpret a bit, we have to know where it comes in a sequence of eight signals. Rather in the way that letters make up words, our binary signal sequences make up larger signals. Like letters, the binary signals are no longer meaningful except inasmuch as they contribute to differentiating words. In fact computers are designed so that they have a basic hardware signal length, and the codes that are fitted to this length are called WORDS.

But compactness of codes has a downside. As we noted above, natural languages are not compact like our eight-bit code for 256 possibilities. Deleting the vowels from written language still leaves most messages intact. This less than minimal coding incorporates redundancy, and is typical of natural communication systems. We talk and write in environments full of random noise—acoustic, electrical, visual noise. This is random energy that is present in the environment superimposed on the signals. With a fully efficient (compact) code, deforming any one signal will always guarantee that we transmit another meaningful message— just that it will be the wrong message. For example, flipping any bit in the eight-bit code for 256 messages mentioned above will always generate another code member.

If we want to be able to communicate reliably in noisy environments, then there must be combinations of signals that are not meaningful. A common scheme for an eight-bit binary code is to have what is called a PARITY BIT. The parity bit is set to 0 if there is an even number of 1s in the other eight positions, and 1 if there is an odd number. On receiving a message, we can examine the parity bit and see whether it is correct relative to the eight bits it comes with. If there are oddly many 1s with a 0 parity bit, or evenly many 1s with an odd parity bit, then something has gone wrong. Of course, there is a chance that more than one error has taken place and the message has been deformed even though the parity bit is correct, but the chance of two independent errors is much lower than the probability of one. Introducing redundancy by "fault-tolerant" schemes such as parity bits means that more bits have to be transmitted, and that some possible messages are meaningless, but it is a price worth paying if we want to communicate in noisy environments. That's why natural language is redundant as we demonstrated above, though its patterns of redundancy are more complex than parity bits.

Shannon and Weaver's framework, simple though it is, helps us to see the abstractness of information. Our technology has become so digitized that the idea of turning anything from product numbers to symphonies into digital codes is all around us. Given the digitization, we can see all sorts of physical IMPLEMENTATIONS of this information. To the bar-code reader, the bar-code is seen as a pattern of light. The reader turns that pattern into voltages, and then into magnetizations on the computer's disk, and half a dozen different technologies besides. When the bar-code on the baked beans doesn't read properly, the assistant types the code. His typing is a pattern of mechanical energy. The keyboard is a device for turning patterns of mechanical energy into patterns of electrical energy. The information stays the same through all these transformations. It is abstract with regard to *implementation*. That is *not* to say that the physical properties of the implementation won't affect the way any mechanisms that process the information will operate. All the physical transformations involved have to fit together into a system. But we can think of equivalent systems that have quite different physics—implementations. In fact, this is what happens as technology develops—the abstract system may stay the same while the physics is completely transformed beneath it.

If we want to completely understand how a device or a creature works we will need to know a lot about the physics of the implementation. But realizing that information can be separated from implementation reveals how there are many levels of understanding in terms of information that are well above the physics. And that for many purposes, it is at those higher levels we need to understand the phenomena of communication. For example, we want a theory of how people use language—not a theory of how they use spoken language and a completely separate theory of how they understand written language. Although the physics of speech and writing are very different, there are huge commonalities between speech and writing that we need to capture. Analyzing at the level of information avoids REDUCTION. A distinctive feature of cognitive science is that it always analyzes phenomena at pairs of LEVELS— an informational level and an implementational level. Sometimes these levels can be stacked several deep, but still this relation remains between adjacent pairs of levels.

2.2 Limitations and Expansions of the Model

But there are severe limitations to Shannon and Weaver's framework. It works only in terms of finite codes. The primitive codes may be used to define other codes—bits can define "computer words," but still only finitely many. We can think of natural language parallels. Letters can define natural language words, and then words can define sentences, and sentences can define DISCOURSES (stories, reports, arguments, . . .). But a curious thing happens when we step up these levels of units. Words are finite in number. Eight-bit computer words define a vocabulary of

256. English has an open-ended but finite vocabulary, as listed in the
Oxford English Dictionary or *Webster's*, of somewhere in the region of
several hundred thousand words, depending on exactly what counts as
a word—a large but finite vocabulary.

But when it comes to sentences, it is no longer sensible to think of
them as listable. It has been estimated that there are about the same
number of sentences in English of less than twenty words length as there
are particles in the universe. Almost all of those sentences have never
been uttered, and never will be. Most of those strings of words are not
grammatical or meaningful. Listing them, or even the meaningful ones,
is not an available approach, either for the linguist, or for the human
brain. We must assume that our grasp of these objects of communication
is through the application of general rules, whether we know the rules
explicitly or not. There are obvious regularities in English that give rise
to open-endedly long sentences. We can conjoin any two sentences by
and and get another sentence. We can embed another relative clause—
The cat chased the rat that ate the cheese that was kept in the house
.... In the end we run out of patience, but there is no clear point at
which it can no longer be a sentence. When we think of units as large as
multi-sentence discourses it is not even so clear what sort of terms the
rules can be couched in.

This infinity or CREATIVITY of language was one of Chomsky's arguments for an approach to language through essentially infinite regularities. Once we reach these levels of unit, Shannon and Weaver's approach breaks down. If the vocabulary of possibilities is infinite, the
information carried by any item is infinite, but then so is the length of
the longest member of the vocabulary. The whole conceptual framework
breaks down. Any actual piece of human communication involves only
finitely long signals, but to capture regularities we have to take seriously
the open-endedness of the affair.

The open-endedness is not just syntactic but is also important at the
level of meaning. Natural languages do not have fixed meanings for their
words. We continually communicate new concepts and meanings through
language. We always have to tailor our language to the context we are in
to transmit the meanings intended. These aspects of communication are
not encompassed by the Shannon and Weaver model. It has no account
of how we negotiate the correspondence that "signal 3" will mean "sell
Ford!"

This is not to say that the framework has no use in the analysis of language. Within the lower levels, finite codes are extremely important to the processors that decode language. The level of sounds, for example, has an important part to play in understanding the "design" of natural language. But as an ultimate framework for understanding discourse, something else must be found.

A discourse is a sequence of sentences each drawn from the indefinitely large population of possible sentences that make up a language like English. When the receiver has decoded a sentence he or she must do something about storing the information it carries if the information is to connect with other sentences, as connect it must. So an immediate consequence of infinite languages is that not all information in the mind is uniformly present throughout. There is a problem of connecting new information with old information in order to base action on knowledge. We will see some concrete examples soon. This process of inference is everywhere in the mind, and everywhere in communication.

Summary

Shannon and Weaver's model of communication, like so much in science, is simple, if not simplistic. But its concepts of sender, receiver, channel, signal, code, and information form a tightly knit web and serve for the elaboration of many insights into communication. Fundamentally, information is a decrease in uncertainty. Redundancy is a diffuseness of coding that can be exploited to give fault-tolerance.

The inadequacies of the model are as revealing as the phenomena it does fit, a common benefit of the simplistic models science entertains. The limitation to finite codes, and the lack of analysis of the message—what is communicated—are the most serious problems and are closely related to each other. A theory of communication that can deal with messages of indefinite length, where the messages themselves build up the context for the messages' interpretation requires memory. An analysis of memory—the storage and retrieval of information during communication—involves us immediately in questions about what the mind of sender and receiver are like.

The only way to deal with essentially infinite possibilities is through capturing generalizations about them. The next chapter will focus on the treatment of rules and regularities in reasoning. We choose an example phenomenon that requires that we take the different perspectives of several disciplines to illustrate how they relate to each other. This will give you some concrete examples of communication phenomena and different accounts of them. The following chapters go on to examine computation and representation—two of the theoretical concepts that underly the cognitive science approach to dealing with generalizations.

Exercises

Exercise 2.1: Find an example from everyday communication where a code is redundant and where that redundancy reduces errors that might otherwise ensue. Find an example where too little redundancy leads to many errors.

Exercise 2.2: What other kinds of behavior exhibit creativity (in Chomsky's sense) other than sentence syntax?

2.3   Further Reading

• Miller, G. A. (1967). *The Psychology of Communication*. New York: Basic Books.
• Lyons, J. (1991). *Chomsky*. London: Fontana Modern Masters.

3 Looking for Certainties

3.1 Introduction

This chapter will take an in-depth look at one very specific experimental situation that appears to show widespread failure on the part of some very intelligent people to understand some simple language. We choose this experiment for such protracted analysis because it can tell us so much about different disciplinary perspectives on communication, and the need for integration—the defining need for cognitive science.

In this chapter we will focus on how people seek evidence for rules that express certainties. In the next chapter we will look at how people manage in a world that is largely made up of uncertainties. We will see that many of the same issues crop up, albeit in different guises.

In what follows, we will sometimes get you to be the guinea pig in informal experiments. We do this because it is crucial to experience these phenomena at a personal level, and only *then* to try to explain them at a scientific level. If you just read about the strange things observed by psychologists you might be inclined to dismiss them as something other people do. Then you would be unlikely to feel the importance of understanding them. We the teachers did these "strange" things in just the same way when we originally were given the same puzzles. Sometimes we will see that scientists' theories about these phenomena (which have been widely accepted) are not much more sophisticated than their SUBJECTS' "errors." Sometimes it is arguable that people's "errors" can be seen as more rational than they at first appear when interpreted in the right context. But you cannot grasp what cognitive science is all about unless you understand this to-ing and fro-ing between the perspectives of personal, subjective experience, and public objective observation and explanation.

We make no apology for spending such a lot of time on what will at first appear as a tiny topic. If we can give you some insight into how the various disciplines approach this one topic, we will have succeeded in our aims. If we succeed we will have changed the way that you reason yourself as a practical activity. We will have given you a better idea of how science works in this confusing area—what is theory and what is data for each of the approaches. You may also have a rather different view of the structure of your own mind. We would feel we have succeeded if you come away with some glimpses of scientific understandings to be had, conjoined with a better grasp of how little we currently understand of some truly baffling phenomena.

Like much of psychology, we will focus here almost entirely on the mental processes of "normal adults" (in fact overwhelmingly undergraduate students), having little to say, for example, about children or abnormal adults. We will say a little about cross-cultural issues in reasoning, and in chapter 18 we will consider differences between learning styles of normal adults. This focus on mental processes in common among undergraduate subjects should not be taken as indicating a belief that everyone's mental processes are the same, or that the differences are uninteresting. Differences can be a rich source of insight into minds. But we believe that going into one approach in depth is more illuminating as an introduction than pursuing a survey. If we are successful, you should be able to transfer this way of thinking to other areas.

3.2   Seeking Evidence for Rules: Wason's Selection Task

We begin by looking at how people reason about rules. In 1966 Peter Wason, a psychologist who worked at University College London, devised the "selection" task for exploring reasoning about "if ... then" rules, or CONDITIONALS as they are known in logic. You the subject are presented with cards, each of which have numbers on one side and letters on the other. Four cards appear on the page before you, one with a vowel showing, one a consonant, one with an even, and one with an odd number.

$$\boxed{A}\ \boxed{K}\ \boxed{4}\ \boxed{7}$$

A rule states about the cards: *If one side has a vowel, then the other has an even number.*

Your task is to decide which cards *must* be turned to see if the rule is true of the four cards. Turn only the minimum number you need to turn.

Write down your choices and some brief justifications for why you chose or didn't choose each card. Keep these notes safe.

This experiment reliably elicits behavior that, according to one widely accepted story about what we *should* do, represents very poor reasoning. It therefore raises acute questions about whether (and if so why) intelligent readers, like yourselves, should reason so poorly. But it also raises questions as to whether this is a good story about what you should have done in this task, and how we are to choose between competing prescriptions. Many different versions of this experiment have now been run in order to test various different explanations, so the selection task represents a good example of how a scientific investigation in this area works. Still more important, it offers examples of how various different disciplines' scientific explanations should relate. We shall visit anthropological, linguistic, psychological, philosophical, and logical questions and theories about this phenomenon in the course of our investigations. We will use the phenomenon to explain something of what each of these disciplines has to say. Our goal is to try to find an interpretation of the phenomenon that is consistent with all of what they have to say.

As mentioned before, the answers to the questions raised here are still highly controversial, so learning to grasp the experiments, the observations, the explanations, and the interpretations is a good way of getting our hands dirty in order to learn how cognitive science is done. One of the morals of this investigation is that the experimenters have often proved as confused as their subjects, and that unquestioning acceptance of what one reads in scientific journals is as unwise as unquestioning acceptance of what one reads in the newspapers. We want to give you a feeling for what it is to adopt a position and to weigh the evidence for and against, from as many perspectives as possible.

Understanding human reasoning requires coordinating two perspectives: the descriptive and the normative. First, in descriptive mode, which cards did subjects actually turn in Wason's original experiment? Almost everyone turns the A card. A few turn the K. Many more turn the 4. But very few turn the 7. The most common response is to turn A and 4 (about 50%). Only about 5–10% of undergraduate subjects turn the A and the 7 and no other cards. These results are highly reliable and replicable—they have been repeated many times on a wide variety of subjects with very similar results.

In normative mode, which cards *should* subjects turn? According to Wason's interpretation of this standard of reasoning, only 5% of subjects got the "right answer," which he held to be to turn the A and the 7 only. We won't repeat Wason's argument for this normative criterion because we don't want to influence you before you read on. But we do want you to think about this general issue about choosing a criterion to measure subjects' performances against. What authority could possibly tell us we were nearly all wrong? After all, this is English. We know what "if ..., then ..." means. Could nearly all the folks be wrong nearly all of the time? Or is their perhaps a failure of communication between experimenters and subjects?

Sometimes in psychology we accept that everyone can be wrong. An example is visual illusions when we all see something wrongly. But in visual perception we have strong independent criteria for veridical perception (e.g. we can measure the length of the two lines and show that they are the same length even when they don't look to be). In reasoning experiments, we rarely have such simple recourse to independent criteria. Wason employed as a normative COMPETENCE THEORY for his task CLASSICAL LOGIC which dictates that we should turn A and 7 only. We return to describe this logic in chapter 5. But this is only one logic for the conditional, and not the one people are most likely to adopt.

Like many experiments in psychology, this one is famous because people don't do what some theory says they should do. There is a discrepancy between behavior and competence model—massive in this case. If they had done what was expected, we would never have heard more of Wason's experiment. On Wason's account of what we should do, these results are surprising. You should ask yourself whether you now agree with Wason that turning A and 7 is the right thing to do. If you disagree, what do you think people should do? And why? Write down your conclusions.

How are we to get evidence about why people do what they do in this task? One of the very first points to emphasize is that we do not automatically know why we did what we did any more than anyone else does. We can collect people's reports of what they think about what they did, but this is just more indirect evidence about what went on in their minds as they made their card choices—more intuitions. People may have forgotten why they chose the cards they chose, and they may not have known why they chose them in the first place. Nevertheless, asking subjects to explain themselves may turn up useful information even if it cannot always be taken at face value.

When we collect this kind of evidence by asking people for their reasons, the reasons given for turning A usually sound somewhat as follows: *I turned the A because if there's an even number on the back of it, then the rule is true.* What people who don't turn 7 say is usually something like: *The rule doesn't say anything about odd numbers.* Were your own explanations similar to these?

Some experiments have tried getting students to list what possibilities there are for the other sides of the cards, and to explicitly judge each possibility for what it means for the truth of the rule. Careful listening indicates that for the A card, subjects typically realize that an even number will make it a positive case, and an odd number a negative one. This will be of some importance as we consider explanations. But there seems to be a real difference with the odd number card. Subjects will list the possibilities for the back of 7 as a vowel or a consonant. Most judge that neither would be relevant to the rule's truth value. What do you think?

Another manipulation that has been tried is to turn the cards over and ask what consequences the discoveries have for the truth of the rule. When the A is turned, a 7 is found. Most people agree that this means that this card doesn't fit and this justifies turning A. Perhaps when K is turned a 4 is found, and most people agree that this means the card need not have been turned. The same is judged when 4 is turned to find a K. When 7 is turned and an A is found, many subjects judge that this is a negative case, but still insist that the card need not have been turned.

This last finding is very striking. The card turns out to be the same card as the first example (an A with a 7), but the initial encounter is from the other face. The card that is seen as decisive when encountered as an A, with an unknown numeral, is seen as irrelevant when encountered as a 7 with an unknown letter. We return to these observations later.

So much for the "facts." Why is this an interesting experiment? Wason took it for granted that there was a single logical model of what people *ought* to do in his task (turn A and 7). According to Wason's logical model of "if ..., then ...," a single exception to the rule means that the rule is false; and if the A card complies (by having an even number on its back) and the 7 card also complies (by having a vowel on its back), then the rule is thereby true, whatever is on the back of the K and the 4, or any other cards. Wason believed that logic provided this unique model with the meaning of "if ..., then ..." sentences and so concluded that according to logic, more than 90% of subjects got the task wrong. If you did not turn A and 7 only, then you should ask yourself whether you now agree with Wason that you made a mistake. Even if you did choose A and 7, you should ask yourself now whether you think he (and you) got the right answer. Or perhaps whether there are other justifiable answers? As usual, record your decision with your notes.

One reason for choosing this experiment as an example is that it focuses our attention on a clash between an account of what people *ought* to do and what they *do* do—between normative and descriptive stances. Psychology generally adopts the descriptive mode—this is what people do and it is science's business to understand it, desirability aside. Logic is often thought of as providing an absolute *prescription* of what people ought to do, though we will see presently that this is not always true. But it doesn't take too much thought to see that these stances are not as separable as they might first appear.

The tension between descriptive and normative stances is not just important because it determines what phenomena psychologists find interesting. It is also important because people themselves have standards by which they judge their reasoning and their behavior is affected by those standards. For example, when some subjects who did not choose the 7 card initially turn the 7 and find an A on the back, they utter some expletive, and proclaim they previously made a mistake. So even a descriptive theory of what people do has to acknowledge the notion of error, because subjects sometimes acknowledge error themselves. Whenever behavior is goal-oriented, there is likely to be both a descriptive theory of what people do and a normative theory of what they ought to do, or are trying to do, and people themselves are likely to have some grasp of this distinction. So psychology is not just descriptive; it at least has to describe normative phenomena. Similarly, modern logic is not a simple prescription of a standard of reasoning. As we shall see, logic models many ways of reasoning and adopts sometimes a descriptive stance, and sometimes a prescriptive one. In descriptive mode, we can ask ourselves which logical system best describes what someone is doing on some occasion. In normative mode, logic may advise, "If you want to reason about this material with these assumptions and these goals, then this is an appropriate system for doing that." Or, "If you are reasoning in this system, then that doesn't follow."

Unfortunately, the history of the study of Wason's task is a history of confusions between logic and psychology, which is why it is such an interesting example for this course. Before we turn to explanations of what people do in this task, we will take a brief trip abroad.

3.3   An Anthropologist Visits a Tribe

Although by this time you may believe that the author of this chapter is a professor of cognitive science who studies groups of students' patterns of reasoning, you might in fact be entirely mistaken. What has been reported to you under the guise of a modern white-coated experimenter in a scientific psychology laboratory recording the card turns and justifications of undergraduate students might in fact be a set of observations made by an anthropologist visiting a tribe in some exotic setting. The subjects might not be undergraduate students but tribespeople. Of course what is presented here must be English translations of these anthropological dialogues, but you should not let that fool you.

From the late nineteenth century onward there have been a succession of studies of the reasoning abilities of other, and particularly "primitive" cultures.[1] These studies are of interest to us partly because they raise issues about social theories of communication, and partly because they bear significant analogies to the situation of the modern experimenter in the psychology laboratory running reasoning experiments on undergraduate subjects.

For convenience we will take our first anthropological example from Sir Edward Evans-Pritchard's (1940) description of the Azande's beliefs. We will lean heavily on David Bloor's (1991) account of Evans-Pritchard and take Bloor's argument for reinterpretation of Evans-Pritchard's claims as our object of study. We make this choice precisely because Bloor has raised, with useful clarity, the issue that concerns us about the relationship between logic, belief, and reasoning.

Evans-Pritchard tells us that the Azande believe that human calamity is the result of witchcraft. Some men are witches and they have witchcraft substance in their bellies which can sometimes even be observed at postmortem. However, the only way to be sure about a witch premortem is to conduct a ritual chicken-poisoning. This is done when disputes about sorcery arise. The unfortunate chicken is given a particular poison and the manner of its survival or death amounts to an oracle's verdict on whether the individual in question is a witch. Witchcraft moreover is inherited through the same-sex line—father-to-son and mother-to-daughter—so if one member of a clan is a witch then all members must be. Nevertheless, only immediate relatives of a known witch are considered witches. In fact, it is self-evident to the Azande that a whole clan cannot all be witches. It was therefore self-evident to Evans-Pritchard, that Azande beliefs about witchcraft are self-contradictory.

Here is an example of some actual beliefs that are claimed by a painstaking outside observer (Evans-Pritchard) to be inconsistent with "developed world logic." A small number of axioms about sorcery, chicken-poisoning, and clan membership lead to a clear logical contradiction. Therefore, there is something radically different about "primitive logic."

To be fair to Evans-Pritchard, he saw such observations of apparent illogicality as peculiarly at odds with other ethnographic observations of the sophistication of primitive thought. Dugon cosmology, to take one quoted example, is of staggering complexity and subtlety, yet is handed down from generation to generation in an illiterate culture without the benefit of physical record. Evans-Pritchard saw the contrast between apparent illogicality of reasoning and obvious cognitive sophistication of cosmology as the puzzle that was in need of solution.

Bloor takes Evans-Pritchard's record of the Azande's beliefs about witchcraft and turns Evans-Pritchard's argument on its head. He uses the logical deduction from the observations as an argument against "logical compulsion" of belief. Logic, he argues, cannot compel belief. He takes as an analogous example our own belief system about murder. "Thou shalt not kill!" is an absolute invocation of most, if not all, human cultures. But it only takes a minute's thought to appreciate that this absolute generalization is no more absolute than the Azande's axiom of the inheritance of witchcraft. In fact, there are military situations in our culture in which it is possible to be condemned to death for *not* killing. There are other situations where killing is condoned if not required—self-defense being one example. Are our own axioms in this regard as inconsistent as the Azande's about witchcraft? A jurist is likely to say not. Our laws are against *murder* rather than killing, and murder is only a subclass of killing—killing with intent, without need of self-defense, in time of peace, not legally sanctioned by the state, etc., etc.

But then the Azande also have just as complex qualifications on their generalizations about the inheritance of witchcraft powers. Anthropologists have gone back to Evans-Pritchard's careful observations and to the Azande and found that indeed the Azande's axioms of witchcraft are also amenable to similar contextual subtleties. Witches can, for example, be active or latent. Most importantly, the Azande never ask the oracle to settle general "theoretical" questions about witchcraft—only practical specific questions about whether this person here has been at this time bewitching that person there? Theoretical questions are beyond the oracle's remit. We return to this contrast between practical and theoretical questions below.

So, complains Bloor, if the compelling nature of logical axioms can always be deflected by additional codicils and exemptions, what is so different about Azande logic about witchcraft and our own about killing people? Moreover, what is so compelling about logic in general? These are important questions. On the first, we would heartily agree with Bloor—the Azande's logic appears to be very similar to our own.[2] Morally, the issue is arguably about whether witchcraft as an institution is a good regulator of Azande social behavior, and that can only be assessed by consideration of it and other social institutions in which it is embedded. But Azande witchcraft institutions are governed by the same logic as our own social institutions.

How can we be so confident on this latter score? And is there any useful sense left to "logical compulsion"? To approach this question we need to look at the work of psychologists such as Scribner and Cole whose studies were specifically about *reasoning* in primitive cultures, rather than about belief systems in general. Scribner records the following dialogue between herself as experimenter (E), and a Liberian villager (S) whom she asks to solve the following problem: *All Kpelle men are rice farmers. Mr Smith is not a rice-farmer. Is he a Kpelle man?*

S: I don't know the man in person. I have not laid eyes on the man himself.
E: Just think about the statement.
S: If I know him in person, I can answer that question, but since I do not know him in person I cannot answer that question.
E: Try and answer from your Kpelle sense.
S: If you know a person, if a question come up about him you are able to answer. But if you do not know a person, if a question comes up about him, it's hard for you to answer it.

Scribner reports another example answer to the syllogism *All people who own houses pay a house-tax. Boima does not pay a house-tax. Does Boima own a house?*:

S: Boima does not have money to pay a house tax.

What is going on here? Do these Liberian subjects lack a logic that we readily apply to Scribner's problems? And how are we to interpret the replies they make? Let's take the second question first. One interpretation of what the first subject is saying is that she is refusing to tell a "story" about a Mr. Smith on the grounds that she does not have first-hand information about this character who is known only to the experimenter. On a similar interpretation, the second subject is agreeing to take up the experimenter's challenge to tell a jointly authored story about some character called Boima unknown to the subject, but possibly (or more likely not) known to the experimenter. If this interpretation is right we can imagine the story beginning with Boima's little financial difficulty, and going on to tell how he resolved his problem with the tax collector.

If these interpretations are approximately right (and of course much more evidence would be required to substantiate them), then what should we say about the *logic* of these Liberian subjects? It seems that their logic may well be impeccable. In the first case, we can interpret the subject as being reluctant to necessarily accept the truth of the generalization that all Kpelle men are rice farmers. Without knowing Mr. Smith it may be impossible to say whether he is an exception. Similarly, the second subject probably interprets the generalization about house-tax as a statement of a law, and understands that just as in our own culture, not everyone obeys laws, either by reason of inability or unwillingness. These responses are perfectly rational, but they do not interpret the task in the way that the experimenter typically intends, which is to decide whether the conclusion is true in all circumstances in which the premises are also true. In other words, to take the words as completely defining of all the relevant situations, without any other knowledge.

Does this mean that these Liberian subjects are just like us developed-world folk? Scribner found that this is, in at least one respect, not the case. Very few undergraduate subjects respond to these problems in the way that these unschooled Liberians respond. In fact, even Liberians with a few years of primary schooling do not respond the same way. These schooled subjects may not "get the syllogisms all correct," but they accept something nearer the logical "game" that Scribner is trying to get them to play. That is, they accept that the offered premises should be *assumed* to be absolutely true, and see the problem as to figure out what logically follows from just these assumptions.

Seen in this light, the unschooled peasant's response constitutes the adoption of a different kind of discourse than intended, though a kind of discourse which we might also engage in in different circumstances. In chapter 5, we shall see that sometimes a different discourse purpose requires a different kind of logic. So does that mean that these unschooled Liberians do have a different logic? Our answer will be "no." Our reason will be that we too engage in these other kinds of discourse with their different logic. In fact, their "storytelling" discourse with all its particularism of interpretation is just what we might indulge in in circumstances different from a psychological experiment. So yes, there are multiple logics for different discourse games, but no, all cultures do use all of these logics. So does this mean that there is no difference between ours and the primitives mind? There are clearly differences. We would look for the differences in terms of the situations that a culture deems appropriate for different kinds of discourse.

Just in case Liberia seems too far away, the same kind of problems arise in developmental psychologists' assessments of childrens' minds. For example, H. J. Leevers and P. L. Harris (2000) have shown that even very young children can be induced to accept some approximation of the "syllogism game" by suitable contextualization. In Harris' experiments, children are given syllogisms such as "All cats bark. Fido is a cat. Does Fido bark?" When four-year-olds are given such problems without any clues as to how they are to be interpreted, they experience the same kinds of clash between their current real-world context and the content of the problem that the Liberian peasant appears to experience. Their knowledge that cats don't bark clashes with the problem content. However, if the child is given some clues that the problem is to be interpreted as being about a world defined by the premises, perhaps by prefacing the problem with the statement, "On this really strange planet ...," then the child is quite likely to conclude that Fido barks.

Harris cites his findings as showing that Scribner must have been

wrong to suppose that schooling is what changes the response from a
particularistic one to a "logical" one, because his four-year-olds have
not been exposed to schooling. We think it's clear that Scribner would
have been quite happy with Harris' findings. She did not claim that
there was *no* context in which unschooled subjects would adopt the
interpretation intended by the experimenter—only that the context she
used in her experiments divided subjects along the lines of schooling
they had received. It is clear that Harris' four-year-old subjects do not
spontaneously adopt the relevant interpretation in Scribner's situation,
not without those crucial extra clues that tell them to isolate their
interpretation from the current real-world context. Nor is it clear Harris'
four-year-olds are really playing the fully fledged "syllogism game"—the
syllogism forms used are particularly simple.

So where does this leave us with the issue about the importance
of discourse and of logic? And with the nature of the force of "logical
compulsion"? And what about undergraduate students' responses in the
selection task—our point of departure for this trip to Africa? Wason
confidently asserted that his undergraduate subjects (or at least 95%
of them) had made a fundamental logic error in their card choices in
the selection task. (Does this sound like Evans-Pritchard?) Is Wason
guilty of a lack of sensitivity even greater than Evans-Pritchard? After
all, Evans-Pritchard at least saw the problem as how to account for
the clash between the extreme sophistication of Dugon cosmology and
the Azande's apparently dismal failure to engage in logical puzzles. And
Evans-Pritchard did locate the problem in the nature of the kinds of
discourse the Dugon were willing to engage in. We might take a more
charitable line with Wason and see him as observing that his subjects
fail to engage in a classical logical interpretation of his task, but if this
is what he meant, then he should have been very much aware that there
were other coherent ways they might interpret his task. He certainly
came down strong on their irrationality.

If you, the (patient) reader, are at all like the undergraduate subjects
who people the extensive literature on the selection task, it is likely
that you accepted Wason's explanation of the "correct" response in the
selection task, and you accepted your initial choices of cards as an error
of reasoning.[3] But perhaps you, the reader, were too quick to accept that
you were wrong on this second count? That is, if you accepted Wason's
account of what you *should* do, then perhaps you were wrong to accept

so quickly that you had made an error and that Wason's criteria of correctness are themselves so obviously correct?

This may seem like rubbing salt in the wound—first students' reasoning is supposed, by Wason, to be wrong, and then when they accept experimenters' explanations of why they were wrong, they are then told that this acceptance may be wrong as well. Many students are at this point willing to accept their initial mistake but not willing to accept the possibility that they are thereby mistaken. Nevertheless, it is this possibility we explore in the next two sections as we review some explanations of the observed card choices in the selection task. As counseled above, you would do well to record your own opinions on these matters so that you can compare them with your considered opinion when we are done.

3.4 Explanations for Observations

Wason, Bloor, and most of the many psychologists who have written on the selection task, have adopted a conception of logic that was certainly current in the late 19th century, but which is definitely not current in the early 21st century. No modern logician would want to defend the *uniqueness* of Wason's particular logical model of what cards people *ought* to select as the only logical model available, and few would even want to claim it as the most reasonable choice. Modern logic provides many models of reasoning in this task. Sometimes the very prevalence in peoples' reasoning of what one logical model calls an error has led other logicians to suspect people have a different interpretation and to invent new logics in which the error is now classified as correct reasoning under this different interpretation. So logicians can be seen as modeling peoples' observed reasoning (a descriptive activity). Logic is nowadays also often used as a framework for analyzing the meaning of natural language sentences (such as "If A then 7"). Logic is then, at least to some extent, a descriptive study of a natural language. As we will see in chapter 5, there are limits to what can count as a possible logic—not just anything goes. We will then revisit Bloor's questions about the nature of logical compulsion.

To take a very simple example of a logical explanation, why do so many people turn the 4 card? An explanation that is sometimes advanced, is that some people understand "if ..., then ..." to mean "if

and only if ..., then ...". This statement form is called the BICONDI-
TIONAL because it is the conjunction of two conditionals, one going each
way. This interpretation may be claimed to be due to some sort of statistical regularity on "ordinary experience" of what "if ... then ..." often
means. Leaving aside the statistical claim about frequency in "ordinary
life," whatever that may be, what do you think of this explanation? How
can we assess it? The most important first question is whether the hypothesis is consistent across the pattern of observed choices? If this is
how these subjects interpret "if ..., then ...," then what other cards
should they turn? Do many people in fact turn those cards?

Work through each card and decide whether you have to turn it if
the rule is *If and only if there's a vowel, then there's an even number.*
This is a good homework exercise that may throw up some questions.
In fact, very few subjects do actually turn the pattern of cards that this
rule would lead you to expect. This is a particularly simple example
of an explanation by offering an alternative meaning for the natural
language, and a good example of how such explanations easily fall foul
of the problem of explaining one error at the expense of creating a host
of other anomalies.

However, this reading of the rule as meaning "if and only if" is not
the only other possibility. There is the rather complicated structure of
the pronouns in the phrases "on *one* side of the card... on *the other*
side..." which are called "variable anaphors" in the trade. They are
called variable because rather like algebra variables, the value of one
(what it refers to) depends on the value of the other and *vice versa.*
Suppose these pronouns cause reasoning difficulties, and faced with these
difficulties, some subjects read the rule as meaning "If there's a vowel on
the visible front side of a card, there's an even number on the invisible
back of that card." This is called by linguists a "constant anaphor"
reading (because the reference of each of the pronouns is fixed—they
are like shortened names). Again, you should work out what cards they
then *ought* to turn—the right choice by this standard is not the same.

Nor does the problem quite end there. If a subject adopted the "if
and only if" reading at the same time as the constant anaphor reading,
then the choice of cards they ought to make is different again. Again,
work out what cards they ought to turn if this is their interpretation. We
will return to deeper kinds of explanation in terms of alternative logical
models presently, but having raised this question mark over Wason's

chosen definition of correct performance, let us now take a look at the explanation he himself favored for his striking data.

Verification and falsification

We now turn to take a look at some of what psychologists who have accepted Wason's standard logical account of the meaning of "if..., then..." have had to say about the selection task. Most psychologists have agreed that most subjects are wrong, and try to explain why. Probably the dominant explanation given is in terms of a contrast between VERIFICATION and FALSIFICATION.   People seek, or so it is claimed, the instances that "make the conditional true" but ignore the ones that make it false, thus betraying a preference for "verification" at the expense of "falsification." Thus, the story goes, they turn the A and often the 4 because a 4 or an A, respectively, will confirm the rule.

Leaving aside whether this is a coherent explanation, let us first ask why verification is supposed to be a bad strategy. The conditional states a universal rule—*whenever* there is a vowel, *then* there is always an even number. Suppose we consider what evidence can be found for and against this universal rule. An A with a 4 is evidence for the rule—in the sense that it is one case of its truth. We might argue whether a Q with a 7 or with a 2 are cases where the card complies with the rule, but at least an A with a 4 is a clear case of compliance. On the other hand, an A with a 7 does not comply with the rule. However, there is an asymmetry between the true case and the false one. Although *one* A4 case might encourage in us belief in the universal rule a bit, *just one* A7 is enough to destroy our belief entirely (or so the argument goes). So this explanation of people's behavior is that they incorrectly seek to verify instead of trying to falsify.

Before going any further, we should note that there is a problem about terminology here. If we believe that the only way to verify a universal rule is to seek (and fail) to falsify it, then verification is *not* what people are doing when they seek only positive instances. In fact, seeking verification on this account can *only* be done by seeking falsification. This terminology could be fixed, but we will argue that the theory underlying it cannot be fixed so easily. If you read the psychological papers, remember that they usually mean "seek positive examples" when they say "verify."

Wason took this explanatory apparatus from the philosopher Karl

Popper—an interesting (and salutary) case of interdisciplinary borrowing. Popper was interested in what distinguished scientific method from pseudo-scientific posturings. In particular, his two ardent hates were Marxism and Freudian psychology which he placed firmly in the second category. Popper's complaint against these two colossuses of the 19th century was that their theories were not falsifiable. Whenever some observation came to light that did not fit the theory, then another wrinkle could be added to explain the apparent counterexample away. Science, Popper claimed, was always about successive falsification of theories which produced a gradual convergence towards truth (but no method of absolute verification).

But Popper was wrong that this criterion can distinguish science from nonscience. The most famous historical case of adding "wrinkles" to a theory was Ptolemaic astronomy—based on the idea that all celestial bodies were situated on spheres that controlled their orbits around the earth. Whenever an inaccuracy in the predictions of planetary motion was noted, another EPICYCLE could be added to the theory—another sphere centered on the surface of an existing one would assimilate the observation. By the time that Copernicus proposed that the sun was in fact at the center of the planets, and Kepler that the orbits were elliptical, Ptolemaic astronomy was a mass of competing conglomerations of epicycles each due to a different astronomer. The data still didn't fit all that well in practice, but it can be shown that, allowed enough epicycles, any observed motion can be generated as "spherical motion." So Ptolemy and his followers were just as guilty as Freud and Marx of holding unfalsifiable theories. There are other differences between their theories, but a strong tendency to nonfalsifiability is something they share. In fact, this expense of huge effort to get data to fit theory is common, and necessary, in scientific practice.

For a theory of how science works that pays more attention than Popper's to the data of science in action, we can turn to the sociologist Thomas Kuhn. Kuhn argues that such responses to anomaly are utterly typical of scientific communities engaged in what he dubbed "normal science." Normal science is the activity that goes on within a PARADIGM when there is general acceptance of a conceptual framework. Normal science is what Ptolemaic astronomers were up to prior to Copernicus' revolution. The Copernican revolution redefined the whole conceptual system of astronomy placing the sun at the center of the universe. The method of seeking falsification might be one tool in the armory of normal science, but cannot be what drives either normal or revolutionary science. Before searching for falsifying instances can be any help, scientists need a paradigm—a set of theoretical beliefs and evidential methods that give a coherent account of a range of phenomena. Without such a framework (such as Ptolemy's system), they get nowhere looking for falsifying data. The main reason is that falsifying data is everywhere. Fledgling theories are usually lousy at fitting data. After the revolution, the new paradigm may be even worse at fitting the data for a long period before "normal" science has worked out the complexities of assimilating data to new theory. Scientists, just like the Azande, don't abandon universal rules at the drop of a first falsification. Although scientists will often seek to explain apparent counterexamples, there are well documented cases of scientists simply choosing to ignore them.

One might suppose that Ptolemy was just part of the bad old days when scientists' reasoning was as suspect as the modern everyman's in the selection task, but Kuhn would disabuse you of this way out, too. All the hallmarks of the period of crisis leading up to Copernicus' revolution were also present in the lead up to Newton's, and in turn they recurred when the crisis in 19th century developments descending from the Newtonian paradigm led to Einstein's revolution.

If we return to more homely examples, we can see that this behavior of scientists is modeled on what we often do in everyday vernacular reasoning. Supposing we know that if the switch is up, then the light is on. What do we then do if, turning the switch from down to up one day, we remain in pitchy darkness? Do we conclude that our rule is false?

Ask yourself what you do in this circumstance. We doubt you make this conclusion. You probably conclude that the bulb is burnt out, and replace it. If the switch still doesn't turn the light on, you test for a power cut by trying some other appliance. If there's power, and a second bulb is no better, you test the fuse on the local circuit—or call an electrician. In short, you behave in a thoroughly Ptolemaic way because you have a (possibly crude) theory of electricity and circuits and bulbs and electricians.... There is almost no evidence that will make you give it up (and quite right, too). Your theory only applies if the circuit is a complete low resistance conductor with a suitable voltage applied across it, and although you may not even be able to specify some of the possible problems with fulfilment of this condition, the theory is so useful in making sense of your world, you do not abandon it lightly. Maybe there are occasions when you never did get to the bottom of the problem and the fault eventually just went away, but you rightly don't think of these as the times the laws of physics were false.

This is not to say that our everyday reasoning is exactly like scientific reasoning. Nor is it to say that scientific training makes no difference to reasoning—that would be an unwise argument for an author of a book on cognitive science to make. But it is to argue that in respect of falsification, our everyday reasoning and scientific reasoning are broadly similar. In neither case do we abandon a general theory on the basis of single counterexamples, and for equally good reasons in both cases. In both cases, we need somewhat general models of regularities before it is of much use expending energy on looking for falsifications. What is often needed in the early stages is exploration and description more than falsification. It is now widely accepted that Popper overstressed falsification at the expense of description, exploration, and discovery. So here is a more subtle divergence of the interpretation of "if..., then..." from Wason's logical model than the biconditional reading we considered earlier. These conditionals are interpreted robustly (with regard to exceptions) whereas in Wason's logical model, conditionals are interpreted as brittle—a single counterexample is sufficient to falsify them.

Now, suppose subjects in Wason's experiment interpret his rule about vowels and even numbers as potentially robust to exceptions. Wouldn't that make the task incoherent? Whatever cards we turn and find to be apparent divergences from the rule *might* merely be exceptions? So isn't the "logically correct answer" to complain to the experimenter that the task is incoherent? We believe this problem is near to the heart of many subjects' difficulties—we return to this below. Perhaps you too can empathize on the basis of your initial experience in the task? Interpreting conditionals as robust to some exceptions is a deeper difference from Wason's classical logic than the earlier examples we saw of "if and only if" interpretations and "constant anaphor" interpretations, both of which can be expressed in classical logic. Robust conditionals are not TRUTH FUNCTIONAL as classical logical connectives are—that is, their truth is not simply a function of the truth or falsity of their parts.

Summary

Falsifying evidence is important in assessing the truth of general rules, but it is only interpretable against a background of beliefs—a paradigm. We don't abandon whole theories, either scientific or everyday theories, at the first apparent counterexample. Part of the meaning of rules such as Wason's is that they are generally robust to some exceptions.

It seems that our investigations need to try another tack. If people are good at realizing that a 7 on the back of an A falsifies the rule, but they are bad at realizing that an A on the back of a 7 does so, then we had better find some way of differentiating these two cases. Let's try a digression into ornithology.

The ravens paradox

There once was an ornithology student who abhorred getting wet. Fortunately, considering his eccentric choice of career, he also chose to concentrate on philosophy during his first year at university. In his elementary logic class he learned that there was a rule for reasoning from conditional rules that went as follows: the statement that P implies Q is logically equivalent to the statement that not Q implies not P. When the first ornithology practical class came around, the task was to find out whether all ravens are black. Our hydrophobe friend saw immediately how to exploit his new found logical law. All ravens are black means "If it's a raven, then it's black" and that is logically equivalent to the statement "if it's a non-black thing, then it's a non-raven." So far so good. When his hardy classmates all piled out on a field trip into the wet Caledonian hinterland in search of white ravens (being good falsificationists to the last one), our friend went for a large pile of miscellaneous objects in the corner of his professor's untidy laboratory. When asked what he was doing, he explained that each non-black thing he found in the pile that turned out to be a non-raven (say something white that turned out to be a tennis shoe) was another piece of evidence for the ornithological law.

But our friend did not stop there. Being both a good falsificationist and a good team player, he explained that a single instance of a non-black thing that turned out to be a raven would prove that the rule was false. And what is more, his evidence would be completely complementary to his class-mates. No worries about accidentally counting the same raven twice. So the thinking philosophers' ornithologist stayed dry. But he failed his practical.

Seeing why ornithology is an all-weather occupation helps to see one of the influences that is at work in the selection problem. How is the paradox of the raven to be resolved? There is first the obvious problem that if the student knows that the pile of non-black things that he searches are tennis shoes, and he knows that tennis shoes are non-ravens, then he is guilty of the drunk-under-the-lamp post fallacy of search[4]. Our student would not be *learning* that they are non-ravens by examining them. Similarly if he knows that ravens are exclusively outdoor creatures, and that there are no stuffed ones in the lab, then he could be accused of the same.

But this is not the real problem with the paradox. There may be ravens in the lab, and it might even be that any white ravens are more likely to be in the lab than outside (because of the professor's interest in them perhaps), and our friend may conduct a genuinely open search for things, and by his reasoning accept each non-black thing that turns out to be a non-raven as a piece of evidence for the blackness of ravens. After all, each discovery of a non-black thing could turn out to be the falsifying white raven. What is wrong with this reasoning? The answer is, "nothing," as far as it goes. The problem is not in the reasoning but in the numbers.

The problem with the student's strategy is not in the logic but in the probabilities. The set of non-black things is so much greater than the set of black things, and especially the set of non-ravens is so much greater than the set of ravens, that the *amount* of evidence offered by the discovery of each non-black non-raven is vanishingly small. The avoidance of weather turns out to let him in for a near infinite amount of hard work for the same amount of evidence as a brief field trip.

Returning from our ornithological digression, how does this field trip help with the problem of explaining selection task behavior? Can we understand this behavior in terms of the different amounts of evidence yielded by making predictions about sets of different sizes? Is the subject just right, on this model, to pick the cards he picks? It has been argued so by Chater, & Oaksford (1994). With some rather reasonable assumptions about what people assume about the relative likelihoods of properties, it is possible to explain a wide range of people's behavior in conditional reasoning tasks. Such explanations assert that the highest proportion of people pick the A to check whether it's a 7 because that is the *optimal experiment* in the sense that it is the card turn that promises to give most evidence about truth value, and so on for the other cards until the least likely turned card is the one that yields least evidence (the false consequent card).

The full technicalities of the argument need not detain us here. What is worth noting is how this explanation transforms the way the selection problem is being conceptualized. Instead of being seen as a DEDUCTIVE problem about the application of logical rules, it is being seen as an INDUCTIVE problem about gathering evidence in the form of instances. This reformulation also transforms our stance toward the rationality assumed by our explanations. Popper's explanation is fundamentally a claim that the untutored unscientific mind is subject to a fallacy of reasoning. Kuhn's attack on falsificationism is an argument that *if* this is error, then the scientist is as prone to the error as is the common reasoner. The argument that sees the selection task as essentially inductive is a stance that makes the behavior of the selection task subject reasonable. With some plausible assumptions, we can understand why people exhibit the observed ordering of preference for the cards.

It is on the basis of the ravens paradox that Chater and Oaksford have argued that the vast majority of subjects treat the task as an inductive task and that their responses are the *correct* responses viewed in this light. Of course, what is different about the selection task and the task of verifying a scientific law about ravens is that Wason carefully crafted the selection task so that the negative COMPLEMENT SETS $< non - vowels >$ and $< non - even - numbers >$ are plausibly at least roughly the same size as the positive sets. He achieves this by the often unnoticed first rule *There is a number on one side and a letter on the other side of all cards*. As long as we accept this rule, nonvowels on the other side of a number are consonants, and noneven numbers on the other side of a letter are odd numbers. So we have a positive characterisation of the negatively defined sets.

So, if we want to use the concepts of optimal experiment and information gain to explain that subjects' performance in the selection task is actually dominantly correct, then we have to make the assumption that subjects have made the error of not realising that the positive and negative sets in the selection task are roughly equal in size. This is a claim that our usual habits of evidence gathering are designed for the case where positive and negatively defined sets are very different in size, and these habits are mistakenly transferred to the experimental situation where that doesn't hold. This is a nice example of an important kind of explanation in psychology—something reasonable in our "natural environment" leads to bizarre behavior in an experimental situation. This is one of the excuses for experiments—by introducing bizarre circumstances they can expose the mechanisms that usually run smoothly and undetectably. So here is another subtly different interpretation of the rule and task from the one that Wason's model demands.

Just before we leave our discussion of people's search for evidence, a word about philosophical paradoxes is in order. Paradoxes may strike you initially as merely irritating. It's pretty obvious that ornithology is an outdoor activity, and so any argument to the contrary is absurd. But absurdity is chief among philosophy's tools. In general, with paradoxes, it is not the absurd conclusion that the philosopher believes to be established by the paradox. Paradox is generally an attack on an *explanation* for some phenomenon. The philosopher is saying that *if this explanation is correct*, then this truly absurd consequence follows. So the *explanation* must be wrong. A famous example is what is commonly known as Bishop Berkeley's argument that the tree in the quadrangle is only there when we are looking at it. In fact Bishop Berkeley had no worries about the flightiness of trees. What he did reject were certain *explanations* of how it is that we *know* the tree is there when we aren't there to see it. Berkeley was responsible for the first proto-psychological theory about how vision worked, 150 years before psychology was recognized. He was among the first to recognize that a different kind of explanation was required. He was a very early cognitive scientist.

3.5   Modifications of the Task: What *is* and What *Should Be*

We have spent quite a bit of time on following out the ramifications of various different kinds of explanation of Wason's original selection task findings in order to reveal the interconnections between theory and data in interpreting the facts. Psychologists' response in the 1970s was actually to seek for modifications of the task that would make it "easier"—in the sense of making it so that more subjects would conform to Wason's chosen logical model. It wasn't too long before they came up with materials that made the task almost trivially easy. To cut a long story short, the same population of subjects were found to be good at problems such as the following:

On each card below, there is the name of a drink on one side and the drinker's age on the other. Your task is to decide which if any of the cards you *must* turn to decide if the drinker obeys the rule.

Rule: *If you drink alchohol, then you must be over 18 years old.*

Cards: whiskey   orange   19   16

In this task, about 85% of undergraduate subjects chose "whiskey" and "16", the cards corresponding to the A and 7 that were so rarely chosen before. This finding led psychologists to some very sweeping conclusions about the relation between logic and psychology in understanding human reasoning. The argument went as follows: This new "drinking-age" version of the rule is of the same *logical form* as the earlier "vowels and consonants" task. Since people find this one easy and the other hard, they cannot be reasoning in virtue of logical form. So logic cannot be the basis for a theory of human reasoning. Cosmides, the originator of the arguments we are about to examine, went on to found so-called "evolutionary psychology" on this evidence. This theory claims to be able to show that our Pleistocene ancestors developed "cheater-detection" modules in their brains and these modules are what allow student subjects to do the second task but not the first.

Johnson-Laird used the same argument about the shared logical form of the two versions of the selection task to develop "mental models" theory that is claimed to be an alternative to "mental logics" as a basis for human reasoning. So this argument is of some importance in psychology.

We believe this argument is completely wrong and comes from a failure of disciplinary communication. Logic, at least since Aristotle (1st century BC), has taught us that the two rules in these two versions of the task, as interpreted by the subjects, have very different logical forms. These two different forms interact with features of the selection task to make the reasoning about one easy and the other hard for simple logical reasons. The consequences for evolutionary psychology and mental models theory are considerable. The necessary logical principles are quite simple and can be explained non-technically. With this heavy hint, you should consider whether you agree that the two tasks have the same form before reading on. If they don't have the same form, note down some of the differences.

The original Wason rule about vowels and consonants is interpreted by Wason as a *descriptive* rule: the drinking-age rule is interpreted as a *deontic* rule. This distinction is closely related to the contrast between descriptive and normative theories we have stressed heavily throughout. Descriptive rules say how the world *is*: deontic rules say how the world *ought* to be.[5] This semantic contrast makes an enormous difference to the ease of reasoning in the selection task. If the relation between rule and cases (cards denoting drinkers) is deontic, then the relation is simple. Cases either comply or not. The status of the rule is completely unaffected by the compliance or non-compliance of the cases. The law may be in force even though everybody breaks it. So, whether one case complies or not has no effect on any other case.

The situation with the descriptive rule is different and very complex. For all the reasons discussed above to do with the robustness to exceptions of our everyday commonsense rules (remember the light switch), it is far from clear whether a single non-compliant case makes a rule false. *If* we do interpret a rule as brittle to single exceptions, then the need to turn a card will be contingent on whether any prior turns have already revealed the rule to be false, so one card's effect interacts with whether other cards' need to be turned. Worse still, it is far from clear even if *all four* cards comply with the rule whether the rule is thereby true. If the cards are thought of as simply a sample of data about a general rule, then their compliance is not enough to show the rule is true, even if each may raise the probability of its truth.

Each of these possibilities makes it hard for subjects to know what to do. None of these difficulties arise with the deontic rule. There are several other problems with the descriptive rule that do not apply to the deontic one—for example the biconditional and anaphora problems mentioned above.

Yet another difference has to do with the peculiar structure of the descriptive selection task as communication. The subject is given a lot of information by the experimenter that they are supposed to take on trust (notably that there is a letter and a number on opposite sides of each card). They are then asked to doubt the main rule, but not to doubt any of this other information. That is, they are asked to trust that the experimenter is being *cooperative* about most of the communication, but to suspend this trust with regard to the rule and treat it *adversarially*. We will see in Part IV that these two stances are important for understanding the pragmatics of language use. For example, if subjects cease to trust the experimenter about the rule they might also doubt whether there are numbers on one side of the cards and letter on the other sides. They would then have to turn all the cards to test the rule. The experimenter is, moreover, an authority figure. If the rule should turn out to be false, the experimenter could be interpreted as lying to the subject. This is an uncomfortable social situation. None of this arises with the deontic rule where the subject is asked to test whether some third parties (the drinkers described) are breaking a law.

On this account, the descriptive and deontic versions of the selection task are just two rather different tasks and one (the descriptive task) should be much harder than the deontic one, as is observed. Unfortunately, no knowledge of our Pleistocene ancestors accrues from this observation. Mental models theory also fails to make this crucial semantic distinction in its explanations of subjects' behavior.

A common response from psychologists to this line of argument is that whereas philsophers and logicians may enjoy such fastidious arguments about the meanings of English sentences, psychologists, along with their subjects, are more down to earth people who just get on with what the task obviously requires. To quote Cosmides:

After all, there is nothing particularly complicated about the situation described in a rule such as "If a person eats red meat, then that person drinks red wine." Cosmides and Tooby (1992), footnote 14, page 223.

Here is a fundamental disagreement. We believe that in coming to adopt one of the many possible (albeit each simple) interpretations of such sentences, subjects actually must engage in rather complex and sophisticated reasoning, even though they may not be aware of what they do, nor have the terminology and concepts to report it even if they are aware. It is a useful homework exercise to note down some of the many different interpretations of Cosmides' example.[6] The fact that in this case we may be able to guess the likely intended interpretation from general knowledge is neither here nor there.

Talking to the subjects—carefully

But how are we to decide between these explanations? The semantic differences between descriptives and deontics are well established, and they do have the consequences for reasoning in these two versions of the task just described. But are they the cause (or among the causes) of the difficulties subjects have in the descriptive task? And how are we to find out? We would certainly agree with the psychologists that there is an extra empirical question here—are these really the problems the student subjects suffer from?

This is a nice example of the importance of being clear about the difference between conceptual and empirical questions. The conceptual differences between deontic and descriptive rules and their implications for reasoning are clear enough; but the empirical question as to whether subjects' reasoning is actually controlled by these factors in the relevant way is an empirical question we cannot settle in our armchairs. Equally, we cannot interpret any set of experimental results without noticing these semantic differences between the tasks. The whole experimental method depends on understanding all the differences between experimental conditions, and these semantic differences have been missed by researchers on the selection task.

Fortunately there are ways of distinguishing possibilities in the laboratory. Two broad approaches have been used. One is to use SOCRATIC TUTORING to elicit subjects' reasoning and the other consists of a program of modified experiments of the traditional kind.

The socratic tutor uses open ended questions without direct feedback to elicit subjects' reasoning. It is an interesting half-way house between getting subjects to make simple introspective reports of their reasoning, and the traditional experimental approach. Socratic dialogues are not best thought of as reports—rather as *arguments* made by the subject. Nevertheless, the elicitation may well affect the subjects' reasoning so it provides at best indirect evidence about subjects' reasoning in the standard task. This variety of methods and their interrelations is an important reason for choosing Wason's task as our example field. All too often researchers stick with a single kind of experiment as a source of information about mental processes—its much easier to run the changes on a single paradigm. We think it is better that converging evidence from as many different methods as possible is brought to bear. That is another aspect of cognitive science.

The following snippets of dialogue come from several subjects in typical socratic tutoring dialogues about Wason's task. They are chosen to bear on some of the semantic difficulties predicted to arise from descriptive rules in the selection task. In each case, the subject is only asked open ended questions and never given feedback as to whether their answers are "right" or "wrong." The tutor starts by asking what might be on the back of each card, and then asks the subject to spell out the consequences of each possibility, and to state what cards they would turn. Finally the cards are turned and the subject assesses their implications. In the dialogues below, "E" stands for experimenter and "S" for subject. The notation "number/letter" means that the number is visible and the letter is on the back: "letter/number" the reverse. A question mark indicates that the value is still unknown to the subject. The snippets are chosen to illustrate the points reviewed above about the semantics of descriptive conditionals.

Subject 18.
S. If I just looked at that one on its own [7/A] I would say that it didn't fit the rule, and that I'd have to turn that one [A/?] over, and if that was different [i.e. if there wasn't an even number] then I would say the rule didn't hold.
E. So say you looked at the 7 and you turned it over and you found an A, then?
S. I would have to turn the other cards over ... well it could be just an exception to the rule so I would have to turn over the A.

In this first snippet Subject 18 demonstrates problems arising from an interpretation of the rule as robust to exceptions. It comes after some of the cards have been turned. The subject clearly recognizes that [7/A] doesn't fit the rule. However, it emerges that he would still want to turn the A to find out whether it too failed to fit, because there could be exceptions to a true rule. You might say that if this is the subjects' problem then they should turn A and 7. This may be true, but remember they are also told to minimize their turnings, and the A is more likely to yield more evidence than the 7. The main point is that if the subject quite reasonably interprets the rule as robust to exceptions, then the task is incoherent. You might say that the subject should therefore reason that the intended interpretation must be "brittle"—that is the rule must be exceptionless—but this is only one of the many problems a subject might have, and there is a problem about which inference to make about interpretation.

Subject 10.
S. OK so if there is a vowel on this side then there is an even number, so I can turn A to find out whether there is an even number on the other side or

I can turn the 4 to see if there is a vowel on the other side.

⋮

S. But if that doesn't exclude the rule being true then I have to turn another one.

E. So you are inclined to turn this over [the A] because you wanted to check?

S. Yes, to see if there is an even number.

E. And you want to turn this over [the 4]?

S. Yes, to check if there is a vowel, but if I found an odd number [on the back of the A], then I don't need to turn this [the 4].

E. So you don't want to turn ...

S. Well, I'm confused again because I don't know what's on the back, I don't know if this one ...

⋮

E. What about the 7?

S. Yes the 7 could have a vowel, then that would prove the whole thing wrong. So that's what I mean, do you turn one at a time or do you ...?

Subject 10 gives evidence of the problem of contingency between the card turnings, information gained, and further turnings. The subject wants to give an answer that takes into account the contingencies between what is found on the back after one turning, and whether any more turnings are needed. You might say that it is obvious that the experimenter is asking what cards must be turned if the information gain turns out to be as uninformative as it can be. But again the instruction to minimize turnings is quite naturally interpreted as implying that the choice of turns should be contingent.

Subject 5.

E. Now turn over those two [K and 7].

S. [Turning over the K] It's a K and 4. Doesn't say anything about this [pointing to the rule]. [After turning over the 7] Aha!

E. So that says the rule is ...?

S. That the rule is wrong. But I still wouldn't turn this over, still because I wouldn't know if it would give an A, it could give me a K and that wouldn't tell me anything.

E. But even though it could potentially give you an A on the back of it like this one has.

S. Yes, but that's just luck. I would have more chance with these two [referring to the A and the 4].

Subject 5 argues that there is a better chance of getting the evidence required by turning A than by turning 7. This subject illustrates the power of the ravens paradox.

Subject 8.
S. [after turning A and finding 7] Well there is something in the syntax with which I am not clear because it does not say that there is an exclusion of one thing, it says "if there is an A on one side there is a 4 on the other side." So the rule is wrong.
E. This [pointing to A] shows that the rule is wrong.
S. Oh so the rule is wrong, it's not something I am missing.

Subject 8 was rather bewildered when upon turning A he found a 7. There is clear evidence that the subject was assuming that the rule was true. Although this may sound similar to Wason's "verification bias," it is actually very different. Wason assumed that subjects would be in genuine doubt about the truth value of the rule, but would then proceed in an "irrational," verificationist manner to seek the wrong evidence. What transpires here is that subjects take it on the authority of the experimenter that the rule is true, and then interpret the instructions as to indicate those cards that are evidence of this. Another similar example:

Subject 22.
S. Well my immediate thought first time was to assume that this is a true statement, therefore you only want to turn over the card that you think will satisfy the statement.

What do these brief snatches of dialogue tell us? On their own very little. First you have to trust us that these are not merely isolated examples, or that the brief quotes are unrepresentative of the complete dialogues. On this point you have our promise—these are representative of common issues that arise in the dialogues with appreciable frequency. If you don't believe us, or even if you do, you could, in the spirit of this course, try some socratic tutoring of your own. Its good fun and very revealing. It helps a great deal if you can tape the dialogues so that you can reexamine what is said.

Second there is the problem that the subject may reason differently in extended dialogue with the "tutor" than they reason on their own doing the classical experiment. This argument is a serious one and can only be responded to by designing experiments, as we shall describe presently.

So what do these dialogues tell us? We regard them as providing *prima facie* evidence that subjects do experience the kinds of problems that our semantic analyses predict. They may remind you of problems that you experienced when you first did the task? If socratic dialogues revealed not the slightest trace of the problems predicted, then although that would not be conclusive evidence against the predictions, it would certainly have motivated us to think harder about the developing theory.

But these dialogues also strongly suggest several important points about the mental processes that go on in doing the selection task that have not emerged from the hundreds of papers that use more straightforward experimental techniques. Although the snippets we quote here are too short to reveal this, the whole dialogues strongly suggest that different subjects have very different reasons for choosing (or not choosing) the very same cards. This suggests that there are what psychologists call *individual differences* between subjects that are as important to explain as the overall group tendencies. Different subjects experience different problems and reason in different ways, and a good cognitive theory should be able to describe and ulitmately explain how and why. Even in the standard experiments, there are several common patterns of card choice but very little interest has been shown in the question what do the differences tell us about the subjects.

One kind of theory of individual differences is that some people are just more intelligent than others and this is what strings them out along a dimension of dumb-to-clever responses. But this doesn't help much in the selection task. Even if we accept a particular theory of what is the "clever" choice, how are the other possible choices to be ordered relative to this standard? And if different subjects make the same choice for different reasons, merely ordering the responses may not help. What we surely ought to seek is a theory about the different mental processes that lead to the different responses?

There are good reasons why psychologists often begin in an area by seeking to describe and explain regularities across groups of subjects. With regard to the selection task, they have chiefly asked what factors control how many people make the selection Wason's particular theory says people should. Remember what was said in the Introduction about different idealisations in science.

A further kind of question that can be raised about the selection task is how do subjects *learn* to do the task correctly? In the socratic dialogues we see subjects changing their mind during the dialogue. These changes are not always in the right direction toward the expected choices or explanations, nor always permanent. Often a subject who is clear about one thing and confused about another at one point, gets into a state of mind in which the clarity and confusion swap around. But sometimes there is progress toward insight into the task, and sometimes insight is lasting. We ought to be able to provide a cognitive theory of this learning. It is very early days in the development of such a theory.

What we do know is that a theory needs to explain how new knowledge is built on old knowledge. Subjects implicitly know a great deal about their language and about reasoning, though not very much of what they know before they start tutoring is explicit. They lack terminology and concepts. Or perhaps it is better to say that they have lots of terminology but they don't always use it consistently. Nor have they always differentiated the many meanings they have for words like "truth" and "falsity."

Experimental corroboration

Returning to our second question, how can we find out whether subjects doing the task as Wason invented it actually encounter the problems that the socratic dialogues reveal? In other words, does the socratic tutoring reveal mental processes that are already going on in the original task (whether or not subjects are aware of them), or does the tutoring radically change what subjects think and how they reason?

One way of approaching these questions is to design variations in the task to alleviate specific problems, and then to see whether these changes actually facilitate subjects' reasoning. If they do, that provides some evidence that subjects do suffer from these problems in the standard task, whether they can report them or not. We will illustrate with three example manipulations. One is an instruction to alleviate misunderstandings about contingencies between card-choice and feedback; one is an instruction to separate the source of the rule from the source of the other information about the task; and the third is a two-rule version of the task designed to induce a brittle interpretation of the rules as intended to be exceptionless.

If subjects are confused about whether they are intended to specify all the card turnings that would be necessary on the assumption that the backs were minimally informative, or whether they should imagine making card-choices contingent on what they find as they go, then simply clarifying this by adding the following to the standard instructions might help:

... Assume that you have to decide whether to turn each card before you get

any information from any of the turns you choose to make.

It turns out that this helps about 15% more subjects to make the Wason's "correct" choices, and raises the turning of the problematical not-Q card from 18% to 47%. Although it may intuitively seem implausible, this is strong evidence that this confusion is an important one in the original task.

The second manipulation is an instruction designed to separate the source of the rule from the experimenter to clarify the communication situation and to remove the discomfort of questioning the truthfulness of an authority figure. Here the following italicized words were added to the standard instructions:

... The rule has been *put forward by an unreliable source.* Your task is to decide which cards (if any) you *must* turn in order to decide *if the unreliable source is lying.* Don't turn unnecessary cards. Tick the cards you want to turn.

This instruction helps 10% more subjects to respond completely "correctly" and increases not-Q turning from 18% to 28%. Again this is strong evidence that these instructions remove problems for significant, though smaller numbers of subjects.

It is not quite so easy to know how to remove the possibility of subjects interpreting rules as robust to exceptions. One way is to emphasize that the task is to choose evidence to decide between alternative rules. The following modification of the standard task does just that.

... Below there appear two rules. One rule is true of all the cards, the other isn't. Your task is to decide which cards (if any) you *must* turn in order to decide which rule holds. Don't turn unnecessary cards. Tick the cards you want to turn.

Rule 1: *If there is a vowel on one side, then there is an even number on the other side.*

Rule 2: *If there is a consonant on one side, then there is an even number on the other side.*

You should first ask yourself what is the "correct" answer in this case? You should then ask yourself, on the basis of your experience of doing this task and the original one, whether you think subjects will find this easier or harder? What do you think they will choose to turn?

Normative performance in this task, according to the Wason's logical model, is to turn only the not-Q card. You should satisfy yourself that this is correct. The rules are chosen so that the correct response is to turn exactly the card that the vast majority of subjects fail to turn in the orginal task. This has the added bonus that it is no longer correct to turn the P card which provides an interesting comparison with the classical task. This is the only version of the task for which choosing the true antecedent card is an error.

By any obvious logical measure of task complexity, this task is more complicated than the original task. It demands that two conditionals are processed and that the implications of each case is considered with respect to both rules and with respect to a distribution of truth values. The normative response is to turn *neither* the true-antecedent nor true-consequent cards. Nevertheless, if this task succeeds in inducing subjects to treat the rules as brittle and exceptionless, then performance should be substantially nearer the logically normative model.

In fact, this task helps 20% more subjects to get the "correct" answer (remember this answer is now different) and it increases not-Q choice from 18% to 30%. So again this is strong evidence that the natural robust interpretation of the rule in the standard task does cause problems.

The socratic dialogues that result from tutoring on this two-rule task are particularly revealing, and it turns out, as one would predict if robust interpretation is a problem in the standard task, that it is much easier to get subjects to reach insight on this task than the standard one-rule task. A few example dialogues will illustrate.

Subject 8.
S. I wouldn't look at this one [7] because it wouldn't give me appropriate information about the rules; it would only tell me if those rules are wrong, and I am being asked which of those rules is the correct one. Does that make sense?

Subject 5.
E. What about if there was a 7?
S. A 7 on the other side of that one [A]. Then this [rule 1] isn't true. It doesn't say anything about this one [rule 2].
E. And the K?
S. If there is a 7, then this one [rule 2] isn't true, and it doesn't say anything about that one [rule 1].

Subjects 5 and 8 have no trouble seeing that certain cards could show particular rules are false, but they still wonder whether the evidence can show that any rule is therefore true. Is simple compliance of the four cards sufficient? Note that it is precisely this difficulty that is absent in the case of deontic rules such as: *If you want to drink alcohol, you have to be over 18.* Such a rule cannot and does not have to be shown to be true; at most we can establish that it is not violated. So in the deontic case, subjects only have to do what they find easy in any case.

As we argued above, the semantic relations between rule and card are complicated in the descriptive interpretation. If a card complies with the rule, in other words "if the rule is true of the card," then some subjects seem to have a tendency to transfer this notion of truth to "truth of the rule" *tout court.* Both are sensible ways of using the word "true" but they are not the same and appear to get confused. One experimental manipulation in the tutorial dialogue for the two–rule task addressed this problem by making subjects first turn A and K, to find 4 on the back of both. This caused great confusion, because the subjects' logic (transfering "truth of the card" to "truth of the rule") led them to conclude that therefore both rules must be true, contradicting the instruction that one was false.

Subject 18 [Initial choice was 4.]
E. Start with the A, turn that over.
S. A goes with 4.
E. OK now turn the K over.
S. Oh God, I shouldn't have taken that card, the first ...
E. You turned it over and there was a 4.
S. There was a 4 on the other side, A and 4. If there is a K then there is a 4, so they are both true. [Makes a gesture that the whole thing should be dismissed.]

This confusion between compliance of card with rule and demonstration of truth of rule by card is a nice example of subjects not having the technical vocabulary and explicit control of the concepts involved when they start the tutoring session. On the other hand subjects who ultimately got the two–rule task right also appeared to have an insight into the intended relation between rule and cards.

Subject 6.
E. So say there were a A on the back of the 4, then what would this tell you?
S. I'm not sure where the 4 comes in because I don't know if that would make the A-one right, because it is the opposite way around. If I turned that one [pointing to the A] just to see if there was an 4, if there was a 4 it doesn't mean that rule two is not true.

Part of the difficulty of the standard task involving a descriptive rule is the possibility of confusing the two relations between rule and cards. Transferring the "truth of the card" to the "truth of the rule" may be related to what Wason called "verification bias," but it cuts a lot deeper.

Of course, we cannot tell from these results how many subjects suffer from combinations of these problems or the several other problems that arise in the descriptive but not the deontic selection task. That is a topic of active research. The question cannot be answered simply by combining all the helpful instructions for reasons you should be able to deduce. But we can tell that the two tasks, descriptive and deontic, are quite different tasks because descriptive and deontic rules have quite different meanings and quite different logical forms.

One final demonstration of the importance of a careful approach to logical form before we move on to the broader implications of these results. In the spirit of broad exploration seeking as many kinds of evidence as we can get, we should ask ourselves, how much of the problem in the selection task is due to the complexities of the meaning of conditionals? One very simple way to find out is to use a different LOGICAL CONNECTIVE. What would happen if we simply substitute the following rule in the standard task:

Rule: *There are vowels on one side of the cards* **and** *even numbers on the other.*

This rule is not conditional but *conjunctive* —"and" conjoins the clauses where as "if ... , then..." makes one conditional on the other. (The bold font is for your convenience–when the experiment is run the font used is normal).

Ask yourself what you would turn in this task? Before you read any further, write down your choices and give your reasons. What does the logical model of language that Wason employed say about this rule? Again write down what you think. What do you think subjects do in fact turn if they are faced with this as a first task, and are not in the middle of a course on thinking, reasoning, and communication?

Wason's logical model demands that subjects should turn *no* cards with such a conjunctive rule—the rule interpreted in the same logic as Wason's interpretation of his conditional rule can already be seen to be false of the not-P and not-Q cards. Therefore, under this interpretation, the rule is already known to be false and no cards should be turned. When this conjunctive rule is given to the same population of subjects as the original task, virtually no subjects adopt the reading suggested by Wason's logical model. Instead, 70% of subjects choose the A and 4 cards and only 3% turn no cards. So it is not just conditional rules that cause substantial problems for subjects (or, looking at it the other way, for Wason's chosen logical model) in the selection task.

We predicted that many subjects would not make Wason's model's interpretation or the corresponding response. An alternative, perfectly rational, interpretation of the experimenter's intentions is to construe the rule as having deontic force (every card *should* have a vowel on one side and an even number on the other) and to seek cards that might flout this rule *other than ones that obviously can already be seen to flout it.* If this reasonable interpretation were adopted, then the P and Q cards would be chosen. An important part of the reasons why subjects adopt this interpretation may be that they feel bound to turn something— after all the experiment is about turning cards isn't it? This is what psychologists call the "demand characteristics" of the task.

Note that this interpretation just sketched is deontic even though the rule is formally *indicative.* It is a general feature of natural languages that deontic rules are often stated with the same sentences as descriptively interpreted rules, and it is often only the context that tells us which the utterer intended. For example, the notice on the lifeboat "Women and children enter the lifeboats first" is interpreted as having deontic force—it is about what should happen—but the sentence is syntactically in indicative mood.

These controlled experimental tests of predicted problems arising from the meanings of descriptive conditionals go a long way towards supporting the idea that the predicted problems initially found in the socratic dialogues do in fact play a role in subjects' reasoning in the standard task setting. It is hard to explain how these instructional and task changes help subjects to construe the task the way that Wason intended (or in the case of the conjunctive rule, give us evidence that they construe the task a different way) unless these are real problems for the subjects doing the original task. This sequence of investigations serves as an illustration of how the different methods (socratic tutoring, controlled experiment) can be used together to support each others' strengths and weaknesses.

3.6 What does it all mean for cognitive theory?

Let us pause now after this long sequence of arguments and ask ourselves what emerges from this minute examination of peoples' behavior with regard to a single sentence in Wason's original task? First, the picture that emerges from the socratic dialogues is of subjects having many different problems (in many different combinations) with interpreting how the experimenter intends the task and materials to be understood. Much of the reasoning going on is reasoning about how to find an interpretation, consistent with all the different information, that makes the task doable. The individual problems created by the semantics of descriptive conditionals interact with each other. Changing one aspect of the interpretation has implications for other aspects. These problems are, properly understood, reasonable problems that intelligent rational people may have in understanding the very strange communication situation that the selection task represents. We have only been able to illustrate a sample of these problems here, we hope you have seen enough to realize that the problems of interpretation are complex. Many of these problems have not been discussed by psychologists concerned with the task.

This chain of arguments has important morals for how the different disciplines' contributions have to be fitted together to gain a rounded account of even a very simple task. Wason's task is centrally about the meaning of a rule and how to gather evidence to support its truth or demonstrate its falsity. The disciplines that study the meaning of natural languages are chiefly logic, philosophy and linguistics. These disciplines have made extensive studies of the meanings of conditionals precisely because general rules are so important in so many fields of human endeavour, not least science itself. In the late 19th century these disciplines subscribed to the view that there was a single correct logic (perhaps even the one that Wason adopted as his standard) but in the early 21st century this is not the view of any of these disciplines. Instead their view of language is that there are many logical models of parts of natural languages and the appropriateness of these models is determined by very subtle contextual cues. It is highly ironic that psychologists who have been most adamant that logic cannot serve as a basis for human reasoning because people do not reason in virtue of form, have in fact adopted the notion that a single logical model can serve as the only standard for correct performance by which to judge subjects' reasoning. In Part II, we will look further into the nature of logical models of meaning and how they can serve as the foundations for a psychology of reasoning and communication.

But first we will turn back and look at the implications of our arguments for psychological interpretations of the selection task. First and foremost, logical treatments of language assign many different logical forms to the same sentence. Although once a FORM and its interpretation have been adopted, then reasoning from that form may be mechanical (blind to content), we cannot ignore the process of choosing interpretations. Interpretation and reasoning are interactive processes. We may interpret something one way, and then when reasoning from that interpretation, we may come to a conclusion that makes us doubt whether we have got the *intended* interpretation. This may lead us to change our interpretation, and to start reasoning again. We see this kind of interaction going on in the socractic dialogues. So logic is made of two parts—an interpretational apparatus and a reasoning aparatus. Taken together, these two parts make logic a theory about how reasoning proceeds differently in different contexts. Psychologists have tended to interpret logic as a theory that reasoning is universally the same in all contexts. This is simply a misunderstanding of logic.

Of course, the fact that so many reasonable interpretations of bits of language are possible makes the study of human reasoning and communication much more complex than it would be if we all spoke a single language with a fixed interpretation. But there are many obvious reasons why this is not possible, and why life (and cognitive science) are so rich and interesting.

There is also a practical reason that the selection task is important. The particular way that the task is abstract relative to more normal communication situations is very common in university level educational situations. Students must learn how to interpret written material abstracted from its world of application. They must learn on the basis of indirect representations how to acquire new concepts in these interpretations, and when to take something on trust, and when to test it against evidence. Logic began in classical Greece as an "educational technology" for teaching the skills of political and legal debate. Its emphasis on making all information explicit, and on making sure that interpretation remains constant throughout an argument is critical in learning how to learn more easily. Logic still can be an important educational technology, though not if it is coneived of as a single fixed normative standard of reasoning.

So where does this leave us with regard to the questions raised on our anthropological field-trip to Africa? There we compared Wason the psychological experimenter to Levy-Bruhl and Evans-Pritchard the anthropologists, accusing their "subjects" of irrationality. We have now laid out arguments to the effect that it was Wason who was deluded about the simplicity of his model of what people ought to do in his task, just as Evans-Pritchard underestimated the difficulty of assessing the rationality of the Azande's witch-craft beliefs. On our account our undergraduate subjects should be seen as struggling to make sense of a very complicated set of information that contains many conflicts in need of resolution. We do not argue that they necessarily succeed in finding a lucid resolution. Nor do we argue that they have perfect and explicit control of their knowledge of the domain of reasoning. Just as we argued that in the case of Scribner's observations of primitive peoples' reasoning, there are kinds of discourse that our students don't readily engage in. Our subjects are neither infallible nor irrational, just human.

3.7   Taking stock

We arrive here at the end of a long and twisting argument. Quite apart from the importance of the particular conclusions that may be drawn, there are some important general conclusions for study skills. Let us review both the specific conclusions and the general ones.

As we have just had cause to note, Wason's experiment shows how people are not accustomed to placing so much weight on tiny words alone—they are quite reasonably much guided by what they take the intentions of the author of the words to be. Science places heavy weight on words, the concepts behind words, and on making intentions explicit in the text. Scientific concepts and terminologies, especially in the cognitive sciences, are often confusable with ordinary uses of the same terms. But the reader should be warned—the exact meaning is critical. This has very direct consequences for the way that this text should be read. If you, dear reader, have arrived at this point in the chapter after one pass through, then it is highly unlikely that you have extracted the moral of our tale. You should expect to have to re-read several times. After all, we have spent forty pages discussing an experiment that hinges on the meaning of a single innocent looking sentence—"If there's a vowel on one side, then there's an even number on the other." Our own language is novel, and not necessarily simpler.

But merely re-reading in the same fashion as a first pass is unlikely to help much. How should the reader go about this task? What is important and what can be discarded? The best answer to this question is that it is the structure of the argument that is crucial, and it is the structure of the argument that determines which details are necessary because they carry that structure, and which can be discarded because they don't. Let's take this chapter as an example and review the structure of its argument.

First an experiment was introduced—Wason's selection task. The task was presented and the results summarized. Second, Wason's interpretation was then described—according to Wason, almost all his subjects got this task wrong. Thirdly, this idea of wrongness was itself described and given Wason's justification. Fourthly, this situation of an observer claiming that almost every one of some subject population got some simple task wrong was likened to anthropologists who put themselves in the same situation when commenting on the reasoning of primitive peoples. Fifthly, we turned to look at Wason's explanations of why his subjects got things wrong in terms of verification and falsification, along with the origins of this explanation in Popper's philosophy. Sixthly, the possibility of a quite different standard of rightness or wrongness of performance was raised through consideration of the ravens paradox—perhaps subjects did what they did because of the arithmetic governing the seeking of evidence in their natural habitat?

At this point, more experimental evidence was introduced. Drinking-age rules make the selection task very easy—at least according to Wason's definition of correct performance. Almost as many subjects from the same population get this task "right" as got the other task "wrong." Yet the tasks look as if they are of identical *form*. With these new observations, came a new interpretation and new explanations—the evolution of "cheating detectors" was supposed to explain the new data. This new explanation is in turn a new argument with new questions. Why can't cheating detectors perform the descriptive task? Are the deontic and descriptive tasks of the same form?

At this point we turned to consider what logic and linguistics had to say about the many meanings of conditional rules. Logic draws a very basic distinction between deontic and descriptive semantics—how the world is and how it should be. Paying careful attention to this distinction reveals how the vowels-and-consonants task poses quite different problems than the drinking-age law. The two rules are interpreted as having different forms. Brittleness to exceptions, contingencies of response on new evidence, anaphora, biconditionality, card-reversibility, the social psychology of authority figures all come into play in the first task but not the second.

Logic can show how the semantics may make the tasks different, but it cannot demonstrate that these differences determine how people act differently in the two tasks. For that we needed to go back to the laboratory, first collecting Socratic dialogues and then controlled experimental evidence. Dialogues are a different kind of evidence with different strengths and weaknesses than experimental evidence. Again the observations are described, and then interpreted, and then explanations based on them were offered. With those explanations we revisited the evolutionary explanations and came to a quite different view of the relation between psychology and logic. Finally we returned to the big picture and argued that Wason's subjects are to be seen as struggling, quite reasonably, to find an interpretation of all the information they have that makes the task sensible to them.

Our different picture leads us to very different conclusions about evolutionary psychology, and about the relation between logic and psychology more generally. Rather than seeing two disciplines competing to give explanations of reasoning mechanisms, we see the relation between logic and psychology as analogous to the relation between mathematics and physics or biology. Logic is the mathematics of information systems, and people, at one level of analysis, are one kind of information system. Psychology is concerned with applying the mathematical descriptions produced by logic to understanding how information systems are implemented in people. This implementation is as likely to be in feelings as in symbols, and does not mean that people cannot make errors in reasoning. This relation between mathematics and experiments is much more typical of science in general than the model that is common in psychology. Logic cannot settle empirical facts by musings in armchairs, but psychological experiments cannot be interpreted without coherent conceptual systems either. Logic and psychology are not in competition—they ought to be in collaboration. A much richer experimental science can ensue, as we hope to have illustrated in a small way.

This has been the structure of the argument. This is what you should be able to produce as a precis of this chapter. Why isn't the chapter replaceable by the precis? Because the devil is in the details. It matters, for example, exactly what wording Wason used in his experiment, and exactly how the drinking-age task is phrased. How can one tell which aspects of Wason's wording is critical? One can't—at least one can't by simply looking at the wording. Does that mean that one should memorize the wording of Wason's original paper? No! because not all the features of the exact wording do make important differences. And, as the "conjunction" experiment shows, it is often not the wording alone that is important. How can one tell the wheat from the chaff? Only by working through what details play what roles in the argument's larger structure. There has to be a continuous traffic between details and argument.

This all sounds like hard work? Why not just remember the details? In Chapter 6 we will show that remembering the details is even harder work. Yes, it is hard work understanding the argument, but once you understand the relationship between the details and the argument you will find the details rather easy to remember—honest. And the argument is the only thing worth having, in the end, because it is the generalizations of the argument that tell us something about how the human mind works—what we set out to find out about.

A common student response at this point is to complain that its all very well the professor stipulating that you have to remember the right details and ditch the irrelevant ones, but the professor has a huge body of specialist knowledge about the hundreds of experimental variations that have been tried and only that knowledge can really tell which details are important. This is a reasonable objection. No student can be blamed for not knowing about Bloggs & Bloggs 1932 article in the Annals of the Transylvanian Society for Parapsychology that shows that such-and-such wording change makes no difference to the results.[7] All any of us can do at any stage is to understand the details we know of, in the matrix of our general explanations, in our current state of knowledge. But none of us has any alternative to trying to formulate what is critical about the details and what is irrelevant surface detail in the light of the arguments as we understand them. The student who produces the best argument for a quite different conclusion than the professor's should always get the highest mark on the course, even if the professor happens to know what is wrong with the particular conclusion that is arrived at because of some piece of information the student could not have known. The quality of argument is all important. Again a student might object that this is not the marking regime that they encounter. If that is the case, then we can only commiserate.

This brings us to the issue of authority for conclusions. A minimal amount of asking around your university or searching a good library or the web will easily reveal that there are many researchers in the field of human reasoning that do not agree with the conclusions reached here. Some of the disagreements have been described here and some not. Aren't we highly irresponsible presenting controversial topics to introductory courses? Shouldn't we be presenting consensus topics so that you can learn the "facts" of the discipline before having to mess with controversial arguments? Our answer is emphatically "no." As we believe we have shown, in cognitive science, often the consensus "facts" of one discipline are false in the next. It is a "fact" in modern logic and linguistics that deontic and descriptive interpretations of rules involve different logical forms. It has been a fact in psychology that they are of the same form. In a young field, the consensus facts may be both hard to come by and rather peripheral when found. What is important is the process of building arguments on data, seeking new evidence and revising arguments—on that much Popper was surely right.

It is a corollary of these "facts" that you the student can very quickly get to the point where you yourself can ask hard questions about how the evidence fits together and design ways of finding answers to new questions that arise. The one thing that is ruled out by the cognitive science "house rules" is to exclude some piece of evidence because it comes from another discipline—unfortunately this move is all too common in academia generally.

Perhaps it is worth reviewing our trip around the disciplines and what it has taught us about both the positive and the negative contributions on this particular small topic? Logic contributes a set of concepts and analytical techniques, and a set of alternative mathematical systems with their own criteria of soundness, designed for modeling information systems such as human beings. Wason adopted a particularly simple such system as his yardstick for correct performance in his task. The psychologists who have followed Wason have simultaneously rejected the relevance of logic to human reasoning, while continuing to accept Wason's chosen logical yardstick. In this they were logically already out of date when they started out. On the other hand, logic, like any other conceptual scheme and attendant mathematics, does not settle empirical questions from the armchair. Mathematics is not science. Logicians may sometimes underestimate the distance between the inspiration for their mathematical systems and their actual application to the world. By and large they have been content to model their intuitions about human reasoning (subtle and interesting as those are) rather than engaging with the messy business of modeling the real data of human reasoning. If the selection task is anything to go by, there are rich logical rewards in paying much closer attention to the data of reasoning collected in carefully controlled (albeit artificial) situations.

Psychology has contributed, above all, a reliably replicable experimental situation in which groups of subjects do things that are not transparently explicable and that get us rather rapidly into deep questions about the meaning of language, social norms, social authority, interpretation, evidence, learning, communication and reasoning. The differences between different versions of the task are radical in their effects yet subtle in their explanation. However, by ignoring what is known by other disciplines about relevant issues in human information processing, psychologists have spent a lot of effort reinventing some old (and rather square) wheels. This has deflected them from some of the really important psychological questions. While holding forth about cheating detectors and mental models as alternatives to logical analysis, they have neglected obviously psychological issues such as conceptions of how memory and emotion relate to reasoning.

Anthropology contributes its hard learned lessons about the problems of interpretation of behavior in other cultures. What may seem utterly and obviously completely irrational to us on initial encounter (certain reasoning about witchcraft), may turn out on closer inspection and interpretation at an appropriate level of abstraction just like the reasoning we do at home everyday. We must drive a course between the immediate reaction that foreign cultures are obviously completely different, and the delayed reaction that they are, after all just exactly the same. Perhaps most valuably of all, we should learn to recognize our own activities in the behavior of others. Interpreting undergraduates' reasoning in the selection task appears to have been at least as difficult for experimental psychologists as interpreting witchcraft practices was for 19th and 20th century anthropologists. The range of interpretational problems posed by the task for naive undergraduates is impressive. On the other hand, perhaps anthropology stands to learn from logic and psychology some limits to the flexibility of interpretation—a modern logic does not assume "logical compulsion" of the kind Bloor targets, but it does impose limits on what can count as a sound language as we shall see in chapter 5.

Linguistics contributes much needed knowledge about the diversity of interpretation of sentences of natural languages and the variety of factors that can influence our choice of the most likely intended reading. Psychologists have no choice but to use natural languages to communicate with their subjects their intentions about what subjects should do in their tasks. These subjects' interpretations of task and materials is the main determinant of their observed behavior. One might have thought it was obvious that psychologists would show an intense interest in linguistic findings about different readings of conditionals. Dismissing linguists' findings on the grounds that subjects are not linguists and so don't suffer from these problems is bizarre. On the other hand, linguistic theory sometimes lulls us into the comfortable illusion that the mind must divide the implementation of linguistic processes into modules corresponding to the modules found convenient in linguistic theory. There is perhaps a tendency to assume that some "literal" meaning of a string of words like Wason's rule is found first, and this is then possibly modified by the details of some particular circumstances. If so, the conjunction condition throws considerable doubt on that assumption. Few linguists would list a deontic interpretation as high on the list of readings of an indicative sentence with two clauses joined by "and." The selection task is more generally rich testimony to the small amount of the reasoning controlled by the words uttered and the large amount determined by situational factors such as finding an interpretation that makes sense of instructions.

Philosophy contributes above all a skeptical attitude to the naive realist's claims that it is obvious that we know what we are talking about. It is not obvious what counts as evidence for generalizations. We do not have to have axiomatic definitions of every word that we use, nor could we have. But nevertheless, sustained effort to be as clear as we can about what we mean is an important part of any science, especially when that science requires conceptual innovation. Philosophy of science has a special contribution to make to cognitive science because science is one well-studied social and cognitive process that leads to knowledge. For example, philosophy of science constitutes the most articulated body of knowledge about what theories are and how they relate to the phenomena that are their objects. Not all knowledge is scientific knowledge, but understanding similarities and differences between common sense and scientific knowledge is one way into understanding something about knowledge in general.

Of course the pathology of philosophy is to assume that conceptual analysis is sufficient to tell us how the world is or ought to be. The history of philosophy is full of such interludes. However carefully we analyze the meaning of conditional sentences and their interactions with the context of the selection task, we cannot tell whether the factors that we find are the cause of the behavior we observe. For that we need observation and experiment harnessed to conceptualization.

This is a review of how the disciplines contribute to our current understanding of one small set of experimental observations of human reasoning and communication. We hope it is clear that our claim is that *all* of these approaches are necessary, however inconsistent their views may appear to be. There is no alternative but to integrate their insights. That is what cognitive science means.

We now turn to another closely related area of communication and reasoning—reasoning about probabilities. Our little bit of ornithology led us straight to probabilities and so will stand us in good stead.

Exercise

Exercise 3.1: Since this chapter has been peppered with "exercises" in reasoning and justification, the obvious postchapter exercise is to review the notes of your own answers that you made during reading. Did you get the task "right"? If not, do you think that your interpretation(s) related to any of those discussed? Did you accept Wason's definition of correctness? If so, was this because of the social pressure of authority? Or was it because Wason was right? Summarize what changes, if any, took place in your thinking during the chapter's arguments, and what conclusions you draw now.

3.8   Further Reading

- Wason, P. (1968). "Reasoning about a Rule." *Quarterly Journal of Experimental Psychology, 20*, 273–81.

The original journal paper that kicked the whole thing off.

- Bloor, D. (1991). *Knowledge and Social Imagery.* Chicago: Chicago University Press. Esp. Chapter 7.

Bloor's discussion of Evans-Pritchard's classical study of the Azande and its implications for logic.

- Scribner, S., & Cole, M. (1981). *The Psychology of Literacy* Cambridge: Harvard University Press.

An introduction to the cross-cultural study of the psychology of reasoning.

- Popper, Karl (1959). *The Logic of Scientific Discovery* New York: Basic Books (first published 1934).

The original statement of Popper's philosophy of science.

- Kuhn, Thomas (1962). *The Structure of Scientific Revolutions.* Chicago: Chicago University Press.

Kuhn's study of the sociology of scientific theory development.

- Leevers, H.J., and Harris, P.L. (2000). "Counterfactual Syllogistic Reasoning in Normal Four-year-olds, Children with Learning Disabilities, and Children with Autism." *Journal of Experimental Child Psychology, 76*, 64-87.

Children doing syllogisms in various contexts.

- Chater, N., & Oaksford, M. (1994). "A Rational Analysis of the Selection Task as Optimal Data Selection." *Psychological Review*, 101:608–631.

Presents the argument that an inductive Bayesian competence model is the appropriate yardstick for judging subjects' performance in the selection task.

- Stenning, K., & van Lambalgen, M. (2004). "A Little Logic Goes a Long Way: Basing Experiment on Semantic Theory in The Cognitive Science of Conditional Reasoning." *Cognitive Science*, **28:4**,481-529.

A more full account of the semantic theory, the socratic dialogues, and the experiments described briefly here, along with a review and a lot more references to the existing literature.

• Cosmides, L., & Tooby, J. (1992). "Cognitive Adaptations for Social Exchange" in J. Barkow, L. Cosmides, & J. Tooby (eds.) *The Adapted Mind: Evolutionary Psychology and the Generation of Culture*, 163–228 New York: Oxford University Press.
A review of the "evolutionary psychology" approach to the selection task.

4 Managing with Uncertainties

4.1 Sequences, Populations, and Representativeness

We shall begin, as we began last chapter's discussion of understanding rules, by looking at some cases of reasoning about likelihoods that commonly cause trouble. Then we will move on to attempts to explain why.

Suppose we take a fair coin and we make a sequence of tosses, recording the outcome of each. Suppose that the first ten tosses all come down heads. What is the probability that the next toss will come down heads?

A common answer among subjects posed this question is that it is now more likely to come down tails. After all, goes the reasoning, the average number of heads has got to come out at 50%, and since we now have a surplus of heads, there will have to be more tails to even out. This reasoning is called the GAMBLER'S FALLACY. This pattern of reasoning has had few defendants among theorists of reasoning in uncertainty.

Another response might be to say that the next toss is more likely to come down heads, because the first ten tosses are evidence that the coin is *not* fair. This response is more reasonable. How long a run of heads do we have to have before we can say for certain that the coin is unfair? Two heads in a row is clearly not enough. No one believes that fair coins have to alternate heads and tails. Fair coins don't show such regular patterns. Ten heads in a row is getting to the point where we might begin to suspect there was something unfair about the coin. But is the sequence of ten heads any less probable (from a fair coin) than any other determinate sequence of heads and tails? Say eight heads followed by two tails, or three heads followed by one tail followed by one head followed by five tails? As usual keeping notes of your answers is a good habit.

We hypothesized that the coin was fair, but what do we mean by "fair"? There are two important elements to fairness. One is that there should be no uneven weighting of the heads and tails sides of the coin. The other is that there should be INDEPENDENCE of one toss from another. To distinguish these two elements we only have to remember our idle schooldays and how easy it was, with a little practice, to get an

ordinary coin to come down heads quite a bit more than tails, especially
if we are allowed to make it spin just a few times. A perfectly fair coin, in
the first sense, in your practiced hand might not behave as a perfectly fair
coin in the second sense. There might be some causal connection between
one toss and the next and so there would be a failure of independence.

It is a short step from the concept of independence to the conclusion
that the gambler's fallacy is a fallacy. The reasoning behind the gambler's fallacy is that there is dependence between different parts of the
sequence of events. If the early parts of the sequence have "too many
heads" then the later parts will have to have more tails. Nevertheless, this
reasoning does have a certain grip. Although you are probably sophisticated enough to see through the simple version of the fallacy, the same
failure of reasoning shows up when the situation gets more complicated.
Besides, unlike the conditional reasoning involved in the selection task,
you are likely to have had at least some elementary statistical teaching
at school. If you are so sophisticated about probability that you don't
see any of this fallacious behavior as plausible, and maybe don't even believe that it happens in experiments, then you should perhaps remember
that these were matters of active debate among Europe's finest mathematicians well into the 17th century. The debate arose in the context
of gambling games, and Blaise Pascal was one of the thinkers associated
with the first deep understanding of these problems. If you are still skeptical that human beings find probability hard to reason about you may
be amused that Amos Tversky demonstrated that professional statisti-
cians still suffer from the same illusion if the problems are a bit harder
and you catch them on their day off.

An example of a slightly harder problem is the question that we
left hanging about the likelihood of different sequences of ten tosses. It
is quite compelling that the ten heads in a row seems freakish. People
would say "Wow! ten heads in a row," but they don't say "Wow! three
heads, followed by a tail, followed by four heads followed by three tails!"
Why not? After all, if we were having to place money on the exact
sequence of ten tosses ahead of time, would you bet more money on the
latter sequence than on ten straight heads? Your answer is probably no,
though there is evidence that in the general population there are many
who still regard the jumbled sequence as *more* probable. But there are
more people who can see the fallacy from the perspective of a question
about a bet on a future determinate sequence, than from the way the

question was put initially.

Why should this be? Why should one determinate sequence seem more probable than another? Just before going into this question, pause and observe that we are in an analogous situation to the one we encountered in the earlier discussion of Wason's selection task. We observe in the population that people make systematic errors of reasoning according to some model of what they ought to do. Again subjects can see, at least when shown different ways of conceptualizing the problem, that these responses are in error. The psychologist's perspective on this situation is that the task is to build a descriptive theory about how people do in fact reason, an explanatory theory about why, and maybe a pedagogical theory about how they can learn/be taught to avoid them. The statistician's (or probability theorist's) perspective, analogous to the logician's in the previous chapter, is rather to seek a normative theory about how they *should* reason.

Those are some of the analogies between the two areas. There may also be important differences. For example, there seem to be differences between the status of the competence theories in the two areas. Logic, as we saw, provided (many) formal models of possible interpretations of Wason's task and materials—Wason's competence theory was a certain language (classical propositional logic), and it turned out the interesting questions were about whether this was actually likely to be how subjects understood the task. There were other possible understandings that made other answers "correct." The probability theory applied to fair coin tossing is a somewhat different kind of competence theory. It is a theory about how a fair coin will behave. The coin does not have to understand the theory, and there are no alternative competence models that yield different coin behavior. The theory is descriptive of the coin, but normative of the subject reasoning. This difference is important. There are issues about how subjects should reason (what is the appropriate reasoning model) as we shall see. In fact, we already touched on Oaksford and Chater's model of "maximum information gain" as applied to the selection task, and that is a theory about how people reason about probabilities and how this sheds light on reasoning more generally. Such theories have to be kept separate from theories of coin behavior.

As the perceptive reader will have noticed in the previous discussion, there are two sorts of questions that we can ask about coin-tossing

events. One is about the probability of specific *sequences* of events.
The other is about characteristics of *populations* of kinds of events.
Many of the problems people have seem to stem from confusing these
two kinds of questions. So, for example, there is a population of ten-
member sequences of coin tosses. This population contains 2^{10} (i.e. 1024)
sequences, of which ten heads in a row is one, ten tails another, and
all the others are mixed sequences of heads and tails. As we have just
argued, if the coin is fair, each of these sequences is exactly as likely as
each of the others. But sequences of the *kind* that have five heads and
five tails (in any order) are a great deal more common than the unique
sequences of ten heads, or of ten tails (because all reorderings of these
are identical). If we plotted the number of sequences containing N heads
(from zero to ten) against N, we would find a bell-curve. One with zero
heads. Ten with one head, ... increasing to a peak at five heads and
decreasing symmetrically from five heads to just one with ten heads.
So muddling these two kinds of questions might be at the bottom of
peoples' confusions.

So why does *H T H H H T T T H T H seem* more likely than ten
heads? Well, have you ever seen a coin yield such a sequence of tosses?
Of course the answer is likely to be "I don't have a clue." Asked the
same question about the sequence of ten heads, and the answer is likely
to be "definitely not—if I had I would remember." The sequence of ten
heads has a significance and a prominence that makes it remarkable
(perhaps because it might indicate a double-headed coin?), distinctive,
and therefore memorable. This is a general property of coincidences.
One of the methods we naturally employ for estimating probabilities is
to ask ourselves how many sequences of events are there that are *similar
in their constitution* to the target sequence. If there are lots, then we
judge the target to have a higher probability. If the target is of a rare
kind of constitution, then we judge it unlikely.

For example, Tversky set people an estimation problem that is
closely related to the bell-curve we have just considered. Supposing a bus
travels a ten-stop route and only stops if there is anyone to pick up or
let off. Since the route is somewhat boring, the bus driver gets to musing
about the number of different kinds of journey (defined by stopping or
passing stops) that can occur on his route. He starts by considering the
two-stop case. How many journeys are there with just two stops? Why
don't you make your own guestimation? He then considers the eight-

stop case. Again you should make your own guestimation. Tversky's undergraduate subjects overwhelmingly estimated that there are more two-stop journeys than eight-stop journeys. The method they use to arrive at this guess appears to be that they see how easy it is to generate distinctive patterns from the population (how AVAILABLE that kind of pattern is) and use the ease of finding such cases as an estimate of how many there are. It is easier to make up two-stop journeys that look quite different from each other (say the journey with the first two stops stopping, and all the rest passed, is quite distinctive from the one in which only the last two stops are stopped at). With the eight-stop journeys, there is much more overlap between the stops visited, and this makes the journeys seem more similar to each other. Peoples' estimates of the size of the two populations puts the eight-stop cases as much fewer.

Of course, you have already noticed that these two cases are equally frequent because they are mirror images of each other, swapping stops for passes is just like swapping heads for tails. Interestingly, people find the symmetry of heads and tails easier to spot than the symmetry of stopping and passing—again an issue of informational perspective and availability of cases in memory. Whatever the reason for the difficulty of reversing perspective, Tversky argued that people judge probability by apparent representativeness. They are rather bad at applying the concepts of probability theory to their reasoning. One particular failing he identified is failure to use BASE RATE INFORMATION —information about how likely an outcome is *regardless of specific predictor information.*

Tversky posed several problems designed to examine his subjects' use of base rate information in reasoning. A witness to a road accident glimpsed a taxi, that she judged to be blue, drive away after involvement in the collision. The accident took place at night under sodium street lights and so this judgment of color is not thought to be totally reliable. Taxis in the town in question are either blue or green. Ninety % of taxis are green and 10% are blue. Tversky asked subjects to judge how likely the witnessed taxi was to be blue. He asked other subjects to make the same judgment of the same problem except that the percentages of the colors of taxis were reversed. From this, and several other experiments, he showed that peoples' judgments of probabilities were markedly *insensitive* to base rate information—the information about background distribution of colors of taxis. Subjects hardly differed in the probability they assigned under the two different frequency conditions. People seem to behave as if the question of what color the witness saw is a matter of the lighting and the goings on in her eyeball, but nothing to do with whatever color other taxis throughout the town are painted. This seems a highly intuitive argument.

The counterargument runs like this. If the witness hadn't seen the taxi at all, and she had to make a guess about its most likely color, she would be sensible to guess the common color. As the witness' glimpse becomes longer, and the lighting better, we should weight the sighting more heavily and the base rate less so. If the witness is not color blind and saw the taxi stationary at ten feet in broad daylight, then we should weight the visual evidence over the base rate entirely. But in the uncertain conditions described in the problem, it is clear that we should combine both kinds of information in assessing probabilities. Tversky assembled considerable evidence that with problems abstracted from their context like the taxi sighting, subjects are not good at taking base rate into account. There appears to be a tendency to try and reason with deterministic scenarios rather than to treat seriously the idea of random variation.

The attentive reader will realize that there is a further issue posed by Tversky's problem. That is the question about what the witness knows about the frequencies of colors in the local taxi populations. One might suppose that if the witness knew that 90% of taxis were green, that this information is already weighted, consciously or unconsciously, in her judgment—it is already "priced-in" as they say in the markets. There is a whole branch of perceptual psychology that deals with the effects of knowledge on perception. To take a classical demonstration, Jerome Bruner showed people brief flashed presentations of playing cards and asked them to identify them. The flashes were shortened or lengthened until reports were accurate with a certain probability. The subject then saw a red ace of spades. This was universally reported as a black ace of spades or a red ace of hearts. Much longer presentations were required before people could actually report what was there.

If the witness was expecting taxis to be blue, then maybe she would have some tendency to see it as blue, even if it was green. The strength of association between shapes and colors in playing cards is much greater than the color distributions of taxis in our examples. In perceptual psychology, SIGNAL DETECTION THEORY investigates the relations between prior expectations, the "pay-offs" associated with false-positive and false-negative errors, and observers' perceptual experiences, in situations which are more akin to the taxi detection example. This body of work shows that people are capable of fine grain adjustment of their judgment to the parameters of probability of occurrence, strength of perceptual "signal," and the penalties for different types of error in a highly rational fashion. What they cannot do, of course, is judge from the nature of the phenomenal experience of one judgment episode, whether they are "seeing" something or judging that it was there because it is most likely to be there or because missing it would incur a heavy penalty. So if the witness is assumed to know about the frequencies of taxis, it might be that this base rate information has already been unconsciously applied in her judgment of the color. It deserves some thought that our eyeballs appear to be able to take account of base rates even though our reasoning seems poor at doing this. It is not uncommon to have some "automatic" processes that appear to be more sophisticated than our more thoughtful processes, but it is important to remember that the former may be very context-bound, and the latter at least capable of dealing with a somewhat wider range of situations. If so, they are doing something more difficult.

The taxi problem is a simple problem for applying base rate information. But the same problem crops up in more complicated guises. Let's have a look at another slightly more elaborate problem about populations of cases. Tversky set his subjects the following problem about genders of births at two hospitals of different sizes. Assume that the probability of a girl is exactly the same as the probability of a boy (not quite, but nearly true in the real world). One hospital has, on average, forty-five births per day and the other only fifteen. The question is about the number of days on which 60% or more of the babies born at one hospital are boys. Specifically, is there any difference in the number of such days expected at the two hospitals? The expected number of boys at the large hospital is 22.5 boys and the same for girls. Sixty % of the expected number births is twenty boys. The expected number of boys at the small hospital is 7.5 and 60% of expected number of births is nine. Should we expect twenty-seven or more boys at the large hospital more, less, or equally often than we expect nine or more boys at the small hospital? Note down your answer. You should perhaps also guesstimate the relative size of the two probabilities.

The correct answer is less often at the large hospital. The actual probability is about twice as high at the small hospital. If you found this easy, then congratulations! You are uncommon in this respect in populations of undergraduate subjects untrained in statistics. If you find this answer hard to believe you are in good company—but wrong. It may help to think about a limiting case. Suppose we consider an even smaller hospital where the expected number of births is just two per day. The expected number of boys will be one, but there will be lots of days when there are zero or two (or even more). Note that two is already a rate 100% above expectation for this small hospital.[8]

The sort of curve we would get for this ultra-small hospital would have a peak at one boy (the mean is always the expected number), but would be much flatter than the same plot for either of the larger hospitals. (This curve would not be a symmetrical bell-curve like our previous example because there is an absolute zero on one side and an open-ended maximum on the other.) But the flatness of the curve for the small hospital explains why divergences from the average are more common than in the large one.

Tversky talks about the fallacy of assuming that the small hospital will have the same distribution as the large one (a fallacy that a huge majority of his subjects exhibited) as belief in the law of *small* numbers. The law of *large* numbers is the one that tells us that on a *long* run of fair coin tosses, half will be heads. But people greatly underestimate how long the sequence has to be to have confidence in getting a result within a specified distance of 50%. Tversky talks about these effects in terms of representativeness. People assume that the small *sample* from a population will be like the larger population—it will be representative—even when the sample is small. This can be seen as just a more elaborate version of the gambler's fallacy—assuming that the sequence will be like common examples from the population from which it is drawn.

Likelihoods in a more natural habitat

Representativeness of samples of tosses from populations of coin trajectories (even deaths from mule-kick in the Prussian army, that is one of the classical sources of one of the distributions we have just been discussing) sound pretty much as dry as dust. But these effects are linked in Tversky's theory to apparently quite distant psychological phenomena such as social stereotyping and maybe even horoscopes.

Consider the following biographical description:

Bill is 34 years old. He is intelligent but unimaginative, compulsive and generally rather boring. In school, he was strong in mathematics, but weak in social studies and humanities. How likely is it that each of the following is true of Bill?

1. Bill is an accountant.
2. Bill is an accountant who plays jazz for a hobby.
3. Bill is a doctor who plays poker for a hobby.
4. Bill is an architect.
5. Bill is a journalist.
6. Bill climbs for a hobby.
7. Bill surfs for a hobby.
8. Bill plays jazz for a hobby.

Try the problem yourself assigning probabilities. Tversky and Daniel Kahneman's subjects rated number 2 as more likely than number 8. Do you agree? Whether you do or not, try writing down your reasoning (roughly is fine). Whether you do or don't, ask yourself what is strange about this judgment?

What is strange is that the judgment asserts that the conjunction of two properties (playing jazz and being an accountant) is *more* probable than either of the properties. People who are accountants *and* who play jazz *just are* people who play jazz. If no one except accountants played jazz, then there could be as many as equal numbers of accountants and jazz-playing accountants. But there could hardly be more jazz playing accountants than jazz players.

If you made this strange judgment you are again in good company— most of us do when we think about this problem for the first time. One counterargument against this interpretation that has been raised is that subjects may not understand the question the way the experimenter intends (shades of the selection task?). Indeed, you may feel that the argument against your judgment has something of the flavor of the Queen of Hearts complaining about Alice: "If you haven't had any sugar, it's odd asking for *more*." One could have sympathy with Alice's argument that if she's had none then its very easy to have more though impossible to have less. This line of argument suggests that subjects interpret option 8 to mean a jazz player *and not an accountant*. It is not clear how much of the phenomenon is due to this kind of misinterpretation, although recent evidence suggests that it is not the whole story. It is clear from options 2 and 3 that professionals can have hobbies and hobbyists can have professions, though it might be thought that listing them as multiple choices inclines us to treat them as mutually exclusive. It has been argued that these errors happen much less when people reason in situations they are highly familiar with. But that is not an argument against Tversky's claim, which is that people are highly susceptible to these errors in certain kinds of rather abstract contexts, and these rather abstract contexts are common in our developed-world culture.

Consider what you wrote in explanation of your judgment (supposing you agreed with most of the subjects in the original experiment). It usually goes something like this: "The description is a dead-ringer for an accountant—especially the boring bit. It's not part of my stereotype that an accountant would choose jazz for a hobby, but maybe hobbies are rather randomly chosen so it's not too unlikely. On the other hand, jazz playing on its own really runs counter to the description, so 8 is very improbable."

What seems to happen is that *adding* the information that Bill is an accountant to the information that he plays jazz for a hobby actually helps us to find a plausible SCENARIO that fits all the data. The information about playing jazz still depresses the judged probability of 2 relative to 1 (Bill simply being an accountant) as we would expect on both scenario and probability grounds. But what we fail to notice is that *adding* information to a prediction (2 relative to 8) always makes it *less* probable. So what seems to be our natural way of assessing these things, constructing a scenario and judging its plausibility, gets us into trouble with the probabilities.

Something like this filling-out of scenarios seems to be what makes horoscopes work. Adding more fairly vague information enables us to find a scenario from our current circumstances that fits (just as adding the fact about accountancy to the jazz player makes it possible to accommodate) the implausible information. It then seems surprising that we can fit our circumstances to such an apparently detailed prediction. Of course much of the interest of horoscopes lies in what we can observe in our own processes of filling in scenarios, and what that tells us about our hopes and fears—an observation that would have pleased Freud but an occupation that perhaps annoyed Popper. So Tversky's theory of representativeness appears to possibly play a role in explaining how we reason in a wide variety of situations. We now look at how some of these same tendencies are used in attempts to persuade.

In the last ten years Tversky's explanations have been challenged, in particular by Gerd Gigerenzer and his colleagues. They have argued that classical probability theory and the competence models for decision based on it are woefully inapplicable in most natural situations, and that subjects in fact are very good at reasoning in these situations by using what they call "fast-and-frugal" heuristics. They have even shown that in some circumstances these heuristics yield better results than application of the classical labor-intensive and knowledge-intensive competence models, and, again in some circumstances, that subjects with less information actually make better judgments—ignorance spawns accuracy (and bliss?). We believe this work is important for what it shows about the "ecology" of everyday decision making, but we feel it somewhat misconstrues Tversky's work. Tversky did not advocate probability theory as the correct theory by which people should reason. He used classical probability theory as a theory of the behavior of independent events. He precisely emphasized the fact that the theory was inoperable by subjects in most circumstances and that therefore people must be reasoning some other way, and his theory of representativeness was the beginnings of such a theory. He also concentrated on rather abstract kinds of situation in which the subject had little knowledge to go on. He did this not because he thought these were representative of real-world situations, but because he believed they were highly revealing of mechanisms developed in more natural situations. This has much in common with our arguments about Wason's task—studying reasoning in a vacuum can be highly revealing, but only if one pays careful attention to the relation between the vacuum and more natural situations. Gigerenzer's work provides much fascinating detail about the ecology of more natural situations.

Base rates and communication

This tendency for us to judge likelihoods by our ease of constructing scenarios on the basis of our knowledge of stereotypical situations rather than by applications of the laws of probability is witnessed vividly in our newspapers each morning. It is quite rare for popular newspapers to talk in terms of generalizations, percentages, or likelihoods of any kind. Rather, what they do is translate generalities into particularities—

a policy we will call *anecdotalism*.

So when a tabloid newspaper asserts that teenage mothers are becoming pregnant in order to jump welfare housing waiting lists, what we do not find in our newspapers is discussion of the relevant statistics. Often this is because such statistics are not available, but even when general information is available it is very rarely cited. Instead anecdotalism is the order of the day. A single teenage mother (of ten, preferably) is found in, say, Cardiff who appears, struggling to be heard above her brood, saying that indeed she only did it to get housed. Anecdotalism is a powerful method of persuasion. The feckless poor are an age-old stereotype. There really are some individuals who conform to the stereotype. And just one is enough for *The Sun*.

What general information is it that we need to assess such generalizations? The number of teenage mothers gaining housing? Their motives in becoming pregnant? But also the number of other people gaining access to housing—what we above called the base rate. After all, the tabloid's claim may be literally true if just two cases can be found, but its utterance as a matter of public concern makes a claim that it is also significant. And this significance rests on the idea that substantial numbers of the homeless are being kept on the street by hordes of wanton girls who would otherwise have eschewed parenthood. It is the anecdotalists' ability to get us to swallow such propositions that deserves our attention.

The reason given for newspapers' use of anecdote is usually that their readers do not understand statistics. We have seen good reason in Tversky's observations that indeed readers have many problems making judgments about probability. There are good reasons why it is unlikely that readers (or even researchers) could ever usefully resort only to a numerical application of principles of statistical reasoning. We may indeed be stuck with reasoning on the basis of paradigm cases known to us, and we would not want to suggest that such reasoning is always pathological. It is often very necessary. You will hear later of many examples of how communication cannot succeed without people "going beyond the information given" on the basis of stereotypes. But what readers can do is to learn to identify the missing information and to make more intelligent estimations of the likely state of affairs, perhaps keeping an open mind where no information is available. This is, of course, what many readers do.

The gap between thinking in terms of probabilities and anecdotal certainties is often made stark when science meets politics in the media. Some of the issues are nicely illustrative of our earlier discussion of the relationship between theory and data, and between science and other sources of authority. A high profile example will illustrate. The example has to be described in some depth to understand the context of communication.

The U.K. is unique in Europe in having had an epidemic of bovine spongiform encephalopathy (BSE, or "Mad Cow" disease), a disease that is believed to be related both to an ovine form known as scrapie, and possibly to a rare human disease called Creutzfeldt-Jakob disease (CJD). BSE is thought to have got into cattle through the feeding of sheep offal to cows, a practice banned until the early 1980s but that grew with the relaxation of government regulations before finally being banned again in the early 1990s. No other European country allowed this practice and no other European country had an epidemic of BSE. One method of transmission of CJD is known to be the ritual cannibalism once practiced in New Guinea in which people eat the brains of their ancestors (the related disease is known as Kuri Kuri in New Guinea). It is difficult to be certain that CJD as known in Europe is exactly the same disease as the New Guinea disease because the method of transmission here is obscure. The agent that is responsible for transmission of these related diseases is somewhat mysterious—variously hypothesized to be a "slow virus" or a strange rogue protein called a "prion." BSE, CJD, and scrapie all have very long incubation periods from several to thirty years.

The question of some public concern is whether BSE is transmissible to human beings as CJD. There has been a significant increase in CJD in the last few years. Although the disease remains very rare, it has roughly doubled from about twenty-five to about fifty cases per year throughout the U.K. However, this may be because of increased attention leading to better diagnosis, a common epidemiological phenomenon. The absolute rate of CJD is still lower in the U.K. than in some other countries that do not have BSE and are not thought to practice cannibalism, for example Austria.

A quite different theory about the cause of BSE is that it is due to organophosphorus insecticides—similar to the ones that have caused concern about nerve damage to agricultural workers who use sheep dips and to soldiers in the Gulf War. The Ministry of Agriculture, Fisheries, and Food (MAFF) ran a campaign in the 1980s to eradicate the warble fly from Britain, that involved heavy use of these compounds that are known to cause nerve damage with symptoms not wholly dissimilar to BSE. It has been shown that organically farmed beef herds do not suffer from BSE. But they neither ate sheep offal when it was permitted, nor were exposed to organophosphorus compounds, so they do not help distinguish these two theories. On the other hand, no known mechanism is understood for the transmission of organophosphorus poisoning from cow to calf, and there is fairly strong evidence that BSE is transmissible.

Here is a scientific problem of some depth, but also a major political and economic one. If BSE is transmissible to humans through eating beef products, and the incubation period is variable between five and thirty years, then we should not expect to be seeing much evidence yet of CJD resulting from humans eating BSE-infected beef products. Reasoning about causal processes that are so slow is known to be especially problematic for human beings, and politicians in particular. I have presented the evidence at this length because it is a case that acutely illustrates some of the differences between political and scientific reasoning. A case that affects us deeply and that is still currently unresolved makes it harder for us to pretend to ourselves that there are easy resolutions to these issues.

Let us concentrate on the evidence from new cases of CJD in the U.K. population. One of the puzzles of the epidemiology is that there is no increased prevalence of CJD among groups one might expect to be vulnerable if BSE is the source of the increase. Up to 1994 there was no case of a slaughterhouse worker, nor a beef farmer, dying from CJD (the disease is relatively rapidly fatal once it becomes evident, but it was not certainly diagnosable before postmortem until very recently). One possibility is that the BSE effects are not yet being seen. Or perhaps only a few who happen to have fast incubation times have yet been seen. Another aspect of the CJD increase is that more young people appear to have been affected than was the case earlier, possibly indicating shorter incubation in younger people, or a different disease. There have been periodical reports in the general press over the last year or so of new cases, with varying degrees of linkage to beef. One was a teenager who had a markedly hamburger-oriented diet. Another was the first slaughterhouse worker.

What significance do such observations have? What extra information do we require in order to interpret these new observations? It is intuitively clear that we need to know something about average teenage diet. If 80% of teenagers eat as many hamburgers as this unfortunate case, we can see that this case alone presents little evidence for a link. If only 0.1% eat this many, then we might look up. Similarly with the occupational hazards. If slaughterhouse workers represented 10% of the population, one case would not be remarkable. In fact, it would begin to look remarkable that there hadn't been such a case before. However, if there are only 0.001% of the population in this work, what then? Well, one case cannot be strong evidence. After all, most CJD cases have a way of earning their living, and we do not accept that an unfortunate couturier who dies of CJD establishes a link between CJD and high fashion? And this remains true however rare couturiers are in the population. This is partly because of the staggeringly large number of ways we have of categorizing people. But what about the next case of CJD in a slaughterhouse worker? Providing there did not seem to be any causal linkage between this and the first case (working in the same factory perhaps might lead us to suspect some joint cause other than BSE exposure) this really would be suspicious. If the two cases are at the ends of the country, and the frequency of this occupation were as hypothesized, then the chance probability of both cases being slaughterhouse workers is about one in a hundred million (0.00001^2).

This is a good illustration of the importance of what we called *base rates* above, for assessing probabilistic evidence. If the base rate for teenage hamburger gorging is high, the evidence of a link is correspondingly low. But if the rate of slaughterhouse working in the population is sufficiently low, then even two cases nationally could be extremely suggestive. It would not in itself establish that BSE was the agent of transmission. Perhaps slaughterhouse workers were exposed to organophosphorous insecticides from the cattle they processed in the 1980s. But it would suggest that slaughterhouse workers' doings would be a good place to look for the cause of CJD. Of course, it is also possible that no more slaughterhouse workers will be affected, but that may be because transmission of BSE to humans requires some other kind of contact to cause CJD—like eating nervous tissue.

I have given this rather extensive summary of the science because it is important to see how complex base rate information is embedded in a real context, the complexity of the background information required, and how hard it is to assess evidence without a well understood mechanism.

Against this background, let us look at what happens when politics meets science. Late in 1995, a minister from MAFF (the ministry of ag. and fish, as it was known) announced that there was *no conceivable possibility* of a link between BSE and CJD. He made this announcement on the basis of advice that he received from the Committee on Infectious Diseases, a group of scientific experts on epidemiology. The first reaction of any scientist (and now I mean anyone who understands about the relation between scientific theory and evidence, rather than someone expert on the interspecific transmission of cattle diseases) reading such a statement must be that the minister has not understood, or willfully misunderstands, the advice. Science has repeatedly demonstrated links between phenomena that were considered "inconceivable." The link was highly scientifically conceivable in 1995. The dominant theory of the origin of BSE in cattle was that it is a bovine form of a sheep disease. It was highly conceivable that this disease might pass from cattle to humans, even if the biological distance is much greater than from sheep to cattle.

On the other hand there was considerable evidence that ran against this theory. There was even an alternative theory having to do with organophosphorus compounds. And the scientists concerned might well acknowledge that it is perfectly conceivable that neither theory is correct—some other agent or agents could be at work.

One might take the view that the politician is simply a liar. The government took a great risk in changing the regulations over feeding offal to cattle. It then dragged its heels over reintroducing regulations to control it. In fact, these regulations were not properly policed, and the announcement just quoted came from a re-reintroduction of procedures to control the treatment of offal. The government has a strong motive in believing, and having us believe, that BSE and CJD are unconnected. Whether this particular politician is lying or not, our interest in the case hangs on the interpretation of scientific reasoning and its comparison with reasoning about policy. What should the politician say about the evidence at hand?

One frequent complaint by politicians about scientific information is that it is so technical no one but an expert can understand it, so it must be interpreted for the public. What the public wants to be told, or so the politician argues, is whether to eat beef or not. Scientists are willing to entertain possibilities so inconceivable to the rest of us that the politician is quite justified in stating that a link between CJD and BSE is inconceivable. J. Public, the politician argues, knows that life is a risky business with which he or she must get on, and the scientists' luxury of focusing on the highly improbable is not an available, or even safe, option. Viewed from the perspective of someone who has to *act*, focusing too much on ill-understood possibilities can lead one to succumb to the blindingly probable—starvation perhaps.

This complaint deserves serious attention. Several of the premises at least are true. Science, at a particular stage of development, frequently makes no judgment on an issue. The issues science remains silent on are frequently the life and death issues that we all do have to make decisions on every day. In fact, one of the defining features of scientific theories is that they choose their own problems rather than having the practicalities decide for them what phenomena they shall encompass. This is not to say that applicability plays no part in what problems scientists spend their time on. CJD was a minor epidemiological backwater, perhaps preserved in the textbooks by the frisson of cannibalism, until BSE emerged. But the theoretical core of the biology that underpins this study is immensely agnostic about many of the everyday particularities with which we all contend.

Here is perhaps one of the greatest contrasts between the humanities and scientific disciplines. The humanities (and in many ways social sciences are in this respect more like humanities than natural sciences) must address the issues of the day. Not every issue in every detail. The humanities do not have to have a position on CJD and BSE. But they do have to have a view on the relation between science and policy. An economics that had a wonderfully detailed and predictive model of the medieval Florentine lace industry, and had nothing to say about unemployment or the business cycle today, would not be a 21st century economics. In the natural sciences this situation is common. Scientists choose problems on which they can make progress and develop their theories, and the criterion of choice of problem is almost entirely that—the possibility of scientific progress. Cognitive science's account of human communication will often strike you like this. It goes into great depth on topics you would not originally have thought to be an important part of the subject, while entirely ignoring others that you may feel to be far more central—say the significance of the media.

Needless to say, this feature of science raises important ethical and political issues. Since as an activity it has become so expensive, what possible justification can there be for allowing the scientist to pursue his nose, guided only by the merest whiff of theoretical insight? One justification may well be in terms of application, but deferred application. Science may have no current settlement of the issue of the link between BSE and CJD, but it has the only approach that has any hope of arriving at a resolution, uncomfortably long though that might take. In some of the less developed areas like cognitive science, one might say that the expected length of time to wait for an articulate theory of, say, the communication of human emotions might be such as to lead us to look somewhere else for a way of living. Indeed, even after such a theory has arrived, we still need practical principles for living, just as we don't generally get around the physical world by using physical theory.

What then is the politician to say in the meantime? His demand for *something* to say is not an unreasonable one. Some interpretation of the expert advice for the public should be possible that is better than the advice to resort to a ouija board. Let us start by examining what it is that the public wants. According to my hypothetical politician, J. Public wants an answer as to whether he or she should eat beef. This may be true, although it is perhaps worth asking whether this *is* what J. Public wants. Some proportion of the public may accept that they themselves are the only ones who can make such decisions. What they want might be to know that the government has taken reasonable precautions in regulating the beef industry in the light of the technical evidence available. What are reasonable precautions? What probabilities are too high, and how are probabilities to be assigned?

The issue is not one amenable to numerical probabilities. The issue has far more to do with impartiality in weighing evidence. Reasonable precautions are ones that have looked at the costs and benefits to all concerned without undue influence of political expediency or direct pecuniary interests. Capriciously announcing that beef is unsafe to eat is damaging to many peoples' livelihoods and many more peoples' chosen diet. But failing to regulate and enforce regulations on an industry that runs such risks with its consumers' lives is irresponsibility of a high order. It is the delay of action that seems most irresponsible from both sides. The feeding of offal cannot have represented a saving of more than a few percentage points of costs for the industry at the outside. Its previous banning was probably based on experience. This saving must be a much slighter effect than the economic costs of a major beef scare, and immeasurably slighter than the human costs of a major epidemic of CJD. In assessing the reasonableness of regulations, one might ask the question—how many potential sources of disaster are there that require regulations to prevent them, each costing a few hundredths of percentage points? This is another kind of higher order base rate problem. Is offal feeding to ruminants banned in all other countries because it poses risks known from historic cases? Or is it banned because it is felt to be *unnatural*? Is it felt to be unnatural because of some even more distant cultural experience of cases?

Thus far this summary was written for a course taught in 1996. In 2000 the rate of CJD cases in the U.K. has risen to about ninety cases. The number of human deaths from what is now called NEW VARIANT CJD (i.e. CJD transmitted from cattle to humans) in the U.K. in 2000 was around twenty-eight, having grown from three cases identified in 1995. This new variant (vCJD) is believed to be the disease transmitted by eating beef products and shows rather different symptoms than what is now known as "sporadic" CJD—the human disease as it was known before the BSE outbreak. The experts are now much more confident that prions are the mechanism of infection. In 2005, as this goes to press, the prevalence of vCJD has been around eighteen per year for the last three years. Let us hope the outbreak is declining, but the experts say it is too early to tell.

The expert estimates of the future extent of the epidemic still range from the hundreds to hundreds of thousands of deaths over the next thirty years, such is the indeterminacy our knowledge of the average length of incubation of this disease. The "good" news, as far as the size of the epidemic goes, seems to be that new variant CJD afflicts much younger people than sporadic CJD. This means at least some incubation times must be shorter. If mean incubation times are shorter, then the epidemic may be at the smaller estimates and be already waning.

We have spent a long time on BSE in order to illustrate some relations between what we know, what evidence we have, and what we communicate. What we know is dependent on what discourse we are engaged in. What is all too easily conceivable to the scientist may be inconceivable to the politician. Learning some cognitive science means asking this question about the relations between theoretical knowledge and practical utterance. Taking an example that is rather topical for at least one readership should bring home the far from academic nature of these issues. A good homework exercise is to write an analogous treatment of the arguments about global warming—a case that illustrates many of the same points. The causal processes are even slower and still more obscure in their totality. The question about what is politically reasonable to do at what stage of development of the scientific evidence, even more acute.

A curious property of the political and policy debate about global warming is the focus on whether the agreed global increase in temperatures is the result of natural or artificial causes. Those who argue against early action before the scientific evidence is unassailable appear to have the moral argument in mind that if it's "not our fault," then we need not try to do anything about it. Of course their argument might be that there is nothing we can do about it, but if their evidence is so strong that we're already doomed, then it would be kind of them to reveal the evidence. Besides, the argument that we should wait for unassailable scientific evidence often comes from those whose concept of unassailability doesn't even accept the evidence for biological evolution as unassailable. The same constituency is only too happy to point out how political action frequently has to be based on hunch rather than proof—with regard to weapons of mass destruction, perhaps.

The politician and the scientist make utterances from different evidential positions, for different purposes, and with different constraints upon them. An understanding of the relations between them is important for all our futures. When Thomas S. Kuhn summarizes what appears to discriminate science from other social institutions he points out that until very recently science has overwhelmingly come from a very few cultures. It seems that only these cultures have produced, or been willing to tolerate, an academy that has a degree of freedom from both political and religious control, and that is largely its own judge of scientific progress. Scientists are as human as others, and are driven by ulterior motive as surely as others, but the albeit partial insulation of the academy from power has meant that economic and political interest are less immediate ulterior motives. Now that science has become so expensive, it is already emerging that the academy can fail to retain the required kind of insulation. Perhaps these social issues are more important in distinguishing science from nonscience than individual psychological issues like Popper's claims about the role of "falsification."

The BSE/CJD problem illustrated the issue of base rates and probabilistic reasoning. People are frequently capable of sophisticated reasoning in familiar contexts (or kinds of contexts), but faced by abstract problems torn out of context (like Tversky's probability problems or the selection task), their performance on formally identical problems is poor. This should remind us of the relation between form and content in human reasoning from the last chapter. The cases are both similar and contrasting. They are similar in that people appear to be better at contentful reasoning embedded in a rich context than they are at reasoning about coin tosses or arbitrary arrangements of letters and numbers. They are similar in that there are some questions about whether the subjects understand the instructions the way the experimenter intends (e.g. the interpretation of the multiple choice options about the bank clerk; the issue about whether the eye witness has already discounted the base rate information about the taxi etc.). They are different in that in the case of the selection task, we came to the conclusion that there are clear formal differences between descriptives and deontics and that difference was actually what was driving the observed difference in difficulty. In the case of reasoning about base rates, it is not so clear whether there is a single formal analysis that can explain subjects' behavior. Nor are there such clear alternatives between competence models for the task.

Reasoning about knowledge

We have just seen that reasoning about likelihoods, and in virtue of likelihoods, is deeply embedded in the processes of human communication because we have to choose between alternative models of the world on the basis of evidence and interest. We will now take a quick look at another dependence of communication on likelihoods that arises from reasoning about others' knowledge. Reasoning about knowledge is a particularly crucial form of reasoning in communication, and will also give us some practice in reasoning about probabilities. Incidentally, the topic will also introduce us to issues about diagrammatic reasoning that will be picked up again in chapter 18. Our first example is what is known as the Prisoners' Paradox, (to be carefully distinguished from the Prisoner's Dilemma, a foundational problem in game theory, that we will also encounter presently).

Three prisoners, A, B, and C have been convicted of heinous crimes. All would be executed save for the fact that it is the empress's birthday and she has decided that one of them will be pardoned. The jailer knows which prisoner is the lucky one. Prisoner A, being the inquisitive type, asks the jailer for information about the identity of the pardoned prisoner.

The jailer says he is not allowed to divulge any information on pain of death (his own), but A reasons as follows. "You can tell me *one* of B or C who is going to be executed without giving me any information. After all, it is a truth of logic, on these premises, that one of A or B will be executed." The jailer accepts this argument, and tells A that B will be executed.

A claims that he now knows much more than he did before, if not the final answer as to whether he will live or die. He reasons as follows. "Before I had a 1/3 probability of surviving because the pardoned one was equally likely to be A, B, or C. But now I have a 1/2 probability of surviving because the pardoned one is equally likely to be either A or C. Therefore the jailer has given me information."

The problem is called a paradox because A's two bouts of reasoning from the same premises come to inconsistent conclusions. Either the jailer has given information about A's chances or he has not. Has the jailer communicated? And if so what? What is your resolution of this paradox? In this highly democratic state, jailers are executed for disobeying orders not to divulge information. Will the empress order the jailer's execution? Of course, it depends on whether the empress understands the necessary reasoning about knowledge, and her birthday mood. So we should revise the question: *Should* the empress, according to her penal code, have the executioner executed?

There are some nice graphical aids to clarifying this problem that are worth mentioning because they exemplify techniques that are useful for thinking about probabilities more generally. The representation in Figure 4.1 is a tree in which each branch represents one of the possibilities of a sequence of events. The first column represents the prior choice of the reprieved prisoner (underlined); the second column represents what the jailer says in response to the prisoner's wheedling. The third column just multiplies the probabilities in the other two columns to get the probability of that branch of the tree. Note that these third-column probabilities sum to one indicating that all possibilities have been accounted for—an important check on one's reasoning.

Remember the question is whether the jailer has given A any information about who is to be reprieved. What is the probability that A can guess who is to be reprieved? Well, if A pursues the policy of always

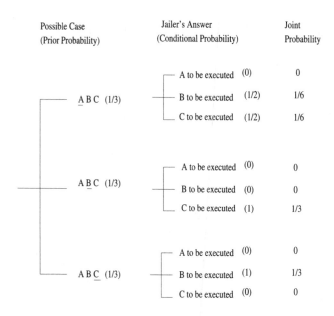

Figure 4.1
The Prisoner's Paradox solved by a tree-diagram of all possible situations.

guessing that the reprieved is whoever of B and C is *not* designated
by the jailer, then the probability of A choosing correctly is 2/3. (A is
always wrong on the top branch, and right on the lower two branches).
So the jailer has given *some* information he was forbidden to give and
the empress, being a lady of impeccable logic, should execute him, unless her birthday mood extends to a further reprieve. Since no one else
volunteers for the jailer's risky job of communicating with prisoners and
spare-time executing, A goes free and there is a happy ending for
him.

Figure 4.2 is an alternative representation. The outer circle represents the jailer's possible utterances, and the inner circle lays out the
corresponding sentence/reprieve. The two circles are aligned so that every radius of the circle represents a joint occurrence of an utterance
and a reprieve, and an angular sector represents a probability of a joint
kind of event. It is easy to see that the policy of picking whoever of B
and C the jailer doesn't mention is correct 2/3 of the time. Experiment
shows that students learning about probabilities find the roulette wheel

easier than the tree—that is more of them get the problem correct. It's an interesting cognitive question why this should be. We return to this problem in chapter 18.

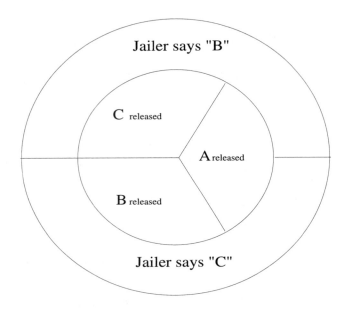

Figure 4.2
The Prisoner's Paradox solved by a "roulette wheel" representation.

There is another well-known problem sometimes called the game show problem that is formally similar to the prisoner's paradox.

A game show host presents his contestant with a choice between three identical boxes in the search for a single prize. The other two boxes contain nothing. First the contestant has to choose a box. Then the host chooses an empty box. Now the contestant must choose whether to stick with her original choice, or to switch to the other so far unchosen box. Sound familiar?

The contestant first reasons as follows: "The host has identified one empty box, but the other two are still equally likely. The box I chose is no better or worse than the others since I chose it at random from a position of total ignorance. Therefore, it is indifferent whether I stick or shift my choice."

But then, being one to look at all the arguments, she reasons as follows: "By choosing the box I chose there is a chance I have constrained the host's choice of box. (If I chose the prize box then I caused no constraint because he could equally choose either empty box. But two thirds of the time I will have forced him to choose exactly the box he chose.) On average, therefore, his choice is giving me information about where the prize is by his avoiding the prize. So I should shift to the other unchosen box."

Here again there are two arguments with inconsistent conclusions. Which one is right? Is there any advantage in shifting to the unchosen box? You should work through applying the graphical representations to the new problem. These problems are hard, the prisoner version generally harder than the game show one. It's interesting to ask why there should be this difference. Both problems demonstrate a difficulty we have with analyzing information and reasoning about information gain.[9] The guard finds reasoning from global considerations about numbers of factual possibilities without regard to knowledge quite natural, and this reasoning suggests that no information has been provided.

Thinking hard about the sequence of events and the choices open at each point to each party is necessary to discover why the guard's (or the host's) choice gives information. Notice that the prisoner's second bout of reasoning actually gets the right answer (the jailer has given information), but gets the quantity wrong, and gives a wrong reason. Reasoning about knowledge appears to present problems of its own beyond those of simply reasoning about probabilities.

Another kind of reasoning about knowledge that is particularly important for understanding communication is reasoning about the mutuality of knowledge. Suppose you are on a bus with a friend, but separated by the crowd, one by the back door and one by the front, so that you cannot see each other. When the bus stops, an acquaintance standing by the bus stop who can see you both yells, "Why don't you two get off and come and have a drink?" Now you have the problem of coordinating your behavior with that of your friend on the bus. Suppose that your priorities are to remain together. You would both prefer to get off and have a drink with your acquaintance, but the worst outcome for you both is that one gets off and the other doesn't. The bus doors open and you must independently decide whether to get off.

In this example, there is an OBJECT-LEVEL of knowledge about the message transmitted by the third person—you both get the message from the party outside the bus. But there is also critical METAKNOWLEDGE about who knows what about who has this object-level knowledge. In order to decide what to do you need to know whether your friend received the message. But a moment's thought is enough to see that you also need to know whether she knows that you received the message. If she got the message but believes you did not, then she will not get off the bus. So she needs to know that you know, and you need to know that she knows. Do matters stop there? There is an argument that there is an infinite regress here—that indefinitely many levels of metaknowledge are needed. What do you think? There is also an argument that the regress in fact "grounds out" after this first round of metaknowledge. And then there is the observation that if you succeed in making eye contact with your friend, you can perhaps establish mutual knowledge and both get off the bus. What do you think? With these paradoxes it is always a good idea to try explaining the paradox to a friend. Two benefits may arise. Sometimes the friend fails to see what is paradoxical and forces you to become clearer in explaining why a paradox arises. Sometimes the friend will immediately see the paradox, and then mutual solution is usually easier than reasoning alone.

It is a hallmark of human communication that it often succeeds (or fails) by the sender of the signal getting the receiver of the signal to realize that the sender intended to communicate by the signal, and intended the intention to be recognized as such by the receiver. Not all human communication has this characteristic—we may unintentionally communicate things (perhaps giving the game away), but much communication has this character. In chapter 17, we will see that Paul Grice was the philosopher who most emphasized the role of the mutual recognition of intentions in communication.

Mutuality of knowledge is also important for understanding phatic communication. Many phatic social rituals have the characteristic that not only shall they be done, but they shall be seen to be done, and this because their function is to ensure mutual knowledge. Such generation of mutual knowledge is important in generating mutual trust. The importance of eye contact in individual-to-individual communication is often to be understood in terms of establishing mutuality of knowledge through joint attention. Many apparently purposeless or downright irrational human activities seem to require explanation in these general terms of the attainment of mutual knowledge. In the next section, we will take a look at a situation where communication is prevented, and see what it can tell us about communication, specifically about how communicative conventions arise and are maintained in communities.

4.2   Where Do Rules Come From?

In engineered systems, or even in legally prescribed systems, there is an easy answer to where rules come from. They are imposed from outside the system. The engineer makes things so that this code item stands for that message, and the legislature similarly makes up the laws. But when we are faced with naturally occurring evolved systems, the question how the regularities of behavior come about runs much deeper. Natural languages are perfect examples. The meaning of English words is not generally decided by a committee. Even in France, the Academy does not try to do more than to influence usage at the edges. The basic structures and meanings of French got to be the way they are, long before the *Académie française* fretted over whether businesses should be allowed to advertise *le hamburger*.

The issue about where rules come from is more often thought about in terms of the origin of CONVENTIONS. Conventions are regularities that could be otherwise. We drive on the left. They drive on the right. It is a matter of convention. That does not mean that flouting the convention only brings the consequences of disapproval of some authority, or that *any regularity* is a workable convention. When they swapped sides of the road in Sweden there was a joke that the public transport would be switched first, and the private traffic the week after. This was not a possible convention. Although it is a matter of convention which side is adopted, it is not a matter of convention *whether there is a convention*, or from what population of possible conventions it is drawn. So conventions (and rules) have an element of arbitrariness but often against a background of necessity.

The rules of language are like this, though the interplay of convention and necessity is far more intricate, and major arguments rage about what aspects are necessary (and why) and which are arbitrary. For example, word meanings are conventional. It is arbitrary which sound is attached to which meaning. However, it is not arbitrary what sounds and sequences are possible, nor what meanings are possible word meanings. Nor is it arbitrary that there is some stability to the pairing, from person to person and from time to time. Words mean what we all mean them to mean, but not what I mean them to mean unless I can get you all to agree. Professors can, and do, frequently make up new words, but only a few catch on, even within the narrow communities of specialists.

We have a large investment in all using the same words the same way, comparable to our investment in all driving on the same side of the road, whichever is chosen. Of course, maintenance of the regularities of our side-of-the-road conventions is commensurate with their simplicity, but maintenance of language regularity takes major effort because of the complexities of the regularities involved.

If regularities of behavior can evolve from groups of people acting without a central legislative body, that has implications for how we can know these rules, and how we infer their consequences. The rule we are given by the experimenter in the selection task has an explicit representation in a way that a rule of our native language's grammar may not—it is easily written down, for example. But we saw in chapter 3 that it was still extremely hard to give an explicit formulation of just what that rule meant to subjects who had to interpret it. So in that sense the rule was as implicit as the rule of grammar, and for similar reasons. Are the regularities in our behavior to be explained by us "following rules," or "behaving as if there were rules?" If we can be shown to behave as if there is a rule, does that mean there must be a mechanism in our brain that corresponds to the rule? If we are shown to behave according to a rule, yet we can also be shown not to know that we do so, what does that mean about our access to our own mental structures?

Separating what is explicit and what is implicit is no easy matter. Even if a regularity such as driving on the right emerges from the distributed activity of a population through history, it may achieve explicitness in being enshrined in the law and the highway code. Conversely, even if we were explicitly given the rule in the selection task in the form of a publicly accessible written sentence, we have seen that our use of that rule depends on implicit knowledge of many linguistic possibilities and subtle contextual cues that easily go unnoticed even by researchers.

One framework for the analysis of the origin and deployment of conventions is the area of mathematics that has come to be called GAME THEORY. Uses of the concepts of game theory crop up in all sorts of areas across the scientific spectrum, e.g. in biology, in psychology, and in economics. Game theory is particularly relevant to communication because it throws light on the interplay of cooperation and competition, and on the relation between what is explicitly known and what arises from interaction. A quick digression into the basics will be useful to our understanding of rules. We will avoid the mathematics—it is the basic concepts that are important to us.

A classical problem in game theory is called the PRISONERS' DILEMMA. Two suspects are arrested in connection with a crime, and both know that both have been arrested. However, they are kept incommunicado, and so cannot negotiate a story for the police. The PAYOFF-MATRIX for the prisoners is as follows. If they both admit to the crime, both will receive a sentence of, say, seven years. If one confesses, and the other doesn't, he turns state's evidence and gets only one year, but the other then gets the maximum sentence of twenty years. If neither confesses, the police have insufficient evidence so they both get off with no penalty. The exact numbers do not matter, but their relations do. The best total outcome for both is mutual silence; the worst total outcome is if one talks and the other doesn't, and this outcome is asymmetrical. If both talk the total imprisonment is intermediate and symmetrical.

Here is a communication problem with a vengeance—except no communication is allowed. The prisoners may wish they could resort to telepathy.... The payoff-matrix of this game is what is interesting about it. Games with a simple pay-off matrix in which players just compete with each other, and the more one wins, the less the other gets, are called ZERO-SUM games. The sum of rewards for all players at the end of the game is always the same, whatever strategy they pursue, and by choosing suitable units of reward and punishment, their sum can be normalized to zero (hence the name). Chess is a zero-sum game: winner takes all and draws split the points equally. The Prisoner's Dilemma is, in contrast, a NON-ZERO-SUM GAME game. The punishments have different totals according to which choices the players make, with a range from zero if they both keep quiet, through fourteen if they both talk, to twenty-one if one keeps quiet and the other talks.

The Prisoner's Dilemma is an extremely important abstract game for understanding social coordination. One reason is that it clearly shows how different ways of defining rationality and their different ways of counting benefits and losses have different consequences. If we define benefits and losses in individual terms and ask what strategy is rational to maximize individual gain and minimize individual loss, then we get one answer; if we define benefits and losses communally and ask what strategy will maximize communal gain and minimize communal losses, then we get another answer. This relation between individual and communal concepts is one of the fundamental issues in the social and biological sciences. Modern economics is overwhelmingly based on the behavior of a theoretical species *Homo economicus* who seeks only to maximize individual benefit. There are arguments that in fact *Homo sapiens* wisely does not fit the theoretical model well at all, except in some limited, important but ill-understood circumstances. The Prisoner's Dilemma is important because it shows how *Homo economicus* loses out.

Life is a non-zero-sum game. Many activities are neither wholly cooperative nor wholly competitive, but an interesting mixture of the two. As the police are well aware, members of the criminal fraternity are quite good at coming out in the optimal cell of the payoff-matrix (that is to say no cell at all). In contrast, randomly chosen pairs of experimental subjects in single-play Prisoners Dilemma situations generally fail to coordinate. In iterated situations where they play repeatedly, they often settle on what is called a TIT-FOR-TAT STRATEGY of trusting their partner unless that partner betrayed them on the previous round. Trust is fundamental to social coordination. Game theory is relevant to social behavior in general and to communication in particular because so much of social behavior consists in coordination. This is another place where phatic and ideational communication come together. Trust and mutual knowledge are often established at least in part through phatic communication—communication that establishes or maintains social groupings. Real criminals may not carry around a black sack marked "loot," but they do have rituals for maintenance of their community.

Some social coordinations are even simpler than the Prisoner's Dilemma. One hallmark of social coordination problems is that the participants may not care about which of several solutions is arrived at, but they nevertheless have a strong interest in some coordinating solution being found. A homely example may illustrate the idea. Supposing you have an arrangement to meet a friend at the theater, but you forgot to arrange an exact place and your cell phone's batteries are drained. You can reason as follows:

We need to decide independently on the same place. What I need to know is how my friend is going to decide this. She is going to decide this by thinking about how I am going to decide this, and so on.... Another of those wretched infinite regresses. So I'll go home.

Alternatively, one could reason:

She's sure to realize that we are both trying to think of a unique kind of place to meet. We don't want to choose entrances because there are usually more than one. It's true that there is only one "northmost" entrance, but there is no reason to pick "northmost" as a direction (even if we happen to know where north is). We could pick the ticket office (usually unique). We could pick the manager's office–also usually unique. But she's more likely to think of the ticket office because people usually don't know where the manager's office is. . . .

and of course you are usually successful.

Sometimes the thinking is more idiosyncratic:

A: I just know he'll go for the bar.
B: She'll just know I'll go for the bar.

But equally this displays an implicit knowledge of the mental processes in "communication," and explains why we get such a feeling of "being on the same wavelength" when we succeed—a powerful phatic achievement. The more idiosyncratic the choice is to the pair of us, the more powerful the phatic effect.

Managing to meet before the theater has much formally in common with managing to interpret each others' communicative intentions. These situations where we are incommunicado throw much light on what is involved in communication, and in particular how explicit communication rests on implicit knowledge. There are powerful arguments that however explicit the framework of communication is made, there is still an ineradicable grounding in a community's implicit shared tendencies to interpret.

Game theory also offers a framework for understanding other sometimes paradoxical aspects of less cooperative communication. One example is negotiation, and the potency of impotence. In an example like a union negotiating with an employer, it is greatly to the union representative's advantage if the employer knows or believes that the union representative has little power to vary the level of offer to be accepted. Unions often reflect this by mandating their negotiators to accept nothing less than some level of settlement. If the employer knows (or believes) that the negotiator cannot settle for less, this may have a bearing on the employer's strategy. A more powerful representative may be at a severe negotiating disadvantage if the employer knows that they are in a position to authorize the acceptance of substantially less. There are examples of real negotiations in which the act of throwing away the ability to take some course of action has been a source of negotiating strength. In fact, the concept of social power has much in common with these other concepts of social coordination. Individuals (or office holders) are powerful if and only if the members of their community generally believe them to be powerful. Banks work similarly. People get their money back out of banks if the depositors believe they will get their money back out. If sufficient people cease to believe this, then they become correct. This self-sustaining (and self-defeating) nature of certain kinds of social coordinations is what makes social science so very complicated, and so very different from natural science.

The evolutionary psychologists' arguments about the selection task that we met in chapter 3 are another example of how these issues about communication and economic exchange come together. The evolutionary psychologists believe that their interpretation of the selection task supports the idea that human reasoning evolved from adaptations for social exchange of goods and services, and their models are the models of *Homo economicus*. The selection task evidence turned out not to support their arguments. The important countermodel of evolution of human reasoning stresses the achievement of general communication skills and trust, and the linkage of ideational and phatic communication in human beings, as a necessary evolutionary foundation for generalized economic exchange. On this argument, being able to speak languages on the basis of trusted exchange of information within communities must have come before generalized exchange of goods and services.

We now turn to more psychological questions about what happens within an individual when new rules are acquired.

4.3   Implicit and Explicit Knowledge

Game theorists and political and social theorists have given accounts of how some behavior that operates according to rules can nevertheless arise without explicit communication from many individuals pursuing local strategies, like the antheap from the local doings of individual ants. Psychologists have been concerned to study what sort of mental access we have to regularities in our behavior that originate in different ways. They make a distinction between IMPLICIT and EXPLICIT knowledge.

We learn "motor skills"—to ride a bicycle or to ski—through a mixture of verbal and nonverbal instructions. Verbal instruction alone is notoriously inadequate, and in many forms worse than useless. The helpful physicist who supplies differential equations for the actions necessary to ride a bicycle is merely an extreme case. We do use verbal instructions, but in particular ways. Apprentice skiers may be taught, and find it useful, to give themselves verbal instructions at particular points of the execution of a maneuver. But the rhythm of the phrase may be as important as its propositional content. Experts at the performance of skills often have extraordinarily poor verbal access to how it is that they perform them. Unless they have learnt how to communicate them to others, they are likely to be the least useful teachers. Often the beginner who has just mastered something is the best placed to pass it on.

A trivial example of poor verbal access to a motor habit is the crossing of thumbs—if you ask yourself which thumb you place on top when you clasp your hands together, you may find you are in some doubt, until you do it, and you then find that there is a very strong feeling that one feels "right" and the other "wrong." This habit is unlikely to be one that originated from verbal instruction (maybe etiquette somewhere dictates?), but another example that does have a clear verbal origin is being able to remember your automatic teller machine PIN number only by poking the keys on the machine—the knowledge is now "only in your fingers," no longer in your verbal memory. Perhaps the most paradoxical examples of the inaccessibility of information to verbal recall are language skills themselves. A good proportion of the formal educational curriculum, including this course, is learning to make explicit knowledge of our native tongue—at the many levels we have been dealing with, and several others. For example, much of the phonetic structure of words remains inaccessible to explicit awareness.

A standard example is to ask yourself (if you are an English speaker) whether there is a difference in the sounds of the "p" in the words *pin* and *spin*. Most people cannot hear this difference. Might you doubt it exists? Try putting your hand in front of your mouth and uttering the two words alternately. You can feel a puff of air released in the pronunciation of "pin" that is not there with "spin." That puff of air is what a phonetician calls *aspiration*, and it makes a difference to the sound that most English speakers do not hear—a breathy sound. In English, although it is a regular phenomenon that word-initial "p" is aspirated but "p" after "s" is unaspirated, which of these sounds is made is never the only thing that makes a difference to what word is meant. There is no MINIMAL PAIR of English words that differ only by this sound, as there is a minimal pair *pin/bin* that show that the *p/b voicing* distinction (see section 2.1) is significant, or as linguists say *phonemic*. In languages where both an aspirated and an unaspirated "p" can occur in initial position and the difference distinguishes words, speakers can hear this sound difference easily. You can train your ear to hear it, as you would have to in a phonetics course, or if you learnt one of these languages in which the distinction is significant. It has even been shown that babies are sensitive to such sound differences *before* they learn a language that does not use them to distinguish words (like English). In learning English they lose the ability to hear what they could hear before. Similar cases could be cited for all levels of language—cases where we cannot say how we behave though our behavior is highly systematic. If we did have transparent access to all our knowledge of communication, I would not be writing this, and you would not be reading it.

You acquired your regularity of behavior with regard to aspirated consonants a long time ago and without explicit instruction. Psychologists have studied the learning of artificial languages by example in order to investigate the development of implicit and explicit knowledge. Subjects learn to judge whether a sequence of symbols of an artificial language is "grammatical," as defined but not divulged by the experimenter. They receive immediate feedback on their judgment. An excerpt from one of these experiments might look something like this:

string	subject	feedback
aa	yes	yes
abab	yes	no
aabaab	no	yes
abaaba	no	yes

. . .

After a long succession of such judgments the subject gets better and better at "knowing" whether strings of symbols are well formed or not—whether they belong to the artificial language. This is supposed to mimic a child learning the grammar of language by example rather than by instruction by explicit rules. It does so in an extremely simplified, and in many ways misleading way, but it illustrates the development of implicit knowledge without explicit knowledge. After this sort of learning, subjects generally cannot say how they are deciding correctly

that a string is a sentence or not. Even if there are simple regular
rules (maybe all mirror symmetrical strings are OK, but no others),
the subject often has no conscious access to the rules.

Similar studies have also looked at the same issue when people learn
to operate devices. A simulation of the operation of an industrial process
produced the same result. People can learn to manipulate complex input
controls to meet an output target, but they do not necessarily then know
what they are doing in the sense of being able to describe it to anyone
else.

There is an important educational issue in these observations. When
is it important for people to gain conscious access to their implicit knowledge? And does their performance change when they do learn to make
the knowledge explicit in some way? Obviously it all depends on what
they want to be able to do. If they want to learn French primarily to hold
a colloquial conversation, then learning to analyze its grammar may be
counterproductive. But achieving literacy, and a self-consciousness about
how language structures work, does make a huge difference to peoples'
thinking and communicating processes. Think back to Scribner's studies of Liberian reasoners in the last chapter. We speculate that certain
of your capacities for reasoning and communication may well change
because studying this book changes them from things only implicitly
known to things you are aware of.

These issues about implicit and explicit knowledge will be taken
up in the discussion of representation in chapter 7. Knowledge learned
from repetitive experience in a certain context on the basis of condition-
ing may be extremely efficient for performing a well-defined task (like
navigating a fixed route), but as soon as the information is needed for
multiple purposes in contexts unpredictable at time of learning (working
out the best route for a novel journey perhaps), then a representational
approach provides more flexibility. When we consider the range of different artificial computational mechanisms we find that some are more
suited to carrying out one of these functions and some to the other. It
seems likely that there is some as yet ill-understood relation between
implicitness or explicitness of knowledge and the kinds of representation
(or nonrepresentation) underlying knowledge.

While the distinction between implicit and explicit knowledge is fundamental to much of psychology, sociologists have a closely related distinction between tacit and codified knowledge. Codified knowledge is

knowledge that is stated; tacit knowledge is knowledge that is not given such explicit expression. Sociologists interested in how organizations (companies, schools, teams, etc.) function have found this distinction essential. They always find that while there is "official" codified knowledge of how things are to be done that participants readily verbalize, actual performance of "the job" relies on peoples' tacit knowledge and practices. The distinction often comes painfully to light when computerization of some function is based on codified knowledge but cuts across the tacit knowledge on which the institution actually relies. Workers then have to develop some "workaround" for allowing the human institution to function despite the machine's imposed system.

Even in science this distinction turns out to be necessary. While scientific theory may be the most extreme case of explicit knowledge, actual scientific experiment relies on a great deal of tacit skill—knowing that the flame looks just thus-and-so when the glass is blown to make the apparatus to do the critical experiment, for example (see Collins 1990). Even theoretical concepts may have an irreducible implicit component— the expert may not be able to say exactly why some things do not count as Xs even though she can reliably recognize that they aren't. It is not clear that everything can in principle be made explicit, even if science is, in general, a sysiphean labor toward that unattainable goal.

The psychological distinction between explicit and implicit, and the sociological distinction between tacit and codified knowledge are different but closely analogous distinctions. They are distinct because someone's tacit knowledge may be verbalizable (and therefore not implicit in the psychologists' sense). The computer operator may be able to tell you exactly what the workaround is that keeps the codified story about what is done up and running. The workaround is tacit but not cognitively implicit. The concepts are nevertheless analogous because they rest on an analogy between institutions and individuals. Just as an individual knows many things that are embodied in their makeup but that they cannot describe, so institutions "know things" that are not accessible at institutional level but only by accessing components (in this case individuals) of the institution. This is a fascinating example of the analogy between groups and individuals, which is a theme always just below the surface in biology, psychology, and sociology.

The distinctions between implicit and explicit, tacit and codified knowledge are related to, though different from, the distinctions between phatic and ideational communication, and between PROCEDURAL and DECLARATIVE knowledge. Phatic communication tends to be implicit in the sense that the communication does not always work by the communicator intending it to work. As we said, ideational communication generally depends on this intention to be seen to intend. Procedural knowledge of how to do something (such as the motor skill of tapping in your PIN number at the cash machine) tends to be implicit, and declarative knowledge (that they drive on the right in the U.K.) explicit.

There are both advantages and disadvantages to having knowledge in one or other of these forms. Implicit knowledge may be automatically accessed in the right context with little cognitive load. Tacit knowledge allows the codified knowledge that depends on it to be succinctly stated. Some sociologists have proposed that social coordination must depend fundamentally on tacit knowledge, and that calculation on codified knowledge could not serve as a basis for coordination. Think of the earlier arguments about trust. If *Homo economicus* announces that he will calculate the advantages and disadvantages to himself of some course of action, be thereby blows any trust that others might have in his public spirit.

4.4   Summary

Starting out from the unpromising consideration of sequences of coin tosses, we have seen how peoples' reasoning in uncertainty connects to a variety of fundamental issues in communication. Distinguishing token sequences of events from abstract types of event sequences is essential to understanding probabilities. Populations of tokens have frequency distributions of types, and led us into considerations of base-rate information as distinct from event-specific information. Base-rates turned out to be key to understanding anecdotalism and a whole range of social and cognitive stereotypes that lurk behind communication. The different notions of what is conceivable politically and scientifically also rest on this foundation.

Reasoning about knowledge and informativeness also turned out to require the tools of probability theory as we saw illustrated in the Prisoner's Paradox. Understanding mutuality of knowledge required the distinction between object- and meta-levels of analysis. Social coordinations such as getting off of buses involve knowledge about what is known by whom. Conventions are mutual knowledge and the process whereby conventions arise is illuminated by game theory. We saw how the Prisoners' Dilemma forces our attention onto tacitly shared knowledge and trust, and onto the difference between individually and group-defined concepts of benefit and loss. Finally, there are parallels between the psychologist's distinction between implicit/explicit knowledge and the sociologist's distinction between tacit/codified knowledge that rest on the important analogy between individuals as systems of components and communities as groups of individuals.

Just as in the previous chapter, you will have noticed how the discussion keeps switching between several perspectives: What do you as a reasoner think is the answer to this problem? Can some mathematical system model the observations of peoples' behavior? Do people know (implicitly or explicitly) about the system? What happens if we teach people the system? This combining of perspectives is characteristic of cognitive science and its attempts to integrate disciplines' contributions. Having reviewed some phenomena of communication, the next part of the book will focus on theoretical approaches to understanding them.

Exercises

Exercise 4.1: Review your notes on your own answers that you gave to the questions asked throughout this chapter. What have you learned by reading it? Review the similarities and differences between this area of reasoning and that reviewed in the previous chapter.

Exercise 4.2: Find a good example of an anecdotal story intended to make an argument from a recent newspaper. What consideration of base-rate information does the story require for the proper assessment of conclusions it invites the reader to draw. What base-rates are involved?

4.5   Further Reading

- Kahneman, D., Slovic, P., & Tversky, A. (eds.) (1982). *Judgment Under Uncertainty: Heuristics and Biases.* Cambridge: Cambridge University Press.

Classical collection of papers on reasoning in uncertainty.

- Gigerenzer, G., & Todd, P.(1999). *Simple Heuristics that Make Us Smart*. New York: Oxford University Press.

An ecological approach to reasoning in uncertainty.

- Schelling, T. (1960). *The Strategy of Conflict*. Cambridge: Harvard University Press.

One of the earliest sociological applications of games theory ideas to issues about convention and negotiation.

- Lewis, D. (1969). *Convention: A Philosophical Study*. Cambridge: Harvard University Press.

Develops ideas from game theory to explain linguistic conventions. Now the classical philosophical account of both the arbitrariness and determination of conventions.

- Chwe, M. (2001). *Rational Ritual: Culture, Coordination, and Common Knowledge*. Princeton: Princeton University Press.

A discussion of the role of social ritual in establishing mutual knowledge.

- Berry, D. C. (ed.) (1997). *How Implicit is Implicit Learning?* Oxford: Oxford University Press.

A collection of papers on controversies about implicit learning in the psychological literature.

- Collins, H. (1990). *Artificial Experts: Social Knowledge and Intelligent Machines*. Cambridge: MIT Press.

A sociological study of implicitness in the foundations of scientific knowledge.

II THEORETICAL FOUNDATIONS

5 Content, Context, and Formal Systems

5.1 Introduction

In chapter 2 the limitations of Shannon and Weaver's finite codes led us to consider the consequences for theories of communication of assuming that languages are essentially infinite. Infinite languages can only be studied as systems of representation and inferences over them, i.e. in terms of computation. Chapters 3 and 4 argued the need for logical, probability, and game-theoretic models (among others) as ways of specifying such infinite systems. We saw that there is generally a plurality of possible models for any naturally occuring task. Interpretation of each new context into the terms of one or another model is a major component of communication. Interpretation, we saw, is guided both by the content of messages and by the context of their utterance. Finding an interpretation and reasoning from it are processes that interact. If our reasoning from our initial interpretation leads to contradiction or implausible conclusions, then changing interpretation is a natural response. So understanding the mind is about understanding how content, context, and formal systems interact.

Although we have seen how it may be controversial determining just what is the model for some particular reasoning in its particular context, nevertheless, some systematization of reasoning is required. Combining the empirical observation of peoples' behavior with mathematical and computational modeling of standards of performance is at the heart of cognitive science. This part of the book provides an introduction to some of these systems for modeling behavior and examines the kinds of issues that arise in fitting them to the data of human behavior. This chapter introduces the system of PROPOSITIONAL LOGIC (the one we saw Wason unquestioningly adopt as his standard of correctness for his task in Chapter 3), and examines the tensions involved in using it to model the behavior of conditional reasoning. This CLASSICAL LOGIC will be contrasted informally with NONCLASSICAL DEFAULT LOGICS, useful for modeling natural language interpretation. Chapter 6 introduces the abstract notion of computation as a quite general framework for modeling behavior, and contrasts abstract computation with the level of its implementation in different kinds of devices—natural or engineered. Abstract computational analysis is applied to structures of natural language in reconstructing Chomsky's original argument for a cognitive approach. Chapter 6 introduces issues that arise in applying computational analysis to understanding the mental representations that underpin discourse understanding.

Cognitive science is all about the tension between formal modeling on the one hand and contentful behavior and experience on the other. FORMALITY is about being free of CONTENT. The modern mind is accustomed to applying formal methods to the physical world, and dissociating the resulting science from our experience of that same physical world. We are happy to model orbiting spheres while experiencing a flat earth.

Cognitive science arose out of the development of new formal methods of computation and their application to some of our most intimately subjective doings like thinking and communicating. Here most people are not yet so prepared to accept the application of formalisms. To them it is just obvious that computers are what come in boxes and perform zillions of operations per second with crystalline precision—whilst human beings are warm, slow, intuitive, emotional creatures prone to error, and, above all, unpredictable and creative. Interestingly, some of the most fervent reactions against the idea that the mind is to be understood on a computational model come from physicists, as we shall see in chapter 19.

This book seeks to chip away at some of these preconceptions about computation and people. Computation understood abstractly is performed by many mechanisms other than boxes with "Intel inside." Human individuals, human social groups, and ant colonies are three examples. Humans compute some things with far greater precision, speed, and reliability than any existing engineered systems. Think of two lines of traffic on the two sides of an undivided highway approaching each other at combined speeds of 100 miles an hour, one-ton boxes of metal, passing a few feet from each other, guided by warm, slow, error-prone humans, daydreaming about the complexities of human communication perhaps. Ask yourself whether you would be happier with the opposing traffic steered by currently available robots? Who is the more capricious in this circumstance? Some of our everyday emotional reactions to the word "computation" may be inappropriate for developing a scientific theory of communication. Here we seek to modify those intuitions.

Chapter 3 reviewed an argument about form and content in human reasoning. The selection task with a descriptive rule and with a deontic rule were claimed by psychologists to be of the *same* logical form. Human reasoning with the two rules was observed to be radically different. Therefore, human reasoning was concluded to not operate on logical form. We reviewed this argument and concluded that it was formally valid but that at least one of its premises was false—the two rules were of *different* forms. What is more, the descriptive rule has multiple possible interpretations varying on a number of dimensions (biconditional/conditional, constant/variable anaphor, brittle/robust to exceptions, etc., etc.). We observed that the content of problems cues people to the likely form intended. For just one example of many, with a conjunctive rule, it appeared that subjects were influenced by the already visible falsity of a descriptive interpretation of the rule to adopt a deontic interpretation as more likely what the experimenter had in mind.

This discussion leaned heavily on unexamined notions of content and logical form. These are two ruling concepts in logical and computational theories. We now present some theoretical apparatus to elaborate exactly what we mean.

5.2   Logic

Some basic concepts

The most fundamental distinction in logic is between TRUTH and VALIDITY. Logic studies relations between sets of PREMISES, that are generally sentences, and CONCLUSIONS that are more sentences. Validity is defined in terms of truth: an argument from a set of premises to a conclusion is valid if *whenever* the set of premises are all true, then the conclusion is true. Logic is about guaranteeing that if we start reasoning from truths, we won't get to false conclusions—valid patterns of argument preserve truth, but they do not necessarily have true conclusions. False premises plugged into a valid argument may yield either true or false conclusions—garbage in leads to the possibility of garbage out. Arguments are vehicles for getting us to new conclusions whose truth we don't yet know. If even one INTERPRETATION of the premises can be found in which the premises are all true but the conclusion is false, then the argument is INVALID.

In these statements, the two words *whenever* and *interpretation* are critical to understanding what logic is all about. In chapter 3, we discussed the interpretation problems of Wason's subjects at length. Here we are going to begin a technical treatment of just what interpretation means in logic. Logic understands languages as having two levels— SYNTACTIC and SEMANTIC. At a syntactic level, languages are just uninterpreted squiggles characterized in terms of sequences of symbols drawn from some vocabulary of symbols. A syntactic definition of a language (natural or artificial) just defines which sequences of symbols are WELL-FORMED sentences, and which are ILL-FORMED or UNGRAMMATICAL. We'll look at such a definition shortly. In order to breath life, or at least usefulness, into such a set of squiggles, we have to give a semantic definition that says what they mean. Usually this is done by saying when sentences are true.

This is where the *whenever* and the *interpretation* come in. We have to give an interpretation to the symbols—to say what objects and properties and relations they are about. But logic is *not* concerned with some particular interpretation onto a single set of objects and relations. It is concerned with *all possible interpretations*. To go back to our light-switch example from chapter 3, logic is not about your switch at home, or my switch at home. It's about all possible situations that are truthfully described by the premises. In fact, it's not concerned with switches. Those are content, and content's only role is to be the same whenever it is named by the same name, in the same argument. So the sentences about switches can get replaced by *P*s and *Q*s, and logic is really about how the little words *if, and, or, not. . .* interact with the VARIABLES marking the recurrence of the same content—about minding one's *P*s and *Q*s.

We have already seen in chapter 3, that descriptive and deontic interpretations of the very same English rule have different logical forms that allow different reasoning patterns, so the subjects' interpretations were not always the same as the experimenter's—the content shifted. Another example was the contrast between brittle and robust interpretations of descriptive rules. These are not cases of the interpretation of particular variables shifting content, but they are shifts of content of whole sentences nonetheless. Assigning logical form is not merely a matter of looking at the sequence of words in a sentence, but also of asking what the sentence is being used to say in context.

In a moment, we will look at a simple example of a logical language.

But first we should stand back and see how different the situation is with an artificial language and a natural one such as English. As we discussed in chapter 4 with regard to the conventional meaning of words, nobody ever constructed English by giving a syntactic definition and a semantic definition. We, and our ancestors, all acquired our mother tongues by being pitched into the middle of a community of speakers, and picking language up as we went along. That does not mean that natural languages are just a mess. They are elegantly structured with extraordinary precision in some aspects of their functioning. But it means that it is hard for us to stand back from natural languages and analyze them, particularly their meanings. Much of our understanding of semantics has come from studying artificial languages and could only then be reapplied to natural languages. The situation is analogous to aerodynamics, which developed from studying built airplanes before it could be applied to birds. In fact, many linguists and philosophers held the position that it was *impossible* to study semantics, until the study of artificial languages made it commonplace. Even today, many discussions of logic in psychology treat only the process of reasoning from artificial languages in virtue of their form, and completely ignore the processes whereby interpretation assigns content. This leads to nothing but confusion. Cognitive science uses ARTIFICIAL LANGUAGE to model aspects of natural ones. As with all modeling, we need to pay close attention to the idealisation—the correspondence assumed between the artificial model and what it models.

When we are done, we will be able to look back at artificial languages and see that in fact, in many respects, they are just like natural ones as long as we look at both kinds of language at the right level of abstraction. We will see that both natural and artificial languages only ever have local interpretations on narrow domains of things, and that these interpretations have to be developed and redeveloped in each new context of communication. People communicate not just new messages, but new local interpretations of languages, too. This is true at the very mundane level at which each utterance of "The cat sat on the mat" requires us to map the mat and the cat and the sitting onto their references in context. It also takes place at the, perhaps, more exciting levels at which words take on new meanings. That natural languages are already interpreted is a common illusion, but not one that we can accept.

Propositional calculus—a simple logic

Propositional calculus (PC) is a logic for analyzing arguments that hinge on the LOGICAL CONNECTIVES: $\&, \wedge, \vee, \neg$.... These symbols connect whole sentences rather than analyzing them into terms for things, properties, and relations. Other more powerful logics (such as predicate logic) subsume PC but also analyze structure within CLAUSES and sentences. So sentences are the contentful part of PC and the connectives are what defines the *form*. The only way the contentful sentences figure in the logic are as *sentential variables*: $P, Q, R, \ldots$ These symbols only constrain content in a very weak way—within an interpretation, the same letter always stands for the same content. The particular version of propositional logic we present here is CLASSICAL propositional calculus. We will briefly mention some nonclassical alternatives because they are cognitively important, and even if we cannot present their technical details, it is important to know they exist as alternatives. Classical logic is not some unique gold-standard of reasoning.

A syntactic definition of PC is usually given by a RECURSIVE DEFINITION. First a finite vocabulary of connectives is listed: $\&, \wedge, \vee, \neg, \rightarrow$. Then a finite but extensible list of sentential variables is listed: $P, Q, R, \ldots$ Finally sentences are defined, usually using meta-variables that range over sentences: A, B, ...where A stands for any sentence variable:

- Any atomic sentential variable A is a sentence.
- If A is a sentence, then $(\neg A)$ is a sentence.
- If A and B are sentences, then $(A \wedge B)$ is a sentence.
- If A and B are sentences, then $(A \vee B)$ is a sentence.
- If A and B are sentences, then $(A \rightarrow B)$ is a sentence.
- Nothing else is a sentence.

The following strings of symbols are sentences of this artificial language by this definition: $(P \rightarrow Q)$, $((P\&R) \rightarrow Q)$, $((P\&R) \rightarrow (\neg Q))$, and $((P\&R) \rightarrow (\neg(\neg Q)))$. We can safely leave out some of the parentheses as we do in writing arithmetic, but technically they are required to be there. You should satisfy yourself that you can see why these are sentences, whereas $(\rightarrow Q)$ is not. So far so good, but so far it's all just squiggles.

For a semantic definition we need to ask ourselves what is a calculus of sentences about? Our answer will be PROPOSITIONS and their TRUTH VALUES. Propositions are what bear truth values. They are expressed by sentences in contexts of use. The same sentence may express different propositions on different occasions (e.g. "It's hot today," uttered as I write, expresses the proposition that it's hot here in Edinburgh on September 21st, 2004)

At first it may seem strange that we only talk of propositions' truth values and not what they are about, but remember that PC does not analyze the internal structure of sentences, and its variables can only mark the recurrence of the *same* content, so truth values are what is significant. Predicate calculus is a more powerful logic that does analyze sentences into terms and relations, and the semantics of predicate calculus is about things and relations between things. PC is just about whole sentences. This should seem more intuitive when we have looked at an example semantic definition.

There are several ways of presenting the semantics of PC. Let's start with TRUTH TABLES. Each connective has a truth table that defines the truth of sentences containing the connective as a TRUTH FUNCTION of its sentential variables. So for $\neg$ the truth table looks like this:

$\neg P$	P
F	T
T	F

Each row of the table gives an interpretation of the sentential variables (in this case there is only one variable). The column headed P gives the truth value of P under the interpretation assigned in each row (T for true and F for false). The column headed $\neg P$ gives the truth value for that sentence, when the sentence P has the value marked in its column on the same row. So the table defines the value of $\neg P$ in terms of the value of P. There are just enough rows to cover all possible assignments, so for a truth table of a sentence with N distinct sentential variables $P, Q, R \ldots$, the truth table has 2^N rows. In this case, $2^1 = 2$.

This particular connective $\neg$ reverses the truth value of the simpler sentence to which it is prefaced. The logical name for this operation is NEGATION. In English, the rather stilted operator *it is not the case that. . .* has a similar syntax and semantics. It can be placed on the front of any indicative sentence, and it reverses the truth value. Correspondences to other ways of expressing negation in English are not quite so straightforward. For example, the sentence *All the circles don't have crosses* is ambiguous, and its two meanings depend on whether *don't* is interpreted as if *it is not the case that* had been appended to the front of the sentence (and the *don't* dropped), or whether the negative only applies to the "verb phrase" *have crosses*. So ¬ models some aspects of negation in English, but by no means all.

The tables for the other three connectives each have two sentential variables, and so have 2^2 rows and look like this:

$P \wedge Q$	P	Q	$P \vee Q$	P	Q	$P \to Q$	P	Q
T	T	T	T	T	T	T	T	T
F	T	F	T	T	F	F	T	F
F	F	T	T	F	T	T	F	T
F	F	F	F	F	F	T	F	F

The usual nearest correspondences to familiar English connectives will be given presently, but first we look at what was done here purely formally. The method of truth tabling allows you to decide for any argument whether or not its conclusion is true *whenever* its assumptions are true—that is to say whether the argument is valid. The central concept is that of a row as one *interpretation* of the sentential variables— a row defines a little world by stating some things that are true and some that are false in that world. Tabling then offers a method of generating a row of table for every possible assignment of truth values to variables, and so cashes out our notion of *all possible assignments of interpretations* mentioned above.

We use this method to assess the validity of an argument formalized in PC. Let's take the example argument that has a single premise $P \wedge Q$ and the conclusion $\neg(\neg Q)$. A table with all possible combinations of values for the atomic sentential variables (P and Q), and with columns for premise and for conclusion then looks like this:

premise	atomic variables		conclusion	
$P \wedge Q$	P	Q	$(\neg$	$(\neg Q))$
T	T	T	**T**	F
F	T	F	**F**	T
F	F	T	**T**	F
F	F	F	**F**	T

In this argument table, the MAIN CONNECTIVE columns for the premise and the conclusion are emboldened to make them stand out. In each row these main connective columns contain the value of the whole complex sentence for the row-valuation of their atomic variables. The truth functions for the connectives come from the earlier cited tables. Note that ¬ can apply repeatedly to a sentence to form new sentences, rather as it is possible to repeatedly apply *its not the case that* to English sentences (e.g. *Its not the case that its not the case that Fred's ill*), even if it is not recommended style.

We can now check off whether our argument is valid. Going back to the definition of validity, we have to answer whether the conclusion is true whenever the premises are all true. Here there is only one premise. So whenever there is a T in the column for the premise, there must be a T in the same row under the column for (the main connective of) the conclusion. In this table, we only have to check the top row, since that is the only one in which the premise is true, and we find that indeed the conclusion is true in that row. The conclusion may be true when the premise is false (third row), but that is neither here nor there.

So the method of truth tabling gives a clear definition for validity. It makes it clear what an interpretation is, and what *all possible interpretations* means. The method literally generates all possible interpretations, and then checks off to see if the conclusion ever fails when the premises are true. The method also helps us to see how syntactic and semantic levels relate to each other.

Now you are probably trying to map all these squiggles on to English, still waiting for the promised correspondences. But not before looking at the importance of having a formal system. That importance is much harder to understand once we start assimilating these squiggles to natural languages such as English.

Metalogic

PC has been initially presented here through truth tables because the most important concept to understand is the distinction between syntactic and semantic levels, and how the two relate to each other. We now proceed to examine this distinction more deeply.

A common alternative to truth tables is to present logic as a set of rules for transforming sentences into others that follow from them, and this is the guise in which logic most often appears in psychological discussions of reasoning. So, for example, we could have presented PC through what is called a NATURAL DEDUCTION SYSTEM. Each connective would be associated with an INTRODUCTION RULE and an ELIMINATION RULE. So for the connective $\wedge$, there would be a rule: *From a premise $A \wedge B$ you can conclude A*. This is an elimination rule for $\wedge$ since the connective appears in the premise but not in the conclusion. The introduction rule for $\wedge$ is like this: *From two premises A and B you can conclude $A \wedge B$*. The rules for $\vee$ are quite different. $\vee$-introduction goes like this: *From A you can conclude $A \vee B$*. $\vee$-elimination is more complex: *if from A you can conclude C, and from B you can conclude C, then given $A \vee B$ you can conclude C*. This is the narrow sense in which logic models purely formal reasoning—you don't have to consider what a sentence means in order to apply a rule.

These rules are syntactic. They are defined entirely in terms of the strings of squiggles and they make no recourse to the meaning. If you didn't know the semantics, you could still apply these rules like a dumb computer. The study of what can be derived from what by using syntactically defined rules is called PROOF THEORY. Given a set of rules for PC, you could set about deriving the argument that we truth-tabled. In other words, starting with just the assumption $P \wedge Q$ using only the rules to transform this sentence and other products of transformation of this sentence, it is possible to derive $\neg(\neg Q)$ as a conclusion.

Truth tables are the easiest way to grasp the semantics. Natural deduction rules give us a way of DERIVING conclusions by sequences of transformations performed syntactically in virtue only of form. When formulas have lots of different letters, truth tables get unwieldy and rules are much more convenient. With this much apparatus, an important distinction can be drawn. That is the distinction between OBJECT LANGUAGE statements and METALANGUAGE statements. When we use PC statements in deriving things, we use the object language. When we use natural language (English here) to define PC or to make statements about PC, then we are making metalanguage statements. The former are system-internal. The latter talk about the system from an external vantage point. In natural language, this distinction is extraordinarily hard to make systematically, because, as mentioned before, we all grew up inside the system and only gradually acquired the ability to stand outside it. Doing linguistics is one of the most obviously metalinguistic activities, but in fact we continually have to extend our language to talk about new situations, and modify parts of our language in more subtle ways, while all the time using it to communicate—the old philosophical metaphor is that of repairing the ship while at sea on her.

The most important development in logic in 20th century involved an improved understanding of the meta/object language distinction. The value of mathematically defining artificial languages is not just so that machines can process them, but because they enable us to study metalogical properties. Some of the most important results for cognitive science are metalogical results about what can and can't be achieved *within* such formal systems. Just to give a flavor of the sort of metalogical properties that are important, we will take SOUNDNESS and COMPLETENESS. Why don't we focus on object-level logic first and then move on to meta-level questions? That is the usual order in a logic class. But the conceptual distinction between talking within a language and talking about a language is more important for cognitive science than most of the details of derivation methods.

Informally, a system of natural deduction rules (a proof theory) such as one for PC is SOUND if it is not possible to derive a falsehood from true premises within the system. Remember how we defined validity? Well, this is an entry-level condition for logical systems. If they aren't sound then they may be lovely squiggles, but they aren't the kind of symbol system that is much use as a language. Slightly more formally, we can observe that we can define deriving a contradiction as deriving a PC sentence $A \land \neg A$ from any true premises, where A is now a variable ranging over the sentence variables $P, Q, \ldots$. We use a variable because soundness is the property of avoiding the derivation of *any* contradiction, not some specific contradiction. Remembering that $\neg$ reverses truth value makes it is easier to see why this formula is going to be trouble. Soundness (not being able to derive contradictions from sets of true premises) is a metalogical property of PC.

COMPLETENESS is another important metalogical property. A system such as PC is said to be complete if it is possible to derive syntactically, by the rules of inference, *all* the sets of premises and their conclusions that are defined to be valid by the semantic definition of the system. So completeness is the opposite side of the coin to soundness. Imagine what would violate completeness. Suppose there was a truth table of a set of premise sentences and a potential conclusion sentence, and examination of the table showed that in all the rows where the premises were all true that the conclusion was also true. That would mean that the inference from premises to conclusion was semantically valid. Imagine further that a given set of inference rules provided us with no way of deriving the conclusion from the premises. Then that set of rules would be *incomplete*. Incompleteness is a certain sort of inadequacy of a rule system to capture all the semantic truths of the system. Sometimes incompleteness is simply due to a missing rule or rules. But sometimes, more fundamentally, *no* set of rules can actually capture all the consequences—in other words, there may be fundamental limits to formalization of semantic consequences.

PC is in fact complete. Much of logic is about the relation between the semantic facts that constitute a logic, and various proof theories that capture all or part of these semantic facts. The proof theory gives a framework for computing semantic facts, but, as we shall see, not everything is computable.

Finally, DECIDABILITY is a third crucial metalogical property. A system is decidable if there is an ALGORITHM (a mechanically applicable method guaranteed to reach a solution in finitely many steps) that can always prove or disprove any target conclusion from any set of premises. PC is in fact decidable. But most logical systems are undecidable. One proof of PC's decidability is based on the truth table method. It isn't hard to see from the description above that any argument that can be stated in PC can be truth tabled in a table of 2^N rows, where N is the number of distinct atomic sentential variables. Although this number gets very large very fast, it is always finite. The basic reason most logical systems aren't decidable is easy to state informally. Whereas the size of the search-space for PC proofs only depends on the number of atomic variables in their statement, most logics analyze sentences into terms, and their semantics is about the *things* those terms denote. Whereas the number of atoms in the assumptions and conclusions is only ever finite, even short sentences may be *about* infinitely many things. "Even numbers greater than two are not prime" is such a sentence. Truth tabling won't work as a decision procedure for these logics with terms and relations because an infinitely large table would be required. Sometimes there are other methods that work. Sometimes it is possible to prove that there is *no* method that will work. In the latter case, such systems are undecidable.

These three metalogical properties (soundness, completeness, decid-

ability) are about relations between syntactic methods of proof and semantic properties. The proofs of these metalogical properties are carried
out in a metalanguage—often English with a bit of set theory thrown
in. The proofs use some rather strange methods. They treat sentences
as objects, and proofs as objects, and arrive at conclusions about what
properties these proofs can or cannot have. These metalogical proofs
cannot be conducted within the systems themselves. The study of what
semantics can and cannot be captured by different syntactic systems
has been a major source of the fundamental concepts of computing as
we will see in chapter 6. This is hardly surprising. Logic is the oldest
program of research to formalize patterns of thinking so that they can
be checked or generated by mechanical means.

The early 20th century gain of insight into the necessity of distinguishing meta- and object-levels and the possibility of studying metalogical properties like soundness has far-reaching implications for the
problem we discussed in chapter 3 about what Bloor called logical
compulsion—remember the Azande's beliefs about witchcraft? Before
object- and metalogic were distinguished, there was an acute problem
about the justification of logics. Why are the rules like that? Why not
like this? Who says so? Bloor rightly rejected the concomitant conception of "logical compulsion."

After the distinction of levels is made, these problems change. Soundness, for example is an obviously desirable property for languages if we
want to use them for reasoning and communication (rather than writing
symbolist poetry perhaps). If our language allows us to derive falsehoods
from true premises it is an unsatisfactory vehicle for thought or communication. So soundness is a "good thing" on quite general grounds.
We're not "compelled" to want to draw valid conclusions, but if we do,
our language and rules had better be sound.

The situation is similar for the other metalogical properties. It may
depend on the kind of reasoning to be done, exactly which metalogical
properties are most desirable, and which ones we may be prepared to give
up. We usually can't have them all. Modern logic is a representational
supermarket—not a monotheistic pronouncement of the one true set
of rules. So, to return to Bloor's critique of logical compulsion, he is
quite right that logic will not easily settle whether Azande beliefs about
witchcraft or ours about killing are consistent. We will need to tease out a
whole network of beliefs and social practices, though local inconsistencies

like the ones that Evans-Pritchard pointed out are essential pointers in that process of interpretation.

But on the other hand, not just any old set of squiggles with any old interpretation will make a language useful for just any old purposes of reasoning or communication. There are metalogical "compulsions" of the most mundane character—for example, "Make sure your language is sound!" These constrain reasoning even though they leave an awful lot of scope for possibly strange beliefs, especially when we want to talk about social practices like witchcraft and the law.

Before we turn to computing, we need to do two things. First, we look at the correspondences between English and PC that have been so assiduously avoided in order to give the advantage of an uncluttered view. Then we turn to applying some of the logical concepts just introduced to arguments in context to see how reasoning and interpretation interact.

5.3   Putting Logic Back into Context

You have probably already derived the main correspondences between PC connectives and English ones. The symbol ¬ has already been likened to *it's not the case that*. Note that the symbol ¬ has a name (*corner*) and its semantic truth function (reverser of truth values) has a separate name (negation). This is the pattern with all connectives and their corresponding truth functions.

∧, pronounced "wedge," stands for the truth function CONJUNCTION. It is closely related to *and*: it conjoins two sentences making one that is only true if both components are true. ∨, pronounced "vee," stands for disjunction and is closely related to one reading of *or*: it disjoins two sentences making one that is true if at least one of them is true. This is called INCLUSIVE DISJUNCTION because it includes the case where both sentences are true. EXCLUSIVE DISJUNCTION is true only if exactly one disjunct is true. Inclusive disjunction is more useful in logic and probably more common in English. →, pronounced "arrow," stands for implication and is closely related, though distinctively different from *if..., then....* This is the connective we saw at issue in the selection task.

There are well known problems with these correspondences. It is easy to find example English sentences that appear to flout them. What is not so easy is to decide how to give a theoretical account of why these divergences appear. Are they due to the overlaying onto a simple classical logic of other phenomena involved in natural language communication? Or are there fundamental divergences between the meanings of the English expressions and their artificial counterparts? We will take a quick look at the most important divergence because it is closely related to our earlier observations of people's reasoning with conditionals. And these problems give a rounder view of the important issues about logical modeling of natural language and human reasoning.

The divergence we will look at is between $\rightarrow$ and *if. . . , then. . . .* The if-clause of a conditional $P \rightarrow Q$, is its ANTECEDENT (P), and the then-clause is its CONSEQUENT (Q). Examination of the truth table for $\rightarrow$ reveals that if the antecedent is false, then the whole conditional is true. And if the consequent is true, the whole conditional is true. Both of these relations hold regardless of any connection between antecedent and consequent. So in our world, a conditional such as *(2 + 2 = 5)* $\rightarrow$ *(Margaret Thatcher was a Trotskyite)* is true, just because the antecedent is false. And *(Margaret Thatcher was a Trotskyite)* $\rightarrow$ *(2 + 2 = 4)* is also true. These effects come directly from the nature of PC in which the truth of a whole sentence is always a simple function of the truth values of its component parts, and from the definition of $\rightarrow$.

Classical propositional calculus is the interpretation of the conditional from which Wason derived his criterion of correct performance for the selection task. You should satisfy yourself that as long as the A has an even number on its back, and the 7 a vowel, then the rule interpreted as a material implication is true of the four cards. You should also go back and check the derivation of the criterion of correct performance for the two-rule task and the conjunctive rule condition from these classical propositional calculus meanings. Wason adopted this criterion despite the fact that material implication was well known to diverge from English conditionals a half a century before the invention of the selection task—interdisciplinary noncommunication. The original paper on these paradoxes is dated 1912, and the arguments were readily available in elementary logic textbooks well before 1968.

These oddities of the right-arrow connective are called the PARA-DOXES OF MATERIAL IMPLICATION (to give this version of implication its full name). These effects have been used by many analysts of natural languages to damn the relevance of logic for analysing natural language and have probably led to more logical development than any other wrinkle. Whole areas of logic exist to model these and related problems.

What is important first is to see that these paradoxes are not quite as strange once one understands what classical logic is about. Remember that our definition of valid inference stated that a valid conclusion is one that is true in all situations in which the premises are true. The important guarantee that validity provides is that we won't derive falsehood from truth. This central definition makes it clear why PC defines implication in the way it does. Conditionals license inference from a true antecedent to the truth of the consequent. The →-elimination rule is: *From P → Q and P you can conclude Q*. So as long as the antecedent is false, nothing follows from a truth, and if nothing follows, then nothing false follows from a truth. And as long as the consequent is true, what follows (the consequent) will be true no matter what the value of the antecedent. To get an intuitive feel, try thinking of a situation in which one of the two problematical sentences about Thatcher could be used to tell a lie. It's quite hard, as long as one is careful. Not being usable to tell lies may not seem a strong qualification for truth, but it is a qualification adequate for PC where we are trying to capture all the things that must be true in any interpretation that makes the assumptions true.

PC rejects the need for any contentful connection between the meanings of the clauses of implications, but guarantees validity despite that. This offends some logicians and psychologists. They argue that people assert conditionals because they know there is some connection between antecedent and consequent, and they want a logical analysis to capture that connection. There is no dispute that people do indeed often have this reason for asserting conditionals, but there is a good question as to whether this is to be modeled in logic. Interestingly, the same people usually do not protest about *vee* as a model of *or*, yet $(\neg P) \vee Q$ is logically equivalent to $P \to Q$. People can use *or* to express implications such as *Either the switch is down OR the light is off*. They do this because they know of connections between these meanings. The evidence we have for a sentence is not necessarily part of what it means, though it may be an important part of what we communicate in using the sentence. These are subtle but important distinctions. We return to them when we discuss the pragmatics of natural language in part IV.

It is also clear that people do sometimes venture to assert conditionals merely on the grounds of their knowledge of the falsity of the antecedent: *If Margaret Thatcher is a Trotskyite, I'll eat my hat.* Neither Margaret's secret leftward leanings nor their absence are causally (or in any other way) related to the speaker's garment-hunger. The speaker exploits her obvious lack of appetite for hats to indirectly assert the falsity of the antecedent. The material conditional analysis fits this case rather well. If we develop this line of argument we can see that there are many things going on besides the bare logic in determining why people assert things in communicating, but the best theoretical approach may not be to try and build them into the logic. In short, the correspondences between PC and English connectives are complex, but not as hopeless as might first appear. As with any mathematical model used in science, fitting the model to the natural phenomenon (here the logic to natural language use) is a complex business.

The paradoxes of material implication are closely related to some of the issues of interpretation of Wason's rule described in chapter 3. If one interprets the "if..., then..." of the rule as the material conditional defined here in PC, then the truth of the conditional for the four cards *is* sufficient to establish the truth of the rule.[10] In PC, the falsity of the rule with regard to a single card is sufficient to establish the falsity of the whole rule. Material implication is what we called brittle with regard to exceptions. The law-like conditionals described in chapter 3 (*All ravens are black, if the switch is up the light is on,* etc.) cannot be completely captured by material implication. Wason's competence model of the conditional is the material implication and from a logical point of view this is strange. It is doubly strange that such a basic model should be adopted by psychologists who were so dubious about the relevance of logical models to theories of human reasoning.

This much logic can also be used to throw light on the central issue raised in chapter 3 about the relation between interpretation and reasoning. We saw there that there was continual interaction between interpretation and reasoning, and we described selection task subjects' reasoning as mostly engaged in making sense of conflicting pieces of information about the many possible intentions of the experimenter. We also observed psychologists arguing that reasoning in logic proceeds only with regard to the form of the premises.

Now that we have some logical machinery we can see how to encompass the first phenomenon and also what is wrong with the second claim. Logic is made up of two parts—assignment of interpretations to sentences, task, and other materials, and reasoning from premises by inference rules. Within an argument interpretation must remain fixed, but, in the larger view, reasoners cycle between assigning an interpretation and reasoning from it. If they come to a conclusion they regard as implausible (e.g. "I don't need to turn any cards, but this experiment is about turning cards," or "This task is impossible because no set of cards will make the rule true") they may change their interpretation and start reasoning over again. This was our theory of what was going on in the selection task, and the psychologists' claims that logic always proceeded mechanically in virtue of form was a misunderstanding of logic engendered by only looking at one half of it.

We illustrate by examining another argument that psychologists have made about how people do not obey logical rules. This argument will allow us to give some idea of the kinds of alternative nonclassical logics that can make sense of natural language conditionals.

The problem is this: given *if the switch is up (P), the light is on (Q)* and the switch is up (P), people naturally conclude *the light is on (Q)*. But then given an extra premise, *if the electricity is off, the light is off (R → ¬ Q)*, they withdraw their previous conclusion from the first premise, that the light is on. How are we to model this observation?

The first part has the formal pattern:

$P \rightarrow Q, P$
therefore Q

This argument is just an example of the rule $\rightarrow$-elimination (often called MODUS PONENS, its medieval name). Adding the new premise $(R \rightarrow \neg Q)$ then makes the following pattern:

$P \rightarrow Q, P$
$R \rightarrow \neg Q$
therefore ?

We observed that most subjects withdraw their previous conclusion. Should we conclude that $\rightarrow$-elimination is not a rule of inference these subjects acknowledge? Surely if people cannot be relied on to comply with *this* rule, then it is implausible that they comply with *any* rules. In our classical logical system PC, *adding* premises never makes a valid conclusion invalid—it is MONOTONIC. We will see these logics later in chapter 16 used to model discourse understanding.

Look closely at how we might intuitively explain this pattern of observations. In particular, is it reasonable to describe this situation by saying that *the light is on* follows logically from the first two premises, but not from all three premises? A logician would give a quite different description of what has happened. Once the third premise arrives, the first premise—*if the switch is up the light is on* is reinterpreted and under its new interpretation is not true any more. That is to say, that the world or worlds described by the sentences is not the same world or worlds anymore. The initial worlds we imagine are ones in which the switch being up, the light is always on (worlds, that is without power cuts, blown fuses, burnt out bulbs, etc.). And the new worlds we get by adding the premise about the possible power cut is one in which the light is *not* always on when the switch is up—only when the power is on, etc., etc.

These observations indicate that the reader's *interpretation* of the premises changes as the information comes in. But classical logic is about what inferences are valid under *constant* interpretation. If the switch the first premise mentions is a different switch from the switch in the second premise, then the recurrence of P in the two sentences does not denote the same content, and all bets are off about any inferences. Similarly, if the interpretation of the conditional is different in the two contexts, then again all bets are off. So the process of systematically changing our interpretation as a discourse proceeds is absolutely commonplace in communication, but if we are going to model things with logic, we must take this into account by acknowledging the cycles of interpretation and reasoning that change interpretations.

Traditional logical education, before the domination of formal logics, consisted almost entirely in learning the skills of detecting subtle shifts of interpretation in arguments—what was called EQUIVOCATION.

People usually interpret conditional rules against a background of suppressed assumptions, or even a whole theory of causal connections. We interpret *if P then Q* as meaning, *if P then Q, other things being equal*—the electricity is on, the fuse hasn't blown, the bulb isn't burnt out,.... In chapter 3.2 we saw this same phenomenon occurring in response not to information communicated to us by some other person (neatly packaged as sentential premises), but coming as a result of experimenting on the world. We saw examples from both mundane experience and the history of science. We saw that we often may not even be able to specify completely explicitly all the *background conditions* that had to hold for some law to hold. Remember Ptolemy's epicycles? We, the language user in the street, certainly cannot do this for the most mundane of situations.

In fact, two psychological generalizations can be made. Human communicators are generally phenomenally good at adjusting their mutual understanding of their interpretations of each others' utterances, intentions, and behavior more generally. They are so good at this that they often do not recognize it as an achievement. This course is full of examples designed to show you how you have unwittingly adjusted your interpretations through heeding subtle cues. The opposite side of this coin is that human communicators can experience severe difficulty in bringing to explicit awareness the processes of interpretational adjustment. Learning classical logic requires one to do this, and elementary logic classes are hard work because they require the unlearning of many automatic habits. This unlearning is practically important for the skills of adversarial argument such as arguing cases in law, or framing laws for a legislature. In such adversarial circumstances, as much as possible about the interpretation has to be made explicit, because people cannot be relied on to voluntarily adopt each others' interpretations.

In chapter 6 we will see a similar phenomenon going on as a reader fills out the information explicitly given in a text from their general knowledge. Logic has to get all this reasoning with implicit information out into the open air. It is an important observation that people use implicit premises in interpreting and reasoning about their world. But if we are to explain this reasoning that remains implicit for the person doing it, then it will have to be made explicit in our theories. And if we are going to get straight about what logic has to do with this reasoning, it will be necessary to understand what premises logic is working on. Logic is made up of two parts, interpretation and reasoning. Interactions between these two parts make logic into a sophisticated theory of how reasoning is sensitive to context and content.

PC is a classical logic. In the 1970s logicians and computer scientists invented formal systems for describing the interactions of reasoning with the effects of the arrival of new premises on old interpretations. These systems are called default systems and their logics are called nonmonotonic logics because adding premises may make previously valid conclusions invalid.

In a default system, the conditional "If P then Q" is read: if P, *and nothing is abnormal*, then Q" and the force of "abnormal" here is that boundary conditions are met. So for each conditional, certain conditions are designated as abnormality conditions (for our light-switch example, the power cuts, blown fuses, etc.) The concept of valid reasoning with these default rules is *non*classical. Instead of an argument being classically valid if, and only if, the conclusion is true in *every* interpretation that makes the premises true (that is every *model* of the premises), here the conclusion is nonmonotonically valid if, and only if, the conclusion is true in every *preferred* model of the premises. Preferred models are ones where nothing is abnormal. Adding a premise that is an abnormality condition can then change whether or not something follows in this new sense of validity.

With this new concept of validity, many things about the logic change. For example, there may be three truth values instead of two—a value called *currently undefined* is added alongside true and false. This nonmonotonic conditional is no longer *iterable*—one cannot keep nesting them with impunity as one can nest material implications $((((P \rightarrow Q) \rightarrow R) \rightarrow S))$. As a hint of the kind of evidence one might bring for this logic fitting natural languages, notice that English conditionals (unlike conjunctions and disjunctions) are often not readily iterable. An example is "If, if John stays then Fred comes, then Percy goes." That isn't the easiest sentence to understand. Sometimes apparent iterations of "if. . . , then. . . " are in fact interpreted as conjunctions: "If the conditional iterates if it's in English, then it might be a material conditional" often just means "If the conditional iterates *and* it's in English, then it might be material." So the noniterability of default conditionals suggestively corresponds to the noniterability of English conditionals. Defeasible conditionals are not iterable because they are not truth-functional—their truth values depend on the abnormality conditions, i.e. on more than the truth values of their component clauses. In fact, "if. . . , then. . . " is no longer a connective but rather a kind of inference-licensing particle.

So going from classical to default logic changes notions of validity (truth-in-all-models vs. truth-in-preferred-models), semantics (two-valued vs. three-valued), and syntax (connective vs. license-for-inference).

Reasoning in default systems is a process that seeks to reduce the number of propositions that are undefined by propagating the values true and false to undefined propositions to derive preferred models.

The reasoning that is being modeled is no longer SKEPTICAL classical deduction where one seeks to eliminate counterexamples, but instead CREDULOUS interpretation where one seeks to believe everything one is being told by finding a model that makes it all true (at least for the purposes of the discourse). This is more like story-understanding than classical logical argument.

So assigning logical form is not just a matter of what sentence is to be translated, but also of what communication task is being attempted— what the communicators are doing with the language. An illustrative earlier example was the Socratic dialogue of selection task subject 22 who just assumed the rule was true (despite the instructions) and then proceeded to identify which cards showed it was true (3.5). One of our claims is that psychologists and their subjects sometimes have different understandings about what they are doing with the language in experimental reasoning situations—literally different logics. Sometimes the experimenters are unaware of this discrepancy.

Although we haven't presented a default logic in the detail we presented PC, we can still use the informal presentation here to revisit the issues about normative and descriptive stances toward subjects' behavior in the selection task, to re-examine the relation between logic and psychology. We now have two possible competence models that can be applied to the task—classical PC and default logic. They give different criteria for what is correct in the task. On the former, we should turn A and 7, and if those cards fit the rule, then the rule is true. On the latter defeasible model, the conditional is robust to exceptions though the subject has no idea what the abnormality conditions are. And even if the A and the 7 both fit the rule, it is not thereby shown to be true (nor false). So the correct response on this interpretation would be to claim that the task is incoherent. The defeasible model is a more plausible model of how student subjects might naturally interpret natural language conditionals in the selection task context. Of course there are also the many other detailed issues of interpretation discussed before, but these are two radically different kinds of interpretation of task and rule.

Do these opposing logics replace psychological theories about the selection task? No. They are mathematical frameworks for describing what constitutes the reasoning in these two very different interpretations of the task. Both require a great deal of psychological specification of how they are implemented to make them into psychological models of mental processes. Those extra psychological details will have to explain how subjects come to make errors and how they learn to distinguish possible interpretations. But without models of what the reasoning is interpreted to be, psychological theory can hardly get started, and gets led into misleading statements about form and content.

The use of such default systems to model communication will be a topic in chapter 16. Whether the interaction between interpretation and reasoning is modeled with classical or nonmonotonic systems, the important cognitive point is that the interaction between interpretation and reasoning is the place where content interacts with form. Logic is precisely a theory of how reasoning is sensitive to context and context is modeled in logic through the process of interpretation.

5.4   Summary

In this chapter we introduced just enough logical apparatus to give an idea of a very simple formal reasoning system—classical propositional calculus. We distinguished its syntactic specification from its semantic interpretation. Reasoning from premises in a formal system proceeds entirely in terms of the forms of the squiggles in the system and the rules that manipulate those squiggles. However, reasoning is only useful in virtue of having an interpretation for the squiggles, and the rules for inference have to respect the nature of the interpretation. Any given set of squiggles can support many interpretations, just as bits of natural language have many interpretations. So form interacts with content and context through the interactions of interpretation and reasoning. Within a bout of reasoning interpretation must be fixed, but between bouts it frequently needs changing. In natural language discourse interpretation changes extremely rapidly—often by the mere addition of a premise.

This distinction between interpretation and reasoning depends on a distinction between the meta-level at which we can talk about languages and other kinds of representations, and an object-level at which we can reason with those same representation systems. Making this distinction radically changes our understanding of logic and logical compulsion. Logic is the mathematical study of information systems and their metaproperties and it has its force through our understanding of the relations between those properties and what we want to do with the information systems. A skeptical classical logic may be appropriate for modeling adversarial argument but not for credulous discourse comprehension. The relation between logic and psychology should be similar to the relation between mathematics and other sciences—an interaction between model and data.

When psychologists observe raw reasoning phenomena it is generally not obvious how to theoretically apportion explanation between meta-level processes of interpretation and object-level processes of reasoning. Just looking at how interpretations change as premises arrive provides simple examples. Metalogical reasoning is not something that just experts do. It's something we all do a good deal of the time. The computations that are involved may be extremely complex, and we are, until we begin to study them, largely unaware of these computations. But computations are not just the processes of boxes with "Intel inside," nor the conscious calculative processes of which we are aware when we think. We now turn toward the question of just what computations are.

Exercises

Exercise 5.1: Is $p \rightarrow q$ logically equivalent to $(p \vee \neg q)$? That is, do they have exactly the same truth values as each other under all assignments? Offer an argument in terms of truth tables and one in terms of rules.

Exercise 5.2: The same question as 5.1) for the pair of sentences $(\neg p \vee \neg q)$ and $(\neg p) \rightarrow q$.

Exercise 5.3: The following is an argument:
"The elements of the moral argument on the status of unborn life strongly favor the conclusion that this unborn segment of humanity has a right not to be killed, at least. Without laying out all the evidence here, it is fair to conclude from medicine that the humanity of the life growing in a mother's womb is undeniable and, in itself, a powerful reason for treating the unborn with respect."
Here is an argument by analogy that the first argument relies on an equivocation:
"The humanity of the patient's appendix is medically undeniable. Therefore, the appendix has a right to life and should not be surgically

removed."

Does the first argument rely on equivocation? If so, can the equivocation be repaired?

The example is borrowed, with full acknowledgment, from:
`http://gncurtis.home.texas.net/equivoqu.html`.

5.5   Further Reading

- Hodges, W. (1977). *Logic*. Harmondsworth: Penguin.

A highly readable introduction to the basics.

- Hofstaedter, D. R. (1980). *Gödel, Escher, Bach: An Eternal Golden Braid*. New York: Vintage Books.

An imaginative and entertaining meditation on the early 20th century discoveries of metalogic.

- van Lambalgen & Stenning (forthcoming). *Semantics and Cognition: Logical Foundations for the Psychology of Reasoning*. Cambridge: MIT Press

A more advanced development of this view of the relation of logic to the study of cognition. See especially chapter 3 on default models of interpretation change.

6 Computation and Representation

6.1 Why Computation?

Computation is a concept as central to cognitive science as information. Representation is another concept that cognitive science returns to again and again—these two are inseparable conceptual twins. Computation serves a theoretical purpose, a technological purpose, and as an application phenomenon of great interest in cognitive science. The fact that people have such trouble using computers has become a major economic issue and therefore, an application problem for cognitive science. A subfield is sometimes called human/computer interaction (HCI—CHI in the U.S.).

For this book, the theoretical usefulness of computation in cognitive science is by far the most important of these three interests, the least familiar, and therefore, the one we will spend the longest time on. Computation provides abstract languages in which communication can be analyzed. These languages have a status akin to the more familiar mathematical languages that have developed in close cohabitation with natural sciences. Computational language allows us to be explicit and precise about our theories. Anyone who has any experience of getting a computer to do anything will know how much has to be made explicit in programming the machine. Most often this need for translation has the immediate result of showing our theories' blatant inadequacies, or narrowness of coverage, or number of required assumptions, but our motto is: "Better an explicit theory that can be assessed, found wanting, and built upon, than an implicit theory that cannot be assessed." In this, at least, we are good Popperians.

The layperson's conception of computers tends to be that they are identifiable as plastic boxes that process numbers, and your initial reaction may be that neither plastic boxes nor numerical treatments of communication are likely to answer the questions about human communication that we hold most dear. But computers are not all plastic boxes and do not just process numbers. From one perspective, people are computers (among many other things). And most fundamentally computers process information—not numbers. The last chapter introduced logical systems that are formal but not numerical. Their content was a great deal more general than numerical systems. The main purpose of this chapter is to broaden notions of computation in the direction of nonnumerical processes, and to show that computation understood abstractly is not just to do with the familiar plastic boxes called computers. One of the major intellectual advances of the 20th century was in our understanding of the generality and limitations of the concept of computation. This advance in understanding is also the reason the ones in plastic boxes exist at all.

Often merely formulating our theories in computable languages is sufficient to our purposes. There are cognitive scientists who do not use computers for much beyond word processing. But many cognitive science theories consist of large bodies of rules (grammars of languages, for example) and it can become impossible to assess all the consequences of a small change in a large body of rules. Here the computer may play a part by actually searching through possible combinations of rule applications to see whether and how a certain sentence is generated by the rules. This use of computational technology takes us into the second use of computation—computation for simulation.

Artificial Intelligence (AI) is defined as an attempt to design and construct intelligent systems. Constructing things has always been a way of understanding them. People first developed an understanding of flight by building flying machines. Efforts at analyzing or imitating biological flying systems were fatally unsuccessful. An understanding of how birds fly had to wait for construction of much simpler systems for which aerodynamic theories could be developed. This approach to knowledge might be sloganized as *understanding by engineering*.

Whereas the Wright brothers were drawn to wood and canvas to build flying systems, understanding mental life and behavior by constructing intelligent systems calls for computation. The reason is because of the generality of computation. Computers process representations of information. So much of human behavior and mental life involves the processing of representations of information, that computation is the obvious medium through which to engineer an understanding. Take a behavior as deceptively simple as navigating around a room avoiding obstacles. We do this on the basis of information carried by light reflected from objects reaching our eyes, reflected acoustic information reaching our ears, along with gravitational information from our middle-ear, and internal PROPRIOCEPTIVE information about where our body parts are relative to each other. We process this sensory information and use it to control our muscles. And the effects of our muscular acts in turn affect the sensory input we get. This feedback between perception and action is through what are known as sensorimotor loops. On our broad view this is computation. The processing of symbolic information may be more obviously computation—reading a book is even more evidently a matter of processing a sequence of symbols—though again we will see that it is not *just* that.

There is a long history in psychology of taking inspiration for theory from current technology. The behaviorists' thinking in terms of developing connections between stimuli and responses may have been influenced by the then latest technology of the telephone exchange. Of course the exchanges of their day contained HOMUNCULI in the form of human operators, but the technology was clearly still stimulating. It is sometimes suggested that cognitive science is analogous in that it was inspired by the "computer analogy" and that it will be replaced when the next wave of, say, biotechnology suggests other analogies.

Our view is different. Cognitive science is not based on an analogy between mind and computer. Cognitive science proposes that mental processes *are* computations. Cognitive science's understanding of computation is not by an analogy to any technology. Cognitive science confidently predicts that when other technologies inspire theories about the mind, in as far as these theories are successful, they will be shown to be explaining mental processes computationally (which is not to say they will not be important novel contributions). Computation has a different status than the telephone exchange because the human mind requires an understanding at an informational level.

As we shall see later, the argument that computation is the concept we need to understand the mind is controversial. Even within cognitive science there are those who rebel against talk of people *processing information* because it smacks too much of the disconnection between engineered systems and their environments. We will argue that these criticisms are important but not generally valid. They are important because they highlight a common source of error in cognitive science—assuming that the sort of computations that engineered computers do are like the computations that people perform. They are invalid because computation is a more general and abstract phenomenon than what artificial computers do.

The complaint from within cognitive science about the information processing model is that it tends to make us think of processing going on in a box that interacts with the environment only in rather weak ways—say through keyboard and screen, whereas people are intimately embedded in their physical environment. When our muscles move to convey us across the room, the light signals into our eyes change as a result—the sensorimotor loop just mentioned. People exploit their embedding and embodiment in the information processing they perform, and so they compute very differently from artificial computers. But it is equally dangerous to reject the idea that computation is what is going on just because it is more tightly coupled to the physical world than current artificial computation. To make headway in understanding this approach to cognitive science, and to understand the criticisms of its detractors, computation must be understood in an abstract way.

The third involvement of computation in cognitive science is through the study of what is usually called HUMAN COMPUTER INTERACTION (HCI). HCI seeks to understand how people interact with computers, and how computers can be designed so that this interaction can be more productive or more pleasurable. Just because computers are such general purpose devices, the relationship between the controls of a computer and the actions they control is generally far more opaque than for most mechanical devices. Faced with a motor car, even the truly unacquainted will probably be able to guess which way the steering wheel turns to go right—though a little reflection on just why this is so reveals it is not quite so obvious. However, faced with a computer, there can literally be *any* relation between inputs and outputs, and for the designer to find the "most natural" relation is no easy task.

Computer interfaces have improved somewhat in the last ten years, but they are still bad enough that you probably have experienced the nontransparency of this relation. In most modern computer systems the interface takes up most of the code. The costs of human computer interaction, and the limitations placed on computers by the limitations on human computer interaction are by far the greatest brakes on development of this technology. Understanding the human operation of computers therefore has a considerable practical value. But the problem also provides a wonderful cognitive laboratory just because of the freedoms for interface design and the opportunity to observe the users' response to them by getting the machine to unobtrusively log the users' actions. HCI is a rather peculiar, and perhaps aberrant form of communication, and therefore of some interest for those interested in human–human communication. Perhaps its peculiarities can throw some light on more natural cases.

6.2 Computation and Implementation

Computation abstracted

Alan Turing (1912–54), English mathematician, was, more than any other single scientist, the founder of our understanding of computation and the originator of AI. A little intellectual history may help in understanding the truly general concept of computation that Turing's work revealed.

Attempts to formalize and mechanize human reasoning are older than Aristotle's logic. If argument can be formalized, then disagreements due to errors of reasoning and calculation can be avoided. Attempts to engineer machines for reasoning also have a long history, and the interaction between the mechanical developments and the mathematical theory is an extremely interesting case for understanding the relation between pure and applied science and engineering. Pascal was responsible for an adding machine in the 17th century. Charles Babbage in the 19th century designed and partially constructed a mechanical machine for reasoning.

The late 19th century was a time of great theoretical mathematical advance. Logic had not changed in its formalization much since Aristotle, but in this period logic suddenly took great mathematical strides in the work of the German mathematician Frege and others. In this context, David Hilbert, another German mathematician, conceived the program of formalizing the whole body of mathematical reasoning. Hilbert's program was entirely theoretical. When Hilbert talked of formalization he meant the demonstration that mathematical problems could be solved by formally defined rules that required no human intuition for their application. The connection between this idea and machine execution is close, but Hilbert was a mathematician, not an engineer. Mathematical logic and METALOGIC, the study of the properties of logical systems, had reached a point where this dream (or nightmare, according to taste), that goes back at least to Leibnitz, was suddenly a plausible research program. Hilbert's program was taken seriously by many of the great mathematicians of the day.

In 1931, another German mathematician, Kurt Gödel proved a strange theorem of metalogic that stopped Hilbert's program in its tracks. Gödel proved what has come to be known as the INCOMPLETE-NESS OF ARITHMETIC. Any formal system sufficiently expressive to represent elementary number theory (the mathematical theory about properties of arithmetical equations) is not completely formalizable. That is, for any formalization of number theory, there are truths of the theory that cannot be proved by internal manipulation of the formal rules. The proof consists of a strange construction for representing the sentences of the formal language of number theory by (Gödel) numbers, and then exhibiting formulas that assert properties of numbers representing formulas. These formulas are demonstrably not provable in the system without proving that the system is inconsistent (because of the propositions that the numbers represent). But if the system is inconsistent, then anything at all is provable and the system is not a formalization of number theory. Gödel's theorem had an immediate effect in logic and metalogic, but its full implications for cognitive science are still a matter of hot debate as we shall see in chapter 19. It is paradoxical that mathematics should be the field of the discovery of fundamentally incomputable problems.

This is the context in which Turing worked. Although Gödel's work had shown that complete homogeneous formalization of even one branch of mathematics was not possible, and his work later had far reaching consequences for the theory of computation, Gödel's proof does not immediately construct a method of computation or a framework for understanding computation as a process. Gödel's own background lead him to see the implications of his theorem as most important for its contribution to the theory of mathematics. For him it demonstrated PLATONISM—the philosophical position that mathematicians have intuitive access to a separate realm of mathematical truth, rather than truth being a construction on their experience of the nonmathematical world.

But construct a framework for computation is what Turing did. Turing worked on a problem derived from Hilbert's program called the HALTING PROBLEM. Is there a way of computing from the descriptions of programs and their data whether or not they will terminate? The details of the problem are not important to us. But the background against which Turing worked is important to understanding what he achieved and what computation is. Turing began by asking what operations constituted human mathematical computation, and whether these computations could be carried out by a machine. He observed that mathematicians write symbols on pieces of paper. They erase them and replace them by other symbols according to well defined rules that are sensitive to which symbol appears where, and what symbol replaces it. They also scan their proofs remembering past bits of working. And that is all, hypothesized Turing.

If that is all, then it is easy to mimic all these operations by a simple machine—what has come to be known as a TURING MACHINE. At this stage this machine is a purely abstract machine—not like Babbage's structure of mahogany and brass wheels. Turing's imaginary machine consists only of an imaginary HEAD and a TAPE. The tape is divided into squares along its length. The head can read and print symbols on these squares. It can erase symbols and print others. And it can move the tape one square at a time in either direction. It can reach a state called HALT, perhaps signified by printing a certain symbol on the tape. The head does these things according to completely specified rules. An example rule would be: *If the square beneath the head has an X, then erase it, print a Y, and move one step left.* A given machine is defined by the set of rules that the head operates by. In the simplest case, only one rule ever applies at a time, so there is no need for any mechanism that decides between options—the whole process is completely DETERMINISTIC.

It is not difficult to describe a particular very simple Turing machine for adding two numbers. The problem is represented by two numbers on the tape—say by two blocks of 1s (simple tally notation) separated by a blank. The machine then processes this starting tape and eventually reaches the halt state. The state of the tape when it halts is the answer to the problem. For an adding program like this, all it has to do in the tally representation system suggested here, is to move the 1s of one number across the blank separating the two numbers in the initial representation (by erasing from one space and moving and rewriting) until it gets to the end of the number it is adding and halts. It will then leave a string of 1s on adjacent squares that represents the answer to the problem (in the same tally notation as its problem was set). Not the most exciting procedure, but as abstract mathematical devices, Turing's machines are immensely productive.

Starting from this notion of a machine whose head-rules compute a particular mathematical function, Turing asked what range of functions could such machines compute? Turing approached this problem not by constructing machines piecemeal to compute some sample of interesting mathematical functions such as sums, products, or square roots. He saw that he could construct a UNIVERSAL MACHINE. That is, he could specify a machine that could have any other machine's head (i.e. its rules) encoded on its tape as data, along with the data for the encoded machine's particular problem. The universal machine could then interpret the encoded machine and mimic its operations on its encoded data.

To simplify matters, Turing supposed that the tape was indefinitely extendable—whenever the head was about to move off the tape, another square would be magically added to it. Such a machine is called an infinite Turing machine. This extension is important because for many problems, the machine's workings may take up much more tape than either the statement of the problem or the answer. Turing's universal machine could be shown to be able to compute any function that could be computed by any Turing machine. Now Turing could ask, are there functions that could not be computed even by this "universal" machine? From his construction, it was a relatively short argument for Turing to show that the Halting Problem is incomputable by any Turing machine. The argument is presented in Turing's highly technical 1936 paper. Roger Penrose has quite an accessible account (see chapter 19). From this result all sorts of logical results eventually followed. For example, there is the idea that predicate logic is undecidable.

Turing's insight was that both the rule-data of the encoded specific machine and its problem-data can just be regarded as data, and therefore written on the tape of the universal machine—all is data and all is just grist to the mill. This same insight is at the heart of the developments that allowed the transformation of his abstract mathematical machine first into the machines that cracked the German U-boat codes, and then into truly programmable computing machines. Although Turing's machine, bumbling back and forth along its single sequential tape, is a far cry from the machine this text is being typed on, there is still a strong resemblance between their two designs. In the general space of possible computer designs, they are still rather close together. Both separate the single active part (the head of the Turing machine; the central processor unit [CPU] of the word processor) from the passive memory of the tape [the core memory, disks, etc.]. The CPU of this word processor contains several million transistors where the smallest universal Turing machine has less than ten rules, but the main difference in design is that this machine's core memory is random access memory (RAM), each cell of which can be accessed by its address equally quickly, saving the long tape traverses that are necessitated by the one-dimensional tape. Nothing of mathematical principle hangs on this difference in implementation.

Notice that this concept of computation has nothing especially to do with numbers. The symbols on the tape can be from any finite vocabulary of discrete symbols. The first of our everyday prejudices about computation already fails.

Computation re-implemented

Now that we have an abstract mathematical notion of computation in terms of the functions computed by Turing's abstract machines, we can see why the relation between abstract computation and the mind is not an analogy like that between telephone exchanges and brains. We can ask how this abstract concept of computation is implemented in biological systems. The answer will be that the implementation is very different, but that the same abstract concepts of computation are relevant to their understanding.

Relatively little is known about biological computers because of their immense complexity and because they evolved rather than being designed. However, some stark differences are clear enough. The brain is composed NEURONS—cells with short fibers called DENDRITES sticking out of the cell body, and one long fiber called an AXON. The dendrites and axons make connections with other cells' dendrites, and axons connect to other neurons' bodies at SYNAPSES. Tens of millions of neurons in the human brain have thousands of millions of synapses with other neurons. Some of the brain's computations are relatively well understood at some levels, particularly the computations involved in sensory processes. This is because it is possible to control the stimulus to an animal's sensory organs, and to record the resulting computations in neurons in the active brain.

From such studies it is clear that neurons are active elements. Far from being a computer with one active element and a large passive store, the brain is a computer entirely composed of active elements, each of which has a rather small passive store. The storage of information resides primarily in the connections between neurons (the synapses) that are adjustable in their resistance. The ensemble of neurons computes by passing electrochemical impulses along axons and dendrites. All neurons are actively firing at some frequency all of the time, though they go through periods of more and less intense rates of activity. They adjust their activity according to the intensity of the impulses they receive at any given time from all their synaptic connections. Nothing could be more different in physical design from a Turing machine. Turing in fact did spend some time speculating and experimenting on biological computation.

So if biological computation is so different from currently engineered computation, why introduce the concept of computation in terms of Turing's machines? The layperson might jump to the conclusion that science adopts Turing's model because artificial computers are so much more powerful than the mere human brain. This should be scratched immediately. The world's most powerful supercomputers are beaten easily for many simple perceptual tasks by rodents' brains. Computer designers are currently engaged in an enormous research effort into how to control PARALLEL computation—they would give their teeth for the brain's facility in massive parallelism. No, the reason is that cognitive science is concerned first and foremost with the abstract concept of computation, and the study of this concept is made much simpler by Turing's abstractions. Cognitive science cannot entirely ignore issues of *implementation*—how the physics of computational devices underwrite the operations that are interpreted as the processing of information. But Turing's abstract concept has proved vital in clarifying what a science of the mind is all about. Psychology attempted a theory of the mind in the first half of this century that tried to cut short this abstract treatment of information and computation, and to base itself on notions apparently more transparently related to the wetware of the brain— connections between stimuli and responses were supposed to be based on neural connections (telephone technology). This movement was known as behaviorism, and it foundered on its failure to appreciate the many levels of account necessary for a theory of mind (see section 2.1). It is this layering that an abstract grasp of computation can help us appreciate.

Giving up computation

What behaviorism sought to avoid was positing mental representations. Not that this was a wholly disastrous thing to have done. There were longstanding problems with the notion of mental representations and peoples' access to them. One historical interpretation of behaviorism is that it was a systematic attempt to see how far one could push a program of eliminating mental representations altogether. Frequently we learn much from such exercises, even if they turn out to be Quixotic journeys in the end. It was the development of the theory of computation, based on Turing's ideas, that established cognitive science and enabled psychology to move on from what had become a rather barren exercise. Not surprisingly, it was human language, a domain in which human behavior consists of the processing of symbols, that was at the forefront of the cognitive revolution. Language is the symbolic activity par excellence, and it was the treatment of language by behavioristic psychologists and linguists that offered Chomsky his opportunity to demonstrate the applicability of Turing's conceptual apparatus to natural behavior.

Behavioristic approaches to language tried to explain it in terms of mechanical RESPONSES to STIMULUS situations. Behavior was seen as a chain of responses to a chain of stimuli. Some of the stimuli might be generated by the animal's own behavior (like the visual feedback from motion mentioned above). But what was theoretically forbidden was any mental representation mediating between stimulus and response. In the case of language understanding, the behaviorist notion was that successive words arrived as stimuli and evoked a determinate response, CONDITIONED by the history of learning of the language. So if the sound "dog" had been heard frequently around dogs but not around candelabra or birthdays, then "dog" became conditioned to dogs and evoked a suitable response when heard again.

This account of language is perhaps made more bizarre from compression, but it is fairly bizarre even at full length. The hallmark of language behavior is that language often happens at a remove in both time and space from the things it describes—dogs and candelabra. But Chomsky's attack in his 1957 book *Syntactic Structures* comes not from the need for this semantic dislocation, but from the syntactic fact that sentences in language are not simply made of words strung like beads on a string—they have hierarchical structure. This is where Turing's automata come in. The theory of abstract computing machines had developed by 1957 so that three main powers of machine were known. By restricting the tape movement of a Turing machine to a single direction, one gets a much less powerful machine called a FINITE STATE MACHINE.

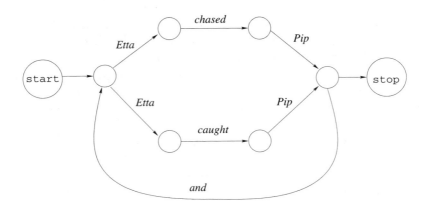

Figure 6.1
A finite state machine.

Such a machine literally has no memory for what its previous computations have been, save for the identity of the last rule applied and the current symbol under the head. Chomsky showed that these machines provide a plausible model for what behaviorists claimed about the structure of the human language processor. Their lack of memory mimics the behaviorists' denial of mental representations. He then went on to show why such a processor cannot compute some of the most basic structures of human natural languages.

Finite state grammars, as automata for producing sentences, are more usually and conveniently represented as node-and-link diagrams than as unidirectional Turing machines. Nodes represent states. Links are possible transitions from one state to another. One node represents the start state and another the halt state. Each link is decorated by an action that represents the output of a word. The machine's current state is represented as a single activated node at any one time. The automaton's lack of memory for the history of its computations is reflected in the fact that the only record accessible to the machine is the identity of the current state. If there are two states from which the current state can be reached, then there is no memory for which route was taken, and therefore, if there is a choice of links out of the current state, there is nothing on which to conditionalize which route should be taken next.

Figure 6.1 represents a finite state machine for generating some English sentences. To restate the rules for interpreting such a diagram: start at start, and follow the arrows. If you have a choice, toss a coin. If you are at stop, you are finished. Each time you follow an arrow, write down the word (if any), above the arrow. By following these rules, you can produce indefinitely many English sentences, consisting of one or more occurrence of *Etta chased Pip* or *Etta caught Pip*, conjoined by *and*.

It is fairly easy to show, as Chomsky did, that there is no way of reflecting simple structures like relative clauses in such a device. A sentence such as "The cat that chased the rat that ate the cheese was a tabby" has an embedded structure—one sentence, "The rat ate the cheese," is embedded inside another "The cat chased the rat," that is in turn embedded inside another, "The cat was a tabby." Any device that can decode this hierarchical structure requires memory for the abstract structure that these three sentences make. Such structure is omnipresent in human languages. *Ergo*, the human processor is not a finite state machine (or, equivalently, a Turing machine with a unidirectional tape). Chomsky also made a further distinction between classes of automata of different power. He distinguished CONTEXT FREE from CONTEXT SENSITIVE phrase structure grammars. Here it is a much more open question whether human languages require the greater power of context sensitivity. But we will leave that distinction and question to the section on syntax and return here to the issue of mental representation.

Chomsky's work shows why Turing's formulation of computation is so powerful an analytic tool. It provides a whole mathematics for describing the structure of processes that had not been available to linguists, psychologists, and philosophers who had struggled to formulate theories of the mind. Chomsky's study of the structure of natural languages (and its implications for the minds that process them) does not resolve the detailed issues about implementation. It does not tell us how a massively interconnected collection of neurons can compute the structure of sentences of English. But it changes the nature of the problem and where to look for solutions.

Those who study neural computation can now show why it is relatively easy for such systems to compute some properties of sentences produced by a finite state machine, but particularly hard to cope with the embedded structures generated by even context-free phrase structure grammars. In fact, the sort of structures like our embedded sentence are just the sort of structures that are difficult to represent in neural computers. So humans definitely aren't like some neuronal implementation of a universal Turing machine—those machines just lap up embeddings. Humans can cope with some very limited embeddings, but are very poor at coping with others—particularly center-embedded sentences such as "The oyster the oyster the oyster bit bit bit," even though such chains of transmitted violence are all too familiar. So human abilities to cope with embeddings may not be a general ability to cope with just any amount of just any embedding, but may be specifically limited by its novel biological implementation. Describing exactly what computations people find easy and difficult and just how they can be implemented in biological systems requires Turing's framework for analyzing computation.

An important evolutionary question is what human mental structures and behaviors were the foundations of language, thinking, and reasoning. Humans appear to have some powers of computation that, described at the significant level, are *not* like their ancestors and stand in need of special explanation—communication capacities prominent among them. One approach to this question is to see the recursive structures of syntax as the innovation in human cognitive abilities—an approach favored by Chomsky and many others. An alternative approach is to claim that these recursive structures underlies lots of computations that our ancestors already could perform, and that human evolution has to be explained as the expression of these capacities in new contexts, mental structures, and behaviors. An example of this approach is the belief that human language comes from the planning abilities of our ancestors, developed for complex motor skills. These skills, it is claimed, already require recursive computations, and what needs explaining is how these capacities gained expression in the many new mental structures people have. This is another central cognitive issue that requires Turing's framework.

The issue how biological systems can implement computations more expressive than finite state systems is now an active area of research— how can connectionist computers inspired by the brain's structure of many interconnected active units do the kinds of computations required by the structures of language and other cognitive activities? Because of Chomsky's demonstration, based on Turing's mathematics, it is much less likely that cognitive scientists will make the mistake of denying that any abstract structure is there. Just what abstractions are there is, of course, another matter. It is now clear that there has to be several layers of abstraction to a complete theory of how people process sentences. Sentences have hierarchical structures, and even the neuronal goings on that underlie our communication have to represent this somehow.

Exercises

Exercise 6.1: What aspects of the dialing mechanism of a touchtone phone could be easily modeled in a finite state machine, and which not?

Exercise 6.2: Explain why a Turing machine whose tape can only move in one direction is equivalent to a finite state machine.

6.3   Further Reading

• Weizenbaum, J. (1976). *Computer Power and Human Reason: From Judgment to Calculation.* W. H. Freeman: San Francisco.
Still an excellent introduction to Turing machines and much else about AI besides.

• Churchland, Patricia S., Sejnowski, Terrence J. (1992). *The Computational Brain.* Cambridge: MIT Press.
An introduction to understanding computation in the brain.

• Chomsky, N. (1957). *Syntactic Structures.* The Hague: Mouton.
The original argument from the structure of natural language to the necessity of abstract structures for understanding the mind.

• Chomsky, N. (1959). "Review of Skinner's 'Verbal Behavior.' " *Language,* 35, 26–58.
A historically crucial polemic that took behaviorism at its word and applies a computational analysis to human behavior.

7 Representation: Inside the Black Box

7.1 Introduction

Turing's definition of computation makes a clear distinction between representations (the symbols on the tape) and operations on them (the operations of the head). We have seen already that at the lowest level of implementation in neural wetware, this distinction may not be nearly so simple to apply to biological computers made of millions of active units as to Turing's machines. Nevertheless, we will argue that we still need the concept of representation, so it is important to remember that representations are themselves theoretical abstractions. A mental representation may not be a localized symbol or string of symbols (in some alphabet) inscribed somewhere in the brain—it may be realized by a complicated pattern of resistances and firings in a large number of synapses. Nevertheless, it will have to have certain gross computational properties, and this is the level that most concerns cognitive science.

The idea of the "black box" is an allusion to the inaccessibility of mental processes. Companies employ "reverse engineers" to work out from the input-output relations of their competitor's complex electronic circuits what those circuits are designed to do. Although one can "get inside" such circuits, simply measuring voltages and currents at particular points doesn't help much in understanding what the whole system is doing—the possible observations are at the wrong level for systemic understanding. Cognitive scientists are very much in the position of these reverse engineers, trying to reconstruct what is inside the black box from its input-output relations. It's just that the human black box is some orders of magnitude more complex and the input-output relations even more indirect.

Our discussion of representation will be divided into two. The first part will take the view from outside the black box and ask why we need to posit internal representations on the basis of what the box can be seen to do from the outside. This is one common psychological/linguistic perspective. In the next chapter we take the synthetic perspective on representations and look at what AI has learnt from the engineering approach of building innards for black boxes.

7.2   The External and the Internal

By *external* representations we will mean physical objects and events
that represent other things, e.g. written text, sound waves, diagrams,
photos, paintings, or bar codes. By *internal* representations we will
mean mental structures that perform computational functions related to
mental processes—very often different forms of memory. When we read
a page, the ink on the paper serves as a stable external representation.
When we finish and close the book, we have some representation (or
maybe many) of what we read. This is an internal representation. It
may or may not be like the external representation from which it was
derived. And there may not be a unique representation that records this
one experience of reading a page. There is much evidence that internal
representations are very different from the sentences on the page. But
they are still representations in an important sense to be explained.
We also have internal representations of regularities that we have learnt
over long periods of time (rather than on one occasion like the event
of reading). For example, there is a representation of the meaning of
the word *travel*, or the skill of riding a bicycle. These are also internal
representations.

Internal and external representations interact in complicated ways.
It is dangerous to suppose that the internal ones merely mirror the external ones—as we shall see that merely leads to regress. We often can
only get at the internal representations (remember something) when we
are in the right external context. Success in the task then depends on
a combination of internal and external representations. Using external
representations (say pencil and paper) may change which internal representations (say working and long-term memories) we use while doing a
task (say arithmetic). Similarly, cognitive processes may be distributed
over a group of individuals (say the crew of a ship), plus a lot of external
representations (say radar screens, charts, etc.) in such a manner that
no one member has all the information needed to do the task (navi-
gate). Nevertheless, we still cannot understand the processes involved in
the team's computations without postulating both internal and external
representations and their interactions.

Language was one of the domains used most powerfully to argue for
the need for internal representations. We now turn to some of the problems encountered by positing internal representations. For this we shift

domains from language to another domain of mental representation—
mental imagery. Our discussion of computation so far has assumed that
the representations processed are drawn from "alphabets" of symbols.
But representation is a much broader issue, and comparing some other
styles of representation will help to broaden the basis of discussion.

The need for internal representations

Let us turn away now from language and look at another area of mental
representation—mental imagery. We do this to review another contribution that Turing's understanding of computation makes to cognitive
science. Philosophers since Plato have written extensively on the nature of mental imagery. Classical philosophers used the metaphor of a
wax tablet receiving "impressions" from the sensory organs and storing
them away until memory recalled them. Plato also used the beautiful
metaphor of memories as birds in an aviary that come to their keeper's
call (sometimes). John Locke based his 17th century theory of word
meaning on the idea that hearing the sound "dog" recalled a mental image of a dog in a foreshadowing of some aspects of behaviorism, but not
denying himself this much mental representation. Psychologists since Sir
Francis Galton in the 19th century have investigated differences in reports of peoples' mental imagery. All these theorists have assumed there
is some similarity between a mental image and a physical picture. Mental
images have been thought of as pictures in the mind.

But there is almost as long a history of objections to this as a theory
of mental representation. The chief objection to the pictures-in-the-mind
theory is what in philosophy is called an argument establishing *infinite
regress*. The argument goes as follows: Suppose you are looking at a
scene—say a desk with a computer and various books and nonsense
on it. Suppose you close your eyes and imagine the scene. The image
theory of mental representation assumes that somewhere in your brain
there is a representation that resembles a picture of the scene. Now how
is the image theory to explain how we process this image that is like the
scene we saw? Well, there must be a *homunculus*, a wee guy who scans
the mental image much as we scan the scene, and makes perceptual
judgments of it. So far so good, but how does the homunculus do this?
Well, the regress argument goes, the homunculus has a mental image
of the scene, and (yes, you guessed!) a wee homunculus scanning it.
Adapting what the old lady said to William James about the stack

of turtles that hold up the world, "It's no good, Professor James, it's homunculi all the way down."

What does this argument to an infinite regress establish? That we don't have mental images? No. What it establishes is that *if* each homunculus has to have *all* the psychological properties of human image processing that we are trying to explain, then we have not explained anything at all, but merely deferred the problem to a theory of homunculus image processing. Such regress arguments have bedeviled theories of mind for many centuries. The problem has not suddenly been totally solved by the advent of concepts of computation. Pylyshyn (1973) is a good recent example of use of regress arguments against modern theories of image processing. Dennett (1991) is a lengthy study of what he calls the Cartesian Theater model of the mind. The problems with theaters are not unlike the problems with images. Some of the most intense contemporary attacks on cognitive science hinge on what are modern forms of these arguments. But concepts of computation do offer the first ever real glimmer of a hope of grounding out these regresses.

Turing's machine is designed to make simple the distinction between active and passive components of computation—what are sometimes called the *mill* and the *memory*. Representations appear on the tape, e.g. representations of numbers in our addition problem, or representations of words in our finite state grammar. But representations are processed by the "head." The head discharges the homunculus. Far from having to project all the properties of the human mental arithmetic processor into the Turing machine head, a few simple rules provide a mechanical account of how the processing is done. Of course, no one is impressed by our being able to discharge the mental arithmetic homunculus. Theories of mental arithmetic have never been the subject of infinite regress arguments, I can conjecture with some confidence. It has always seemed easier to imagine how languages, either natural or artificial—strings of symbols—can be processed by mechanisms that embody general rules without resort to the intuitions of homunculi. This seeming may be an illusion as this course attests with its examples of how difficult it is to specify language processing. But because Turing was able to show that his improbably simple apparatus is in principle capable of any computation, he holds out the possibility of discharging homunculi in general. He does not perform this discharge—he merely holds out the hope that we can get theories of mental processes to bottom out in the operation of computational mechanisms. Of course, this hope is just what many critics of cognitive science see as the wrong move. Where has the *feel* gone if it's all abstract information? We return to this question of the subjective in chapter 19.

The attractions of images and sentences to theorists of mental representations are complementary. Where sentences hold out the hope of being able to define formal rules and therefore mechanical devices that can process them, they pose the problem that it is hard to connect them with what they mean. An arbitrary symbols' meaning is just that— arbitrary. Where pictures are, at least apparently, easy to connect with what they mean (remember Locke's attraction to them to ground out the meaning of the word "dog"), they are correspondingly hard to process with mechanical rules. Images are what have traditionally thrown up regress arguments and brought out into the open the need for theories of the processors of mental representations. Of course, it is not a matter of deciding between images and sentences. Most cognitive scientists would now accept that there is considerable evidence for a diversity of mental representations, and mental imagery is again taken seriously scientifically. The point made here is that understanding computation abstractly has given us a *potential* route out of regress in the theory of mind. That is what establishes the cognitive science program.

Computation does not mean that homunculi are all doomed to unemployment, or that there are no finite regresses—multiple-layered systems of systems of computation. Cognitive scientists have tended to focus their attentions so far on mental processes that apparently go on within a single system of representation. Psychologists and AI researchers have considered language behavior within the confines of a single grammar, or theorem proving within the confines of a single logic. Understanding single systems is quite hard enough. But there is much evidence that human mental processes frequently switch representations during reasoning. One example is the subjects in Wason's task switching interpretations of the materials.

Another example of the part that the plurality of representations plays in thinking comes from mathematical problem solving that is highly externalized and therefore available for scrutiny. If we look at a book like George Polya's *How to Solve It* we see a working mathematician writing about the numerous tricks of the trade for solving novel problems. We are perhaps never convinced that the master has managed to externalize more than a few of his tricks. But what is presented is an inventory of ways of re-representing problems. Polya exhorts us all the time to think of a familiar problem that we do know how to solve, and use it as an analogy for the new problem. Analogies are methods of representation and re-representation. Polya leaves us with the feeling that what is absolutely crucial, and what is largely still hidden by his treatment, is the skill of knowing when to use which trick.

Polya's picture of the experienced mathematician seems to me quite a plausible model of much of human thinking. It is quite unusual outside highly formalized professional performances to get long sustained trains of reasoning within a single system of representation. But it is quite common to see cases of problems being cast and recast into other representations. A problem starts as one stated in terms of distances, but is recast into one about times, and then is turned into a diagram in which it is finally easy to solve. In fact, quite a good dictum for describing much of human thinking might be, "If you can't find a way of representing the problem that makes it trivial to solve in a few steps, then give up!" The effort seems to go into finding the system of representation, not on the steps within it. The expert's skill is in "just knowing" which re-representations will help.

If anything at all like this view is right, then cognitive science requires a theory of mental processes that has at least two levels of systems in it. At one level there are systems of representation like natural languages, artificial languages, diagrammatic systems, etc. These systems each come with their own rules of inference to animate them. But then there must be a level of the mind that corresponds to ways of choosing representations suitable to the task at hand. For example, our discussion of the content effects in the selection task suggested that being able to re-represent the problem about truth as a problem about lying can sometimes make all the difference to its solution.

On this view, one metamechanism must treat other object-level systems as *objects* of its own computations. This picture is highly speculative. Some work along these lines has gone on in AI. But the reason for drawing such a speculative picture here is that it will play an important part in answering some of the critics of the computational theory of mind in our discussion below.

But before turning to criticisms of the computational theories of mind, we must take a closer look at representation. Although most cognitive scientists now accept that there are many kinds of representation involved in mental processes, it is doubtful how useful the pictures-in-the-head analogy is for understanding mental imagery. Seeing how this can be consistent requires a look at representations at several levels of abstraction.

Representation exemplified

Representations are things that stand for other things. The sentence "Napoleon entered," or an oil painting of the French general striding through the door, are representations of an event that occurred many years ago. There are aspects of the representations that are critical to them as representations—they are aspects we interpret. And there are other aspects that are quite irrelevant and that we do not interpret. If the sentence were "Napoleon centered," we might be away from military history and off on a soccer commentary. The little curved line we interpret as a "c" placed in front of the "entered" is one of the properties of the representation that *is* interpreted. On the other hand the font of the sentence is not. "`Napoleon entered`" has the same interpretation, unless we establish some special code—defining teletype font as email addresses perhaps. What is or is not interpreted can be shifted around at will, but nevertheless, the line between significant and insignificant must be drawn somewhere. Not everything can be significant. If everything were significant, the thing could not function as a representation but only as itself.

So far we have been discussing *external* representations—ones that are out in the world rather than inside the mind or the brain. Of course the brain is in the world, but its contents are private to all but the individual concerned and so representations that are *internal* to the person using them cannot be examined by other parties to communication. This makes them elusive entities indeed. So much so that many psychologists, more even than just the behaviorists, have rejected the coherence of internal representations as playing any part in theories of mental processes.

No such skepticism about internal representations here. Representational theories of mind are critically different from nonrepresentational theories, and some of them at least are right. But the skeptics are correct that it is terribly easy to talk nonsense about these elusive constructions. We have already seen something of the part internal representations can play in generating infinite regresses if they are not accompanied by computational mechanisms that store and transform the information in them.

If they are so much trouble, why should we give these things theoretical space? Because we get into worse trouble if we try denying them altogether. The simplest, though not the only reason why internal representations are required to explain the workings of the mind, is the same reason Turing machines need tapes that move in both directions— because they allow separation in time and space of stimulus and response.

Human mental life is full of such separations. We use information that arrives smeared across widely separated times and places, and we put it together as a basis for action. We acquire enormous amounts of information that we never knowingly act on at all, as witnessed, for example, in feats of trivial pursuit. We base actions on information that did not foresee being used for that purpose at the time of receiving it. We need representations to do all these things. What better example of this phenomenon to take (especially in a book on human communication) than you reading this text now? Well, matters will be easier with a somewhat simpler text, but text comprehension is one of the areas in which these truths are most self-evident. Consider the following paragraph:

Napoleon entered as the door opened. The commander strode across the room to the fireplace. He stood in front of the ginger-haired woman seated on the sofa. The mud-spattered man addressed his immaculately dressed cousin....

How do you think you represent and remember this short paragraph of forty words? Is each word a stimulus evoking some response before you pass on to the next? It's pretty obvious that the words are structured in a certain way to create the message that they convey. Scramble the words within each sentence and something quite different will result— either "word salad" or some other quite different message. If the units are not independent words, what are they? And what are you doing as you read them?

Before we set about these questions, without looking back at what you read, judge which of the following sentences occurred in the paragraph.

1. Napoleon was mud-spattered from his travels.
2. The mud-spattered man addressed his immaculately dressed cousin.

3. The commander walked across the room to the fireplace.

4. Napoleon addressed his immaculately dressed cousin.

5. He stood in front of the woman with ginger hair seated on the sofa.

6. As the door opened, Napoleon entered.

7. The woman crossed the room from the fireplace.

8. He stood in front of the ginger-haired woman seated on the sofa.

9. He stood in front of the ginger-haired woman seated on the sofa to the right of the fireplace.

This sort of memory experiment we have just conducted is one of the methods that psychologists have used extensively to analyze what happens as we comprehend text. Sentences like sentence 7 are generally easy to reject. Sentence 7 is in direct conflict with the scenario described. All of the other sentences are broadly consistent with the original, and your likelihood of getting them right is much lower. Sentence 3 has a changed verb, but one that expresses a similar idea—"walked" replaces "strode." In fact, people are quite good at detecting such changes of words, even when the meanings are only subtly different. One gets a rather different idea of Napoleon's action according to which word is used, and perhaps it is the assertiveness of "strode" that we remember. That does not mean we remember it *as a word*—perhaps we have a "mental film" of his swashbuckling. All we can conclude is that whatever we have in memory is sufficient to discriminate between "walks" and "strides" in *this* context.

With a number of the sentences, the problem is to remember which term was used to refer to Napoleon. It's quite easy to remember that the entrance happened first, and it isn't hard to figure out that Napoleon was introduced as Napoleon before he was redescribed as the commander, the mud-spattered man, etc. But it is much harder to remember precisely which description goes in which sentence unless it makes some substantive difference to the message. Maybe it is easier in 4 because "mud-spattered" is directly contrasted with "immaculately dressed," but whether it was someone described as the commander who strode across the room or someone described as Napoleon by name might be harder.

Then there is 9 that provides a spatial relation not provided in 8. Some people describe what they experience in understanding a paragraph like this as the construction of an image of the scene. They "see"

Napoleon striding across to the fireplace, and they "see" the sofa in some definite relation to the fireplace. Such people, if they happened to have put the sofa on the right and have no other memory than their image, will have trouble distinguishing which of 8 and 9 they read. On the other hand, if they definitely put the sofa on the left, they may have no trouble rejecting 9. Even if you do have this kind of imagery, it is also possible that you can remember somehow that you supplied the spatial information and that it wasn't in the text. And we shouldn't forget that there are those who experience no such imagery.[11]

Although this kind of imagery may be optional, there are other integrative processes that are at work in reading that are absolutely not optional. You probably read the paragraph and equated Napoleon, the commander, and the mud-spattered man on the one hand, and the woman and the cousin on the other. If you look back, there is no explicit statement of these identities anywhere in the text. You happen to bring with you to this reading task the knowledge that the most likely Napoleon (the French general rather than the pig in *Animal Farm*) was a commander. You surmise that he has perhaps just traveled and hence is mud-spattered. And most importantly, there are no other characters available to fill the descriptions in this fragment of story. You realize that Napoleon is unlikely to be talking to himself and can't be his own cousin, and there isn't anyone else around to be cousin other than the woman. If you go back to the text, and you imagine some quite different context for it, perhaps by adding a few sentences before the paragraph starts, then you will have no difficulty constructing interpretations in which Napoleon is not the same person as the commander, and perhaps the cousin is actually a fourth character (or maybe the commander), all without changing a word inside the original text.

What we cannot do is proceed with comprehending such a text without assigning identities and nonidentities. Finding identities as we process discourse will be a major topic in chapter 14. Mostly, with well-written text, we do this without even noticing. Only occasionally do we make a mistake, perhaps with hilarious results. An extreme example of such problems is often encountered with the following story:

A father and his son were driving down the motorway late one night when they were involved in a collision with another car. An ambulance rushed them to the hospital. The son was badly hurt though the father was only slightly injured. The father was admitted to a ward. They took the son immediately to the operating room, where the surgeon waited. The surgeon took one look at the boy and said, "I can't operate. That's my son."

You may well have heard this before, but if you haven't, the chances are that you will entertain various hypotheses about stepfathers, or family trees of amazing convolution. The surgeon was, of course, the son's mother. Many people jump so firmly to the unwarranted inference that the surgeon is male that they become quite unable to find any consistent interpretation for the story. *Going beyond the information given* is something that we have to do all the time in making sense of the information we get, and occasionally we get royally stuck, betraying our beliefs and prejudices in the process. Think back to the discussion of anecdotalism in chapter 4.

In understanding our Napoleon scenario we have to infer identities. But we may go far beyond this in making the fragment meaningful. Old movie freaks (on either reading) among you might well associate the scene described with Greta Garbo's film *Marie Walewska* in which Napoleon, retreating from Moscow, is billeted on a countess in a Polish castle. This particular association might be unlikely, but the general tendency to assimilate such decontextualized fragments to the things we know is powerful and can be shown to have direct implications for our memories. For someone who did associate this paragraph to that film, the identity of woman and cousin does not fit. In the short term this is likely to make the discordant information in the paragraph "stick out" in the memory and be *better* remembered. But in the longer term, it is likely that the more powerful older memory will lead to the loss of this particular information from your memory for the paragraph you have just read. We tend to "rewrite" our memories, usually in the direction of making them more consistent with our general experience.

So your representation of this simple paragraph is indeed a complex thing. Far from being a sequence of word-by-word responses, or sentence-by-sentence constructions, understanding integrates the information both within the paragraph, and between paragraph and prior general knowledge. In general, this integration removes detail of the wording of the sentences of the text, but retains the *gist*—the significant aspects of the story. There are ways we can artificially train our memories to retain the wording (see Alexander R. Luria's *Mind of a Mnemonist*), but in general, they tend to make it more difficult to process the all important gist. In normal comprehension we represent the gist in some way very different from the string of words we read. This is a powerful argument for representation. But it takes careful thought to realize what it does and doesn't establish. It means there has been some change inside us such that we can now discriminate between the story we read and the others that we do not confuse it with when tested. It does *not* mean that we have a *discrete thing* that represents just this story separate from anything else we know (like the text of the story), nor that our memory for this story will operate the same in all external contexts. In fact, all the evidence is that our representation of the story is intimately interwoven with a whole lot of other general and specific knowledge that can be cued by all sorts of external circumstances.

The observations and arguments we have just been through about what your memory does and does not retain about the story you read, illustrate one of psychology's "reverse engineering" methods for studying mental representations. Some information is presented (the paragraph) and then removed so that it cannot be reprocessed except on the basis of internal representations. The reader's memory is then tested by seeing what changes to the information can be recognized as changes, and that are not reliably detected. The argument is then as follows: if a change in information can be detected, then the information represented in memory must discriminate the change. If the change cannot be detected, then the representation that is stored is *invariant* with regard to the difference.

Studying language comprehension brings this message home powerfully because the way the information arrives is so indirect. With language, we have to make inferences to establish identities, whether we notice making them or not. If we were instead to see a film of our scenario, the identities of the characters are supplied for us much more directly by the film image, at least in such a short clip. It would be hard to make a film of the scene without making it clear whether Napoleon was the commander, and whether the woman was the cousin. It would be hard (though not impossible) to make a single film have the alternative interpretations in the way that we can make the paragraph bear other interpretations by prefacing it with a few sentences.

That is not to say that our memory for the film is like a film. If we try the same sort of experiment with memory for film that we have just conducted with text we would find that our memory was a great deal more schematic than a movie. We rapidly jettison our memory for much of the filmic detail of camera angles, pans, and zooms in the same way we jettison memory for sentence structure. We are generally extraordinarily poor at regenerating images even of scenes we have seen many thousands of times—the standard example is to ask the question, "How many windows does the front of your home have?" Most people do not report answering this by inspecting a "mental photograph," but rather by adding up the number of windows in each of the rooms that they know look out at the front. Such reports have to be interpreted skeptically, but this doesn't sound like image inspection, even if it is accompanied by some experience that shares some "feel" with seeing your home.

Mental representations are essential whenever the arrival of information is separated from the occasion of its use and no external record is available. Having looked at the process of text comprehension, we can now see this separation at work, and also some of the other pressures for representation in mental processes. The most obvious pressure is to reduce the amount of information that we have to retain. It is not difficult to restructure each of the sentences in Napoleon's paragraph in twenty different ways. There are four sentences in the paragraph, so this would give 20^4 rewritings. The same sort of arithmetic applies to the resolution of identities. As phrases like *Napoleon, the commander, the mud-spattered man, his cousin, he, etc.* proliferate, the potential number of assignments of identity/nonidentity between them grows exponentially. But here there is a real need to store the information. They are not all just different wordings of the same sense. If the woman turns out to be the commander, the story is substantially different.

Representations achieve data-reductions. Because representations are *not* like what they represent in so many respects, they are selective. Evidently they have to be selective of the right kind of information—the information that their user may want to act on in the future. Using representations implies an active approach of committing to the future use of what is currently being learnt—deciding what is wheat and what is chaff, or even filling in beyond the information given in order to be able to construct a representation at all. If our mental representation of the story is image-like, at least in the crucial property that it demands that all identities are resolved, then we may have to make informed guesses about identities even when the information is not explicitly supplied.

And sometimes we inevitably make wrong guesses, as with the surgeon.

This need to decide what use information will be put to, and so what information to preserve is, however, ameliorated by another achievement of representations. They are multipurpose. The example of navigational information will illustrate. This is one of the domains that was historically important in arguments about the existence of mental representations. The behaviorist approach to explaining how an animal stored information about its environment was to think of routes through space as sequences of stimuli and responses, rather like route directions. This mechanism was supposed to wheel itself into action as the rat ran through its maze, but the information was thought of as only available when triggered by a particular motivation. One can get a flavor by thinking of the situation as we remember a route we know as we reach its choice points but are not able to "run it beforehand like a movie" from memory.

The cognitive theorists pointed out that this mode of functioning would be extremely inefficient since the information held was held only for a single purpose—navigating this single route in one direction. Taken literally, it was for navigating this single route with a particular sequence of muscle contractions. In contrast, a representation like a map represents a whole space. All navigators in Edinburgh can buy the same map regardless of which routes it is that they wish to travel. They do not need to know when they purchase their map where they will want to go within the city. Although choosing a representational system commits us to deciding what information we retain and what we discard, it also frees us from committing to a single *use* of the information within that system.

A digression on assessment

Because the separation in time of receiving information and deploying it can be so great in human learning, the issue of how to represent it for the use it will be put to is acute. Studying university courses is a good illustration of this problem. Students who succeed can be shown to develop their own personal representations of information that retain what is important to them, and that necessarily jettison lots of other information. This active process of making information one's own by relating it to the other knowledge and interests one has, contrasts starkly with the unsuccessful strategy of trying to rote learn the surface of the information without commitment to any significance. As every lecturer knows, the design of assessment procedures is crucial in triggering the right strategies of encoding, and the right kind of retrieval strategies for success. Of course, the larger goal is to design assessment methods that will engender the kind of learning that will be useful beyond the course. And of course, very often what is most important is the strategies for learning other material rather than the material itself.

Designing such assessment is not easy. Sometimes information has to be learnt before its significance can be appreciated by relating it to something else. Then there is the problem of deciding what information needs to be retained in memory, and what will be readily available from reference sources and so can be left to be looked up. It is the principles that need to be internalized, and the details that can be left to reference sources. Except, as we saw in reviewing the arguments about the selection task, the principles have to be supported by the right details.

Take the episode of learning you have just been engaged in. You have been presented with information and arguments about what happens when you read a paragraph. What is essential in this information? Is it important that the paragraph was about Napoleon? That it described two characters? Well, no. What is important is that you should be able to take another paragraph, say, picked from today's newspaper, and use it to illustrate the processes that have been reviewed here. This ability to re-apply principles to new examples is a highly efficient way of testing one's understanding (and also the reasonableness of the principles!).

Another important test of understanding of principles in science is whether you understand the evidence for those principles. If you can explain how psychologists have produced evidence for the principles, then you know a great deal more about what their real significance is, what limitations they have, and how you can assess counterclaims about related but different situations. What was essential about the reverse-engineering methods involved in our memory experiment with the Napoleon paragraph?

A common student complaint is that examinations are a dumb method of assessment because they are quite unlike the real world tasks to which learning will have to be applied. In particular, it is often said that having no access to reference material, and to be working against the clock, is highly artificial. Sometimes these complaints are perfectly sustainable. If the exam can be passed by rote learning a lot of inessential detail just before the exam, and if one cannot judge the students' grasp of principles from their answers, then that exam is probably a poor assessment. But exams can be highly realistic assessments. If you ask any professional whose practise is based on a body of formal learning, how they use reference material in their practice, you will find that it is used for retrieving certain kinds of detailed information. But most of the time, practice has to be based on internalized knowledge of principles and the critical details that support them. There simply isn't *time* for anything else. The demonstration that you can apply the principles you have learnt, to use example material provided in the question, against the clock, may be a highly realistic assessment of what you have learnt and whether you have made it your own. And of course, in any course based on this book, we would have to assess whether you had applied what you learnt about human learning to your own learning.

Internal representations and the blackness of the box

The comparison of maps and route directions is a simple illustration of the efficiency of using representations that are in a different format than the input (in this case a text). Of course, it does not settle the issue of how animals do represent their environment. That question is more complex. For one thing, animals have to learn their environment from the experience of traveling routes rather than by buying a map. There is evidence for both route and map kinds of organization of information, but there is clear evidence that people can construct map-like representations of their familiar environments that display some of the efficiencies of external maps. Readers who had an image of where the sofa was relative to the fireplace in the scenario we considered above were probably using some kind of spatial representation.

How are such mental images similar to external images? One very abstract but important way in which they are similar is that they both *enforce* the representation of spatial relations. Sentences can remain vague about whether Napoleon was on the countess' left—images cannot. Similarly, sentences can remain vague as to whether two mentioned individuals are the same person or not—images cannot depict the countess and the cousin without deciding whether they are the same individual or not. This enforcement is a rather abstract property of images, but it is the crucial computational property that distinguishes images from sentences. In chapter 18 we return to look at the consequences for inferential tractability of this enforcement of information.

The reader may by now be willing to accept the case for mental representations in explanations of human information processing, and have the beginnings of an understanding about the sort of approach to understanding communication to which this acceptance leads. But the attentive reader will have noticed a considerable gap between what we know about external representations, and what the methods and arguments just described can tell us about internal representations. The business of cognitive science is to close this gap, but it is extremely important not to lose sight of its existence and its current breadth.

But as you will have noticed, the result of this exercise is more a characterization of *what* is represented than exactly *how* it is represented. For example, we saw that the reader determines the identity relations between the characters mentioned in the story, and represents this information somehow, because the information is retained. This is a tremendously important insight into the process of reading. It may appear utterly obvious with hindsight, but it hasn't always been utterly obvious. These abstract specifications of what is represented are vital to developing theories about how memory is implemented.

In the 1950s, engineers set about trying to process texts like our paragraph (in fact, Russian chemistry papers) by computer. They thought that it should be a ten-year research project to get a computer to translate Russian scientific abstracts into English. Half a century and many billions of dollars later we know a great deal more about why translation is so hard, and are several steps nearer to what is still a fairly distant goal. Many of the difficulties of extracting meaning from text hinge on the problem of finding identities, and that problem is hard because people do it by deploying large amounts of general knowledge— that Napoleon was a commander, for example. Computers have trouble with general knowledge, not because they cannot be given facts, but because they can't be given *all* the facts, and so they have to infer facts from other facts (as people do), and the question how they do this is an extremely deep one. We saw some of the complexities involved in representing generalizations (rules) in Wason's selection task. The answer hangs on how facts and generalizations are represented, and therefore what computational processes can be applied to combine and analyze their representations to create new ones as they are needed.

So appreciating, for example, that identities have to be found, and that they have to be represented, is an important advance for cognitive science. But it does not tell us what the representations of these identities are like in the way that we might answer that question for examples of external representations, or even computers' representations. This gap is a trap for the unwary cognitive scientist. Sometimes it is filled by simply assuming that whatever mental representation people have *must* be like the external representations that we know and understand. For example, at one time in visual perception it was common for psychologists to assume that the visual part of the brain was doing calculations of the trajectories of moving objects by estimating subsequent distances from binocular disparities (the differences between the two eyes' images) and doing the required geometry.

James Gibson showed that the representations and the computations we perform on them when we estimate the trajectory to catch a ball is actually quite different from these calculations. Instead of calculating from, say, a known size and a sensed-image size a distance at a first time t, and then repeating the calculation for a time t', and then using the two positions to interpolate a track and velocity, Gibson showed that the eye/visual brain does a much more "direct" computation. It measures the rate of change of the diameter of the retinal image of the ball. If this image is getting smaller, the ball is traveling away. If it is getting bigger then it is approaching. It is possible to get people in cinemas to duck by projecting the right sort of rate of retinal image size increase on the screen. And this is despite the fact that they "know" the "projectile" is an image on the screen. There is a relatively simple function from the rate of change of retinal image to speed of approach and time of contact. Rate of change of image is also much easier for the (single) eye to estimate. So the first moral is that there is more than one way of skinning a cat or catching a ball, and what is convenient for a theorist may not be convenient for the brain. Careful study of creatures doing tasks in the environment is needed to understand how biology has "engineered" them.

But Gibson is sometimes interpreted as arguing that there is no representation and no computation—that the perception is just "direct." At best this is muddled—at worst mystical. There is a great deal of information processing required—witness the difficulties engineers have had in implementing Gibson's methods. The computation is a lot more "direct" than the suggestions it replaced, but it is computation nonetheless. And it takes place on representations of such things as image size and verticality.

A second way of falling into this trap is to deny that it is there. Having noticed that identity information, for example, is extracted and represented in understanding texts, we can name whatever does this representing a *mental model* of the text, and treat this as a *kind* of representation. If we remember that this is merely a name for whatever achieves a function, then no harm is done. But the problem is that this function can be achieved in many different ways. Just think of the kinds of external representations that could perform this function. Pictures or diagrams or perhaps clips of moving pictures can easily represent the identity relations in our scenario of Napoleon's entry. But so can text. In fact, there is something of a paradox here. Computational accounts of mental representations tend to be couched in terms of sentences in artificial languages—logics or programming languages. These have the advantage mentioned earlier that they are precisely defined and so, once interpreted, they can be manipulated mechanically without resort to the human intuition we are trying to analyze. But they present a certain paradox in the current context. They represent identities in texts by identities in texts. It looks initially as if all our arguments about why you have not represented the surface of the wordings in your memory of the text must be wrong if computers can do this representation in terms of languages internally, and those internal representations have just as rich a set of surface features.

This paradox is not a deep one. And it is resolved by asking ourselves about the computational mechanisms that work on the representations, whether of texts or of something else. Suppose the representation is in terms of some artificial logic. And suppose that the inference mechanisms that work on this logic can extract information about identities (say answering "yes" when posed the question whether Napoleon and the commander are one and the same). There is no reason why such a mechanism also has to be able to answer questions about the form of the sentences in the representation—"Did it say $P \wedge Q$? Or $Q \wedge P$?" for example. Nor is there any reason why the form should bear any simple relation to the sentences of English in the text. For example, all English sentences might be translated into some canonical form in the logic so that all superficial English syntactic information was lost. Even if the internal representation language were English, there could still be some normalization of sentence form that destroyed all trace of the surface wording.

So are our internal representations of discourse "linguistic" or "imagistic"? Or both? These are hard questions to which we don't yet know the answers. One approach is to specify some of the logical characteristics of our representations of gist at a level of abstraction that does not distinguish between linguistic and imagistic representations. Reverse engineers have to start with abstract functional characteristics and only later narrow down their implementations. We have already seen that our internal representations of scenarios could share with images the property of enforcing the representation of identity information. In chapter 18, this proposal will be taken further by asking about differences between diagrams and sentential languages. The gain in specifying such theories in logical languages is that they enable us to analyze the functional properties of the representation system with some precision, independently of the experiential features of the representation.

The psychologist's reverse engineering provides valuable insight into what the mind represents, but only weakly constrains questions about how this is achieved. Much of our knowledge about the "how" of representation comes from engineering—from AI's attempts to engineer mental functions. Combining the methods of psychology and AI (and a lot more besides) is our only hope of understanding the mind. The next part of the course looks at some of these techniques applied to understanding the structure of natural language and how it is processed by human beings.

Exercises

Exercise 7.1: Why are image-based theories of mental processes more prone to regress arguments than language-based theories?

Exercise 7.2: Do the arguments put forward here for representations in theories of mental processes mean that each memory has its own mental representation?

Exercise 7.3: Find a paragraph from a recent newspaper and use it to illustrate the same phenomena as the paragraph about Napoleon.

7.3   Further Reading

• Pylyshyn, Z. (1973). "What the Mind's Eye Tells the Mind's Brain: A Critique of Mental Imagery." *Psychological Bulletin* 80(1), 1–24.
A modern example of a skeptical argument against the role of imagery in mental processes.

• Dennett, D. (1991). *Consciousness Explained.* Boston: Little, Brown and Co.
Dennett's concept of the Cartesian Theater as an architecture for the mind is another interesting discussion of related issues.

• Bartlett, F. (1932). *Remembering: A Study in Experimental and Social Psychology.* Cambridge: Cambridge University Press.
The classical study that established that human memory is an active construction on the basis of cultural knowledge.

• Luria, A. R. (1968). *The Mind of a Mnemonist.* New York: Basic Books.
Important argument often taken to be against representational theories of mind—more usefully taken to be an argument that the wrong formal theory can lead to bad representational theories, and a good formal description to much better representational theories.

III MODELS OF LANGUAGE

Parts I and II of this textbook have focused largely on human reasoning—both its idealized form (see the discussion of logic in Section II) and how it's done in practice, e.g. Wason's four card problem and Tversky's jazz-playing accountant. Indeed, we saw how observations about human reasoning within controlled experimental settings reveal that there are differences between the "reasoning ideal" and human practice.

One way to view the role of human reasoning in an overall account of human communication is that it models how people handle the propositions that are conveyed in that communication, be it via conversation, text, graphics, or some other medium. People perform various inferences on the basis of those propositions, forming new beliefs or new intentions to act (including the intention of saying something) as a result. Recall, for example, that the phenomenon of anecdotalism exposes that often people infer more general conclusions than perhaps they should on the basis of what was said in a text. And Wason's four card experiments and Tversky's jazz-playing accountant experiments exposed that sometimes people perform quite surprising inferences on the basis of what was said. In the case of the jazz-playing accountant, people drew conclusions from the text that flout the fundamental laws of probability.

However, while parts I and II provide us with the means to discuss human inference from the content or propositions conveyed in a conversation, we have so far largely ignored the very important question of how humans work out what the content of a conversation is in the first place![12] So how does one map the markings on a page or the acoustic waves of speech into representations of their meaning? In other words, how do we work out what was said? On the face of it, this might seem like an odd question. Humans are generally unaware that there is anything to work out at all since we understand language with such apparent ease, and in all but very rare circumstances there is no conscious thought or effort in conversing. These initial impressions are deceptive, however. One aim of this part and part IV is to demonstrate this. We will show that thanks to ambiguity being pervasive in natural languages such as English, the link between a sentence and its meaning involves quite complex processing, which humans happen to be very good at. We hope that by the end of this part you will be in awe of how easily humans handle the complex processes involved in understanding conversation.

Working out what was said in a conversation is clearly a prerequisite to forming new beliefs or intentions on the basis of it. For example, consider the following very simple discourse: *John is rich. He has two million dollars.* One fails in some fundamental way to understand this discourse unless one works out that *he* refers to the same person as *John*, and arguably also that having two million dollars is evidence that John is rich. This is to be contrasted with, for example, another inference one might draw upon understanding the text: that John could afford to buy a nice car, for example. While this is a perfectly reasonable inference, it is not an inference one *must* draw as part of the process of working out which propositions were conveyed in the discourse. Rather, one draws this inference on the basis of those propositions and world knowledge about the price of cars.

This part of the course therefore examines the problem of working out what was said. We aim to answer two questions:

• *How can we describe language? In particular, how can we model the mapping between language and its meaning?*

• *How can descriptions of language be used either to understand human processing of language or to develop technology based on those descriptions?*

Addressing these questions has been delayed until now because much of the research on models of language draws on formal modeling techniques such as logic, which we were not in a position to introduce until part II. In essence, logic is not simply a tool for describing (idealized) forms of human reasoning; it is also a tool that is useful for describing human artifacts such as natural language. This shouldn't be surprising, since one can view the task of understanding text or conversation as a reasoning task.

We will focus in this part and in part IV on a theory for constructing a representation of the meaning of a discourse that's known as *Discourse Representation Theory*. This theory is quite representative of current thinking about how one might use logic to model the mapping from discourse to a representation of its meaning. Since it adopts a logical approach to the problem, it uses notions such as truth conditions and model theory which we discussed in chapter 6. These logical artifacts are useful because they can make very *precise* predictions about language and its meaning. As we will see in the subsequent chapters, ambiguity is pervasive in language, and logic is very good at representing that ambiguity, as well as the reasoning involved in resolving it.

All the disciplines in cognitive science address the mapping between linguistic signals and representations of meaning. Psycholinguistics is largely concerned with how people access words in their "mental lexicon" on the basis of what they hear, how the memory is structured, at what points during processing certain information is accessed, what data is stored in memory when processing a sentence, and so on. Linguistics is concerned with how language is structured, how it exhibits regularities, and how those regularities provide information about meaning. Computational linguistics and AI are concerned with how one can model the mapping between language and meaning within bounded computational resources. In this part and in part IV, we will focus mainly on the linguistic and computational linguistic approaches to the problem. This is because one of our main aims is to demonstrate the extent to which the analysis of natural languages such as English can be subjected to mathematical modeling (hence our focus on a logical approach to the problem). However, we will also touch on certain research results within psycholinguistics (see chapter 13), as well as how this research connects to the models of language developed in the other disciplines (see, for example, section 15.5).

8 Describing Language

Popular beliefs notwithstanding, language is *systematic*, and so can be described in terms of rules and general principles. We investigate its dual nature, considering both its physical, external forms—the words we speak, hear, read, or write—and the less observable—the thoughts or propositions those words inspire.

We will examine the nature of meaning in language and investigate representations of meaning that allow us to characterize—at least in part—the interpretation of simple sentences. We will show how these representations of meaning can be computed systematically from the way words are grouped into larger units, such as simple sentences. We will also see a variety of difficulties that arise in developing a theory of linguistic meaning, especially in characterizing the meaning of multi-sentence text and conversation.

In developing the model of language, we will be driven in part by insights relating to the study of ANAPHORA: anaphora is reference to an entity that has been previously introduced in the text or conversation, and the expressions that exhibit such reference are called ANAPHORIC expressions. For example, observe how the pronouns *she* and *him* in (1)a, the definite description *the dog* in (1)b, and the phrase *did too* in (1)c all refer back to things that have been mentioned already (e.g. *she* in (1)a refers to Mary, and *did* in (1)c is interpreted as *cried*):

(1) a.   John insulted Mary and then she insulted him.

    b.   John owns a dog and a cat. The dog is called Fido.

    c.   John cried. Mary did too.

A major challenge for any model of language is to state the principles that govern how the discourse context influences the interpretation of anaphoric expressions.

We will also see that human language is surprisingly ambiguous: elements of natural language, such as words or sentences, have many alternative interpretations. How can we model such alternative interpretations? And how can our models of language arrive at a choice between them?

Explicit models of language allow the development of a range of technology for the computer-based manipulation of human language.

We will consider examples of such systems, performing tasks such as the retrieval of information from databases.

A discussion of recent advances will provide both a point of contrast with psychological models and a perspective on the long-active debate between the symbolic, rule-based (or "rationalist"), and statistical (or "empiricist") views on human cognition. One crucial difference between the performance of humans and that of machines is in the ability of humans to deal effectively with the ambiguity pervasive in human language.

8.1   Preliminaries

We spend a great deal of time talking and listening, encountering tens of thousands of words in a typical day. Our native languages are so familiar and such an essential part of the environment we inhabit that we generally don't reflect on our use of language. Like breathing or walking, it's only in rare circumstances that we have to make an effort, perhaps when we are trying to express or understand a complex idea.

Every science needs to make assumptions about the things that it studies. These assumptions tell us what kinds of thing we can (and can't) expect to learn about our object of study (cf. section 1.2). In the case of physics for example, one has to assume that there is in fact a world that is ordered by principles that can be uncovered by experiment and argument. It's just the same with the study of language—we have to have a set of ground rules that tell us what we're studying and what methods are appropriate for conducting experiments. In this section, we'll discuss some basic assumptions of linguistics.

8.2   Languages and Language

You'll be aware that there is something called "English." A speaker of English can exploit his or her ability to interact with other speakers of English to exchange information and to accomplish other goals. Similarly, there are other languages and speakers of those languages. With extremely few exceptions, all humans have command of at least one language. When we say that our goal is in part to "study language," we're referring to a general phenomenon, namely the particularly human trait (and perhaps underlying genetic predisposition) for using linguistic systems.

One justification for using the more general term is that, despite their superficial diversity, languages seem not to vary particularly widely. Much work in linguistics over the last thirty years has been devoted to the search for constants that underlie that diversity, with a reasonable amount of success in areas such as the ordering of words, and the range of possible configurations (see section 9.4) in different languages. Building on this point, even though we'll use examples drawn exclusively from English, the same phenomena can be found in many other languages (in fact, we would hazard *all* languages). If you're fortunate enough to speak another language in addition to English, you will probably find it interesting to look in that language for the kinds of phenomena we will investigate here, and that we will illustrate with examples from English.

8.3   Description, Rather than Prescription

One of the things people often report about themselves is that they don't speak their native language properly. Why should they make such a statement? There seem to be a variety of reasons. First, they might believe that there is a set of rules (perhaps written down somewhere) that dictate what counts as "good English," and that their speech doesn't conform to this. Second, they may be aware of so-called standard forms of a language (for example, English as spoken by the middle classes in areas around London, or by the talk-show host David Letterman) and of differences between their speech and the standards they perceive. A consequence of this is that many people outside linguistics believe it should be a normative discipline: It should tell people which rules to follow in order to speak or write "good English." This mirrors the discussion of human reasoning from parts I and II of this book, where we suggested that the reasoning people *actually* do is just as interesting as the (prescriptive) reasoning that would be the ideal, as defined by formal logic.

In fact, those rules that people sometimes point to are most likely inventions of people in the 18th century who mistook English for Latin. It was true of Latin, for example, that sentences didn't end with a preposition, that is with words such as *above, to,* or *of.* So we couldn't take the individual English words in the following sentence, replace them with the words that correspond to them in Latin, and end up with a Latin sentence:

(2)   *The Brothers Karamazov* is a book I've never gotten to the end of.

We can't do that because of rules that govern how Latin sentences can be constructed. English doesn't obey the same rules as Latin. The following example is decidedly strange in English,[13] but the original is of course fine as a Latin sentence.

(3)   Gaul   is   all   divided   into   parts   three.
        Gallia est   omnis   divisa   in   partes   tres.

Sometimes, ensuring that a sentence doesn't end with a preposition results in something that sounds decidedly awkward compared with the alternatives: compare (4)a with the much improved (4)b:

(4) a.   This is the kind of English up with which I will not put.

     b.   This is the kind of English which I will not put up with.

So different languages obey different rules as far as the ordering of words goes. What we will try and do is uncover some of the rules for English that you use in constructing sentences. We will not in general take a stand on whether such rules correspond to any of the standard forms of English. (See also p.195 for an example of differences between dialects of English.)

    Another kind of example that attracts derision from some commentators on language is shown here:

(5)   I never did nothing.

Many commentators assert that double negatives cancel each other out, and that therefore this sentence means "I did something." Such a comment would be fine if we were dealing with a system such as arithmetic where, for example, two minuses standardly cancel each other, but in the case of language the assertion is patently false. You may have studied French, in which case you'll recognize the following two sentences, both meaning "I haven't eaten":

(6)   a.   Je n'ai pas mangé.

    b.   J'ai pas mangé.

You may also know enough to recognize that the first of these is the type of sentence one would see in relatively formal speech or writing, while the second is more informal. So French in this respect is the converse of English: two negative elements *ne* and *pas* are required in the more formal, and perhaps more prestigious, style of speech. What we can see from this is that the association of certain constructions such as "double negatives" with particular social groups is arbitrary; two languages may be the exact converse of one another.

Taken together, the economic privileging of standard forms of a language and an educational system that rewards adherence to a set of relatively arbitrary rules are a powerful mechanism by which linguistic prejudices develop and are perpetuated. You may have been following the ongoing debate on the teaching of English in schools. Current advice to teachers is that they should emphasize the economic advantages of speaking "standard English." What's left unsaid here is that in changing one's speech to be more like some standard form of English, one will most likely make one's speech less like that of one's peers. Unless your peers also change their speech in the same way, you will be sending out the phatic message that you don't want to be in the same group as them (for more details about phatic communication, see section 1.1).

The novel and film *Trainspotting* provides a useful example of how adherence to a particular set of linguistic norms can be advantageous. Renton and Spud have been caught shoplifting. The judge asks for statements from them both before sentencing them. Renton talks posh, and mentions Kierkegaard. He gets off with a suspended sentence. The judge turns to Spud and says *you are a reprobate*. Spud replies *Spot on, man* and gets six months. This scene is a powerful reminder of how one's linguistic behavior is a factor in advertising membership of certain groups, and of the practical effects of perceived group membership in interactions with the institutions of society.

As an aside, we are *not* saying here that English and other languages are haphazard; we'll see that there are rules that govern how English sentences can be put together. Nor are we saying that, in writing, or in speaking in formal situations, you can get away with jumbled up sentences or poorly worded ideas. The practical effects of failing to adhere to certain norms have been discussed above. You can be certain that you will at times be judged according to how you speak and write.

Linguistics, as a discipline, has generally taken an explicitly descriptive rather than normative (or PRESCRIPTIVE) approach (cf. section 1.2). Put another way, we should attempt to describe how people actually speak, rather than how they ought to speak. We want to study the regularities of language as language is actually used. Look at the following examples:

(7) a.   John's bedroom is not a good place to play in.

     b.   John's bedroom is not a good place which to play in.

     c.   John's bedroom is not a good place in which to play.

Before reading on, think carefully about these three sentences, and try to answer the following questions. Are any of them "odd," in the sense that they are not something you would expect someone to say, or to write down? Can you find other respects in which these sentences differ?

The consensus in this case is that the second of these sentences is decidedly strange, certainly when compared to the other two. (You may also be aware that you're more likely to come across the third sentence in writing than in speech.) By now you shouldn't be too surprised by this result. As demonstrated in section 2.1, there are rules that people follow in their speech that have never been taught to them or set down as a prescription for "good English." In the next section we'll see how judgments of oddness like the one you've just been exposed to form a valuable tool in determining the rules that speakers of English and other languages use in constructing and interpreting sentences.

Exercises

Exercise 8.1: Try out the sentences in (7) on other people and note their reaction.

Exercise 8.2: Example (2) above shows a sentence that ends with a preposition. How many different ways can you find of rewording the sentence so that its meaning is preserved? Can you correlate those rewordings with particular kinds of situations? That is, does one rewording seem more likely to be found in written versus spoken English? Do any of your rewordings seem more likely to be used in a casual conversation than the original?

8.4 Competence vs. Performance; Grammaticality Judgments

The following sentence is taken from the *Map Task Corpus* about which
you'll hear quite a lot in subsequent chapters of this book. Philip is
trying to guide Neil along a route drawn on a map. Neil can't see the
route on Philip's map. At one point, Philip says:

(8)   Yeah. 'Til you're at th...just beyond the f...the far...the
         bottom left-hand side of the fallen pillars.

Observe the false starts and hesitations; "..." indicate places where
there were pauses in the conversation. In spite of these, Neil is able
to extract a more or less complete description of a location from what
Philip says, which is something like: *'Til you're just beyond the bottom
left-hand side of the fallen pillars.*

If we're interested in examining rules and regularities of language, we
need to find a way of making a similar kind of idealization. We'll use the
word UTTERANCE to refer to a particular act of speaking. For example, I
may go to the sandwich store every day and say, "I'd like a BLT please."
There is clearly a sense in which I speak the same sentence every day,
even though the physical properties of the situation and of the sound
waves I produce may vary quite widely. I may have a cold one day, be
chewing a piece of gum the next, and so on. If someone else utters the
same words, we will again take this to be a different utterance of the
same sentence.

A standard position in linguistics takes the view that we often want
to abstract over different utterances of the same sentence (see also
section 2.1 for discussion of an analogous distinction between system
and implementation). This is in order to analyze those aspects of the
sentence's meaning that are independent of the time and place where
they were uttered, and who uttered them. Clearly, words like *here* and *me*
take on a meaning that is utterance-dependent; for example, *here* refers
to the *place* where the sentence is uttered. But there are many words
and groups of words whose meanings don't depend on the circumstances
of utterance in this way. And so it often makes things simpler to ignore
differences among different utterances of the same sentence.

The assumption here is that speakers of a language have access to a collection of rules that define the language that they speak. We can access these rules by tests of the kind shown in examples 7 and 9 (note that these judgments are about the sentences and not their utterance, since regardless of the circumstances in which they are uttered, the judgment about them remains the same). These examples are relatively clear-cut, and one seems to get more or less unanimous judgments that one of each of those sets of sentences has something wrong with it. We'll term these judgments GRAMMATICALITY judgments. They seem to diagnose whether particular sentences are consistent with the rules speakers of English have. We can then use such judgments in order to determine what sentences our models of grammar should allow and which ones they should rule out. To refer back to the discussion of section 2.1, such an approach may help us to uncover a single *system* underlying different implementations. Consider the examples here:

(9) a.   Which article did you file?

     b.   Which article did you file without reading?

     c.   *Which article did you file the letter without reading?

     d.   Which article did you file without reading the letter?

The * here is notation used by linguists to reflect the judgment that that sentence is odd. This fact remains, regardless of the accent in which the sentence is pronounced, whether it is written or spoken and so on. If we set up a model of language, we would want it to reflect such judgments.

So our use of intuitions allows us to group sentences into those that are grammatical and those that are not. To introduce some jargon, we take such judgments to give us information about the underlying grammars people have, their linguistic COMPETENCE. We distinguish this from the study of PERFORMANCE; that is, of particular sentences spoken by people in actual situations. Again the claim is that there are properties of sentences that hold regardless of the situations in which they occur.

We've chosen our examples here quite carefully, and it's worth taking a slightly wider perspective, to see how easy it is in general to apply the criterion of grammaticality. The exercise 8.4 asks you to consider random permutations of a sequence of words such as *John ran up a big bill*. One such permutation is

(10)   A up John bill big ran.

This is clearly not something anybody would take to be a sentence of English. You can probably find examples using those words that are less clear-cut. Here's one with different words:

(11)   These are the kinds of cars that when you leave them outside you have to be careful that there's someone to look after them.

You may hear or produce such sentences. Taken in isolation, what's your grammaticality judgment? Can you see what might be at issue as far as the grammaticality of such a sentence is concerned?

There are other sources of data derived from intuitions, for example about meaning:

* *Mary has a green bicycle* implies *Mary has a bicycle.*
* *John jogs* and *John doesn't jog* are contradictory.
* *Every student who worked hard got an A* and *If a student worked hard, he or she got an A* mean the same thing (or are PARAPHRASES).

We also have intuitions about whether or not discourses "work" (or COHERE). Observe, for example, that there's something odd about the following:

(12)   She left.

(13)   Mary knits jumpers. He's very good at it.

(14)   Every child has a dog. It's called Pip.

These are judgments of a different kind to those above. Each sentence is well-formed, but there are difficulties in interpreting what was meant overall, or why the sentences were juxtaposed.

One source of variation in judgments is that different dialects exploit different rules. How do you react to the following two sentences?

(15)   My shirt needs ironed.

(16)   My shirt needs ironing.

The chances are that if you're a speaker of Scots English, or of Midwestern U.S. English, you'll think of the first as the way you'd normally say it, but you may also be aware that the second is the way a speaker of English from Southeast England is likely to say it. Conversely, someone from Southeast England may well judge the first to be ungrammatical, and indeed it probably is, *with respect to most varieties of English spoken in Southeast England*. It's worth reflecting on what the reasons might be for this asymmetry in perception. This kind of variation is relatively rare in English, surprisingly so for a language spoken so widely. This means that the rules we use in this book are unlikely to produce results that are contentious.

So we've seen some of the assumptions we can make to get our study of language off the ground, and some of the factors that we may have to take into account in judging the grammaticality of sentences. These assumptions, together with others about the nature of form and meaning discussed below, provide linguistics with, as it were, its laboratory conditions, ways of controlling for factors that might otherwise disturb what it is we're trying to study.

Exercises

Exercise 8.3: Description vs. prescription.

For each of the following statements, say whether it is a prescriptive or a descriptive rule:

- A sentence in English can consist of a name, such as *John* or *Mary*, followed by a verb, such as *walks, snores,* or *vanished.*
- No word in English can begin with the sequence of letters *ng.*
- Writing should be concise.
- Don't start a sentence with a conjunction, such as *and* or *but.*
- Avoid repeating words.

Exercise 8.4: Consider the following two sentences:

1. John ran up a big bill.
2. John ran up a big hill.

As each of these sentences is five words long, we can reorder the individual words in 120 different ways. Pick out some orderings at random and evaluate the resulting sequence of words. Are they grammatical?

Can you find examples in which the individual words seem to have different interpretation relative to 1 and 2 above?

What is odd about the permutation *John ran a big hill up*, and what does this tell you about the groupings of words in the second sentence above, as contrasted with the first?

8.5   What We'll be Leaving Out

Before moving on to more technical topics, it's worth pointing out aspects of language and linguistics that we will downplay or ignore in this book.

Phatic Communication

As discussed in chapter 1, there are many aspects of communication that are phatic in nature. Consider the following conversation:

A: *Hi, how's it going?*
B: *Good, how are you?*
A: *Fine. Nice day, eh?*
B: *Yeah, fantastic.*
A: *Anyway, see you around.*
B: *Yeah, see you.*

This type of interaction doesn't seem to have the communication of information as its goal. At the end of this conversation, we can expect the participants to have renewed their social bonds to some extent—after all, they stopped to talk to one another—but we don't expect them to have learned much about each others' opinions, desire, etc. This suggests that in this example the communication is phatic—it serves to indicate and reinforce social groupings. This kind of observation is one aspect of work in SOCIOLINGUISTICS, while the study of ETHNOMETHODOLOGY examines interpersonal aspects of language. In the example above, speaker A indicates clearly that he or she thinks the conversation could be brought to an end, and awaits confirmation from B that the conversation is over. There is a lot to be said about this aspect of language use, but we won't have the space for it in this book.

We will nevertheless make a couple of points about phatic communication with respect to language. On the one hand, we'll emphasize often that one's linguistic ability allows the expression of an effectively unlimited range of ideas, attitudes, etc. In other words, from an ideational point of view, we can communicate anything we want. On the other hand, phatic communication with language seems to be more "controlled," and controlled in different ways. For example, there are aspects to everybody's speech that indicate the kinds of social groupings to which they belong. Consider how Eminem speaks, and contrast that with the speech of someone like Bill Clinton. Both of these "accents" (we use the word here in its everyday sense; it's not used in this way in linguistics) indicate that the speakers identify in some way with America. On the other hand, you are likely to associate these accents with very different social groupings, with different aspirations, and so on.

Just as people can to some extent advertise their group membership via their speech, so they can also, by varying their accent, indicate the extent to which they are willing to go to enter into social relations with one another. For example, we obviously speak differently to babies and bus drivers! Imagine speaking to a two-week old baby and saying: "Good afternoon. How are things?" The comic effect of this derives from the fact that the speaker doesn't adopt the usual conventions about how we interact with babies. More generally, we have a choice about the extent to which we alter our accents towards or away from that of our conversational partner, but the range of possibilities is, arguably, relatively limited. Even though we do this unconsciously, people still register such variation, and will take it as an indication of whether the interaction is proceeding well.

Other areas of linguistics

In place of the question, "What is English like?" we might ask: "How did English come to be the way it is?" Despite their inherent interest, historical explanations of language seem to be less relevant for cognitive science. Humans grow up speaking their native language regardless of its history—you don't need to know that the word *nice* derives from the Latin *nescius* in order to use that word appropriately. Nor do you need to know that there is a continuous history of language that relates speakers of English and speakers of Gujarati to groups of humans that lived near the Black Sea about six thousand years ago. We'll consequently ignore historical aspects of language in this book.

More relevant are the areas of PHONETICS, PHONOLOGY, and MORPHOLOGY. In phonetics, one studies the vocal tract, how it's used in the production of speech sounds and the resulting acoustic effects. It's a phonetic fact about most dialects of English, for instance, that no sounds are made by moving the tongue back so that it makes contact with the pharynx (the back wall of the top of the throat). However, such sounds are commonplace in Arabic.

Phonology studies the patterning of sounds in language. Some consequences of the phonology of English are that no word starts with the sound written (in English orthography) "ng," and that there could not be words such as *sring or *bnil.

Morphology looks at the way in which the form of words varies according to the other words it combines with (put more technically, according to its syntactic context). So in most dialects of English, one says: *I am, You are, She is, I was. . . .* Here we see a particular word "be" taking on different forms, *am, are, . . .* as the subject (*I, you, . . .*) varies. "Be" is quite unusual in English in having so many different forms—more typical are verbs such as "walk" (*walk, walks, walked, walking*).

We won't have time here to say anything much about these three areas, and this is obviously an unfortunate gap—if we wanted to give a complete account of the mechanisms by which people speak and hear, we would obviously have to talk about how sequences of words are realized, or how the acoustic signal is related to our perception of words. Similarly, we would have to describe the relation between the different forms of a word in the language in question. Although we'll briefly touch on some of these issues in the course of this book, we will not examine them in detail.

8.6   Summary

We've argued that there are fundamental regularities about how words in a given language can be grouped together to form sentences within an "idealized" setting of language use, abstracting away from hesitations, slip-ups, pauses, and false starts, all of which occur in spoken conversations. These regularities are what speakers have to know in order to know English. But how can we describe them? Certainly not by listing each acceptable sentence of English individually in a list. This isn't possible, since the number of acceptable English sentences is unlimited. Instead, we need to write down a finite number of rules that govern the way words can be combined to form sentences. We also need an accompanying set of rules that tell us how these sentences are *interpreted*; i.e. these rules must tell us what these sentences mean. In the next chapter, we'll begin to examine these linguistic regularities and suggest ways in which rules can accurately express them.

8.7   Further Reading

O'Grady et al. (2004) provides an excellent introduction to general Linguistics, including theories of phonetics, phonology, morphology, syntax, and semantics:

- O'Grady et al. (ed.) (2004). *Contemporary Linguistics: An Introduction.* London: Longman (5th Edition).

O'Grady et al. covers the topic of prescriptive vs. description English, that was discussed in section 8.3. The evolution from Latin to rules of how English should be used, including the use of double negatives (see also section 8.3), is described at greater length in Pinker (1994) from p.373 onwards:

- Pinker, Steven (1994). *The Language Instinct.* New York: W. Morrow and Co.

The differences in the ways we communicate with different social groups (e.g. babies vs. bus drivers) is covered in Aitchison (1976, 1987):

- Aitchison, Jean (1976). *The Articulate Mammal: An Introduction to Psycholinguistics.* London: Hutchinson.
- Aitchison, Jean (1987). *Words in the Mind: An Introduction to the Mental Lexicon.* Oxford: Blackwell.

We will be focusing mainly on the subareas of Linguistics known as syntax, semantics, and pragmatics in this book. For an excellent introduction to the theory of syntax and its interface to semantics, which presents a more advanced approach to these subjects than O'Grady et al. (2004), consult Sag and Wasow (1999).

- Sag, Ivan A., and Tom Wasow (1999). *Syntactic Theory: A Formal Introduction.* Stanford: CSLI.

Levinson (1993) gives an overview of the various areas in pragmatics:

- Levinson, Steven (1993). *Pragmatics*. Cambridge: Cambridge University Press.

And Davis (1991) is an edited collection of some of the seminal, original papers in pragmatics, including papers by Grice and Searle, whose work we will examine in chapters 16 and 17:

- Davis, Steven (ed.) (1991). *Pragmatics: A Reader*. New York: Oxford University Press.

9 Words, Phrases, and Meanings

9.1 A Simple Introduction: Arithmetic

Before looking in detail at ways of describing a human language such as English, we'll start with a simpler example: an interpretation of arithmetic equations. This relatively simple system will provide an introduction to some of the techniques we'll use in the description of English.

The structure of arithmetic expressions

A set of rules for defining arithmetic expressions is shown in Figure 9.1. Observe how some expressions—namely, 2, ×, and others—only appear on the right hand side (RHS) of these rules. These are known as TERMINAL SYMBOLS, and they correspond to the "words" of the language. The other symbols are called NONTERMINAL SYMBOLS: they're not expressions of the language of arithmetic itself, but rather they express clusters or generalizations over such expressions. In each of these rules, the RHS of the arrow ($\rightarrow$) is an ordered list of one or more terminal or nonterminal symbols, while to the left of the arrow is a single nonterminal symbol expressing some cluster or generalization.

Now, you can think of this set of rules in one of two ways: as a device for generating all the well-formed equations of arithmetic, or as a device for assigning a STRUCTURE to a given equation. As a generator, we can read the $\rightarrow$ arrow as "rewrite the symbol on the left with the string of symbols on the right." You keep rewriting the symbols you have written down, until all of the symbols are terminal ones.

The sequence of rules you use to generate an equation can be equally

$$Eq \rightarrow Ex \ = \ Ex$$
$$Ex \rightarrow (Ex \ Op \ Ex)$$
$$Ex \rightarrow (N \ Op \ N)$$
$$N \rightarrow 1, \ 2, \ 3, \ \ldots \ 9$$
$$Op \rightarrow +, \ \times, \ /, -$$

Figure 9.1
A set of rules for generating arithmetic expressions.

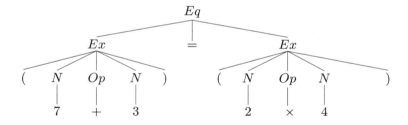

Figure 9.2
Structure associated with the equation $(7 + 3) = (2 \times 4)$.

well viewed as a DERIVATION of that equation. It is common to represent
a derivation by a TREE (commonly shown inverted, with the root symbol
at the top). For example, the tree for (1) is shown in Figure 9.2.

(1) $(7 + 3) = (2 \times 4)$

This tree shows in a succinct way the sequence of applications of the
rules in Figure 9.1 that you would have to perform so as to generate
the equation (1). Notice also the distinction mentioned earlier, between
the terminal symbols that appear in the arithmetic expressions, such as
=, (, 1, +, ... and the nonterminal symbols that are to do with overall
structuring, e.g. of the equation symbol Eq.

Some sequences of characters, for example)2+)(−1, are ILL-FORMED
according to this grammar. There is no way we can draw a tree using the
rules above so that that sequence of characters appears at the bottom of
the tree. On the other hand, if an equation is well-formed, such as that
in Figure 9.2, there is a corresponding tree and *vice versa*.

A second point to notice is that this set of rules allows us to analyze
expressions that are arbitrarily complex, for example:

(2) $(((6 \times 2) + 1) \times (2 \times 9)) = (1 - 2)$

We can do this because of the second rule in Figure 9.1 which states that
an expression can consist of two expressions separated by an operator.
Such a rule is *recursive*: the same symbol occurs on the righthand
side and the left. Recall from section 5.2 that logic contained recursive
definitions, too. And we'll see examples of such rules for describing
English in section 9.6.

The interpretation of equations

So we've seen that we can produce equations. The equations happen to be in a language whose INTERPRETATION you already know. How can we describe the interpretations of the equations? Or provide rules that will allow you to work out the interpretations of sentences in a language that you don't know? We'll see in this chapter that *logic*, such as the propositional logic that we discussed in chapter 5, is an effective way of representing interpretations; logic models inference, and through using logic to encode what sentences mean we encode the inferences that one can draw from them.

To illustrate the idea, let's first focus on the interpretation of arithmetic equations, and observe the ways in which logical notions such as *truth* and *falsehood* can play a role. In interpreting an equation, our goal is in effect to determine whether the equation is true or false. We'll do this by giving a set of rules for replacing part of a tree with a number derived from the part of the tree we're replacing. Here are those rules: Starting at the bottom of the tree, make the following replacements until you can't make any more:

(3)   *labels*   *replacement*
         N   the number below in the tree
         Op   the operation below in the tree
         Ex   the result of applying the operation to the
                    two numbers and erasing the brackets
         Eq   *true*, if the number on the lefthand side is
                    the same as that on the righthand side; *false*
                    otherwise

Figure 9.3 shows some of the steps involved in computing whether the given equation is true or false. (We've left out quite a few of the steps.) As you can see, by following those rules we end up with the symbol *false*, indicating that the equation is not true.

Some observations and conclusions

First of all, notice that there are two parts of the system of rules above. These two parts deal with different kinds of things. First, there are rules dealing with the structure of expressions, how they are organized into larger units, and ultimately how they correspond to marks on paper.

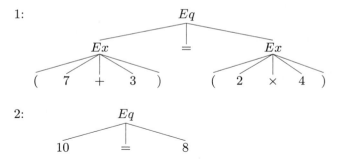

Figure 9.3
Computing the truth or falsity of an equation.

Second, there are computations over numbers, and ultimately whether equations between expressions are true or false. We can make this point more strongly by pointing out that we could have used the following as rules:

(4) $N \to$ *one, two, three, … Op → plus, times, …*

which would allow us to produce the equation:

(5)   *(seven plus three)* = *(two times four)*

In this case, we'd also need to say that *one* corresponds with the number 1, *times* with multiplication, and so on.

Another point to note about this example is that we could consistently change the symbols in any way and not alter what the system does. We could say, for example, that the symbol $\otimes$ (instead of $\times$) refers to multiplication, or we could replace the symbol Eq by XXX throughout. Furthermore, this system operates purely in terms of symbols. To introduce some terminology, this system is FORMAL in the following sense: it is explicit about the rules involved and there is no guesswork involved in applying the rules. In other words, all that matters is the *form* of an equation or expression (rather, say, than any interpretation a human might come up with).

Finally, notice that we can:

- define well-formedness for unlimited collections of expressions,
- define interpretations over them, and
- distinguish between the well-formedness and the truth of an equation.

Exercises

Exercise 9.1: Write out all of the steps involved in Figure 9.3.

Exercise 9.2: Draw the tree for example (2) and compute the truth of the equation.

Exercise 9.3: Can you satisfy yourself that for any sequence of symbols drawn from those that can appear in equations, you can

- determine whether the sequence is well-formed, and
- apply the rules above to end up with an equation between two numbers?

What problems might you encounter if division is included in the set of operations?

Exercise 9.4: Sketch an argument that shows that the number of equations that can be processed by our rules above is unlimited.

Exercise 9.5: We've used brackets in the expressions defined by the rules above. If you take the brackets away, an expression can be ambiguous. As an example, if we omitted the brackets, the sequence $7 - 2 \times 2 = 5 + 5$ is ill-formed: It can't be generated using the rules of the grammar. If we left out the brackets from the rules, sequences like the above would be ambiguous. Standard arithmetic has ways of resolving the ambiguity in unbracketed expressions. What are they and how could you alter the rules we've given to conform to the rules of standard arithmetic?

9.2 Building Grammars

In this section, we'll look at how we can model some aspects of English by writing explicit rules for describing how words can be arranged into sentences, and for relating sequences of words to representations of meaning. It's important to be clear about what such models (or GRAMMARS) are intended to do, and what they cannot be expected to do.

From the perspective of this book, one function of the grammar that we'll develop is to get you used to manipulating systems of this kind. Such grammars are formal in the sense defined above (section 9.1). As an analogy, consider the following statements:

A sonnet is a poem of fourteen lines. Allegory is the use of fictional, broad brush characters in representing, for example, powers such as gods, or personality types.

Which of the above statements can we apply in a formal way to determine whether we're looking at a sonnet or an allegory or something else? It should be obvious that we can look at a poem and see whether it contains fourteen lines—we can just count them. On that basis, Elizabeth Barrett Browning's "How do I love thee" clearly is a sonnet, while Marvell's "To his coy mistress" is not. On the other hand, it's much less clear that we can easily tell whether something is an allegory. We might agree that Bunyan's *Pilgrim's Progress* is an allegory, but in so doing we'd probably have to make assumptions, for example, about what we take "personality type" to mean. Note that one can also quibble about the definition of allegory given above, something that's more difficult to do with the definition of sonnet. We will be restricting our attention to those aspects of language structure and meaning that are amenable to formal definitions, such as those given in grammars.

A second function is to introduce you to ideas that have been influential within this field. The language model we'll develop through the course of this book is closely related to one that has been prominent for the last twenty years or so, and so to some extent you'll see what the workings of one of the latest theories are like. One of the crucial points here is that, having set up our grammar, we can then use it to make predictions about the meaning that corresponds to a particular sequence of words. In some cases, the grammar will get it wrong—it may fail to permit the analysis of a particular sequence of words, or it may assign a meaning that we judge to be incorrect. Some of these faults may be simple to correct. We may for example have failed to define a particular word in the grammar. Some of them may be deeper rooted and indicate that some of the rules in the grammar have to be changed. You can think of this as the linguistic analogue of scientific experimentation. On the basis of some data, we define a model that we hope will capture that data. We can then test the model against other data to see how well it performs, perhaps refine the model, and continue the cycle. To take up the discussion of section 3.4 again, one can view the assumptions made above and the formal tools we'll discuss here as a paradigm, within which we can investigate phenomena in language. It might be that the whole approach is, like Ptolemaic astronomy, founded on an incorrect assumption, which will have to be revised in order to gain a deeper understanding of the phenomena in question. We won't inflict such radical changes on you. We will however develop the model as we go. From part IV onwards, for example, we redesign the way we express some aspects of the theory in order to unify the treatment of a range of phenomena.

A further reason for looking at this kind of grammar is that, even though it deals with a limited number of phenomena, it serves to reinforce the point that human interpretation of language is a complex process involving different kinds of rules that appeal to different kinds of information.

Any scientific model has limits on what phenomena it accounts for— you wouldn't expect a model of a pendulum or a transistor to tell you how raindrops form. Our grammar will employ a sense of the word "meaning" (to be explored below) which is likely to be very narrow compared to the sense you're used to. How our narrow notion of meaning is related to broader ones will be tackled in later chapters. Relative to current research in the field, we will also make simplifications to the kinds of rules we will use. One motivation for this is to allow you to understand the basics of the model without looking at the mathematics that underlies it. We'll also limit the kinds of linguistic data we'll be looking at, in order to keep the number of rules manageable. These simplifications and other shortcomings of the grammar are discussed in section 10.3. It makes sense to try and predict what we'll say in that section, as you read the remainder of this chapter.

It is worth saying something about the kinds of sentences the grammar will cover. We will be able to analyze and describe the meaning of "simple past tense" sentences, such as *Pip barked* or *If Etta chased a bird, she caught it.* We'll also be able to analyze sequences of sentences, or DISCOURSES, such as *Etta chased a bird. She caught it.* We will limit ourselves to the simple past tense for several reasons. There are complications in saying how sentences such as *Pip is barking* are constructed. Other present tense formulations, for example, *Pip barks*, seem to refer to habitual actions, and this is a kind of meaning that is not easily captured in the system we develop below. Sequences of past tenses sound more natural than sequences of simple present tense sentences (unless one is speaking in "soccer commentator English": *Cantona dribbles to the edge of the box, he shoots, he scores.*)

9.3   Words and Meanings

From a linguistic point of view, we want to distinguish between the external (directly perceivable) and internal (not immediately perceivable) aspects of language. We can probably agree that there are things called "words"; for example, as seen in collections of marks on paper, or as we perceive them when someone speaks to us. It's more contentious to assume that there is something called "meaning." After all, meaning is something we can't see or measure. In section 6.2, we saw some of the reasons for assuming the existence of mental representations. We will assume that part of what you do, when you understand a sentence of English, is form a mental representation of the meaning of it. In other words, people are very good at working out what was said, even if they are not very good at working out the *logical consequences* of it (cf. the fallacies in human reasoning that we discussed in chapter 3). We must be careful not to confuse the process of constructing a representation of the meaning of a sentence with the process of *interpreting* that representation or reasoning with it.

In this section, we will talk first about how we understand the notion of "meaning," and what mental representations of the meanings of sentences might look like. We then turn to the issue of words, and how they group into larger units. This serves as an introduction to the topic covered in the following chapter, namely how we can make the connection between form and meaning.

Meaning

What is "meaning"? This is a question we can't answer, at least not without being more specific and making a lot of assumptions. We could for example ask what the meaning is of a sentence such as the following:

(6)   "All the world's a stage, and all men and women merely players."

One could give a variety of answers. Any of those answers is likely to be rather complicated, perhaps focusing on the overall topic of the sentence, the context in which it's said, its consequences, its connotations, and so on.

The position we are going to take here is that every sentence of English is associated with at least one LITERAL MEANING: what the sentence means in virtue of the words it contains and how they're put together. This assumption helps us to abstract away from how such sentences are interpreted in particular contexts (and so is another part of our "laboratory conditions," see p.196).

So a sentence like (7) has a literal meaning to do with being a fiend and with coming from a particular place:

(7)   Etta is a stick-crazed fiend from hell.

A person who utters (7) may, on the other hand, intend to convey something different from this literal meaning; for example, among other things, that Etta is a nuisance (because she likes sticks so much). Working out this intended meaning depends, however, on working out the literal meaning, and so there is still some value in having a rigorous and systematic way of analyzing literal meaning.

Some other examples involving nonliteral interpretations are shown here:

(8)   Did you forget the door?

(9)   David Beckham literally took off down the left wing.

While (8) is "literally" a question, it can be used to convey a *request* to shut the door (or open the door, depending on the context in which it's uttered). The person who utters (8) doesn't want an answer to his question about forgetting a door (whatever that means), but rather he wants the action of closing the door to be performed. We will examine this kind of "nonliteral" use of language in chapter 17. Sentence (9) exhibits another way in which what a person means may be different from "literal" meaning. The soccer player David Beckham is unlikely to be flying during a soccer match, and so despite the claim for literalness made in the sentence, we have to interpret it nonliterally. From here onwards, the word *meaning* will refer to literal meaning, unless otherwise indicated. Later on, in chapters 16 and 17, we'll return to the issue of how literal and nonliteral meanings might be related.

Representing literal meanings

Let's simplify things a little, and assume that we're dealing with conversations between a couple of individuals, A and B. Suppose that A informs B of something by saying *Pip barked*. If B believes what A says, then they now have something in common: they both believe the proposition that amounts to the meaning of the sentence. Perhaps what they have in mind is something like the picture in Figure 9.4.

That's fine as far as it goes, but presents us with a few problems. For a start, it's not obvious how we can interpret pictures to say what their meaning is. As discussed in section 7.1, there can't be a person inside our head interpreting such a picture. Furthermore, there's a lot about that picture that is irrelevant to the sentence in question. Why is the dog facing right rather than left? What are all those bones doing there? In sum, as a representation of the meaning of the sentence, the picture doesn't seem to capture what is constant across different utterances and seems to include a lot that is not implied by the sentence on its own.

It's also the case that language provides resources for combining meanings. How would you draw a picture of a sentence such as *Pip barked, and then Etta chased sticks*? Is it a single picture? If so, how is the sequence of events to be indicated? If not, how are the pictures related? And how would one draw a picture for a sentence containing the word *or*, such as *Pip chased Etta or he chased a stick*?

We therefore need a way of thinking about meaning that better reflects the meaning of sentences. One very influential proposal is the following:

(10)   You can know the literal meaning of a sentence by knowing the conditions under which it is (or would be) true.

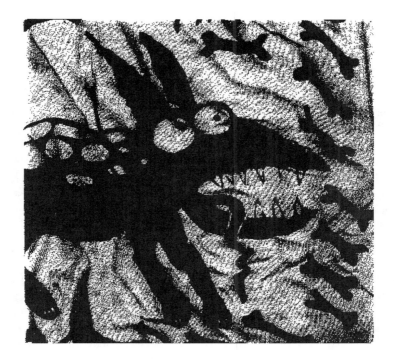

Figure 9.4
Is this what *Pip barked* means?

So we need a way of representing such conditions, and a way of determining whether those conditions are true.

What we are going to do is adopt a specific proposal about the representation of meaning (due independently to Hans Kamp and Irene Heim), namely that we represent literal meanings in terms of the individuals under discussion and conditions that hold true of and between those individuals. This work extends earlier work in semantics by Alfred Tarski and Richard Montague, the extensions being explicitly designed to handle anaphora.

Why the emphasis on individuals? Clearly, language can be used to talk about groups (e.g. *lottery winners*), amorphous masses (e.g. piles of sugar or sand), stretches of time (*three to five is when I can make it*), and many other things that are perhaps difficult to construe in terms of single entities, well-distinguished from others. But for the sake of

$$\boxed{\begin{array}{l} x \\ \hline \mathrm{dog}(x) \\ \mathrm{bark}(x) \end{array}}$$

Figure 9.5
An example of a discourse representation structure (DRS).

simplicitly, we will ignore the technical complexities that are necessary for describing groups. Instead, we will focus on modeling anaphoric references for simple cases involving individuals, so as to demonstrate how the meanings of words interact with the context in which they are used (see section 10.2). For example, consider (11):

(11)   Etta's in the park. She likes chasing sticks.

We can think of the first sentence *Etta's in the park* as providing a context in which the second *She likes chasing sticks* is interpreted. If we were to omit the first sentence, you wouldn't be able to tell who *she* refers to. We can take this to indicate that a word like *Etta* introduces an individual into the conversation, and a word like *she* refers to an individual that the speaker assumes has already been introduced. We will want our grammar for English to reflect these facts.

In order to make the distinction between the individuals under discussion and the conditions that hold of those individuals we'll use DIS-COURSE REPRESENTATION STRUCTURES (DRSs) of the kind shown in Figure 9.5. As a first approximation, we can read the contents of 9.5 as "we're talking about an individual, call it x, and the conditions hold that x is a dog and x barked." For the time being, we will assert that this is a semantic representation of the English sentence *a dog barked*. This semantic representation can in fact be *constructed* in a systematic manner from the sentence *a dog barked*. (We'll show how to construct the semantic representations of English sentences in chapter 10.)

Some terminology associated with DRSs is shown in Figure 9.6. In such diagrams, the area above the line contains the DISCOURSE REFERENTS, that is, symbols that stand for the individuals under discussion in the current discourse. Below the line you see the CONDITIONS that hold of those individuals.[14] These are called discourse representation structures because they aim to be able to represent the meaning of sequences of

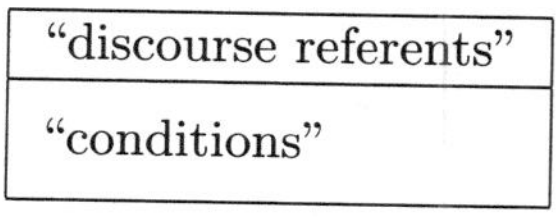

| "discourse referents" |
| "conditions" |

Figure 9.6
Terminology to do with DRSs.

sentences as well as that of individual sentences.

More formally, the definition of discourse representation structures is given as follows:

DEFINITION 9.1: **Discourse Representation Structures**

A discourse representation structure (or DRS) K is a pair of sets, where:

1. The first set is a set of discourse referents: x, y, z, x_1, x_2,....
2. The second set is a set of DRS conditions.

DRS conditions are defined as follows:

1. If P is a predicate symbol that takes n arguments and x_1, x_2,...,x_n are discourse referents, then $P(x_1, x_2, ..., x_n)$ is an atomic DRS condition.
2. If K_1 and K_2 are DRSs, then $K_1 \Rightarrow K_2$ is a DRS condition.

Atomic DRS conditions are things like bark(x) (which can be read as "x barked") chase(x,y) (which can be read as "x chased y") and so on. The so-called conditional DRS conditions given in item 2 above is used to handle English sentences containing the words *if* and *every*. We will study this type of condition, and the words *if* and *every*, in chapter 10.

The above definition says that DRSs consist of two sets; the box-style notation of a DRS given in Figure 9.6 is simply a way of showing the two sets graphically. Using this box-style notation will make it easier to see how constructing DRSs as semantic representations of simple English discourses proceeds, a matter we return to in chapter 10.

We now need to say something about how we interpret DRSs. We can make a start on this by giving rules under which we say whether or not a DRS is true.

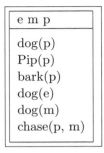

Figure 9.7
An example model.

Models and truth

In discussing the literal meaning of sentences, we used the term "true" in section 9.3, and this clearly requires a definition. One way of being true is to correspond to how the "real world" is. So the following is true:

(12)   This sentence was typed on a computer in Buccleuch Place around 12 noon on a Thursday.

There are obvious philosophical problems in talking about the "real world" (whatever that might mean) and what is true within it. We are going to side-step these by relating meanings not directly to the "real world," but rather by relating meanings to collections of facts that might, but don't have to, correspond to the way the world is. We could think of such collections as representing (a small part of) what someone knows, or of some pertinent facts from a situation we're interested in.

We'll call such a collection of facts a MODEL,[15] and an example is shown in Figure 9.7. You can think of a model such as this as a snapshot, a collection of facts that indicates a possible state of affairs at a moment in time. We can read these facts as "there are individuals e, m, and p, p bears the name Pip, p is a dog, the individual p chased the individual m," and so on.

So in Figure 9.7, we have a snapshot, something that could in principle correspond to a state of affairs, and, relative to that, we can ask the question: Is the DRS in Figure 9.5 true? Notice that in a sense, the DRS is "contained" in the model. That is, for each condition in the

DRS, we can find a corresponding fact in the model. More particularly, by replacing x in Figure 9.5 with p, we end up with precisely the fact shown in the model.

We can now say that a DRS is TRUE WITH RESPECT TO A MODEL if every condition in the DRS is in the model, substituting individuals in the model for referents in the DRS. We'll have to make this slightly more complicated when we come to look at "conditional" sentences in section 10.2. But for now, let's work with this very simple definition. Note that, in doing this, we accomplish two things. First, we provide a notion of truth that is mechanically interpretable. To check whether a DRS is true with respect to a model, you just have to check whether there is a mapping from the referents in the DRS to the individuals in the model such that: (a) no referent is identified with more than one individual in the model (note that if you did, you wouldn't have a mapping anyway), and (b) all of the conditions on the referents in the DRS also appear in the model on the individuals that the referents are mapped to. Second, we have severed any explicit link between "the real world" and our collection of facts. As discussed above, this neatly sidesteps some philosophical issues. It also allows us a way of cashing out the proposal on p.212 that the literal meaning of a sentence corresponds to the conditions under which it is true. With the mechanisms to be developed in chapter 10, we'll be able to go from a sequence of words to the corresponding DRS, and we can then evaluate that DRS against possible models to see whether or not the DRS adequately captures the literal meaning of the sentence.

We've set up our models so that they are as similar as possible to DRSs. We draw them differently, so that we're reminded that they're not exactly the same kind of thing. There are two respects in which models and DRSs are different. First, as we'll see below, we'll need to express in a DRS the condition that two referents are identical (we will do it with the condition $x=y$). In the models, we'll assume that all the individuals are distinct. So models won't ever feature the equals symbol "$=$," and a DRS condition $x=y$ will be satisfied only if the mapping from the discourse referents to individuals in the model map both x and y to the same individual. In the case of 9.7 then, there are three distinct individuals, e, m, and p. We can now think of the referents in a DRS as REFERRING to individuals in the model. A second difference is that facts are the only things that can occur within a model. In a DRS, we will use not just atomic conditions, but also "implications" (see definition 9.1 and also section 10.2). You may have noticed another minor difference: We generally use letters such as x, y, z to stand as referents in a DRS, while we use other letters, for example e, m, p, to represent individuals from a model.

For those readers who would like to see the formal definitions of models and truth of a DRS with respect to a model, here they are:

DEFINITION 9.2:   **Models**
A **model** M is a pair of sets, where:

1. The first set D_M is a set of individuals; and

2. the second set F_M is a set of facts, where each fact is expressed as an n-place predicate symbol followed by n individuals from D_M.

DEFINITION 9.3:   **Truth**
A DRS K is **true** with respect to a model M if there is a mapping f from the set U_K of discourse referents in K to individuals in D_M in the model M, such that all the DRS conditions C_K in K are satisfied by the model M and mapping f.

A DRS condition is satisfied by a model M and mapping f just in case:

1. When the DRS condition is an atomic DRS condition $P(x_1, x_2, \ldots, x_n)$, then $P(f(x_1), f(x_2), f(\ldots, x_n)) \in F_M$.

2. When the DRS condition is an equality of the form $x=y$, then $f(x)$ and $f(y)$ are the same individual (i.e $f(x) = f(y)$).

3. When the DRS condition is of the form $K_1 \Rightarrow K_2$, where K_1 and K_2 are DRSs, then for *every* mapping g such that:

   (a) g is like f, save that it is also defined for the discourse referents U_{K_1} in the DRS K_1, and

   (b) K_1 is satisfied by model M and mapping g,

there is a mapping h such that:

   (a) h is like g, save that it is also defined for the discourse referents U_{K_2} in the DRS K_2, and

   (b) K_2 is satisfied by model M and mapping h.

In other words, the interpretation of conditional DRS conditions stipulates that *every* way of making the right-hand side DRS K_1 true (by finding suitable mappings from the discourse referents in K_1 to individuals in the model) must be such that you can also make the left-hand side DRS K_2 true as well. We will study the interpretation of these conditional DRS conditions in more detail in section 10.2, where we will show that this interpretation matches our intuitions about the interpretation of words like *if* and *every* in English.

Exercises

Exercise 9.6: Consider the model shown in Figure 9.7. Of the following DRSs, which are true with respect to that model?

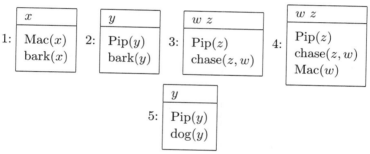

In all cases, be explicit about how you came to your decision. To what sentence of English might the last DRS correspond?

Exercise 9.7: Suppose you have a DRS just like Figure 9.5, except that the order of the conditions is reversed (i.e. the one having to do with barking appears above the one having to do with Pip). Can there be any models that make the example shown in the text true, and the reversed version false (or *vice versa*)? Explain your reasoning.

Exercise 9.8: Even though we have sidestepped some thorny issues, they haven't gone away. Think about the following claims.

1. The world can be represented as a set of facts.
2. Your knowledge of the world can be represented as a set of facts.

3. The literal meaning of a sentence is given by the conditions under which that sentence is true.

4. In hearing the sentence *A dog barked*, you construct something in your brain (or head or mind) that is the same as the diagram in Figure 9.5.

What arguments could you use for or against these claims? (As you may expect, this exercise is challenging.)

There is a large body of work on models of meaning of the kind we examine here. Obviously, we can't give you all the technical details, but one technical aside may help some of you. In expressing a condition in a DRS such as $\text{dog}(x)$, a more technical way of interpreting this is to say that the individual for which x stands is an element of the set of dogs. Looking at Figure 9.5, we can read the whole DRS as "We're talking about an individual, and that individual is contained in the intersection of the set of dogs and the set of things that bark."

There are also considerable disadvantages with the very simple view of a model as a snapshot collection of facts about individuals. All of the following phenomena require a more sophisticated view:

- sentences that refer to several times, or on-going activities: *John arrived after Mary blew out the candles; Alice is studying for her degree.*
- sentences that talk about possibilities: *John might be late.*

As a final word of warning, we haven't said anything about models and consistency. Later on in this book, we'll be interested in the difference between *she* and *he* (and *her* and *him*). With a few exceptions, the former is used for female animals and humans, and the latter for males. We'll want to say that in a discourse like

(13)   John kissed Mary. She kicked him.

She has to refer to Mary because Mary is the only female mentioned. However, nothing we've said rules out either of the following as models:

(14)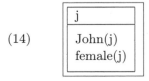

Figure 9.8
An alternative semantic representation of *A dog barked*.

(15)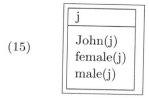

As these examples show, we haven't required models to obey conventions about names and gender or pronouns and gender. However, at various places below, we'll assume that models are in fact consistent in the assignment of gender. We'll see how conventions of names and gender can be implemented later in the book.

The semantic representations of words

In the examples used above, one aspect that may seem unsatisfactory is the way in which we represent the meanings of individual words. We've generally asserted that, if we see a word like *barked* in a sentence, the symbol that appears in the DRS is "bark," and likewise for *dog* and "dog." At first pass, this doesn't look particularly insightful. So let's look at an example to show that something more interesting is going on.

Suppose we say that the semantic representation of the noun *dog* is the symbol "aaaa," and that of *barked* is the symbol "bbbb." This means that for the sentence *A dog barked* we'll get a DRS as shown in Figure 9.8. Now, this DRS isn't true with respect to the model in Figure 9.7, because we've broken the connection between the symbol that we used in representing the meaning of the word and the symbol that appears in the model. If we were to make the same substitution in the model, the DRS would be true with respect to the new model. This emphasizes that, as with the situation with symbols in grammar rules, the choice of symbols is unimportant—they have no content of their own. What *is* important is their role in the system as a whole. In section 10.1, we give one reason why such an approach is justifiable. It does, however, leave you with the practical question, "What convention should I adopt for choosing the symbols that will be part of the semantic representation of particular words?" The convention we use is that described in section 10.1.

Symbols like "dog" and "chase" do tell us something about dogs and chasing, however. We have stipulated that "dog" takes just one discourse referent as an argument while "chase" takes two. This indicates that being a dog is a *property* of an individual, while chase is a *relation* between two individuals. Generally, the number of arguments that a predicate takes indicates the number of individuals involved in its meaning.

We've seen how we can approximate some aspects of the meaning of sentences in natural language, namely part of the internal aspect of language. We'll now turn to methods for characterizing external aspects.

9.4 Linguistic Form

We'll use the term FORM to refer to properties of sentences that are constant across utterances of the same sentence. So in the case of the sentence *Pip chased Etta*, one thing that's constant across different utterances is that it contains three words in a particular order. Another constant is the organization of those words into larger units, as we will see shortly.

One way of getting a grasp on the notion of form is by analogy with a piece of music and its score. How does this help? Well, a piece of music is in some sense defined by its score—the score is a set of instructions telling you how to realize the piece of music, and different people playing the same piece will be executing (almost) the same instructions. If there's a mistake in execution—a wrong note is played, perhaps—that doesn't alter the piece of music the performer is playing.

Exercise

Exercise 9.9: How far does this analogy go? Are there ways in which the performance of a piece of music is not like speaking?

As we'll see in the next section, words also go together in a particular way. In order to describe aspects of form having to do with the words used, their grouping, and ordering, we'll use SYNTACTIC RULES.

Grouping words; order and constituency

Consider the following permutations on a simple sentence:

(16)   Etta bit the vet.
         The vet was bitten by Etta.
         What Etta did was bite the vet.
         Who Etta bit was the vet.
         The vet bit Etta.

From these examples, we can see that certain words, e.g. *the* and *vet*, tend to go around together. Furthermore, such words go together in a particular order. Sequences of words such as *∗vet the* or *∗bit Etta the vet* are ungrammatical in modern English.

ORDER and CONSTITUENCY are two of the crucial concepts in discussions of linguistic form at the level of phrases and sentences. Order refers to the linear order of words within a sentence (progressing from left to right in the writing system we use, or corresponding to the passage of time in speech). Constituency refers to the way in which the words in a sentence group together into larger units. The rules we saw for arithmetic in section 9.1 provide an appropriate way of talking about both these aspects. Looking at the examples above, the words *the* and *vet* go together in that order, and so we could write a rule:

(17)   X → *the vet*

where the symbol X determines what context the whole expression can occur within. That's fine as a rule, but we might notice that we could replace *the* with *a* in any of the sentences in example (16) and still end up with a sentence of English. (The sentence might mean something different, but that's not at issue here.) In the jargon, we can SUBSTITUTE one sequence for another without affecting grammaticality. One or more words that may undergo substitution we'll term a CONSTITUENT.

We could write another rule like (17) for *a vet*, but then we'd find ourselves having to write many more rules, for example, for *a dog*, *the dog*, and so on. An alternative way to proceed is to say that the words *a* and *the* fall within the same CATEGORY (and similarly for *vet* and *dog*). We'll call the category for *a* and *the* DETERMINER (or Det for short),[16] and that for *vet* and *dog* NOUN (or N). Now we can write the following rules:[17]

(18)   NP → Det N
        Det → *a, the*
        N → *dog, vet, cat*

With these rules, we can now produce (or GENERATE) a variety of sequences, including all of the ones discussed in the paragraph above and some others as well. We've also replaced the symbol X with the symbol NP for NOUN PHRASE. We use this term because we're here dealing with a PHRASE (i.e. something perhaps involving more than one word) that includes a noun.

Compare the first and the last sentences of example (16). It suggests that the sequences *the vet* and *Etta* must have something in common. In particular, if the first is of category NP, so must the second be. We'll add the following to our growing list of rules.

(19)   NP → PN
        PN → *Etta, Pip, John, Mary*

Here we use the symbol PN to stand for PROPER NAME, i.e. a name such as those shown above. Our rules now say that any position in which the phrase *the vet* occurs is also one in which *Etta* may appear and *vice versa*.

How do the other words in the sentences above fit together? Consider the example: *Etta threatened to bite the vet, and <u>bite the vet</u> she did.* A conclusion from this example is that a VERB such as *bite* forms a constituent with a following NP, in which case we can write the following:

(20)   VP → V1 NP

(21)   V1 → *bit, chased, caught*

We'll use the convention of V1 for TRANSITIVE verb. Contrast this behavior with an INTRANSITIVE verb, such as *Etta slept*. For this second kind of verb, we can write a rule such as

VP → V0
V0 → *slept, ran, barked*

(As a mnemonic, a V1 verb goes around with one NP, and a V0 with none.)

So we've seen how to construct two kinds of phrases. We can add the statement that a noun phrase and a verb phrase can go together to form a sentence (S) in the following way:

(22)   S → NP VP

Our rules will now allow us to analyze sequences such as *a dog chased a cat, the vet loved Mary,* or *Etta slept.*

Exercise

Exercise 9.10: How many sentences do the syntactic rules allow?

One general comment is in order here. The syntactic rules that we supply are in general incomplete, in the sense that we don't give all of the words for a particular syntactic category. We'll see in section 10.1 some reasons why this would be difficult. We also don't give all the rules for forming sentences of English. For example, our grammar doesn't handle relative clauses, such as that in the perfectly grammatical sentence *A dog which has brown fur slept.* There are of course many other kinds of English constructions that our grammar ignores. But that's not important for now, since we simply aim to give you a flavour for what grammars are like. Extending grammars to handle a larger variety of English constructions is in many cases very straightforward.

9.5   Rules and Trees

As we saw in our discussion of arithmetic, there is a close correspondence between syntactic rules and trees. We can draw a picture in the manner of, for example, Figure 9.9, to represent the syntactic groupings within a sentence as a whole. The fact that we can draw such a tree using only the rules in the grammar indicates that the sentence is well-formed according to the grammar.

Words for describing the parts of a tree follow in part the analogy of real trees (even though we draw them upside down), and in part

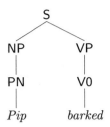

Figure 9.9
An example syntactic structure.

that of family trees. The labels that we saw in rules appear at the NODES of a tree. Nodes are linked by BRANCHES. The top-most node of a tree is its ROOT. When a node appears above another, linked to it by a branch, the first is the MOTHER of the second, and the second a DAUGHTER of the first. The relationship between a mother and its daughter(s) essentially expresses the information that there's a rule in the grammar where the mother is on the left hand side (LHS) and the daughters on the RHS (in the order they appear in the tree). As we mentioned in section 9.1, viewing the grammar rules as a device for generating all well-formed sentences of the language is a legitimate alternative way of thinking about the grammar system. And under this view, the relationship between a mother and her daughters amounts to the relationship of REWRITING or EXPANSION. Nodes that share a mother are SISTERS.

Exercises

Exercise 9.11: Draw trees for the following sentences:

1. Etta loved Pip.
2. The vet caught Etta.
3. The vet slept.

Exercise 9.12: On the basis of the rules given above, say what categories the underlined elements in the following sentences have to be:

1. <u>Peter</u> bit the vet.
2. The vet <u>hated</u> John.
3. The vet <u>hesitated</u>.
4. Mary <u>saw</u> the vet.
5. The <u>saw</u> caught Etta.
6. Etta caught <u>every</u> bird.
7. Etta loves the <u>doctor</u>.

You may have come across the terms SUBJECT, PREDICATE and OB-JECT. For our purposes, we can define them in terms of the grammar rules we're using. The subject of a sentence is the NP that is sister to VP, and VP is the predicate. Objects are sisters to V1. An ANALYSIS of a constituent is the corresponding tree.

9.6 Recursion

We'll now introduce a rule that shares an interesting property with the second rule in Figure 9.1, and also with the rules discussed in section 5.2. In this rule,

(23)   S → *if* S S

we can see that the same symbol S appears on both the left- and righthand sides of the rule. What are the consequences of this? In terms of sequences of words that the grammar generates, we can now produce examples like:

(24)   If Etta chased a bird Etta caught the bird.

Thinking more generally, you should be able to see that our grammar now shares with human languages the property that there is no limit to the length of sentences we can analyze. To repeat some jargon introduced earlier, we are dealing with a *recursive definition*; what may constitute a sentence involving *if* is itself defined in terms of sentences. Taking the grammar as discussed so far, we can make an unlimited number of sentences, for example *If Pip caught Etta Etta barked* or *If John loved Mary (then) if Etta caught a bird (then) Pip barked*. (Adding the word *then* sometimes helps to make such sentences clearer).

Exercises

Exercise 9.13: The syntactic rule for conditionals given here allows some pretty bizarre sentences, particularly if you use the rule for *if* a lot. Find a few such examples. What is your judgment of their grammaticality?

Exercise 9.14: What rule would you have to add in order to allow sentences involving *then*, e.g. *If Pip barked, then Etta ran*?

Exercise 9.15: Draw the trees associated with the last few examples.

Exercise 9.16: Summarize in your own words the arguments why:

1. We cannot set a limit on the number of sentences in English, and
2. the kind of grammar shown above is suitable for capturing an unlimited number of sentences.

In this section, we've seen how we can describe some aspects of the form of sentences, specifically how words can be grouped into larger units, and those units into still larger ones. In the next chapter we'll turn to the topic of how we can use the form of a sentence to determine its literal meaning.

9.7 Further Reading

This book bases the model of grammar—and in particular, of semantics—on a semantic framework known as *Discourse Representation Theory* or DRT. For a comprehensive introduction to DRT, see Kamp and Reyle (1993):

• Kamp, Hans, and Uwe Reyle (1993). *From Discourse to Logic: Introduction to Modeltheoretic Semantics of Natural Language, Formal Logic, and Discourse Representation Theory*. Boston: Kluwer Academic.

The interpretation of DRSs that we gave in section 9.3 is largely taken from Kamp and Reyle (1993). However, DRT affords itself an alternative *dynamic* interpretation. Dynamic semantics has proved very useful in modeling many of the communication phenomena that we will discuss in this book—particularly the phenomena discussed in part IV—but for reasons of space and simplicity, we don't introduce dynamic semantics in this book. Van Eijk and Kamp (1997) provide an excellent overview of this exciting area:

- Van Eijk, Jan, and Hans Kamp, "Representing Discourse in Context," in J. van Benthem and A. ter Meulen (eds.) (1997). *Handbook of Logic and Language*. Amsterdam: Elsevier, 179–237.

Word meaning—or lexical semantics as it's also known—is currently a hot topic in linguistics and computational linguistics. The following article lays out some of the challenges we face in analyzing the meaning of words:

- Pustejovsky, James (1991). "The Generative Lexicon," *Computational Linguistics*, 17.4, 409–441.

The following articles also give an overview of the phenomena in lexical semantics, but in a more introductory style than Pustejovsky:

- Briscoe, Ted (1991). "Lexical Issues in Natural Language Processing," in E. Klein and F. Veltmann (eds.) *Natural Language and Speech*. Berlin: Springer-Verlag, 22 pages.
- Copestake, Ann (1995). "Representing Lexical Polysemy," *Proceedings of the AAAI Spring Symposium on Lexical Semantics*, 21–26.

For further details about lexical semantics, consult Pustejovsky (1995):

- Pustejovsky, James (1995). *The Generative Lexicon*. Cambridge: MIT Press.

For an introduction to syntax, consult O'Grady et al. (2004), and Sag and Wasow (1999):

- O'Grady et al (2004). *Contemporary Linguistics: An Introduction*. London: Longman (5th Edition).
- Sag, Ivan A., and Tom Wasow (1999). *Syntactic Theory: A Formal Introduction*. Stanford: CSLI.

Both of these books give details about the various tests for syntactic constituency, which are mentioned in section 9.4.

10 Linking Form and Meaning: Grammars

We'll use the term GRAMMAR in the following technical sense: a formal system for relating form and meaning (see p.206 for a definition of the term "formal"). So the term here is distinct from other senses such as "reference grammar." We already have mechanisms for describing both form and meaning, and the question this chapter addresses is the way in which we can link the two. By the end of this chapter, you will have learned a formal and systematic way of constructing a representation of the meaning of simple discourses, such as *Etta chased Pip. He barked.*

You've seen many of the techniques we'll use here in section 9.1, both in general terms, where we use a set of syntactic rules to produce an analysis of a sequence of symbols which can then be interpreted to produce the "meaning" of that sequence, and in the specifics, where we will produce that meaning by taking apart the tree that represents the sentence's analysis. Our point of departure will be a discussion of general principles that might underlie such a process.

10.1 Arbitrariness and Compositionality

There have been two key insights into the relationship between form and meaning in natural language. Both date to about one hundred years ago, and have to do with the extent to which meaning is predictable from form.

What's in a name?

Take a word, or to be more precise the sounds (or letters) that constitute that word's form or external aspect. The relationship between that word and what it means (its internal aspect) is ARBITRARY. That is, if you know a word, for instance *span*, has such and such a meaning, you can't use that information to predict the meaning of other words that are similar in form, for example *pans, swan, scan, Stan, scran,* or *shan*. You may not know the meanings of some of these words and that should reinforce the point made here. Even though these words are very close in form, the greatest change being the replacement of two letters, their meanings have very little, if anything, in common.

Conversely, the following words do have something in common as far as their meaning is concerned: *mǎ*, *Pferd*, *cheval*, *ippo*. All of these words are translations of the English *horse* (in Mandarin Chinese, German, French, and modern Greek respectively). Again, if there were any direct connection between the sounds (or letters) of a word and its meaning, we should expect all of these words to be similar in form.

What's in a name? That which we call a rose by any other name would smell
as sweet.
Shakespeare (*Romeo and Juliet*, II.i.43)

As the above quote suggests, there is complete arbitrariness between the form of a word and its meaning. It took a while for this idea to find favor with linguists. Ferdinand de Saussure coined the term *l'arbitraire du signe* to describe this phenomenon around the turn of the 20th century.

To give one further example, suppose all speakers of English agreed one day to replace the word *table* with the word *plurk*. It's clear that this wouldn't have any effect on the things *table* used to refer to, and it's also pretty clear that, apart from this change, the grammar of English wouldn't be affected either.

One of the many amazing things about human facility with language is that we are able to learn so many arbitrary associations. Because they're arbitrary, there's no rhyme or reason to particular pairings of form and meaning and so there are no general principles that can aid the process of memorization. One estimate, and there are good reasons to think that it's a conservative one, is that typical English-speaking students at age seventeen know 60,000 such pairings. If you've read a fair bit, you're quite likely to have topped the 100,000 mark. In order to achieve even the lower figure, you have to learn a new arbitrary pairing every ninety waking minutes or so from the time you're one year old. The glossary at the end of these notes contains on the order of 250 definitions, and that's probably a good estimate of the number of new words, or new senses of words you'd already come across, that you will have learned in reading these notes.

Two objections are common at this point. First, what about words that sound like what they describe? Well, cases of such onomatopoeia are vanishingly few (at most a few hundred) compared to the typical case. Onomatopoeia is also conditioned to a large extent by available sound patterns in the language: *cock-a-doodle-doo* translates as *cocorico* in French. Second, what about words such as *doorknob* that describe the knobs of doors? In this case, there's a mismatch between two definitions of words. If you take "word" to mean "a sequence of characters without intervening blanks" (an entirely *formal* definition, by the way), then *doorknob* is indeed a single word. We've implicitly adopted a definition of "word" as a sequence of characters whose meaning is not predictable (what's known to linguists as a MORPHEME). Under that definition, *doorknob* consists of two words, as do, for example, *de-ice* or *quartermaster* as each has identifiable subparts with determinate meaning.

You may have noticed that a consequence of this discussion is that whenever we use the term "word" we're being a little imprecise. We could be intending to refer either to the form of a word or to its meaning. We avoid being more precise, because in general the context in which we use the term makes it clear which aspect of a word we're talking about. We'll also make use of two technical terms: LEXICAL to refer to information to do with words and LEXICON to refer to the collection of information about words. For the reasons just discussed, we can assume that part of the language system in humans consists of a large lexicon, giving information (at least) about the form and meaning of words and about the kinds of syntactic configurations that words can appear in.

We saw in section 9.3 that we will need to provide a representation of the semantic contribution that individual words make to the content of sentences that contain those words. In fact, our present goal is a relatively humble one: we aim to account for how the meanings of words *combine* to form the meaning of sentences overall, rather than focusing on the meanings of the lexical items themselves. Accordingly, we can in fact use an arbitrary symbol to stand for the semantic representation of each word, providing we do so consistently; what's important is the account of how these symbols combine to form a semantic representation of larger linguistic units, such as individual sentences or multisentence discourse. In fact, assigning each lexical item an arbitrary symbol is not as stupid as it might first seem, because of the arbitrary nature of the form-meaning relationship at the lexical level. Thus, the convention we will adopt here is that the semantic representation of words such as proper names, nouns, and verbs involves a symbol of the same form as the word itself, except that, in the case of verbs, we won't use a form that indicates, for example, past *versus* present tense. Some examples of words from different categories and the kinds of conditions they are associated with are given in Figure 10.1.

category	examples	predicate symbols
PN	*Etta, Pip*	$\text{Etta}(x)$, $\text{Pip}(z)$
N	*cat, dog*	$\text{cat}(w)$, $\text{dog}(y)$
V0	*walked, ran* (or *walks, runs*)	$\text{walk}(z)$, $\text{run}(x)$
V1	*caught, loved* (or *catches, loves*)	$\text{catch}(w,x)$, $\text{love}(y,z)$

Figure 10.1
Examples of predicate symbols for words of different syntactic categories.

Note that we consistently distinguish between the form of words (given in *italics*) and their corresponding PREDICATE SYMBOLS (given in an upright typeface). Observe also that variance among the number of arguments that these symbols take (e.g. love takes two arguments while Etta takes one argument). This, in fact, represents an extremely important aspect of the meaning of these words: It shows that a proper name like *Etta* is a property of an individual (i.e. any given individual either has the property of bearing the name Etta, or it hasn't), while a verb like *love* expresses a *relation* between two individuals. This semantic information is crucial when it comes to combining the meanings of words to form the meaning of sentences, as we'll shortly see.

Compositionality

We've just seen an example *doorknob*, in which the meaning of some expression (in this case written as a single word) can be determined from the meanings of its subparts (*door* and *knob*). What kind of regularity or principle might govern the way in which subparts of an expression contribute to the meaning of the whole?

The concept of COMPOSITIONALITY is attributed to Gottlob Frege, working towards the end of the 1800s. A textbook definition of the term goes like this:

(1)   A system for relating the form of an expression to its meaning is compositional if *the meaning of an expression is a function of the meanings of its parts and their manner of combination.*

For our purposes, we can identify the term "expression" with "constituent," and "manner of combination" with the syntactic configuration in which an expression appears, or (in other words) with the "shape" of the tree the syntactic rules tell us to draw. It's probably worth qualifying the above quotation with "and nothing else can affect the meaning of the expression as a whole," to emphasize that, in a strictly compositional system, only the meanings of subparts and their manner of combination affect the overall meaning.

Let's first investigate the definition relative to the rules from the arithmetic grammar (Figure 9.1). This says that the meaning of an expression labeled Ex is the result of applying the operator beneath that label to the two numbers beneath the label. This is compositional, because each time we use this rule we compute the result by seeing what operation (multiplication, division, *etc.*) corresponds to the operator $(*, /, etc.)$ and by applying that operation to the two numbers. So the meaning of an equation (i.e. whether it's true or false) is computed from the meanings of the arithmetic expressions that make up the equation and how they are combined. So we can say that the arithmetic system is fully compositional.

Note that arbitrariness still holds at the level equivalent to that of words. It's a convention that the symbol $*$ represents the operation of multiplication. We could alter that convention, for example to use $\times$ instead, without affecting the system as a whole. On the other hand, we have to have some convention, otherwise we would not be able to write down equations involving multiplication. Things are much the same in natural languages; words are a necessity for talking, but there is no essential connection between the sounds of words and their interpretation.

So is a natural language such as English compositional? We'll see later that English can't be strictly compositional, but before we get to that conclusion it's worth considering some extreme cases. Suppose English followed these rules:

(2) a.   The phrase *milk a cow* refers to a situation in which someone gets milk from a bovine, except on Saturdays when it refers to a situation in which someone runs quickly.

b.   If the words *green* and *toadstool* appear within a sentence, then the whole sentence means "My bicycle has been stolen."

c.   If the words *red* and *pajamas* appear within a sentence, then the whole sentence means "I have red pajamas."

These examples have been chosen in part for their bizarreness, and each of them represents a violation of compositionality. In the first case, we take into account factors entirely outside the sentence—i.e. whether today is Saturday—in determining the meaning of *Eddie milked a cow*. In the second case, while the words in the sentence may affect its meaning, they don't affect it in a way that takes account of the meaning of those words. The third does take account of the meanings of words, but not of how those words are put together. If the sentence in question is *I have red pajamas*, things are not so bad. The cases of *I don't have red pajamas*, or *While dressing gowns are typically red, pajamas are often blue* show that how words are grouped into larger units must be taken into account.

In a world where language were noncompositional, predicting the meanings of an utterance would be much more difficult. Given the unlimited number of sequences of words that constitute well-formed sentences, we rely on considerable regularity in the way in which the meaning of words and phrases contribute to that of sentences as a whole. Without this regularity, we would see the same arbitrary relationship between sentences and their meanings as holds between words and their meanings.

The examples above have been deliberately extreme in order to drive home the possibilities (or, more to the point, the limits) of completely noncompositional systems. You should have a strong intuition that English is not like the more extreme examples in (2). In fact, assuming that the meaning of an expression can be characterized in terms of what that expression DENOTES or REFERS TO (and this is a standard assumption in models of meaning that exploit formal systems such as logic), there are a number of interesting ways in which English is not completely compositional. Consider, for example, the following statements:

(3) a.   The phrase *today* means "Monday" on Mondays, "Tuesday" on Tuesdays,. . . .

     b.   The phrase *the bucket* refers to a previously mentioned bucket, except in the context *kick the bucket*, where the whole phrase means "die."

     c.   The word *she* refers to a female mentioned somewhere else in the sentence or discourse.

While you might quibble with details, these statements sound plausible as descriptions of English, much more so than those in examples (2)a–c. Each of them violates compositionality more or less severely. According to the first, in order to know the meaning of *today*, you have to appeal to something outside the sentence, namely whatever day it is. In the second, the meaning of *kick the bucket* is not predictable from the meanings of its parts: in the jargon, it is IDIOMATIC. This case also appeals to the notion "previously mentioned." In this respect, it's a similar case to the third. There you're not told where to look for a previous reference to a female, and that reference could be outside the sentence you're currently interested in.

We won't have time to go into the details of some of these cases. Words like *today* and other so-called INDEXICALS pick up their meaning from the context, location, or other aspects of the situation. Idioms can have an arbitrary meaning relative to their subparts. Both of these topics are the subject of considerable ongoing research.

We will look in detail at the behavior of words such as *the* and *she* and the principles that appear to govern their interpretation, within a framework that is broadly compositional. Put another way, it seems reasonable to suppose that English is for the most part compositional, and that violations of compositionality fall into some reasonably well understood classes. You should assess this claim for yourself as we work through the grammar.

Exercises

Exercise 10.1: Consider the rules given in the grammar for English. Say which aspects of the rules are compositional and which are not. Explain your reasoning.

Exercise 10.2: How do you interpret the example *Peter kept an eye on Pip*? What are the consequences of this example for compositionality?

10.2   The Semantic Rules in Detail

The previous sections have served to set the scene for the work that our grammar will do for us. Recall that we're interested in relating sequences of words to their literal meanings. Our approach will be broadly compositional. We'll use the techniques in our description of arithmetic to produce the meanings associated with sequences of simple English sentences. That technique is based on rules that exploit the syntactic structure of an expression in constructing a representation of its semantics. This representation is known as a LOGICAL FORM; it's so-called because the logical forms of discourse are expressed in a language over which we also provide a "mechanistic" way of performing logical inferences. Different researchers within the field of linguistics and computational linguistics choose different languages with different logics for expressing logical forms. As we said in the previous chapter, we'll use DRSs (see p.215 for the definition of DRSs and their interpretation). We will at various points stop to consider how the meanings we compute and represent in DRSs are related to models that make those DRSs true or false. In this way, we ultimately link a natural language discourse with the models—or equivalently, the conditions—that make it true.

General rules for constructing DRSs

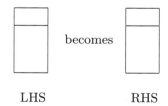

LHS   RHS

Figure 10.2
General form of semantic rules.

Our job now is to provide a systematic way of constructing from a (relatively) arbitrary discourse of English its logical form, expressed as a DRS. To do this, we will exploit the syntax of the sentences; in particular, we'll provide rules that stipulate the semantic contributions that various parts of a given syntax tree make to the overall content of the discourse. Accordingly, the rules we will use to construct the DRSs for discourses will all have the general form shown in Figure 10.2. There is a DRS on each side of the figure. On the LHS of such a rule, you will see a part of a tree, including one or more syntactic categories. On the RHS, you will typically see a different tree (or no tree at all), and an indication of information to be introduced into the DRS. The following general rules should be borne in mind:

- The tree on the LHS indicates a part of the tree to be removed.

- Any tree on the RHS indicates what should replace the portion of the tree that is removed.

- In the lower part of the box on the RHS, you will see any conditions that have to be introduced.

- If you see a discourse referent at the top of the RHS, this indicates that a new discourse referent has to be introduced. Assume that you have a collection of referents from which you can draw at will. Unless otherwise stated, you should choose a referent that doesn't occur elsewhere in the DRS and introduce this at all the relevant points within the DRS.

- If you're processing a discourse, add the syntax tree for the first sentence to a box, and use the rules to construct its DRS. Then add the syntax tree for the second sentence to the *same* box and continue applying the rules, so that you *add* conditions to the DRS that was constructed for the first sentence. Then add the syntax tree for the third sentence and so on.

- If you introduce an identity condition between two referents (i.e. a condition of the form $x = y$), you can replace one referent by the other throughout a DRS (in this case, you can replace all occurrences of x with y, or *vice versa*), and eliminate the identity condition.

From these general rules, you can see that, in a sense, a tree within a DRS represents "work to be done"—we have to take away parts of the tree as we specify, in the form of newly introduced discourse referents and additional DRS conditions, how those parts affect the content of the discourse. If we end up removing the last part of a tree from a DRS, then we have finished composing the logical form.

Figure 10.3 shows an actual rule, that for intransitive verbs. We can paraphrase this rule with the following set of instructions:

- Pick any discourse referent (that hasn't been used yet; in this case we chose z).

- Substitute that discourse referent for the tree whose root is labeled

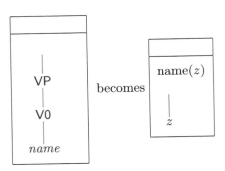

Figure 10.3
The semantic rule for intransitive verbs, e.g. *ran, slept.*

VP.

- Add "name(z)" to the DRS's conditions, where "name" is the predicate symbol associated with the word whose form is *name.*

In other words, this means an intransitive verb *name* contributes the following semantic information to the discourse: it introduces a condition that some individual, denoted by the discourse referent z, has the property "name." In fact, thanks to other semantic rules for processing NP nodes and S nodes that we will introduce shortly, this discourse referent z will denote the same individual as the one that's introduced by the subject NP. Replacing the VP node and everything beneath it with z will ensure this, given the way the other rules for NP nodes and S nodes are stated. Note that we do *not* introduce z into the top strip of the box. This is to capture the idea that intransitive verbs (and indeed, verbs generally) do not introduce new individuals that are being talked about. NPs do this, and we'll shortly see that the rules for converting various kinds of NPs into semantic information will reflect this.

In other rules, you may see a discourse referent in the space at the top of the RHS box. This indicates that, in applying the rule, you will need to add the referent to the top of the DRS you are creating.

The semantics of verbs and *a*

Let's take *A dog barked* as a concrete example. Our first step in composing its logical form is to find a syntactic tree for it, as licensed by the syntax rules in the grammar. The syntactic tree is shown in Figure 10.4.

We start by adding this tree to a DRS, to get Figure 10.5. We can now

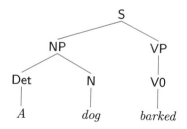

Figure 10.4
The syntactic tree for *A dog barked.*

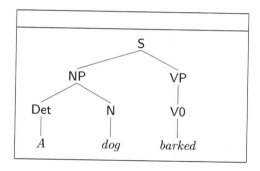

Figure 10.5
The first step in applying the semantic rules for the sentence *A dog barked.*

ask the question: can we apply the rule shown in Figure 10.3 to the DRS
shown in Figure 10.4? The answer is *yes*, because we can find the tree
shown in the rule within the DRS we're processing. In that case, we can
follow the steps described above to produce a new diagram, as shown in
Figure 10.6. Here, we have chosen y as the discourse referent to introduce, and assumed "bark" is the predicate symbol that's introduced by
the English word *barked.*

To proceed further with this example, we need to introduce another
semantic rule. The next rule will deal with configurations involving the
word *a*, and is shown in Figure 10.7. Note that this rule is intended

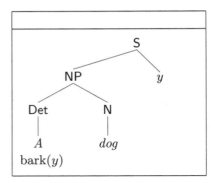

Figure 10.6
Step 2 in applying the semantic rules for the sentence *A dog barked.*

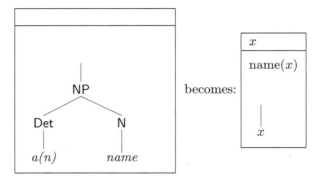

Figure 10.7
The semantic rule for *a.*

to work with both forms of the indefinite article, that is both *a* and
an. This is why we write *a(n)* as the letter(s) standing for the word
in question. In other words, this rule captures the following intuitively
compelling information: an indefinite NP introduces a new individual
that's being talked about in the discourse (that's why we introduce a
new discourse referent x into the top of the box), and this discourse
referent has the property specified by the noun (this is captured by the
condition name(x)). Furthermore, the fact that this rule replaces the NP
node with x, in combination with the way the sentence node S is treated

(we'll give the relevant rule shortly), will ensure that the individual denoted by x (i.e. the individual denoted by the subject NP) will be the same individual as the one who is assigned the semantic conditions that are derived from the VP.

Note that this rule involves a more complex tree than the rule we saw before (it consists of a mother node with two daughters, rather than one daughter), but the principle—whether we can find the tree on the LHS of the rule within the DRS we are processing—remains the same. So we can apply that rule to the diagram in Figure 10.6, and this will produce Figure 10.8.

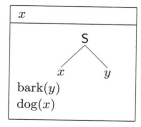

Figure 10.8
The next step in processing *A dog barked.*

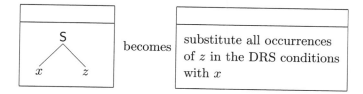

Figure 10.9
The semantic rule for sentences.

The final stages in processing will involve a rule that looks a little different from the preceding two, namely Figure 10.9. Here, the rule tells us to substitute one discourse referent for another. This captures the idea we mentioned earlier, that the individual introduced by the subject NP is the same as the individual who is assigned the properties conveyed by the VP (e.g. in this case, the property of barking). Indeed, we can apply that rule in our example to give Figure 10.10. Observe how

Figure 10.10
The DRS for *A dog barked.*

the discourse referent y that was the argument to the predicate bark has now been replaced with the discourse referent x; that's what the rule in Figure 10.9 instructs us to do. In fact, this DRS is exactly the one we were aiming for in Figure 9.5 (p.214). We saw at that point how a model would need to look to make the DRS true, and you may want to review that discussion now.

We introduced the rule for intransitive verbs above before that for *a* because the rule for verbs is simpler. You may have noticed that we could have done things in another order; we could have chosen to process *a dog* first, before *barked.* Does it matter which order we do things in? The answer is: it depends. In this case it doesn't matter. Using either of the possible orderings produces the same result. We'll see later on, in section 11.3, some cases where applying the semantic rules in different orders produces different results.

Exercises

Exercise 10.3: Satisfy yourself that, in processing the last example,

- there are only two possible orderings in which to apply semantic rules (even considering all of the rules in Appendix B.2), and
- you obtain the same result regardless of which ordering you choose.

Review your answers after considering the following exercise.

Exercise 10.4: We haven't been explicit about why some orderings are possible and others not. Give one or more reasons why, for example, it

is not possible to start composing the DRS of a sentence by applying
the sentence rule.

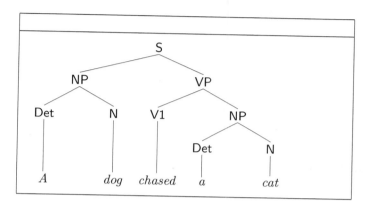

Figure 10.11
The first step in applying the semantic rules for the sentence *A dog chased a cat.*

Let's consider another example, *A dog chased a cat.* Some aspects of
the processing will be quite similar and so we'll omit some details this
time. First of all, you'll notice that the rule for noun phrases involving
a can be used regardless of where that noun phrase appears (that is, it
may appear within S or VP). So we can cut short our description here
and say that, on the basis of the syntactic tree shown in Figure 10.11
and two applications of the rule for *a*, we can arrive at Figure 10.12.

At this point, we need to introduce a new rule, namely that for
transitive verbs, shown in Figure 10.13. Note that this rule is a bit more
complicated than previous ones; there are two distinct referents in this
rule, and we'll need to keep track of which referents are which. (We chose
to use the referents u and v above to help make things clearer.)

We can see the tree shown in the rule within the DRS, and so we can
apply the rule, taking w in the rule to be the same as u in the DRS. We
can also see that the predicate symbol for *chased*, assumed to be "chase,"
will appear in the result of applying the rule. That means that the DRS
(so far) will look as shown in Figure 10.14 *before deleting the part of the
tree in question,* and as shown in Figure 10.15 afterwards. At this point,

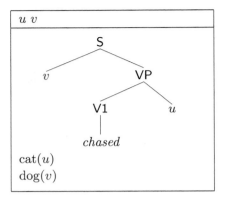

Figure 10.12
A dog chased a cat after processing the NPs.

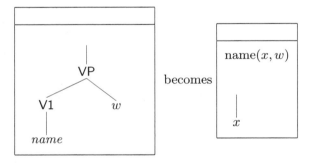

Figure 10.13
The semantic rule for transitive verbs, e.g. *loved, chased, caught.*

we have now gotten to the same stage in constructing the DRS as that
shown in Figure 10.8 for the previous example, and it should be easy for
you to see the steps involved in completing the example.

Exercises

Exercise 10.5: Complete the above example, and write out *all* of the
steps involved (including the two steps leading to the stage shown in
Figure 10.12).

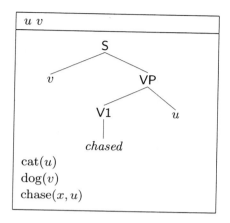

Figure 10.14
The next step in processing *A dog chased a cat*.

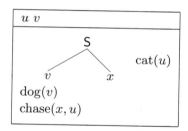

Figure 10.15
A dog chased a cat after deleting the tree rooted in VP.

Exercise 10.6: Is the DRS you compute true with respect to the model shown in Figure 9.7? Is it true with respect to the following model?

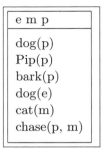

We've now seen how we can compute DRSs for simple sentences involving transitive and intransitive verbs, and noun phrases involving *a*. In the following sections, we will build on this to cover more examples.

Exercise

Exercise 10.7: For each of the semantic rules, rephrase them in English, as we did for the V0 rule above.

Proper names, discourses, and *the*

Our syntactic rules allow us to generate sentences such as *Etta barked*, which use a name to refer to an individual. What do our semantic rules have to say about such sentences? Let's notice first that, in many respects, processing this sentence will be the same as that for a sentence like *a dog barked*. We'll concentrate then on what the name *Etta* contributes to logical form. The relevant semantic rule is shown in Figure 10.16. The rule here is different in one way from rules we've seen before. There is an additional instruction about how to interpret the rule: *Reuse a referent, if you can.* By reuse, we mean identify a referent currently in the top of the DRS and use that as the referent introduced by the rule.

The tree for this sentence is shown in Figure 10.17, already placed in a DRS, the first step in the process of constructing logical form. We can use the PN rule as follows:

- Search for a referent to reuse, but there's no referent within the DRS, and so there's none to reuse.
- So introduce the condition "Etta(x)" where x is a new referent.

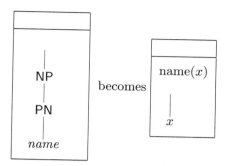

Reuse a referent, if you can. Otherwise introduce the referent at the
top of the box.

Figure 10.16
The semantic rule for proper names, e.g. *Etta, Pip, Mary.*

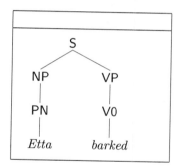

Figure 10.17
Start of the process for constructing the DRS of *Etta barked.*

• Delete the part of the tree rooted in NP (where this NP has the PN
node as its daughter) and leave x behind.

• Introduce x at the top of the box (because otherwise the DRS wouldn't
reflect the fact that the proper name introduced a new individual to be
talked about in the discourse).

This will leave the diagram as shown in Figure 10.18. From this point
in, composing logical form will follow essentially the same steps as those
discussed in section 10.2, so we omit them here. The resulting DRS will

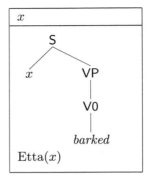

Figure 10.18
Step one in composing the logical form of the (one-sentence) discourse *Etta barked*.

be very similar to that shown in Figure 9.5. The circumstances under which the difference between the rule for *a* and the rule for proper names results in very different DRSs will be discussed in the next section.

Exercise

Exercise 10.8: Complete the process of composing the logical form for *Etta barked*. Ignoring whatever letter you use for the discourse referent, what is the single difference between this DRS and that for *A dog barked*?

The semantic rule for noun phrases involving the definite article *the* is shown in Figure 10.19. You'll notice the instruction about which discourse referent to use is the same as the one in the semantic rule for proper names. That is, unlike *a*, we are told to reuse a referent if we can, thereby reflecting the fact that the semantic contribution of NPs containing *the* is often (though not always) to *refer back* to individuals that have already been talked about in the discourse. Whether *the* has this co-reference effect or not depends on the prior sentences in the discourse, as we'll see in the next section.

Exercise

Exercise 10.9: Construct the DRS for the one-sentence discourse *The dog barked*.

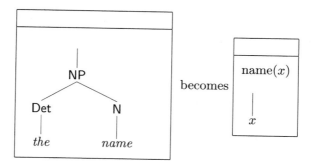

Reuse a referent, if you can. Otherwise introduce the referent at the top of the box.

Figure 10.19
The semantic rule for *the*

Discourses and models

We have looked so far at the logical forms of sentences in isolation. What happens if we want to look at larger groupings of sentences, in other words at discourses? We saw above that, if we process sentences involving definite and indefinite articles in isolation, we end up with pretty similar looking DRSs. So when are the DRSs different? Consider the following examples of very simple discourses:

(4)   A dog barked. A dog ran.

(5)   A dog barked. The dog ran.

The difference here seems to be that in the second case we can only be talking about a single dog (or, in the jargon, the discourse only refers to a single dog). Do the rules we have so far capture this? Well, first of all we have to be a bit more specific about what a discourse is. We'll give the following definition, which functions rather like one of the syntactic rules for the internals of a sentence:

DEFINITION 10.1: **Discourse**
A discourse is a sequence of one or more sentences, each terminated by a full stop.

And, in order to provide its logical form, we need to give a semantic rule. It goes like this:

DEFINITION 10.2: **How to construct the logical form of discourse**

To process a discourse, process the first sentence. This will involve creating a DRS. Process the remaining sentences in order, adding them one at a time to the DRS containing the first sentence.

How will these rules operate? By our syntactic rules, the following is a sequence of two sentences, and is consequently a discourse by Definition 10.1:

(6)   A dog barked. The dog ran.

So our semantic rule, as given in Definition 10.2, says that we can process this by taking the first sentence and processing that. We already know what the result will look like (see Figure 10.10). Definition 10.2 stipulates that the first step in processing the second sentence in the discourse is to add its tree to the same box. This is shown in Figure 10.20.

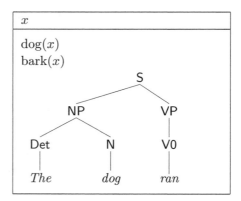

Figure 10.20
Processing the second sentence in a discourse: step 1.

If we think about the instruction "Reuse a referent, if you can," it's clear that we are in a different situation from the analysis of the previous example, where *the dog barked* was the first sentence of the discourse (recall the discussion of Figure 10.18). In the current case, when we come to process the NP *the dog*, we will be doing this in a *different context*; this time there is a referent, and so we can reuse it as instructed by the rule. Therefore, processing the noun phrase in this example will result in the diagram shown in Figure 10.21. Crucially, then, when composing the

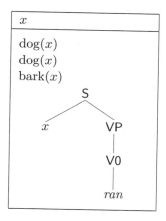

Figure 10.21
Processing the second sentence in a discourse: step 2.

logical form of the sentence in context, we are able to link the individual referred to by the first occurrence of *dog* with that referred to by the second. That link is made by the reuse of a referent. You should think about the consequences of this for models that make this DRS true (or false).

The remaining steps in constructing the DRS follow closely examples we've already seen. The overall result is shown in Figure 10.22.

Exercise

Exercise 10.10: Complete the process of constructing the DRS for *A dog barked. The dog ran.*

$$\boxed{\begin{array}{|l|}\hline x \\ \hline \mathrm{dog}(x) \\ \mathrm{dog}(x) \\ \mathrm{bark}(x) \\ \mathrm{run}(x) \\ \hline \end{array}}$$

Figure 10.22
The result of processing *A dog barked. The dog ran.*

You'll notice that we've followed the letter of the rules, and ended up with two occurrences of the condition "dog(x)" in the DRS. Is this important? If we think about the models that make such a DRS true (or false), you should be able to see that having both occurrences of the condition is redundant. If we were to delete one occurrence, exactly the same models will make the DRS true (and similarly for DRSs that fail to make the DRS true).

Exercise

Exercise 10.11: Satisfy yourself that all of the claims in the following discussion are true.

Let's consider a range of sentences, and what our grammar currently has to say about them. You should check what we have to say against your intuitions about these sentences.

(7)   A dog barked. A dog ran.

Here, the DRS of the first sentence will introduce a referent. The second sentence will introduce a referent, too, but according to the rules of our system, this should be a different referent. (To speak in terms of what will appear in the DRS, we will use different letters or symbols for the two referents.) What that means is that, relative to a model, the two occurrences of *dog* in this discourse could refer to different individuals in the model. In the following model, they do:

(8)

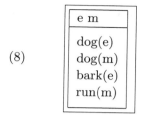

In this model, one individual "e" is associated with the conditions to do with being a dog and with running, while another individual "m" is associated with the conditions to do with being a dog and with barking. Contrast that with this model:

(9)

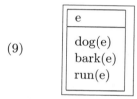

You'll see that a single individual is associated with all three conditions. Therefore, with respect to this model, the two referents in the DRS for the sentence in question refer to the same individual, because there's nothing else they could possibly refer to.

What if we reverse the ordering of the sentences of our first discourse, so that we have:

(10)   The dog ran. A dog barked.

In this case, there is nothing preceding the first sentence and so it will get processed as if it were in isolation. Consequently, there will be no existing referent within the DRS to reuse. The grammar therefore makes the same prediction as in the case with two indefinite articles: the two referents in question may refer to the same individual, but they don't have to.

So far, probably so good. It's quite likely that you'll agree with what our grammar predicts. Let's take a look at some sentences where things don't work out quite so well:

(11)   John ran. The dog barked.

In processing the first sentence, there can be no referents to reuse, and so *John* will introduce a referent, say x. When we come to process the second sentence, the referent x will be around, and so according to the rules of the grammar, we should reuse that referent in processing *the dog*. In other words, *John* and *dog* have to refer to the same individual. If the DRS for this discourse is true with respect to a model, then that model must look (at least in part) as follows:

(12)

i
John(i)
dog(i)

First of all, check your intuitions about this prediction. If it seems plain wrong to you, try to say why.

What can we learn from this example? First of all, it's a useful reminder that we are mechanically following rules. For better or for worse, we can mechanically work out what the grammar predicts. In this case, it forces *John* and *the dog* to CO-REFER, that is they must be taken to refer to the same individual. We'll be pleased if what it predicts, co-reference in this case, accords with our intuitions. If what it predicts seems odd, then we have to try and work out what that oddness is, and whether it represents a good reason to revise the grammar (or perhaps discard it altogether).

A second useful reminder is that the grammar "knows" only what we've told it. We haven't said anywhere that *John* is quite an unusual name to give a dog. The grammar is not permitted to hypothesize a scenario in which, say, John is a human and has a dog. All the grammar can do is relate sequences of words to DRSs and all we can do with a DRS is offer models with respect to which that DRS is true or false. We could choose to build a constraint into our model (cf. p.221), to the effect that no individual is associated with both the conditions "John" and "dog."

What intuitions do you have about reference in the following example?

(13)   A dog chased a bird. The dog caught the bird.

There are in fact two things that go wrong here. Before reading on, see how many problems you can spot. Let's deal with the perhaps more obvious one first. Suppose *a dog* introduces the referent x, and *a bird* the referent y. When we come to process the second sentence, both of these referents can be found at the top of the DRS, and so what is there to stop us reusing x for *the bird* and y for *the dog*? (This amounts to the claim that one possible interpretation of this discourse is that the thing that did the chasing is the thing that got caught.) The answer is: there's nothing to stop us. We haven't put any constraints on how you pick from the referents that are available, and so any way of choosing them is allowed. You should note that, under that interpretation, this DRS can only be true with respect to a model in which there are individuals that are both dogs and birds. With the example of *John* and *the dog* above, it seemed that our grammar was too strict in forcing us to reuse a referent. In this case, it seems too liberal in allowing us to reuse referents in ways that are not the "most obvious." For the time being, we'll leave things in what may seem to you to be an unsatisfactory state of affairs. This topic will be taken up again in considerably more detail in chapter 15, where a lot of the problems we have just described will be solved by amending the rules given here.

What's the second problem? It's one that will violate your intuitions probably more than any we've seen so far. Consider the situation shown in Figure 10.23.[18] At this point, in processing *the bird* we can ask the

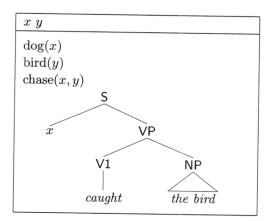

Figure 10.23
One point in processing the discourse *A dog chased a bird. The dog caught the bird.*

question, is there a referent we could reuse? Obviously there are two referents we could reuse. There's the "obvious" one y, which would say that the thing that was chased is the thing that got caught. But then again, there's no reason why we can't reuse x instead. This would in the end give us the DRS (14):

(14)

x
$\text{dog}(x)$
$\text{bird}(x)$
$\text{bird}(y)$
$\text{chase}(x, y)$
$\text{catch}(x, x)$

So the thing that got caught was the thing that did the catching. In other words, someone caught himself! This is, most people will agree, clearly wrong. Bear this problem in mind, and we'll return to it in the next section.

Exercise

Exercise 10.12: Repeat the kinds of analysis we've attempted above on the following examples. That is, assess the kinds of DRSs each gives rise to, in terms of the models that make those DRSs true, and your intuitions about what the discourses mean.

(15)   A dog ran. Etta barked.

(16)   Etta caught a bird. The dog barked.

(17)   John chased Etta. Etta chased John.

Pronouns and anaphora

Consider the following example:

(18)   He barked.

This example is pretty odd as the start of a discourse, unless its speaker is pointing at someone while he says it. This is because one has no idea to whom *he* might be referring. We have encoded this intuition in the rule for pronouns, shown in Figure 10.24.[19] It should be clear that if (18) is the first sentence of the discourse, then the semantic rule in Figure 10.24 will predict that it's uninterpretable. This is because when we reach the

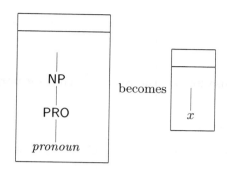

You *must* reuse a referent.

Figure 10.24
The semantic rule for pronouns, e.g. *she, her, it, he, him.*

instruction "You *must* reuse a referent," there is no referent around to reuse and we are unable to finish constructing the DRS for this sentence, and so, by our rules, cannot go on to process any later sentence.

That inability to proceed captures nicely the double take we feel on hearing such sentences as that above. We should be explaining why sentence (19) is odd in a similar way.

(19)   She chased Etta.

But here we run into a problem: if we process *Etta* first, then the referent we introduce will be available for *she* to reuse. Most people have the very strong intuition that that shouldn't be allowed, and so our rule for pronouns as it stands doesn't make the right predictions about (19). Things are perhaps even worse here:

(20)   Etta chased her.

It seems to be the case that co-reference is impossible in this example.

In order to fix this problem, we will introduce a restriction, the ANAPHORA CONSTRAINT, which will govern how we may reuse referents. One bit of terminology will help in phrasing it. In an atomic condition in a DRS, such as "love(x, y)," x and y are the ARGUMENTS to the condition. The Anaphora Constraint goes like this:[20]

(21)   In constructing a DRS, a referent cannot appear more than
          once in the arguments to an atomic condition.

How can we apply this constraint? Most obviously, in a sentence such
as (22), if we reuse for *her* the referent that *Etta* introduces, we will
violate the constraint.

(22)   Etta loved her.

We've already seen another case in which the Anaphora Constraint will
help out, namely in the discussion to do with Figure 10.23. There we
saw the possibility of reusing the same referent for both noun phrases in
the sentence *The dog caught the bird*. Again, if we were to do that, the
constraint would be violated.

Exercise

Exercise 10.13: Go through the details of the above claims.

There are some interesting consequences that follow from this constraint. Here are a couple of them:

• A pronoun like *he* and *her* cannot occur within the first sentence of
a written discourse. For the pronoun to reuse a referent in this case
there are only two possibilities: It could reuse a referent from a previous
sentence, but there is none, or it could take a referent from something
else in the same sentence, but that would result in a violation of the
constraint.[21]

• A proper name occurring in the first sentence of a discourse always
introduces a new referent. If a proper name doesn't introduce a new
referent, it behaves in effect like a pronoun.

• In the discourse *Mary loved Etta. Etta loved her*, either *Mary* and *Etta*
refer to different individuals in a model, or the individual known as Mary
is also known as Etta.

Exercises

Exercise 10.14: Justify the preceding claim.

Exercise 10.15: Discuss the following discourses:

(23)   Etta barked. She ran.

(24)   Etta chased Pip. He ran.

(25)   Etta chased Pip. She caught him.

(26)   The vet loved Pip. She bit him.

(27)   The vet chased a stick. She bit it.

Be certain to consider all possible ways of re-using referents. Which ways of re-using referents strike you as odd?

Exercise 10.16: Consider the possessive pronoun *her*, as in *Etta caught her ball.* Provide a treatment based on the following syntactic rule: Det → Pro[possessive], and assuming that one of the conditions associated with the pronoun is "possess(x, y)," meaning that x possesses or possessed y.

(You may want to review this exercise after covering the materials to do with pronouns in section 14.2.)

Even with the Anaphora Constraint in place, the grammar still allows a lot of discourses that are decidedly odd. Consider the following:

(28)   John chased Mary. It ran.

Here, *it* can be taken to co-refer with either of the two preceding noun phrases. In

(29)   Mary loved John. He loved her.

there are two possible pairings, but one of them results in the second sentence having the same meaning as the first. We'll return to these problems in chapter 14, where we will show how to amend the grammar so that it no longer makes these wrong predictions.

Conditionals and *every*

We've seen above how we can represent the meaning of a discourse as a DRS containing a collection of conditions, and how we can determine the truth (or falsity) of a DRS with respect to a model. In the cases that we have examined so far, that amounted to checking whether we could match each condition in a DRS to a fact in the model, substituting discourse referents for individuals in the model.

However, not all meanings in natural language are like this. Conditional sentences, on which we spent some time in section 3.2, seem to express a relation between situations: *If it's raining, I'll take an umbrella* doesn't mean "It's raining" is true, and the discourse *Etta chased a bird. She caught it* means something different from the conditional *If Etta chased a bird she caught it*. We discussed the syntactic rule for *if* in section 9.6, and repeat it here:

(30)   S → *if* S S

Before we get on to the semantics of sentences involving *if*, let's consider a few points about their meaning.

Under what circumstances would we say that the sentence *If Etta chased a bird, she caught it* is true? First of all, we'll assume the pairing where *Etta* and *she* co-refer, as do *bird* and *it*. Now let's think about some models, for example, the ones shown in Figure 10.25. Which of these models do you judge make the sentence true? Let's look at them one by one. Here, we'll speak rather loosely and say, for example, "Etta" for the referent introduced by *Etta*. In model 1, we see that there is a bird, "b_1," that Etta chases and which she catches. There isn't a bird that she chases but doesn't catch and so the conditional seems to be true. In model 2, there is a bird, "b_2," that she catches, and a different one, "b_1," that she chases. So "b_1" is a bird that she chases but doesn't catch, thus the conditional is not true. In model 3, she doesn't chase any birds. We'll leave it to your intuition whether you think that makes the conditional false. In model 4, there are two birds that she chases, and she catches both of them, so the conditional seems to be true.

How does this discussion relate to DRSs that might represent the meaning of two halves of the conditional? The two DRSs corresponding to the left- and right-hand sides of the conditional can be seen in Figure 10.26. One way of generalizing the discussion above is the following:

(31)   The sentence "*If* S_1 S_2" is true, provided that any way in which the DRS for S_1 is true is also one in which the DRS for S_2 is true.

One way of making the lefthand DRS true, with respect to model 4, is to take x to be "e" and y to be "b_1." In that case, the righthand DRS is also true. There's another way, involving "b_2." Again the righthand DRS

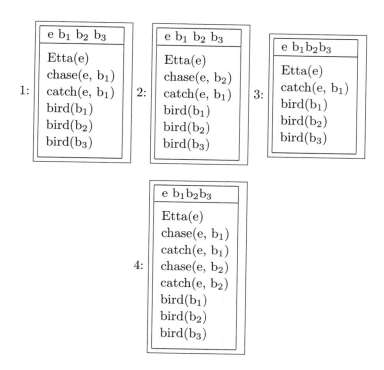

Figure 10.25
Some models involving Etta and birds.

is true. Now we have exhausted the ways of making the lefthand DRS true, and seen that each of them is also a way of making the righthand DRS true; therefore by the rule given above, the conditional is true with respect to model 4.

Exercise

Exercise 10.17: Go through the models applying this test.

So how can we represent, within a DRS, the "conditional" relationship between two DRSs, as expressed in the above truth conditions? We'll do this by adopting a symbol to indicate this relation between two DRSs, as shown in Figure 10.27 (recall also the Definition 9.1 of DRSs on p.215). The last thing we need to do now is to provide a semantic rule to allow

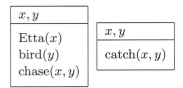

Figure 10.26
The DRSs for the left- and right-hand side of the conditional.

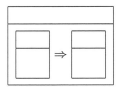

Figure 10.27
Representing conditionals in a DRS.

us to construct DRSs for conditional sentences, and this is shown in Figure 10.28. We can read this rule as follows:

- Insert two DRSs within the larger DRS linked with $\Rightarrow$.
- Process the first sentence inside the lefthand DRS.
- Process the second inside the righthand DRS.

Note that we include the VP nodes under the S nodes in these rules, even though the rule doesn't change these parts of the tree at all (we have rules for intransitive and transitive verbs that do that). We include these nodes here as a way of imposing an *order* on the application of the semantic rule for *if* with respect to those for processing verbs. We do not want the rule for processing verbs to be used before this rule for *if*. This is because otherwise, the semantic condition imposed by the verb (e.g. bark(x) or chase((x),(y))) will not appear in the correct DRS. These would appear outside the conditional DRS structure, in the main box. This would allow for an interpretation of a sentence like (32) where this sentence would be true *only if* a dog did indeed bark, which is clearly wrong.

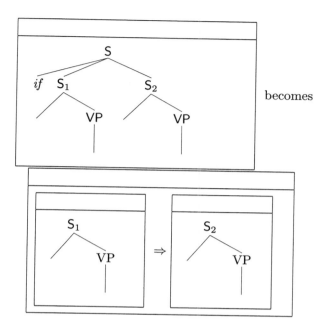

Figure 10.28
The semantic rule for *if*.

(32)   If a dog barked, Etta slept.

We leave it as an exercise to the reader to satisfy themselves that this
would happen if we could apply the rule for verbs before that for *if*.
The above rule for *if* ensures that we can apply this rule only if the VP
nodes are still intact. And they are still intact only if the rules for verbs
haven't been applied yet. This stops us from ever constructing a DRS for
sentence (32) that looks like that in Figure 10.29. Note, however, that
we *do* allow NP nodes to be processed before *if*. The reason for allowing
this will become clear in chapter 11, when we discuss an important type
of ambiguity known as scope ambiguities (see p.284).

In general then, composing the logical form of a conditional, once split
into two DRSs, will proceed much as if the sentences were in isolation or
part of a discourse. Let's go through the analysis for the sentence *If Etta
chased a bird, Etta caught the bird*. In Figure 10.30, we don't show the
sentence-internal structure in the first step. We have four choices as to

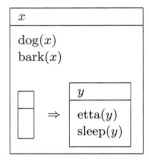

Figure 10.29
A bizzarre interpretation of sentence (32).

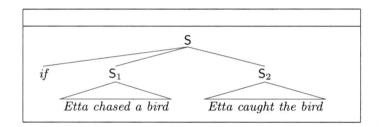

Figure 10.30
Step one of constructing the DRS of a conditional.

what our first move might be: we could apply the rule for proper names
to the *Etta* in the first sentence, or we could apply it to *Etta* in the second
sentence, or we could apply the rule for indefinites to the NP *a bird*, or
we could apply the rule for *if*. For now, we'll choose to apply the rule
for *if* first (analyses which adopt one of the alternative first steps is left
as an exercise to the reader, but see p. 11.3 for more discussion). This
move will break up the conditional and place each sentence within its
own box. See Figure 10.31. Now processing of the LHS in this example
will be much like others we've seen before; see for example Figure 10.11.
We'll omit all these steps. One comment is necessary. As you will see
in Figure 10.32, we have placed the referent introduced by the left-hand
sentence into the top of the left-hand box. This mirrors our rules for
translation within the main DRS.

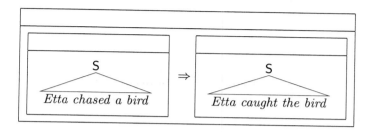

Figure 10.31
Step two of constructing the DRS of a conditional.

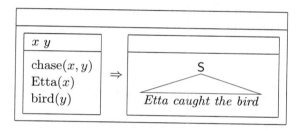

Figure 10.32
Step two of the translation of a conditional.

We can now go ahead and process the second sentence from the conditional. The main question that will arise now is in the instructions to reuse referents associated with *Etta* and *the bird*. For now, to make things as simple as possible, we assume that one can reuse a discourse referent that was introduced *anywhere* within the DRS so far. We'll present more sophisticated constraints on which discourse referents you can legitimately reuse in section 14.2, and these more complex constraints will better capture some of the linguistic data. But for now, let's assume you can reuse any discourse referent in the DRS. Under that rule, we can process the second DRS to produce the final DRS shown in Figure 10.33. This is not the only DRS because, for the reasons discussed in section 10.2 above, we have a choice about how we choose to arrange the co-reference. This representation uses the "obvious" correspondence, in which both occurrences of *Etta* have to refer to the same individual. Other DRSs also arise as possible analyses of this sentence from apply-

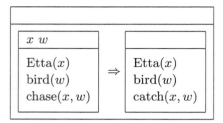

Figure 10.33
The final DRS of the conditional.

ing the semantic rules in a different order. This will be studied in detail in section 11.3 on p. 11.3.

Exercises

Exercise 10.18: Work through this example completely.

Exercise 10.19: Produce a DRS for *If Etta chases a bird, she catches it*. If you take *Etta* and *she* to co-refer, is there any model with respect to which this DRS is true and the DRS we constructed in Figure 10.33 for *If Etta chased a bird, Etta caught the bird* is false, or *vice versa*?

There is a very close connection between conditional statements and so-called UNIVERSAL sentences involving the word *every*. To see this, consider the following examples. Ask yourself the question, can one of these sentences be true and the other false?

(33)   If a farmer owns a Mercedes, the farmer is rich.

(34)   Every farmer who owns a Mercedes is rich.

The consensus is that these two sentences are true under exactly the same conditions. If that is so, then our analysis of sentences involving *every* should look similar in many respects to those for conditionals. We've seen semantic rules for other determiners, and so we may well expect similarities between them and the semantic rule for *every*. Bearing those facts in mind, look at Figure 10.34.

Relative to the previous determiner rules, what's different about this rule is that, like the *if*-rule, it takes a tree apart and arranges the subparts

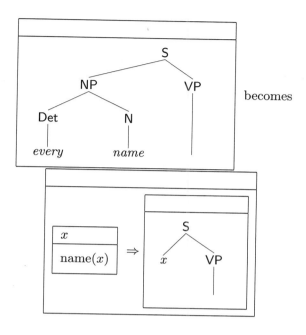

Figure 10.34
The semantic rule for *every*.

in smaller DRSs. Processing then continues within the smaller DRSs. Figure 10.35 gives a complete sequence of steps in the processing of *Every dog barked*.

Exercises

Exercise 10.20: Sketch a model in which *Every dog barked* is false, and one in which it's true.

Exercise 10.21: The syntactic rule for conditionals given above allows some pretty bizarre sentences, particularly if you use the rule for *if* a lot. Find a few such examples. What is your judgment of their grammaticality?

Exercise 10.22: What are your intuitions about the truth or otherwise of conditionals in which the first sentence is not true?

Exercise 10.23: The semantic rule for *every* can only allow us to interpret configurations in which that word appears in the subject NP (i.e. the one directly below S). Sketch a semantic rule to provide an interpretation of NPs appearing as objects of transitive verbs (i.e. appearing next to V1). Can you then give an interpretation for *Every dog chases every cat*? Explain your reasoning.

Exercise 10.24: How does the interpretation of conditionals above compare with human interpretations of the four-card problem?

Exercise 10.25: We haven't given an analysis for *Etta is angry*. What rules would you need to supply to do this? Hints: *Angry* is an adjective, and you will need a new syntactic rule to introduce *is* and the category of adjectives.

Exercise 10.26: Consider the sentence *Every angry dog barked*. Write down a DRS and construct models that should allow you to assess whether the DRS is a good logical form of the sentence (i.e. the models that make the DRS true should match your intuitions about how the world would be if the sentence were true). Do the semantic rules that you devised for the previous exercise allow you to construct the DRS you have written from the syntactic tree? Why not?

Exercise 10.27: Compare the interpretations of the two sentences *If a dog chased a bird, a dog caught a bird* and *If a dog chased a bird, the dog caught the bird*. What relationship holds between models in which these sentences are true, and why?

10.3   Evaluation of the Grammar

In this section, we assess how good our grammar is and in what respects it's deficient. First, let's accentuate the positive aspects of the grammar we've developed so far. One thing we can do is generate simple discourses, a little like children's stories, although with no claim to any literary merit. Allowing a few more words into the grammar, one such story is:

(35)   Etta loved Pip. He loved her. If Etta chased a bird, she caught it. If Etta caught a bird, Pip ate it. Etta chased a bird. She caught the bird. Pip ate it.

We can tie together the uses of different referring expressions within the sentence. Even though the grammar is much too liberal in the ways it allows us to do that, we can still be confident that the interpretation of those referring expressions that is obvious to us humans is also an interpretation that is allowed by the grammar.

A second positive point is that, while we have restricted ourselves to a very small number of words, and syntactic and semantic rules, they are still quite general in what they could potentially cover. In case you are doubtful about this claim, consider the following exercise.

Exercise

Exercise 10.28: Here is a model:

j p g r s_1 s_2 s_3 s_4
song(s_1) song(s_2) song(s_3) song(s_4)   Yesterday(s_1) Tell-me-why(s_2)   Yellow-Submarine(s_3) Norwegian-Wood(s_4)   write(j, s_2) write(j, s_4) write(p, s_1) write(p, s_3)   John(j) Paul(p) George(g) Ringo(r)   beatle(j) beatle(p) beatle(g) beatle(r)   sing(p, s_1) sing(j, s_2) sing(j, s_4) sing(r, s_3)

You should now be in a position to apply the grammar rules so as to decide the truth or otherwise of sentences and discourses such as *Paul wrote a song. George sang it.* And *If a Beatle sang a song he wrote it.* Stipulate which grammar rules you need, and use these to produce DRSs for these discourses. Produce groups of sentences which are true or false according to this model.

There are many aspects of natural languages that we have not been able to cover, even within the limitations set out in section 8.5. We can cover only simple sentences. This means that we are unable to process sentences like *The dog that caught the bird barked*, as well as many other kinds of sentences. In general, it seems to be the case for English that we can give quite a thorough characterization of its syntax only using context-free rules. Below, we'll mention some other phenomena that are of importance to cognitive science, but for which this simple kind of rule seems inadequate.

Syntax

Within linguistics, a substantial effort has been devoted over the last forty years to the description of the syntax of human languages, looking in particular at variations seen within and across languages, and attempting to account for that variation by means of general principles. You'll notice that, above, we've talked of phrases within a language such as English. There's a fair amount of evidence to suggest that phrases of different kinds (e.g. noun phrases and verb phrases) share a number of properties: for example, they both contain a "most important" element (its HEAD, the noun or the verb) and that element determines to a large extent the syntactic configurations within which the corresponding phrase can occur.

Across languages, substantial progress has been made in describing variations in word order. In Japanese, for example, one can make the single statement that the head of a phrase always occurs last, while in English (with some qualifications), verbs come first in their phrases while nouns come last. The sort of grammar rules we have used make it difficult to express these kinds of generalizations. They also make it difficult to state constraints that hold between different words in a sentence. As we saw in section 8.5, the form of the verb "to be" varies according to the subject: If the subject is *I*, the verb must appear in the form *am*, and so on. Our sentence rule (S → NP VP) doesn't express this fact; it says any way of being a noun phrase followed by any way of being a verb phrase is a legitimate sentence. This means that sentences like *A dog chase a bird* are allowed by the grammar, when for most dialects of English they should be ruled ungrammatical. As we'll see in chapter 14, we can improve on this situation by annotating our syntactic categories.

A theme running through the study of grammars of natural languages has been the question of the power of the formal apparatus required to describe their syntax and semantics. We saw above (on p.155) that systems without memory, or finite state machines, are unable to describe the kind of embedding seen in sentences such as

(36)   The person that the dog that <u>the cat chased</u> bit snores.

Finite state machines may be drawn as we saw in Figure 6.1, and the sequences such machines generate can also be characterized by rewriting rules of the form

(37) $X \rightarrow yZ$

where y is a word to be output and Z is a single symbol from the grammar.

The grammar rules we have used, so-called CONTEXT-FREE phrase structure rules, are able to describe the embedding seen above. Notice in general terms, we would want to write rules whose overall effect is the same as the rule shown here:

(38) $S \rightarrow \ldots S \ldots$

Because there is material to both sides of the symbol S, we can't write this rule in the format of example (37). In the jargon, this kind of rule allows CENTER EMBEDDING.

Over the course of the last couple of decades, there's been a lot of discussion as to whether the syntax of human languages can be completely described in terms of only context-free rules. It now seems quite clear that there are phenomena that require greater than context-free power. To give one example, some sentences in Dutch, such as the translation of *I saw Jan feed the hippos*, require a configuration in which parts of different sentences are interspersed with one another. This situation is shown in (39).

(39)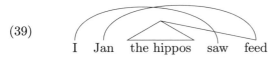

We have drawn in lines linking subjects and objects to the verbs they form sentences with. You can see from this that we are no longer dealing with the kind of tree that our grammar rules have allowed. In order to generate such configurations, a more powerful type of rule, called CONTEXT-SENSITIVE rules, are required. (See the glossary for information about such rules.)

A consequence of this discovery is that, even though the simpler rule format may be sufficient for English, human languages in general are more complex than can be described using a context-free grammar. On this basis, we can argue that the human processor in language is able to deal with the more complex, context-sensitive rule format.

Semantics

Just as our simple grammar will not cover most of the syntactic phenomena in English, there is a large amount of work in the area of semantics that we have ignored. In some cases, we have to do this because of the simple nature of the models we've used. If a model only represents a snapshot of the world, or of some state of affairs, we won't be able to talk about what was true in the past, or what might be true in the future, or about situations that are ongoing, e.g. *building a house*, but that are not true at the very moment our snapshot depicts. These issues, referred to under the heading of TENSE and ASPECT (see section 16.4), have been crucial in the development of apparatus for the description of the semantics of natural language.

Exercises

Exercise 10.29: Our models are very simple collections of facts. In what way does ignoring tense assist that simplification? Put another way, what information would have to be present in our models in order to correctly distinguish between *Pip is barking* and *Pip was barking*?

Exercise 10.30: Why can't we use the grammar as it stands to model negative sentences *Pip doesn't bark* or ones involving *or*, e.g. *either Pip is in the park or Etta is in the park*?

Much of current research in semantics develops models of the meaning of natural language sentences and logics that describe those models. Chapters 14 to 17 will go into greater detail about some of these topics.

To review the contents of this chapter, we have developed a system that is able to:

- construct a collection of English sentences, and

- provide an interpretation for those sentences as DRSs.

We have examined what predictions this system makes, for example, in the interpretation of discourse, and what elements may (or may not) refer to the same individual. In the next chapter we will turn to the question of ambiguity in human languages.

10.4   Further Reading

The theory of semantics we have presented here is part of a much larger area of linguistics known as *formal semantics*. The concept of compositionality, which we discussed in section 10.1, is fundamental to all theories of formal semantics. The Gamut books provide an extensive introduction to formal semantics, and in particular to an alternative way of modeling semantics known as Montague Grammar:

- Gamut, L. T. F (1991a). *Logic, Language, and Meaning, Volume I: Introduction to Logic.* Chicago: University of Chicago Press.
- Gamut, L. T. F (1991b). *Logic, Language, and Meaning, Volume II: Intensional Logic and Logical Grammar.* Chicago: University of Chicago Press.

Gamut is a pseudonym for Johan van Benthem, Jeroen Groenendijk, Dick de Jongh, Martin Stockhof, and Henk Verkuyl.

The following is also a very good introduction to formal semantics:

- Chierchia, Gennaro, and Sally McConnell-Ginet (1990). *Meaning and Grammar: An Introduction to Semantics.* Cambridge: MIT Press.

As we mentioned in the previous chapter, the particular formal semantic approach that we take in this book is based on *Discourse Representation Theory*, or DRT. For a comprehensive introduction to DRT, see Kamp and Reyle (1993):

- Kamp, Hans, and Uwe Reyle (1993). *From Discourse to Logic: Introduction to Modeltheoretic Semantics of Natural Language, Formal Logic, and Discourse Representation Theory.* Dordrecht: Kluwer Academic.

This book devotes a lot of attention to the semantics of *pronouns* (see section 10.2), and our analysis of pronouns in this book will be based on this work.

The interpretation of DRSs that we give in this book is taken from Kamp and Reyle (1993). However, an alternative interpretation within the framework of *dynamic semantics* is also possible. Van Eijk and Kamp (1997) provide an excellent overview of dynamic semantics:

- Van Eijk, Jan, and Hans Kamp, "Representing Discourse in Context," in J. van Benthem and A. ter Meulen (eds.) (1997). *Handbook of Logic and Language.* Amsterdam: Elsevier, 179–237.

In section 10.2 we discussed the semantic analysis of the definite article *the.* Definites have been studied extensively over the years: Russell and Stalnaker offer seminal papers—and conflicting views—on the semantics of definites from the perspective of philosophy of language:

- Russell, Bertrand (1905). "On Denoting," *Mind*, 14, 479–493.
- Stalnaker, Robert (1978). "Assertion," in P. Cole (ed.) *Syntax and Semantics, Volume 9: Pragmatics.* New York: Academic Press.

A more recent analysis of the definite that brings these two conflicting views together, and that also offers a more linguistic perspective, is described in the following book by Gennaro Chierchia:

- Chierchia, Gennaro (1995). *Dynamics of Meaning: Anaphora, Presupposition, and the Theory of Grammar.* Chicago: University of Chicago Press.

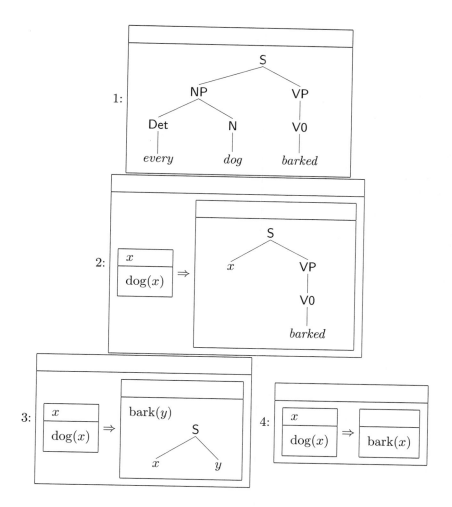

Figure 10.35
The DRS of *every dog barked*.

11 Ambiguity

AMBIGUITY refers to a situation in which a word or larger unit can have more than one interpretation. Or to put it another way, it's a situation where a linguistic expression gives rise to more than one meaning representation (or DRS). In this chapter we examine the kinds of ambiguity seen in human languages, and ways of modeling these within the grammar we've seen so far.

A concept closely related to ambiguity is that of VAGUENESS. But linguists differentiate between the two. Like ambiguity, vagueness can make it difficult to determine what to do with a particular input based on its meaning representation. But vagueness does not give rise to multiple semantic representations in the way that ambiguity does. For example, what exactly is the threshold distance between the restaurant and theater that one needs to assume in answering the question (1)?

(1)   Is there a restaurant close to the theater?

Well, it depends. Is the questioner on foot? If so, and if he's at the theater and asking the question because he wants to find somewhere to eat, then the distance you might consider would probably be smaller than if he has a car and is prepared to drive to the restaurant. There is no single, absolute distance that we can associate with the meaning of the word "close." In this sense, its meaning is vague. But we nevertheless would not want to construct multiple logical forms to the question (1). At most, we would want to include an argument to the predicate "close" that stands in for the context in which the word is used (and from which we could perhaps determine more precisely the distances being talked about); and when nothing is known about the context, that argument isn't filled in. Since we don't derive more than one logical form, this is an example of vagueness, but not of ambiguity. Needless to say, it's sometimes difficult to distinguish ambiguity from vagueness. See section 11.6 for further discussion.

Typically ambiguity will be the result of there being a choice of syntactic and/or semantic rules to apply. Apart from the semantic rule for *if* (see section 10.2), we've been careful so far to set things up so that you haven't had to worry about situations in which more than one rule can apply (or to arrange things so that the order in which we used rules

wasn't important). On the other hand, we did see, in the last chapter
for example, how using the rules for pronouns and proper names often
led (incorrectly in some cases) to a choice of discourse referents to reuse,
with corresponding differences in interpretation. The computer science
term NONDETERMINISM is often used to describe a situation where we
have a free choice between rules. Here we will see cases where different
choices of rules lead to alternative interpretations of words and larger
units. We'll also see some perhaps surprising things that the grammar
of the previous chapter predicts.

As an indication of the sorts of topics we'll discuss here, we'll start
with a few examples. Think carefully about them before reading on and
try to locate the source of the ambiguity. Think carefully about how
you would interpret these sentences *if you hadn't been told that they are
ambiguous*. The following classified advertisement was reported in the
The Scotsman, November 22, 1996.

(2)   For sale. Four poster bed. 101 years old. Perfect for antique
         lover.

And here's an old joke:

(3)   Every day a pedestrian gets knocked down on Princes Street,
         and he's getting really fed up about it.

Here are some newspaper headlines and other examples:

- Iraqi head seeks arms.
- Neighbors complain about sex between parked cars.
- Queen Mary to have bottom scraped.
- Tonight's program discusses stress, exercise, and sex with Celtic forward Scott Wedman, Dr. Ruth Westheimer, and Dick Cavett.
- Visiting relatives can be boring.
- Vegetarians don't know how good meat tastes.
- Remove and examine the screw that holds the wing on. If it's worn, replace it.

Finally, consider how you would interpret the words *service today* if
you found them on a note

- pinned to a church door,

- on a post-it on a VCR,
- on a post-it on a locker in a tennis club, or
- pinned to a ewe's stall.

11.1 Categorial Ambiguity

Words with the same form may often be associated with different syntactic categories, and we'll call this situation CATEGORIAL AMBIGUITY. The word *service* above provides an example. In the sentences (4), we can see the word being used as a noun and transitive verb, respectively (we have used present tense in the second example to ensure that the form of the word is the same in both sentences).

(4) a.   A minister conducted a service.

b.   Repairmen service radios

We can model this kind of ambiguity straightforwardly in our grammar; for example, using the rules:

(5)   N → *service*

(6)   V1 → *service*

As a consequence of this way of modeling categorial ambiguity, each time we draw a tree for a sentence involving a word that is ambiguous in this way, we will in fact remove the ambiguity, through having to choose a category with which to label the word. So if we were to draw a tree for the first example above, it would have to contain in part the subtree shown below:

(7)

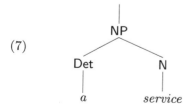

In fact, we used just this kind of justification above when we decided that one instance of the word was a verb and the other a noun. As we'll see in section 12.1, this observation will come in useful when we talk about automatically determining trees for sentences of English. Categorial ambiguity may also be present when a sentence as a whole is associated with more than one tree, a situation discussed in section 11.4.

In this instance, the different categories for *service* are associated with different meanings: when a minister conducts a service, something different happens from when a repairman services a TV. It would be highly unusual to describe the situation of a minister officiating in worship as the minister "servicing a congregation." We'll look at ambiguities involving the meaning of words next.

Exercises

Exercise 11.1: Find other examples of words that can be of more than one syntactic category. Construct examples in which each word is forced to have a particular category. Can you find examples where this doesn't happen? Is there always a difference in meaning associated with the different categories?

Exercise 11.2: Repeat the above exercise using words taken from a few sentences in a novel or newspaper article.

11.2   Sense Ambiguity

Consider the word *set*, in the sentence *Let's finish the set*. If you hear this sentence out of context, there are a variety of ways you could interpret it. In particular, the word *set* could mean any of

- a part of a game of tennis,
- a stage or film set,
- a session of music, or
- a part of a dance,

and quite possibly many other things. In certain contexts, for example when two musicians are speaking, one interpretation is more likely than others. In other cases, things are less clear. In the example

(8)   Iraqi head seeks arms.

the words *head* and *arms* are ambiguous in their meaning. The first can refer to a body part or to a head of state (and this doesn't exhaust the possibilities), while the second can refer to a body part and also to weapons. We'll term this phenomenon SENSE AMBIGUITY, as we have a choice about which sense of a word to use in our interpretation.

In constructing DRSs so far, we have tacitly assumed that each word has a unique predicate symbol associated with it. These examples show quite clearly that this assumption is false. To model this kind of ambiguity, we need to have ways of providing predicate symbols for representing the meanings of words. We could do this quite simply by annotating our rules, for example:

- N → *head* where the predicate symbol used in logical form may be "head-of-state" or "head-of-body" or....
- N → *arms* where the predicate symbol used in logical form may be "weapon" or "arms-of-body" or....

A consequence of this, following this proposal through, is that the symbols we use to represent individual words must also be the symbols that occur in models (cf. section 9.3).

Exercises

Exercise 11.3: If we adopted the proposal above, how many interpretations will the sentence *head seeks arms* have?

Exercise 11.4: Go through a few sentences from a novel, a newspaper article, or these notes, finding as many instances as possible of words that have more than one meaning. How many of those meanings are relevant to the context of the discussion? Are there any cases where you think it reasonable to believe the author was aware of the ambiguity?

As we commented above, categorial ambiguity often goes together with sense ambiguity. In examples like

(9)   The planes bank as they come in to land.
(10)   The bank will refuse checks not drawn in U.S. Dollars.

the syntactic context helps us to sort out whether *bank* is a noun or a verb, and the corresponding choices in interpretation are narrowed (but not removed entirely).

So in order to model the kinds of ambiguity discussed so far, we can introduce rules to our grammar that specify a word's meaning, and there may be many rules for a particular form to indicate different possible syntactic categories. The following example is not exhaustive for the case of *bank*:

(11)   N → *bank* with predicate symbol "river-bank" or "financial-institution."

(12)   V0 → *bank* with predicate symbol "tilt."

(13)   V1 → *bank* with predicate symbol "deposit" or "cause-to-tilt."

The predicate "cause-to-tilt" is intended to capture the use of *bank* in sentences like *The pilot banked the plane.*

Exercise

Exercise 11.5: Find other examples to do with *bank*.

Recalling the discussion of section 10.1, the existence of sense ambiguity offers further evidence in favor of the claim of arbitrariness of the form-meaning relation at the lexical level. The senses or meanings that are related to some particular form need not be, and typically are not, related to each other. As far as the modern user of English is concerned, there is no connection between the sense of *service* meaning "act of worship" and that meaning "repair."

The kinds of ambiguities we've seen so far have just been to do with the behavior of individual words. We'll now turn to other forms of ambiguity that result from choices in the application of semantic rules, and of syntactic rules involving units larger than the word. The first example we'll see has in fact been a prediction of our grammar all along.

11.3   Scope Ambiguity

Consider the tree shown in Figure 11.1. With appropriate rules for *man* and *woman*, this sentence is well-formed according to our grammar rules.

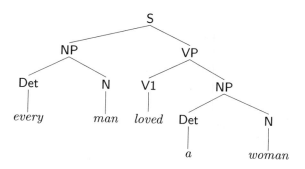

Figure 11.1
The syntactic structure of *Every man loved a woman*.

What semantic rules can we apply at this point? The answer is that we have a choice. We can either apply the rule for *every* or that for *a*. So how do the choices we make affect the final DRS that's constructed? Let's see what happens if we use the rule for *every* first. This will result in the DRS shown here:

(14)

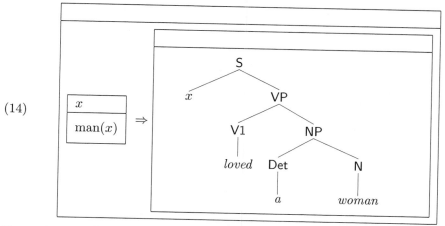

Processing can then continue within the smaller right-hand box, to yield:

(15)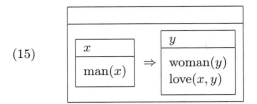

On the other hand, if we use the rule for *a* first, our first two steps will produce the DRSs below:

(16)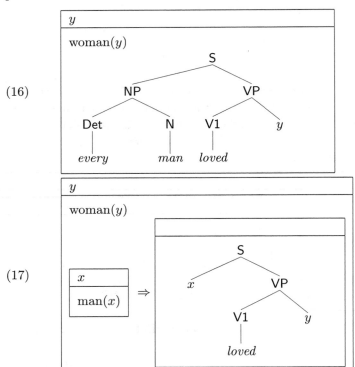

(17)

This process will ultimately yield this DRS:

(18)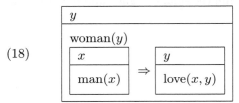

So are the two DRSs that we have computed different? Will there be models that make one true and not the other? The crucial difference is that in the second case the condition associated with *woman* appears in the outermost box. So a model that makes this DRS true must contain at least one individual of which the condition "woman" holds. Furthermore, the other condition must also hold, namely that for every way of making the LHS in the implication true there must also be a way of making the RHS true. In this case, then, our choice of individual for y is fixed with respect to choice of individuals associated with the condition "men." In other words, there should be (at least) one woman that all the men love.

Turning to the second DRS that we computed, things are different. The condition "woman" ends up in the box on the RHS. Our rules for $\Rightarrow$ say that any way of making the LHS true should also be a way of making the RHS true. In this case, for each way of being a man, you have to be able to find a woman, such that the man loves the woman.

In the light of the previous discussion, consider the following models:

(19)

m_1 m_2 m_3 w_1 w_2 w_3
$woman(w_1)$ $woman(w_2)$ $woman(w_3)$
$man(m_1)$ $man(m_2)$ $man(m_3)$
$love(m_1, w_1)$
$love(m_2, w_2)$
$love(m_3, w_3)$

(20)

m_1 m_2 m_3 w_1 w_2 w_3
$woman(w_1)$ $woman(w_2)$ $woman(w_3)$
$man(m_1)$ $man(m_2)$ $man(m_3)$
$love(m_1, w_1)$
$love(m_2, w_1)$
$love(m_3, w_1)$

(21)

m_1 m_2 m_3 w_1 w_2 w_3
$woman(w_1)$ $woman(w_2)$ $woman(w_3)$
$man(m_1)$ $man(m_2)$ $man(m_3)$
$love(m_1, w_3)$

The first model here makes the first DRS we computed true: For each man we can find a woman that he loves. It doesn't make the second DRS true: We can't find a single woman such that all men love that woman. On the other hand, this last condition is met by the second model, which therefore makes the second DRS true. The last model fails to make either DRS true. From these models we can see that any model that makes the second DRS true will also make the first DRS true. A further case is worth considering, namely that where the model contains no men and no women. That model makes the first DRS, but not the second, true.

Some people find it difficult to see that there is more than one interpretation for sentences like this. You may like to think about the following sentences:

(22)   Every worker must take part in a fire drill next week.

(23)   Every student has to come to a meeting next week.

(24)   Every person in the village has a friend (in the subpost-mistress).

(25)   Every officer was present at the arrest of a highly dangerous criminal.

On the other hand, a sentence such as

(26)   Every student has access to a state-of-the-art computer.

seems to require an interpretation where there is not just one computer.

The kind of ambiguity we have investigated here is termed SCOPE AMBIGUITY. It is more pervasive than you might at first think; any sentence involving more than one determiner is potentially ambiguous with respect to scope. Consider the following examples:

(27)   Three lawyers bought a house.

(28)   Three lawyers bought two houses.

How many lawyers and houses could there be in each case?

Exercises

Exercise 11.6: Provide the details of how the logical forms for the two sentences above are composed.

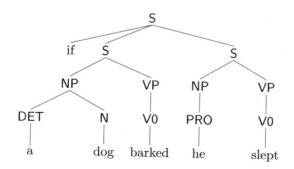

Figure 11.2
The syntactic structure of the sentence (29).

Exercise 11.7: What does the phrase *a certain* do, in *Every man loves a certain woman?*

Exercise 11.8: What does the phrase *each* do, in *Three lawyers bought a house each?*

Sentences involving the word *if* can also exhibit scope ambiguities. Recall from section 10.2 that the semantic rule for *if* is like *every*, in that it introduces a conditional DRS structure. Now consider the following sentence:

(29)   If a dog barked, he slept.

The syntactic structure for (29) is given in Figure 11.2. Note that there is a choice of rules that we can apply first: the one for the indefinite article *a*, or the one for *if*. If we apply the rule for *a* first, we obtain ultimately the DRS on the LHS in Figure 11.3. If we apply the rule for *if* first, we get the DRS on the RHS.

These DRSs are satisfied by different models. The LHS DRS can be paraphrased as: there is a dog such that if he barked, he also slept. It's true in a model, for example, where there are lots of dogs that bark but don't sleep, and yet there is one dog that does neither—this latter dog makes the DRS true. The RHS DRS is true only if *every* dog that barked also slept, and so this DRS wouldn't be true in the model we've just described. However, unlike the LHS DRS, it would be true in a model that contained no dogs! These different interpretations of the

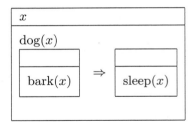 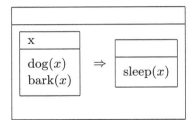

Figure 11.3
Two possible DRSs for sentence (29).

same sentence are just another example of a scope ambiguity.[22] Recall from section 10.2 that our semantic rule for *if* was stipulated so that it must apply before the rule for verbs, but no order was imposed relative to the rules for NPs. The need to capture scope ambiguities within the grammar was the motivation behind this.

Exercise

Exercise 11.9: Sentence (29) exhibits a scope ambiguity where the two alternative interpretations have different truth conditions; i.e. they are true with respect to different models. Is the same true of the following sentence, which also exhibits a scope ambiguity?

(30)   If every dog barked, he slept.

If not, why not?

11.4   Structural Ambiguity

The ambiguities in the last section arose because we had a choice of orders in which to apply semantic rules. In this section, we will see a situation involving a choice between syntactic rules. These ambiguities will typically give rise to different trees associated with a sentence, and we call them STRUCTURAL AMBIGUITIES.

The arithmetic grammar of section 9.1 again serves as a useful point of departure. Recall that grammar uses rules that produce expressions such as $(1 + 3) = (3 * (4 - 2))$. In the case of these arithmetic equations, their structure is worn on the sleeve, as it were. The fact that we see parentheses in the sequences of characters that the grammar allows means that we can see, in virtue of these sequences, what the grouping of elements are, and it's easy to apply the rule (which is captured in our instructions for interpreting equations) that we process the innermost set of parentheses first.

In the case of natural languages, there is nothing that corresponds in an obvious way to the parentheses, nothing to tell us explicitly how to group words into larger units (with the notable exception of punctuation, but quite often there are choices of how to group things when punctuation is absent). We can exploit the rules of the grammar to tell us how to do this. For the purposes of this discussion, we'll have to introduce a few more rules. They go like this:

(31)   V1 → *hit*

(32)   N → *hammer*

(33)   P → *with*

(34)   NP → NP PP

(35)   VP → VP PP

The symbols P and PP stand for "preposition" and "prepositional phrase," respectively.

With these rules, we can analyze a sentence such as *Etta hit the man with a hammer* in one of two ways, corresponding to the fact that there are two trees associated with the sentence.

(36)

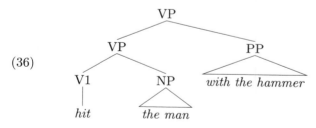

(37)

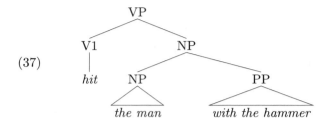

In the first tree shown here, we have used the rule that allows a PP to follow its sister VP. This structure is assumed to go together with the meaning in which Etta used a hammer to hit someone. The second tree, where the PP groups with the NP, shows the analysis whose interpretation is that Etta hit a man who had a hammer.

The example here relies on syntactic rules for phrases to induce ambiguity. In some cases, categorial ambiguity may also be involved:

(38)   Pip saw her duck.

This sentence could either mean that Pip saw an animal belonging to some female, or that Pip saw some female bob down. In the first case, we interpret *her* as a pronoun indicating possession, functioning in a manner similar to Det. In the second case, the pronouns *her* is of the kind we've seen before.

11.5   Ambiguity in the Groupings of Sounds

When we speak we don't leave gaps between the words. This means that in hearing speech we have to work out which groupings of sounds correspond to words. There is what we might call PHONETIC AMBIGUITY. Here are some examples in which things go wrong:

(39)   A: How are you?
         B: Fine. I've got a week off.
         A: Oh, I'm sorry to hear that, dear.

(40)   People can easily wreck a nice beach.

(41)   Eugene O'Neill won a pullet surprise.

(42)   A girl with colitis goes by.

(43)   I'd like to offer you a nude eel.

(44)   Gall, amant de la reine, alla, tour magnanime.
         Galamment, de l'arène á la tour Magne á Nîmes.

(45)   Ça me dit. ("That's fine for me.") Samedi.

(46)   Remember,   a spoken   sentence
         Ream ember   us spoke can   cent tense

         often   contains   many   words
         off in   men knee

         not intended   to   be heard.
         knot in ten did   bee herd.

As with sense and structural ambiguity, these examples, which have been called ORONYMS, indicate that the choice of how we group sounds into words may result in different interpretations of a sentence. The examples from French show that, in that language, there are cases where no such grouping can be definitively made. As with the other kinds of ambiguity, the different groupings result in the sentence as a whole having more than one interpretation.

We seem to work out with ease how sounds should be grouped into words in languages we speak. On the other hand, this task is at the limit of current computer technology. Until very recently, commercial automated speech recognition systems required you to leave gaps between words when you speak, effectively bracketing off each word with silence. A further consequence of speaking with gaps is that the machine doesn't have to deal with the phonetic effects that result from the sounds used in one word affecting those in another.

This completes our survey of the topic of ambiguity. Before we move on, it's worth pointing out some things that follow from our discussion. First let's consider ambiguity in another domain, that of drawings. Figure 11.4 shows a "Necker cube," an outline drawing of a cube that has two interpretations, according to which of the two vertices towards the center of the diagram we perceive as nearer. You can reinterpret the diagram, to "flip it over in your head," alternately seeing the higher of the two vertices towards the center as nearer or as further away. In thinking about the meaning of sentences, you should be able to get a similar effect. Thinking of someone saying the sentence *Take me to the bank*, you should be able to interpret what you "hear" alternately as meaning something to do with money, or something to do with rivers, or some

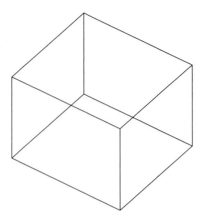

Figure 11.4
A "Necker cube."

other meaning. The effect is less striking, because it doesn't relate to an ongoing external stimulus—there is no picture that we're looking at against which to correlate our interpretation—but we venture that the effect is there all the same.

This observation provides some useful input into a longstanding question, namely the issue of the relationship between language and thought. Some people will tell you that "thought is the same as language." The existence of ambiguity provides one method of arguing that these people are wrong. We can entertain different interpretations of the same word or sentence, and that implies that there's some difference between a word or sequence of words in a sentence and the thought that that word or those words inspire. Put another way, the fact that I can choose how to interpret the word *bank* or the sentence *Peter arrived at the bank* implies that there is no simple, direct correspondence between those units of language and whatever thoughts are made of.

Ambiguity represents one crucial respect in which human languages differ from artificial languages, for example those developed in maths, logic, or computer science. If a sentence is ambiguous and intended in a certain way by a speaker, the possibility exists for a hearer to interpret in a way not intended by the speaker. So the existence of ambiguity represents in principle an impediment to communication. If language were not ambiguous, speakers would be more certain that the goal of communicating some meaning is achieved by some utterance. On the other hand, we often don't perceive ambiguity, even though we can demonstrate its existence in many cases. It's probably fair to say that the ubiquity of ambiguity in natural languages was barely suspected until people attempted to get computers to process language. We'll see in the next two chapters that ambiguity is problematic for machines, but easy for people to deal with. The obvious interest is why that should be so.

Exercises

Exercise 11.10: Go through all of the examples in chapter 11 categorizing the ambiguities you can find. Which examples do you think would be difficult to model in our grammar, and why?

Exercise 11.11: What ambiguities are present in *How did you find the steak?*

Exercise 11.12: Before reading these notes, what was your opinion about the relationship between thought and language? Where did that opinion come from? Has it been altered, and if so, how, by the discussion above?

Exercise 11.13: Some of the examples at the beginning of this chapter come from advertising. Why do you think the advertisers (or their agencies) opted to use ambiguous sentences? Find more examples of ambiguity in advertisements, song lyrics, novels, and any other instances of language that interest you. Do you notice any differences in the way ambiguity is used in these different kinds of language?

Exercise 11.14: If someone says to you *A Scottish Assembly would have the power to raise taxes* as opposed to *levy* or *vary taxes*, what could you conclude about their attitude to a Scottish Assembly, and why?

11.6   Further Reading

The literature on ambiguity is vast, largely because it is one of the main problem areas in linguistic study and linguistic processing. We mention here only very brief highlights.

At the beginning of this chapter, we discussed the distinction between ambiguity and vagueness. It's not always easy to tell the difference; Zwicky and Sadock (1975) provide a useful set of tests that can be used as diagnostics:

• Zwicky, A., and J. Sadock (1975). "Ambiguity Tests and How to Fail Them," J. Kimball (ed.). *Syntax and Semantics, Volume 4*, 1–36. New York: Academic Press.

Lexical ambiguity—of both the categorial and sense variety—is discussed in the following (where Levin focuses on verbs):

• Levin, Beth (1993). *English Verb Classes and Alternations*. Chicago: Chicago University Press.
• Pustejovsky, James (1991). "The Generative Lexicon," *Computational Linguistics*, 17.4, 409–441.
• Briscoe, Ted (1991). "Lexical Issues in Natural Language Processing," in E. Klein and F. Veltmann (eds.). *Natural Language and Speech*, Berlin: Springer-Verlag, 22 pages.

Scope ambiguities are discussed in detail in Gamut:

• Gamut, L. T. F (1991a). *Logic, Language, and Meaning, Volume I: Introduction to Logic*. Chicago: University of Chicago Press.
• Gamut, L. T. F (1991b). *Logic, Language, and Meaning, Volume II: Intensional Logic and Logical Grammar*. Chicago: University of Chicago Press.

And structural and phonetic ambiguities are discussed in O'Grady et al:

• O'Grady et al. (2004). *Contemporary Linguistics: An Introduction*. London: Longman (5th Edition).

Recently, computational linguistics has approached the problem of resolving ambiguities of various kinds through machine learning over online linguistic data. The advent of new statistical models and larger computers have made this approach possible. For a general overview of this work, consult Manning and Schütze (1999):

- Manning, Chris, and Hinrich Schütze (1999). *Foundations of Statistical Natural Language Processing.* Cambridge: MIT Press.

12 Language in Machines

We've seen in the last couple of chapters how we can give a description of some aspects of language that's formal in the sense defined on p.206. In exercises, you've practiced constructing sequences of representations that capture some aspects of the meaning of simple discourses. To a large extent, this involves the mechanical application of syntactic and semantic rules.

In this chapter, we look at ways of getting computers to do a similar kind of processing at the level of syntactic rules. We'll see a set of instructions that are sufficient (in many cases) to produce one or more trees from a given sequence of words. We'll see that ambiguity is a major problem, and demonstrate this by the exponential growth in the number of syntactic analyses of relatively simple sentences. In the next chapter, we'll use this as an argument against a simple view of how humans process language.

The large amount of background knowledge that humans bring to the task of understanding language has to a great extent frustrated attempts to use grammars of the kind we develop to produce computer systems for automatically processing language. In short, grammars of language exhibit ambiguities that humans rarely perceive, because very often all but one of the analyses that are licensed by the grammar amount to silly interpretations given general world knowledge (i.e. knowledge outside the grammar). Humans are therefore very good at resolving ambiguities, by bringing extralinguistic knowledge to bear. Machines are very poor at this task. We'll see that one engineering response to this problem is to rely on statistical properties of language. We'll use these concrete examples to reexamine the discussion of Turing machines vs. biological computers from chapter 6.

12.1   Processing Language: Parsing

In the book so far, you have often been given the task of going from a sequence of words to a DRS, and we have claimed that this process can be mechanizable. It's now time to cash out that claim. Let's look first at how we've gone about this task. The following captures the overall process:

(1)   Step 1: Produce a syntactic tree.

                   Step 2: Apply the semantic rules.

This statement isn't particularly explicit. It says that we should perform
two different tasks in a certain order, but it doesn't say how we should
go about the individual tasks. Example (2) gives details of an algorithm
that will allow us to accomplish the first of these tasks.

(2)   • Start off with a sequence of words, which we'll call the
                   INPUT, and with the current symbol set to S.

                   • Repeat the following until you've run out of words:

                     1. Choose a rule whose LHS is the current symbol.
                        Remember all of the other choices you could have
                        made, and be prepared to consider alternative choices
                        if you come back here.

                     2. Draw in the tree.

                     3. Work from left to right through the daughters.

                        –If the daughter is a word, and it's the same as the
                         first word in the input, erase that word from the
                         input, and move on to the next daughter.

                        –If it's not a word, set the current symbol to be the
                         one you're looking at and continue at step 1.

                   • If you get stuck, go back to your last choice of rule and
                   try a different one. Erase any tree you've drawn in as you
                   go, and put any words you erased from the input back
                   again.

                   • If you've completely run out of rules to try, there is
                   no analysis of the sentence (or no other analysis if you've
                   already found one).

                   • If you run out of words, and you are not looking for
                   any other categories as a result of rules already chosen,
                   the tree you have drawn so far is a possible analysis of the
                   input.

What we have here is an explicit set of instructions to cash out the first
step of the overall process—that of constructing a syntactic tree for the
sentence. This operation of assigning a tree or structure to a sequence

PN → *John*   S → NP VP
PN → *Mary*
PN → *this*   NP → PN
Det → *a*   NP → Det N
Det → *his*   NP → Det AP N
Det → *the*
Det → *my*   AP → AP A
Det → *her*   AP → A
N → *dog*
N → *boy*   VP → V0
N → *girl*   VP → V1 NP
N → *home*
N → *garden*
V1 → *is*
V1 → *loves*
V0 → *walks*
A → *angry*
A → *beautiful*

Figure 12.1
Syntactic rules used in parsing example.

of words is known as PARSING.

Let's assume that we're dealing with the grammar shown in Figure 12.1 and that our task is to analyze the sentence *Mary loves her dog.* (We'll refer to the sequence of words we have to analyze as the input). We can now use our algorithm to work out the individual steps in creating a tree for the sentence. Each step will consist of rewriting (or expanding) the symbols in the tree. Notice how we work from left to right in the tree as a consequence of step 3 of our instructions. We'll assume that the program attempts to use rules in the order shown in Figure 12.1—if you have a choice of rules and using the first one doesn't work, try the next in order from top to bottom.

Following our instructions, we'll construct a sequence of diagrams as shown in Figure 12.2. In some cases, for example in this grammar when we want to expand the symbol S, we won't have a choice between rules, and so we won't have to remember alternative rules at stage 2 in the

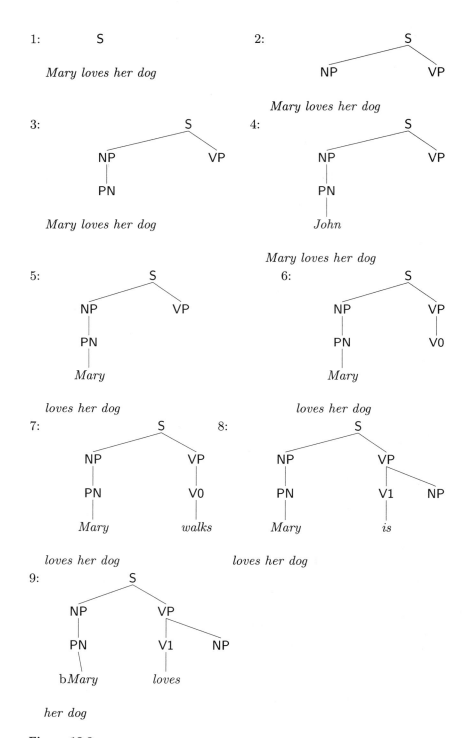

Figure 12.2
Steps of the parsing algorithm.

parse (where the stage number is as shown in Figure 12.2.) On the other hand, at stage 3, the program has to remember that there are other ways of making an NP (even though those ways won't be used at this position for this input). Likewise at stage 4, the program has to remember the other ways of making a PN. Once the program reaches stage 4, it has to check that the word introduced into the tree matches with the word (here, the first word) in the input. In this case the words don't match, and so the program has to revisit the last choice that it made. That last choice was of the rule for PN. Using the next choice of rule results in the picture shown in stage 5. The program can at this point match up *Mary* with the first word in the sequence to be analyzed, and we have come up with an analysis for the first part of the input. Following the instructions of the algorithm ("work from left to right through the daughters"), the program then switches its attention to how to expand the VP. It first considers the possibility that VP expands as V0, adding in the corresponding tree. When it gets to stage 7, it fails to match *walks* to the input and so revises its choice of rules. As *walks* is the only choice for V0, it goes back to its choice for VP. The parts of the tree introduced for the VP → V0 rule are erased as the program reconsiders its choice of rule. (Notice that several individual steps are omitted between stages 7 and 8.) In stages 9 and 10, first *is* is tried as a V1, and then *loves* is. The next steps will be to attempt to expand the NP. If it can analyze what's left (*her dog*) as an NP, then we will have an analysis for the whole sentence.

Exercises

Exercise 12.1: Complete the sequence of diagrams that will produce a syntactic tree for this example. Be certain that you notice all the blind alleys that the program gets into and that you don't skip any steps.

Exercise 12.2: Think of some other sentences that the grammar allows, and repeat the previous exercise.

The program here defines a PARSER. To be technical, it's actually a left-to-right, TOP-DOWN, BACKTRACKING parser. In situations where there is a choice of rules, i.e. where the grammar is nondeterministic, our parser actually operates in a deterministic way, by choosing the first possible

rule, and in being willing to revise that choice, or "backtrack", if things
don't work out further down the line. In general then, backtracking is
one way of taking a nondeterministic specification of a problem, and of
turning that into a deterministic process that a computer can implement.

The term "top-down" refers to a style of processing in which what
you know in general about a problem is used to search for a solution
to that problem. Our parser starts from the assumption that it's trying
to find an S and uses information from the grammar to work out what
trees might correspond to the input. Because of this, it doesn't take into
account what words are in the input until it has filled in a large part
of the tree. (It's coincidental that we also draw the tree in from top to
bottom.) A BOTTOM-UP parser starts by attempting to group the words
seen in the input into larger units, and those units into larger units still.

Suppose we were dealing with an ambiguous sentence. In that case, we
could get the parser, when it reaches the end of the sentence, to keep a
record of any complete trees found so far and then backtrack to check
whether other combinations of rules also result in an analysis.

Notice how the process of drawing the tree results in a syntactic
category being drawn above each word. In other words, one consequence
of constructing a tree is that, in the case of a word with multiple syntactic
categories, we work out which category is appropriate for the word within
the sequence of words and the tree as a whole. In other words, parsing
sometimes resolves categorial ambiguity, because alternative syntactic
categories for a given word yield no syntactic analysis of the sentence at
all.

The parser defined here only operates on a single syntactic tree at any
one time, i.e. it operates in SERIAL. One alternative is to have the parser
operate on several trees at once, i.e. in PARALLEL. In this case, every time
we have a choice of rules, rather than picking one and seeing how far we
can get with that choice, the parser keeps a record of the consequences of
using all rules. (The other instructions remain the same.) So how would
a parallel parser work on the example above?

Well, stages 1 and 2 in Figure 12.2 would be the same as for the serial
version, as there are no choices of rule in those cases. So far, then, we'd
just be working on a single tree. When we get to the next step, things
are more interesting. Because there are three ways of making an NP, we
will then produce three trees, one in which NP is a PN, and one each
for the other two rules. In the next step we'll produce a large number of

trees, thirteen to be precise:

Three because there are three ways of being a PN, plus

five because there are five ways of being a Det for the rule NP → Det N, plus

five because there are five ways of being a Det for the rule NP → Det AP N.

When we apply the rule that words introduced by a rule must match words at the right place in the input, we can junk all but one of these analyses, i.e. the one in which *Mary* appears as a PN. A parallel parser would then go on to look at all ways in which VP can be expanded, resulting in a collection of two trees. The process can then continue until we reach the end of the sentence. In the case of an ambiguous sentence, when we reach the end we'll have more than one tree in our collection.

Exercise

Exercise 12.3: Get a large piece of paper and write down all the steps that a parallel parser would go through for this example.

We've seen then how we can define a mechanical procedure that will find trees associated with sentences, and so fulfill part of the overall process of constructing a DRS. The process is laborious, but as we have specified the process in more or less complete detail, we can in principle get a computer to do this kind of processing for us. This may seem fine and dandy, but, as we'll see in the next section, ambiguity will seriously test the limits of computers and our patience.

12.2 Ambiguity

Recall the example we discussed in chapter 11, concerning the words *service today* written on a scrap of paper and then

- pinned to a church door,
- on a post-it on a VCR,
- on a post-it on a locker in a tennis club, or

- pinned to a ewe's stall.

This example is intended to highlight the immense amount of knowledge we can bring to bear in interpreting bits of language. According to the situation in which we find the words, our interpretation of them differs radically. This example gives you something of a feeling for the kinds of choices that a computer would have to consider in order to determine what the appropriate interpretation of some word is. We will deal with this topic in detail in part IV of the book. For the time being, let's note that ambiguities are pervasive in natural languages, and second that ambiguities within a single sentence interact multiplicatively. Let's look at an example:

(3)   I   1
                                      saw   ×2
                                   a star   ×2
                        with a telescope   ×2
                        with a large lens   ×2
                        with my friends   ×2

Here we have choices about, for example, what sense of a word is used in a particular case or how to group words together. The word *saw* could mean either "to have seen someone in the past," or "to cut something with a saw." Recall that in the treatment we gave in section 11.2 each sense of a word is associated with a different syntactic rule. Either "I" or "a star" had the telescope (in some sense of *had* or *have*). One interpretation might then be: "When I'm with a group of my friends, I use a telescope with a large lens to cut through a famous person." That's clearly a very odd thing to say, but it's also a possible interpretation of this sentence.

Each two-way ambiguity here doubles the number of interpretations a sentence can receive. (Note that some categorial ambiguities, for example *saw* the noun vs. *saw* the verb, may be resolved in virtue of the syntactic context in which a word appears, as discussed in the previous section and in section 11.1.) That suggests that there are at least $2^5 = 32$ interpretations of this example, and that's twice the number of words already. If we add another ambiguity, for instance by replacing *friends* with *set*, we will again at least double the number of interpretations. As you can tell, this means that even for innocuous-seeming sentences there are likely to be many analyses and, if we use a model of grammar like that developed earlier, and the parsing algorithm described above, to find those analyses, we could be in for a long wait. Let's see just how long.

Exercises

Exercise 12.4: Work out a few more of the different interpretations of this example.

Exercise 12.5: Justify the claims made about the number of ambiguities above, and categorize them in terms of the kinds of ambiguity seen in the previous chapter. Is there more ambiguity in this example than we've claimed?

Exercise 12.6: Construct other ambiguous sentences, and attempt to compute just how many ways they are ambiguous. Note which of these reading are plausible and which are absurd.

In this example (as in many others), the number of different interpretations of the sentence doubles with almost every word. This spells trouble for syntactic processing. In other words, if it takes us one unit of time, using the instructions in example (2), to produce one analysis of a sentence that is n words long, it will take something like 2^n units of time to find all analyses of the sentence. Even if one unit of time is very short (say one hundredth of a second), parsing a ten-word sentence would still require over ten seconds to produce all parses, an eleven-word sentence over twenty seconds, a twelve-word sentence over forty seconds, and so on.[23] For reference, it's worth pointing out that the previous sentence was about forty words long and so, by the reckoning above, it could take over three hundred *years* to process. Even if we take a lower figure, supposing for example that there are only five ambiguities for every fourteen words (which is the ratio seen in our example above) we still predict that it will take several minutes to process, assuming we can produce one hundred analyses every second.

What this means is that even with the fastest computer there is, we're still going to reach a limit of sentence length beyond which complete syntactic analysis will take too long. And, of course, it flies in the face of our intuition that, while it might be a bit more difficult to process long sentences, it's not *that* much more difficult. In the next chapter, we'll see other reasons for the implausibility of a model that produces all syntactic analyses in the human case. In the meantime, let's assess the current model to see what's good about it and what might be wrong with it.

12.3 Modularity

The model in example (1) has at least one thing going for it—it's very simple. In particular, we can design simple processes for parsing sentences, safe in the knowledge that the application of semantic rules can't affect the operations of the parser.

As a consequence, it's easy

- to write a computer program to use as a model, and
- to predict what the behavior of the program will be.

In the jargon, this kind of organization is MODULAR. In artificial systems, modularity is a useful property; it allows one to be more certain in one's predictions of the behavior of some systems. To take one example, consider an electric car clock. It must be connected to the car electrics to work, but should be on a different circuit from the ignition. After all, you don't want the clock to stop when the car is turned off. In a well-designed car, the operation of the clock should not affect the operation of the remainder of the car. You wouldn't want the engine to rev when you advance the time. In general then, because the relationship between the clock and the rest of the car is (or ought to be) stable, changes in the clock shouldn't affect the behavior of the rest of the car. The only thing that should affect the clock is the complete removal of power from the electrical system. On the other hand, the braking system of a car is less strictly isolated from other systems, as a result of the legal requirement that your lighting system indicate to road users behind you that you have applied your brakes. When the brake pedal is pushed, a circuit is closed to light the brake lamps, in addition to various bits of hydraulics operating so as to bring the braking surfaces into contact. According to the state of the brake pedal then, the state of both the electrical and hydraulic systems change. A consequence of the more complex arrangement is that faults can be more complex and more difficult to diagnose. It's possible to imagine a fault in the brake lamp circuit that results in the engine cutting out when the brake pedal is depressed (especially if the fuses fail to do their job). As the relationship between two components in a system becomes more intimate, so it may be more difficult to diagnose where a fault lies, and more difficult to predict that, for example, replacing a particular component will cure a fault.

As another example of a highly modular system, consider a production line. At each step in the production process the output of the previous step is altered in some way and passed on to the next step. Such a system maximizes throughput, by splitting the overall task up into very simple steps, with consequent economic benefits, including accurate estimates of the amount of time that it will take to produce one unit of output. The system specified in example (1), in which syntactic rules are used to construct a tree which is then passed along for processing using the semantic rules, clearly falls under the production line model. Where our system seems to break down is that the syntactic part of the system has to do too much work—we can't guarantee that it will finish within a reasonable time.

An example of a much less modular system is the production of a book with multiple authors. As the text develops, one author may say to another, "I don't like what you've done here—rewrite it." It may be the case that the authors have to negotiate amongst themselves in order to reach a decision about the text. In a piece of text on which a group of people have worked closely, it may be impossible to decide which author is responsible for a certain piece of text.

Relative to the model of example (1), a less modular system would allow the application of semantic rules to affect the operations of the parser. A famous example of this is a program called SHRDLU. In processing sentences that are potentially ambiguous, such as *Put the red block on the blue block next to the pyramid*, SHRDLU was able to consult its model of the world to check whether it could find a red block on a blue block, or a blue block next to the pyramid, to work out which grouping of words is appropriate.

As an engineering consideration then, modularity is a useful property of systems, but strict modularity of the production line model may not always be achievable. In the case of cars, the braking and electrical systems have to be linked in some way in order to comply with the law. In the case of artificial processing of human language, strict modularity seems to be ruled out because of the consequences of ambiguity. In the next chapter, we'll see a human perspective on modularity, and results from psychological experimentation that indicate what kinds of modularity may exist in humans.

12.4   Processing with Semantic Rules

For completeness, we'll give a brief description here of an algorithm for processing with semantic rules. With syntactic rules, we construct trees from words. To use a term from computer science, the "data structures" we use there are very simple: symbols for words and syntactic categories, and branches that link such symbols. In the case of semantic rules, the process is rather more complex, most notably in the way in which we decide whether or not a particular rule can apply.

The following instructions approximate one way of automatically applying the semantic rules:

Repeatedly do the following, until you end up with a DRS that contains no tree.

If you're looking at a DRS containing a tree T,

- choose a semantic rule, with tree t in the LHS box;
- if T matches t at some node,
    - find the predicate symbols of any words,
    - add in appropriate conditions and discourse referents as specified in the RHS box, and
    - delete that part of T that corresponds to t, replacing it with the tree t' that's in the RHS box.

In order to make these instructions more explicit, we'd have to say what is meant by "contains," "matches at some node," and "add in conditions ...as specified in the RHS box." The notion of matching should also make certain that when we see a referent in the LHS of a rule, rather than a symbol from the syntactic rules, a referent indeed appears within the analysis we're processing.

Exercises

Exercise 12.7: Try to make "add conditions ... as as specified in the RHS box" more explicit.

Exercise 12.8: Apply the above programs for parsing syntax and applying semantic rules, to construct a DRS for the sentence *Mary loves a dog*.

You'll recall that there are some semantic rules (for example, those for *every* and *a*) that interact; if one could apply one or other of the rules, the order in which you apply them is significant—the different orders give rise to different interpretations. So the semantic rules can themselves introduce ambiguity. In this case we can do the same thing as we did for alternative syntactic rules: remember the other choices of rules you could have made and be prepared to use the other ones. In other words, we could use a backtracking processor that remembers alternative rules for later investigation.

12.5   Applications of Language Technology

Demand for automatic processing of language is increasing with the amount of text in electronic form. There are billions of words out in cyberspace, putting considerable economic pressure for progress in the automatic processing of language. Companies have important information "locked away" in reports and other texts in natural languages. If we could process those reports in one of the ways mentioned above, the information in them could be accessed much more efficiently and effectively.

Computer processing of language also holds out the promise of offering access to electronic information by people who are unfamiliar with formal programming languages. Interacting with a computer might be a lot easier if you could talk to it in a language you already know, than if you have to learn some new, perhaps badly designed system for interacting. One of the less pleasant future scenarios is one where we live in a "technocracy" with power concentrated in the hands of the computer-literate. Using language processing to broaden access to computers may help to prevent that.

There is a third motivation for looking at technology: Successful language technology may give us clues as to how humans go about processing language. As we saw in section 5.2, our understanding of aerodynamics came in large part from studying artificial rather than natural wings. Perhaps successful language technology will help in our understanding of humans.

Once we have a model of grammar that can be manipulated by a computer, there are many uses to which automatic processing of language could be put. Even the simple grammar we've looked at so far can be exploited by systems that perform various language-based tasks. Applications that typically exploit rules of the kind we've seen so far include database query, machine translation, and dialogue systems (e.g. tutorial systems). Other applications for language technology include:

- text retrieval
- question-answering systems
- information extraction systems
- command and control
- prosthetics for speech/hearing-impaired
- text analysis
    - assessing readability
    - digesting
    - automatic categorization and indexing
    - email routing
- knowledge engineering and acquisition
    - inputting knowledge to intelligent systems
    - explaining the reasoning of intelligent systems
- computer-aided instruction
- automated customer support (e.g. by automated email replies)

Exercise

Exercise 12.9: Add to the list above.

The problem of ambiguity is a bottleneck for all of the applications we've mentioned. For some of them, to varying degrees, the problems can be lessened by limiting the domain in which the applications operate. For example, a system could only answer questions or process texts to do with a particular kind of industrial process, say welding. In that case, one needn't program the computer to understand every possible sense of the word *spot*; programming it to understand the sense of *spot* as it's used in *spot weld* will suffice (usually). You could also design a speech system that requires users to leave gaps between words, thereby eliminating some of the phonetic ambiguities that arise in continuous speech.

Exercise

Exercise 12.10: For some of these applications, it will be easier to enforce these limitations. You might like to think about which.

12.6 Nonsymbolic Approaches

At least in part because it has proved so costly to formulate rules of the kind we've looked at to cover a large amount of a language like English, and also because it has proved very difficult to find any general principles by which humans cope with ambiguity, a trend over the last twenty years has been to move away from "symbolic" approaches of the kind we've looked at in this part of the book, and towards approaches that are based on the statistical, or "nonsymbolic" analysis of large bodies of text. A contrast between these two styles of approach can be seen in two ways of attempting to translate automatically between languages. In the symbolic approach, we attempt to come up with an analysis that utilizes rules that explicitly stipulate general principles of grammar and of semantic interpretation. These rules can get quite complex precisely because of the complexities in language, including its ambiguities.

In the second, nonsymbolic case, we can sidestep the problems involved in formulating appropriate rules. Such systems can, for example, "learn" appropriate correspondences between words in different languages, and use what is learned in computing translations from one language to another. Such approaches have been used in a number of different applications, often with better performance than their symbolic counterparts.

To take a particular example, one way of translating by machine between human languages would be to set up rules for, say, English and French, such that we could create a DRS for a sentence of English and then work out to what sentence of French that DRS corresponds. This would be a symbolic approach. All the information manipulated by the system is in terms of explicit rules. An alternative, nonsymbolic approach to the problem of translation might be to look for statistical correspondence between texts that are known to be translations of one another. For example, many researchers use the Canadian *Hansard* corpus to automatically acquire a probabilistic model of English-French translations (this is a corpus of reports on parliamentary debates, where each report is written in English and in French).

An obvious question that arises is: if such approaches are technologically successful, then is this evidence that we should view human processing as being statistically based? There are a number of assumptions that lie behind this question. It assumes for example that successful technology diagnoses successful science.

Exercise

Exercise 12.11: Do you agree with this claim?

To what extent should natural language processing be modeled with statistics, and to what extent should it be modeled with symbolic rules? There are many possible answers to these questions. Let's summarize two "extreme" answers here. The view that all of language processing (and cognition more generally) can be explained in terms of statistical behavior, or in terms of groups of neuron-like units linked by connections of different weights, is one that has the apparent attraction of biological realism—the kinds of computation that happen are (in general) ones that can be performed by real neurons. Because of their statistical basis, a well-defined notion of induction from a group of cases can be applied—in other words, such systems are capable of learning regularities. Another consequence is that the categories that are induced are flexible—a word can be a better or worse translation of another, according to relative probabilities. The abilities to learn regularities and to apply categories in a fuzzy way are, for many people, important advantages of this style of computation. Because of the use of induction from data, such approaches are sometimes called EMPIRICIST. The system "knows" only what can be induced from the data.

In contrast, a RATIONALIST approach to cognition holds that human information processing is symbolic in nature, and is founded on explicitly represented rules. These rules are processed in ways that generally conform to logical laws, and can be simulated relatively directly by devices like Turing machines. What we see as statistical generalizations over behavior are in fact the result of complex interactions between many rules (and perhaps many processors, cf. modularity). To give an analogy, economic transactions are discrete—a definite amount of money is exchanged for goods or services—but give rise to complex phenomena at a macroeconomic level.

Put as barely as this, both sides have a lot of explaining to do. In section 6.2, we discussed how human information processing is implemented in terms of neurons. We also saw that giving an account of some phenomenon purely in terms of the behavior of neurons is likely to be unsatisfactory. From a symbolic point of view, it's relatively easy to give an explanation of why it is that French texts containing the word *attendu* have something in common with English texts containing the word *expected*. The words correspond to closely related mental representations (or even perhaps to the same representation), and so texts that use those words stand a better chance of being translations of one another. Notice that here we can go relatively straightforwardly from a symbolic statement of what's going on to something like a statistical prediction (even if getting all the details right might be a lengthy business). Going in the opposite direction is much more difficult. If all we have to go on is the brute fact that *attendu* correlates with *expected* with some factor, we don't have any purchase on what it is we're describing. And this link from symbolic representations to statistical correlations has in fact helped to improve language technology; the trend now in computational linguistics is to use a *combination* of symbolic techniques and statistics in so-called HYBRID models of language—the symbolic models help to provide a useful model of abstraction, which is then exploited by the statistical model to obtain better estimates of linguistic behavior from the training corpus (see below for further discussion). Statistical modeling in parsing, for example, is essential for achieving practical ambiguity resolution; one estimates the relative likelihoods for applying syntactic rules given the (parsing) context and the parser applies only the most likely rule, according to those estimates.

We also saw, in chapter 6, that there are difficulties in getting neuron-based models to process variables and structures. We've seen how we need things like variables (discourse referents) to indicate the individuals under discussion, and that we need to be able to say that two referents stand for the same individual. Similarly, we've used DRSs to represent meaning, and these have a substantial amount of internal structure, for example, boxes may appear in other boxes. At the moment, it's unclear whether such operations can be partially implemented in nonsymbolic approaches. Again, what we're missing here is a notion of abstraction, i.e. that the same function can be implemented in many different ways on different styles of computing devices, and that the function needs description just as the details of implementation do.

The same point can be made in connection with rationalist approaches; they still owe us an explanation of how it is that the kinds of representations and processes they claim to discover can be implemented in terms of the biological resources available to the human brain.

In our current state of knowledge, the conclusion of this discussion has to be unsatisfactory; we want descriptions at both the level of neural computation and more abstract functionality. At the moment, there is a large amount of work in

- combining statistical and symbolic information in processing, resulting in *hybrid* models, and
- relating more abstract functional descriptions with statistical or connectionist systems.

In fact, these two strands of work are closely related. Statistical models are constructed on the basis of counting the number of events of various kinds that have taken place: for example, one might count the number of times that *bank* is a noun vs. a verb in some online corpus. In general, choosing exactly what to count is *crucial* to acquiring a statistical model that performs well on the language processing task that you have in mind. In other words, statistical modeling is effective only if we exploit useful abstractions, which enable us to represent the sample space (and its events) in appropriate ways.

Rule-based models of language provide very detailed linguistic analyses, but are brittle and often fail to give an analysis of the data at all.

In contrast, statistical modeling tends to provide less detailed analyses, but it's more robust in that it will always gives some analysis for the linguistic data it encounters. Thus the advantages and disadvantages of these two views on language modeling seem largely complementary. And as a result, many researchers in cognitive science believe that building hybrid models of language processing may be a route forward.

Exercise

Exercise 12.12: In rejecting quantum mechanics, Einstein said, "God does not play dice with the Universe." Commentators have taken this to mean that he could not conceive of our universe as being governed by physical laws that are statistical in nature. His rejection of quantum theories was therefore based not on experimental evidence but on beliefs that come before and prejudge the bounds of explanation in science.

In what way does Einstein's opinion line up with the symbolic vs. nonsymbolic debate? What is your opinion on whether we can expect to find laws that are strictly true or false? Where does your opinion come from? What would you count as evidence for or against your opinion? Are there other beliefs you hold that are closely related to that opinion? How do these questions relate to the claim that "science chooses its own problems"?

12.7   Further Reading

The computational linguistics literature is vast. So we mention here some introductory textbooks where the ideas presented in this book are discussed in much more depth. The following focus largely on symbolic or rule-based approaches to language processing:

• Allen, James (1987). *Natural Language Understanding.* Menlo Park: Benjamin Cummings.

• Jurafsky, Dan, and James H. Martin (2000). *Speech and Language Processing.* Upper Saddle River: Prentice Hall.

We presented in this chapter just one algorithm for parsing, but there are many other varieties. Perhaps the classic reference for parsing algorithms is Aho and Ullman (1972):

- Aho, A. V., and J. D. Ullman (1972). *The Theory of Parsing, Translation, and Compiling.* Englewood Cliffs: Prentice Hall.

Although the focus of this book is the parsing of programming languages, the parsing algorithms they describe have all been applied to natural language as well.

Introductions to nonsymbolic approaches to natural language processing are given in Charniak (1993) (which focuses mainly on parsing) and Manning and Schütze (1999) (which surveys machine learning as its used in a wide variety of linguistic applications, as well as providing a comprehensive overview of the various machine learning techniques that are used):

- Charniak, Eugene (1993). *Statistical Language Learning.* Cambridge: MIT Press.
- Manning, Chris, and Hinrich Schütze (1999). *Foundations of Statistical Natural Language Processing.* Cambridge: MIT Press.

13 Language in People

In this chapter, we will review some experiments that shed light on the mechanisms that humans use to understand language. Ambiguity is an important topic again, both because humans seem to cope with it so well, and also because of the scope it provides for the psychological investigation of human processing. Other important topics are the overall design of the human processor, in particular whether and to what extent it does its processing in parallel, and whether different kinds of knowledge interact, in other words the modularity of the processor.

The experiments we discuss in this chapter complement the ones we discussed in part I. The latter were designed to discover interesting properties of human reasoning. The ones we discuss here are designed to discover interesting properties of how people process language. Once again, we see that this part of the book is about how people identify the propositions and ideas that are conveyed in a conversation, while part I was about how people reason with such propositions and ideas.

13.1 Ambiguity

One of the most striking things about human processing of language is that it works so well in the face of ambiguity. In the course of speaking and listening, people rarely notice ambiguities. On the other hand, if you go looking for ambiguities, you find them everywhere. As we saw in the last two chapters, there are many potential sources of ambiguity, and we claim innocuous-seeming sentences to be perhaps hundreds of ways of ambiguous. Still, in the task of processing language, we humans don't normally get hung up on attempting to sort out which interpretation to opt for.

How can we square these two perceptions? Is it the case that we've manufactured our ambiguities by looking at language the wrong way? Or can we demonstrate that at least some of these ambiguities are detected and processed, even if we're unaware of that processing? We'll see that the latter answer is the right one in at least some cases.

We can show that humans consider at least two of the types of ambiguity discussed in chapter 11. We'll use data from an experiment based on a technique called CROSS-MODAL PRIMING—"cross-modal" because it uses both the modalities of vision and hearing, and "priming" because it makes use of the fact that, when processing a particular word, say, *dog*, related words (such as *cat*) can be retrieved from memory faster.

In that experiment, subjects were played a tape with a sentence on it, and at some point shown some characters on a screen. They have to indicate by pressing one of two buttons whether or not the characters on the screen form a word of English. The sentence in (1) might be presented aurally, and we have also marked with $\boxed{1}$ and $\boxed{2}$ the points in the aural signal where the characters are displayed on the screen to the subject.

(1)   The gypsy read the man's palm $\boxed{1}$ for only $\boxed{2}$ a dollar because he was broke.

The word *palm* is of course sense-ambiguous: it can refer to a tree or to an area of the hand. The experiment proceeds by presenting the words *hand, tree*, other unrelated words, and sequences of characters that aren't words at all visually at one of the times marked $\boxed{1}$ and $\boxed{2}$ in the example above. The subject's task is then to judge whether they see a word of English, and their reaction time (RT)—that is, how long it takes the subject to make the required judgment—can be noted.

The results that we get from this experiment, using a variety of different sentences and tests are as follows:

• At time $\boxed{1}$, RT for related words (e.g. *hand* and *tree*) is the same, and quicker than that for unrelated words.

• At $\boxed{2}$, RT for *hand* is quicker than RT for both *tree* and unrelated words.

From the reduced reaction time, we can argue that, at point $\boxed{1}$ in processing the sentence, all of the senses of the word in question are available to the processor. The same result is obtained for words of differing syntactic categories (e.g. the noun *tyres*, which also sounds like the verb *tires*, with corresponding related words *wheels* vs. *wears out*, respectively).

This result is very important for three reasons. First, it reminds us that we have only limited introspective access to processing in the mind or brain. We may not be aware that we "access" the implausible sense for *palm* (i.e. the sense related to *tree*) in this context, but this experiment shows that we do. Second, it demonstrates that there is at least some degree of parallelism in human processing of language—we access both senses of *palm*. Finally, the sense ambiguity for *palm* is resolved very rapidly: the time between $\boxed{1}$ and $\boxed{2}$ is just a few milliseconds.

13.2 Parallelism in Syntactic Processing

The issue of whether similar parallelism exists at the level of syntactic processing has been an issue of great contention over the past couple of decades. There isn't time here to do justice to this subject, and we'll have to content ourselves with looking at just a couple of aspects of the discussion.

The following examples demonstrate the phenomenon known as GARDEN PATH SENTENCES:

(2)   The man who hunts ducks out on weekends.

(3)   The cotton shirts are made from grows in Mississippi.

(4)   The old train the young.

(5)   The daughter of the king's son loves himself.

The consensus intuition is that, on hearing such sentences, one experiences a mental hiccup. Things are going fine until you hear a word that somehow doesn't fit with the rest of the sentence. You may then have to go to a bit of effort to work out how the word does in fact fit.

Exercises

Exercise 13.1: For each of the above cases, work out which word causes the problem, and why. Rephrase the sentence so that the hiccup disappears.

Exercise 13.2: Try out some of these examples on a friend or two. Note their reactions.

Exercise 13.3: Make up some garden path sentences of your own. Can you see any variation in how strong the garden path effect is?

One way of modeling this phenomenon would be to design a parser that is only able to work on a single analysis of the input. When faced with a choice of rules, the parser chooses a rule (perhaps on the basis of a number of general principles that tell it which rule to choose). In choosing this rule (unlike the parser defined in section 12.1), the parser makes a commitment to using that rule—it is not able to backtrack and revise a previous decision. In the jargon, we've changed the processor from a nondeterministic to a deterministic one: Once a choice is made, you have to stick with it.

The behavior of such a parser will then approximate what we see in the human case. If the parser makes the wrong choice of rule, it will sooner or later come to a grinding halt. Note that this may not happen immediately. In the case of the *cotton shirts* example, the crucial choice of rule is whether to group *cotton* and *shirts* or to group *shirts are made of*. We seem to lean toward the former, and to interpret the words *are made of* as the main verb of the sentence. That is, when our parser processes the word *are*, it has already assumed that we have reached the "main" verb phrase of the sentence, rather than continuing to parse the subject noun phrase (so that *are* starts a relative clause that modifies *shirts*). We get stuck when we reach the real verb in the sentence *grows*, and this is considerably after the point at which the parser made the wrong choice.

So the phenomenon of garden path sentences might be taken as some evidence in favor of the view that humans compute a single syntactic tree when processing language. This is clearly a tempting hypothesis—it provides a very simple explanation of some striking data. The question is: can we make it stick? We'll review some alternative explanations in section 15.5 below. For the time being, note the following examples, and observe the way in which the sequence of words at the start of a sentence (in this case *Have the police*), which is ambiguous, can be disambiguated in the basis of the subsequent words:

(6)   Have the police...   eaten their supper?
                                                     come in and look around.
                                                     taken out and shot.

For example, in *Have the police eaten their supper?*, the police are the *subject* of the verb *have*. But in *Have the police come in and look around* they are the object. We can also delay the point in the sentence where this subject vs. object ambiguity is eliminated; for example, we could replace "..." to end up with a sentence *Have the police who are investigating the hideous murder come in and look around.* It may be that you "garden path" when you hear the word *look.* For some sentences, though, that effect doesn't seem to be there.

One way of eliminating processing difficulty is to eliminate the ambiguity. For example, one could eliminate the subject vs. object ambiguity in the phrase *have the police* by replacing *the police* with *they* if the meaning required is the subject one (e.g. *Have they eaten their supper?* vs. **Have them eaten their supper?*), or *them* if the meaning required is the object one (e.g., *Have them come in and look around*). But articulating sentences that generate no ambiguities is almost always impossible, and even when it is possible it's often not helpful. This is because, as these examples suggest, humans often expect to consider multiple possible analyses, and are sometimes willing to "simultaneously" entertain two different hypotheses about the organization of the sentence (although if the ambiguity isn't resolved at some point, humans encounter difficulties in processing the sentences further). The ease or difficulty that people experience in resolving ambiguities is a highly complex matter, dependent on many interacting factors: the type of ambiguity, the words used (and in particular whether the word often appears in the kind of syntactic structure encountered or whether this is relatively rare), the context in which the conversation is situated, etc. They all have an important role to play. Psycholinguists design experiments in which the impact of these various factors on human sentence processing can be explored.

13.3   Modularity and Human Processing

We considered in section 12.3 how modularity makes sense from an engineering perspective—if you want to have a simple model, it makes sense to build it out of smaller components that don't interact strongly with each other. Each gets on with its own task and is affected as little as possible by the operations of other components. From a human perspective, one can take this engineering consideration and elevate it into the hypothesis that the overall organization of the human mind is in terms of distinct modules. Included in these modules would be the traditional five senses, a language module, and (more controversially) components that allow humans to reason about numbers, biology and botany, danger, and perhaps many other areas.

This hypothesis has the potential to explain a number of aspects of the human capability of language. It may, for example, offer an explanation for how such capability can arise evolutionarily. It may be supported by evidence such as the localization of language processing within the brain. It's probably fair to say that most researchers in human language processing believe in modularity to some extent. What is most controversial is the "size" of the modules. Is there a module whose task is just to compute syntactic trees? Or is there a larger module that operates at both syntactic and semantic levels? If the former were true, we'd end up with a model like that seen in section 12.1. We've already argued that, under that model, we end up with a bottleneck if the syntactic module produces all analyses. Hence, there is a tendency among people who believe in a separate syntactic module to believe also that the human parser doesn't operate in parallel. That is, it discards potential analyses that look implausible at certain stages in parsing. As noted above, this seems to offer an explanation for the garden path phenomenon.

On the other hand, there is also contradictory evidence that the human processor operates simultaneously on syntactic, semantic, and perhaps other aspects of the speech being processed. Some of the most impressive evidence for this come from the experiments involving SHADOWING.

In the shadowing task, a subject listening to a tape repeats what he or she hears. Some people can perform this task with a delay, between the recording and their repetition of it, of half a second or less. The time scale is important here, because it tells us that humans don't have to wait until one linguistic unit (say a noun phrase, or a verb phrase, or a sentence) is complete before the processing of parts of that unit can start. Still more impressively, a wide class of errors, purposely introduced into the recording, can be corrected by speakers as they go. For example, the speaker might replace an occurrence of *cigaresh* with *cigarette*.

The fact that shadowers can correct mispronunciations so that they make sense in context suggests quite strongly that processing is taking place at a pragmatic level, at more or less the same time as syntactic and semantic processing. In the next section, we'll see further evidence that this is so. It also leaves us with a paradox. The language model we examined in previous chapters assumes that one builds the syntactic structure of a sentence and then exploits that to construct a semantic analysis of it. But if semantics affects the choices we make in resolving syntactic ambiguities, people must be constructing semantic representations in the absence of a complete syntactic analysis. How do they do this? And what impact does this have on modularity?

Exercise

Exercise 13.4: Try the shadowing task yourself.

13.4 Looking at Cards

EYE TRACKERS represent a technological development currently influencing studies of human processing of language. They are used to work out what aspect of a scene a subject is attending to. By studying where people look in a particular scene, we can make inferences, for example, about how much of a sentence has been processed.

In one such experiment, people are asked to move playing cards around a table. The layout of the table might look something like Figure 13.1 A possible instruction to a subject might be: *move the six of clubs to*

4♠		6♣
6♡	3◇	
		K♣

Figure 13.1
Cards on the table in an eye-tracking experiment.

beneath the three of diamonds. One result obtained from this experiment is that, with this instruction and in a configuration like that shown in Figure 13.1, the subject's gaze alights on the 3◇, just as, or even just before, the word *diamond* is said.

One conclusion one might draw from this experiment is that, as with shadowing, people can allow their knowledge of the context to allow early processing of semantic and discourse information. In this case, the uniqueness of the 3 allows the subject to work out which card is being referred to.

There are a number of open questions that these experiments raise, however. For example, the tasks the human subjects are asked to perform are "unnatural," in the sense that identifying a particular card out from a small set of different cards is not something one does everyday (although arguably we do closely-related tasks frequently). Recall that the experiments from part I, especially Wason's four-card experiment from chapter 3, also involved somewhat unnatural tasks. This "unnaturalness" is often a feature of psychology experiments, and the extent to which this affects the way humans perform is not really known. Another relevant issue concerning the tasks in the experiments we have described here is that they are highly repetitive; subjects do the same task again and again in these experiments, and so their performance improves with practice. To what extent do these factors affect the conclusions that we can draw from the experimental results? Right now, there are no clear answers.

13.5   Conclusions

The modularity of human language processing, the size of the components involved, and the extent to which those components may operate in parallel all represent open research questions in this area. We can make some tentative conclusions.

The mechanisms by which humans process speech involve some parallelism in the sense that they are willing to entertain several different analyses of some linguistic unit. This certainly occurs at the level of words, and perhaps also at the level of syntactic analyses. Those mechanisms don't conform to the strictest version of modularity (at least, when the "levels" over which modularity is defined distinguishes syntax from semantics from pragmatics). There can be relatively large-scale interaction between different sources of knowledge, for example in the way that knowledge about context may affect our interpretation of words with multiple senses.

Exercise

Exercise 13.5: 'Twas brillig, and the slithy toves
Did gyre and gimble in the wabe;

All mimsy were the borogoves,
And the mome raths outgrabe.   Lewis Carroll, *Jabberwocky*
   Think about Lewis Carroll's poem, and assess what it tells us about

- the notion of well-formedness in English (and other natural languages),
- human abilities in interpreting utterances in terms of their form, and
- the overall process of arriving at a meaning for utterances.

13.6   Further Reading

There are some excellent textbooks that cover either psychology in general or cognitive psychology and psycholinguistics in particular. For a general introduction to psychology consult the following:

- Gleitman, Henry, Alan Fridlund, and Daniel Reisburg (1999). *Psychology*. New York: W. Norton.

Chapters 7, 8, and 9 of the above book cover issues concerning human sentence comprehension and production, which are discussed in this chapter. But this book also includes information about other areas of psychology, such as psychology in education and social psychology.
   The following textbooks cover cognitive psychology and psycholinguistics in particular. They give more details about the cross-modal priming, completion tasks, and shadowing as experimental methods for investigating human sentence processing. They also discuss eye tracking (as used in the experiment discussed above where the task is to pick the card that's being described).

- Anderson, John R. (1995). *Cognitive Psychology and its Implication*. W. H. Freeman, 4th Edition.
- Harley, Trevor (2001). *The Psychology of Language: From Data to Theory*. Hove: Psychology Press.
- Parkin, Allen (2000). *Essentials of Cognitive Psychology*. Hove: Psychology Press.

Chapters 1, 3–5, and 10–12 of Parkin (2000) are particularly relevant to the issues discussed in this chapter.

The human comprehension experiments involving eye tracking, where the task is to pick the card that's being described, were conducted by Michael Tanenhaus and his colleagues. The following papers give more details about those experiments:

- Tanenhaus, Michael, M. Spivey Knowlton, K. Eberhand, and J. Sedivy (1995). "Integration of Visual and Linguistic Information in Spoken Language Comprehension," *Science*, 268, 1632–1634.
- Tanenhaus, Michael, J. Magnuson, D. Dahan, and C. Chambers (2000). "Eye Movements and Lexical Access in Spoken-Language Comprehension: Evaluating a Linking Hypothesis between Fixations and Linguistic Processing," *Journal of Pscyholinguistic Research*, 29, 557–580.

The following paper combines statistical natural language processing techniques, which were outlined in the previous chapter, and experimental methods coming from psychology to develop models of ambiguity resolution:

- Lapata, Mirella, Frank Keller, and Scott McDonald (2001). "Evaluating Smoothing Algorithms against Plausibility Judgments," *Proceedings of the 39th Annual Meeting of the Association for Computational Linguistics and the 10th Conference of the European Chapter of the Association for Computational Linguistics*, Toulouse, 346–353.
- Pickering, Martin, M. Traxler, and M. Crocker (2000). "Ambiguity Resolution in Sentence Processing: Evidence Against Frequency-Based Accounts," *Journal of Memory and Language*, 43, 447–475.

There are many differing explanations of the garden path phenomenon, which we discussed in section 13.2. Two opposing models of the phenomenon are given in the following papers:

- Crain, Stephen, and Mark Steedman (1985). "On Not Being Led up the Garden Path: The Use of Context by the Psychological Parser," in L. Karttunen, D. Dowty, and A. Zwicky (eds.). *Natural Language Parsing*, 320–358. Cambridge: Cambridge University Press.
- Fodor, Janet, and Lyn Frazier (1980). "Is the Human Sentence Parsing Mechanism an ATN?" *Cognition*, 8, 417–459.

The former paper argues that the discourse context can ameliorate a garden path, or create it, and on that basis they argue that processing these sentences provides strong evidence that semantic representations are constructed before the syntactic analysis is complete, and indeed influence the construction of the syntactic analysis. In other words, there is no autonomous syntax module. The latter paper argues that there is an autonomous syntax module, syntactic analyses are built in series, and garden paths occur because of default choices that are made for resolving structural ambiguities within the syntax module.

The following is a more advanced overview of current research in human sentence processing:

- Tanenhaus, Michael, and John Trueswell (1995). "Sentence Comprehension," in J. Miller and P. Eimas (eds.). *Speech, Language, and Communication*, 217–262. San Diego: Academic Press.

IV COMMUNICATING IN CONTEXT

In part III, we examined in some detail the syntax of languages such as English, and how that syntax reveals information about meaning. We provided a simple model of this by constructing a grammar, which uses DRSs to represent meaning. We also observed that ambiguity in language is pervasive, and we discussed what impact this has on processing language from the perspective of both machines and humans.

But the link between syntax and semantics is only a small part of the story, since syntax is not the only source of information that contributes to interpreting language. Life is too short for people to make explicit every single piece of information that they want to convey, and perhaps surprisingly, this isn't a problem in practice, because people are very good at "reading between the lines." People can infer more about meaning than is revealed by the sentences' syntax, because they are very good at making sensible assumptions about what the speaker or author *intended* to communicate. These assumptions are often based on factors that are present in the context of the conversation. They lead one to augment the meaning that is revealed by syntax, and they can also help one choose among the different interpretations of ambiguous expressions.

Communicating with languages such as English thus contrasts with communicating with computer programming languages, where all the meaning must be made explicit in the syntax and symbols used in the program. If a computer is to communicate using human languages such as English, then it must be programmed in these explicit programming languages to use contextual factors, in addition to the sentences' syntax, to compute what's being communicated in a conversation.

The study of how information sources other than syntax contribute to meaning is known as PRAGMATICS. The information sources in the context that contribute to inferences about the interpretation of a text are wide and varied, ranging from knowledge of the world to assumptions about the hearer's beliefs and desires. The fact that such information sources influence the interpretation of a conversation helps speakers and authors leave certain things they want to convey unsaid, while feeling sure that the hearer will be "sensible" enough to infer them anyway. Accordingly, the influence of context on meaning also helps hearers and readers work out what someone is really getting at, from what he or she has said or written.

One can argue quite persuasively that almost *every* example of communication with language involves pragmatics, i.e. some form of reasoning about how the context influences its meaning. At first, this may seem strange, because very often one isn't even conscious that one infers more about meaning than is derivable from syntax alone. But it happens all the time. To illustrate this, let's look at a particular example in some detail, and study what's left unsaid, but the hearer infers anyway. The dialogue (1) below is taken from the Map Task Corpus.[24] The method used to obtain the dialogues in this corpus is to present a map each to a "giver" and a "follower." The giver's map has a route drawn on it, and the follower's map doesn't. The giver and follower can't see each other's maps. The giver's task (which is known as the MAP TASK) is to describe the route to the follower, so that the follower can draw that route on his or her map. The features on each map may differ, and so the two participants may have to talk about those features in order to work out the routing. With this now in mind, consider this extract from the corpus:

(1) a.   *Neil*: Right. Start from the sandy shore.

     b.   *Chris*: Okay.

     c.   *Neil*: Moving down... straight down.

     d.   *Chris*: How far?

     e.   *Neil*: Down as far as the bottom of the well.

     f.   *Chris*: I don't have a well.

     g.   *Neil*: fg—Ah. Right, fg—eh. Move down, fg—eh, vertically down about a quarter of the way down the page. Move to the right in... Do you have local residents?

     h.   *Chris*: I do.

     i.   *Neil*: Right, well, move up and round and above them.

     j.   *Chris*: Okay.

There are several things that are part of the dialogue's content, but that are not derivable from the syntactic forms of the sentences on their own. For example, the NP *the sandy shore* is felicitous only if the context contains a unique salient object that satisfies the description that it's a sandy shore. So when Neil uses this phrase in (1)a, he must be assuming that Chris has one, and only one, sandy shore on his map; moreover, Chris must know that Neil assumes this through observing that Neil has used this NP. But Neil doesn't make this assumption explicit. He doesn't say *You have one, and only one, sandy shore on your map*. This content is "hidden" in his use of *the sandy shore*. Also, Chris has to work out *what* he's supposed to start from the sandy shore, because Neil doesn't tell him explicitly. Start running from there? Start cleaning up the environment from there? Start shouting from there? Chris will assume Neil means *start drawing*. Moreover, Neil knows Chris will assume this, because of their shared knowledge about the purpose of the conversation, which is to do the Map Task. So here we see that the background knowledge people have about the world and each other influences the message that they extract from an utterance.

We can go further. In utterance (1)c, Chris interprets Neil to mean *Moving down from the sandy shore*. But Neil doesn't say this explicitly; he just says *Moving down*. Nevertheless, Chris reasons that this is what is meant, because (1)c follows on from (1)a. In other words, through thinking about how (1)a and (1)c connect together, Chris gets an additional piece of information, which is where he's supposed to move down from.

In (1)f, we see that Neil's use of the noun phrase *the well* in (1)e failed to have the desired effect of enabling Chris to pick out the relevant object on the map. We know there is this "breakdown" in communication because Chris lets Neil know that he can't find what Neil wants. This is an example where Neil's assumptions about what Chris knows and what he's able to do have gone wrong. Through using *the well*, Neil assumed that Chris had one, and only one, well on his map. Neil and Chris never negotiated about whether Chris had exactly one well on his map. Instead, Neil just took this assumption for granted (and exploiting such assumptions without checking they're valid beforehand is extremely commonplace in conversation). Even so, Chris is aware from Neil uttering *the well* that this is what Neil was assuming, and so he tells Neil in (1)f that this assumption was wrong. In other words, what a person says reveals information about what he assumes the other agent believes, and when these assumptions are wrong, corrections of them can surface in the dialogue. One couldn't interpret such corrective moves without a theory of how utterances connect to beliefs and *vice versa*.

In (1)g, we infer, as presumably Chris does too, that Neil wants him to move a quarter of the way down the page, *and then* move right. But this temporal relationship between the two actions isn't explicitly stated. Neil doesn't use the words *and then*, or *after that*. Rather, Neil is assuming that Chris can work out that this is what he means, in virtue of the *order* in which Neil has said these instructions. In other words, because Neil has said move down *before* he's said move to the right, Chris should do the actions in this order.

Utterance (1)i means *move up and round and above the local residents*. Neil assumes Chris can work this out, that he will interpret *them* as referring to the local residents even though many other things have been spoken about in the dialogue, and so could conceivably be referred to again, such as the well, the sandy shore, the map itself, the page the map is on, and so on. This preference for interpreting *them* as the local residents as opposed to any other group of things that have been mentioned already in the dialogue must arise from the way (1)i connects with the previous dialogue.

If a computer is to participate in a dialogue like this, then it is clear that it would need to reason about the way the context influences interpretation. It would have to compute that *them* is the local residents, and not the well and the sandy shore, for example. Otherwise, the computer would draw the wrong route! It would have to know what the speaker is assuming when he uses a DEFINITE DESCRIPTION (that is, a phrase of the form *the X*), so that the computer can produce the necessary utterances when these assumptions are wrong (e.g. as in (1)f). It would have to work out that the instruction in (1)c amounts to *move down from the sandy shore*. And it would have to work out that the instruction in (1)g means *move down and then move to the right*. None of these things are explicitly stated. And yet we infer them. Indeed, we infer them in an apparently effortless manner.

The above discussion is an indication of just how powerful an effect context has on the way we interpret talk. Life would be intolerable if we had to make explicit in dialogue everything that's been described in the preceding paragraphs about (1)'s interpretation. You probably felt that spelling out what (1) meant in this way was all a bit laborious. But we would have to communicate in this laborious and time-consuming manner if we were forced to make explicit everything we need to convey.

Luckily, people don't have to do this. They are very good at working out what people mean, even when it's not all explicitly stated. They use all kinds of knowledge to work it out: knowledge about the world, the speaker, the way language is used in conversation, the purpose of the conversation, and so on. Computers, in this sense at least, are stupid. They can't work out what people mean unless we tell them in explicit programming languages how to do it. We've already discussed in this book how one might get a computer to extract meaning from the SYNTACTIC FORM of a sentence. But the discussion of the above dialogue shows that several other knowledge sources also provide essential clues about meaning. So a computer must know how the meaning derived from a sentence's syntactic form is extended and refined, in the light of these other knowledge sources.

There are four central pragmatic phenomena that we will examine in this book that are directly related to the above observations about dialogue (1):

- **Finding antecedents to pronouns**
In chapter 14, we will examine how we compute what pronouns like *he* and *them* denote. This in effect addresses the problem of predicting that *them* in (1)i refers to *the local residents*, as opposed to some combination of the well, sandy shore, and the page.

- **Presuppositions**
The utterance *Down as far as the bottom of the well* in (1)e PRESUPPOSES there's one, and only one, well. In chapter 15, we will examine how such presuppositions contribute to the overall meaning of text.

- **Juxtaposing sentences**
When a speaker juxtaposes sentences, he relies on the assumption that the hearer will reason about *why* he did this. The fact that (1)c is said after (1)a results in the added meaning, move down *from the sandy shore*. In chapter 16, we will study how mechanisms developed in AI for reasoning in commonsense ways can help formalize how one computes the "hidden" message behind juxtaposing sentences.

- **Processing dialogue** Even though "Can you pass the salt?" has the syntactic form of a *question*, it is usually interpreted as a *request* that the hearer engage in the action of passing the salt. So simply responding to the question with "yes" is unhelpful, because it ignores what the questioner wanted—the salt, not information. In chapter 17, we will examine the interaction between language on the one hand, and the beliefs, desires, and intentions of the agents engaged in the conversation on the other. We will examine this interaction in the context of simple dialogues involving questions and answers.

In each case, we will examine specific, formal theories about how information in the context augments the (compositional) semantic representations that are derivable from syntax, and how it resolves ambiguities. We aim for formal procedures, because this is a requirement for getting a computer to do the task. We will find in the course of studying these four central phenomena that they are closely related to one another. For example, the inferences about what a person wants, given what he or she has said, is often logically codependent on the inference concerning the denotation of a pronoun or a definite description; that is, one often cannot perform one inference without also performing the other.

The specific proposals we will examine all have one thing in common: They're inadequate and can only deal with very simple texts and dialogues. This simplicity is analogous to the simplicity of the grammar we examined in part III, for modeling the FORM-MEANING RELATION (see chapters 9 and 10). Nevertheless, just like studying the simple grammar, studying models of pragmatics, however simple, has benefits. Here, we mention two of them. First, it will hopefully demonstrate the utility of developing a formal approach to pragmatics. Things that seem arbitrary at first glance will in fact turn out to be the result of rational and systematic reasoning. Second, observing counterexamples to the formal models often exposes gaps that you wouldn't have anticipated had you not tried to develop a formal model of the phenomena in the first place.

In fact, to keep things as simple as possible, we will model the interpretation of pronouns and the interpretation of definite descriptions by extending the method we used in part III for constructing representations of meaning (see chapters 14 and 15 for details). Thus we will extend the DRSs that we used earlier, and show how information other than syntax can contribute to the construction of a DRS for representing the meaning of a text or conversation.

14 Finding What a Pronoun Refers To

14.1 The Problem

Pronouns are words like *he, it, his, she, her, himself, one*, etc. They refer to things, but you only know exactly what they refer to by identifying which entity that's already been mentioned in the context the pronoun refers back to. Thus a word like *he* differs in meaning from an NP like *a dog* in that its referent is determined by the context in which it's uttered. If the context fails to provide such a referent, the sentence containing *he* sounds odd. For example, text (1) makes a lot more sense than a written text that *starts* with the sentence *he barked*:

(1)   Pip found a bone. He barked.

That's because the first sentence in (1) sets up a context in which we can work out what *he* refers to; namely, it refers to the same individual as *Pip*.

We now introduce some terminology that will help us talk about the phenomena involving pronouns (and other expressions like them). Reference to an entity that has been previously introduced into the discourse is called anaphora (see chapter 8 for our first introduction of this term), and the referring expression is anaphoric. We say that two referring expressions that are used to refer to the same entity CO-REFER (i.e. *Pip* and *he* in this example co-refer). We call *Pip* the ANTECEDENT to *he*—we may also call the discourse referent that's introduced by *Pip* into the DRS the antecedent to the discourse referent that's introduced by the pronoun.

In section 10.2, we offered a semantic rule for pronouns in our grammar. But as we highlighted in that section, a lot of its predictions about the antecedents to pronouns are wrong, in that they don't agree with our intuitions about what a pronoun in a given text refers to. So in this chapter, we will study the semantics of pronouns in much more detail, and offer ways of improving the analysis we have given so far.

The fundamental questions we ask are: How does the context affect what a pronoun refers to? What principles govern these effects? Accordingly, when can one use a pronoun to refer to something? And if there is more than one possible referent for a pronoun—as there is in text (2), for example—how do the different choices get ranked:

(2)   John met Bill. He asked him a question.

Observe how although one could interpret this text so that it means that Bill asked John the question, there seems to be a preference for interpreting it as John asked Bill a question.

Answers to these puzzles should ideally provide us with a systematic procedure for finding the antecedents to pronouns. That way, we gain an understanding of the rules by which languages work. And we also come closer to being able to get machines to understand pronouns in the same way as humans do. Pronouns appear very frequently in text. To convince yourself of this, just pick a newspaper article at random, and compare the number of sentences that feature pronouns to the number that don't. Now, to see how useful pronouns are as a communication device, try to paraphrase that newspaper text so that all its pronouns are removed, and observe how the result is odd and very difficult to understand. Here is an example, taken from the BBC News website:

(3) a.   Tony Blair praised his wife and accused the media of "distortion" over its coverage of her dealings with fraudster Peter Foster.

    b.   Tony Blair praised Blair's wife, and accused the media of covering the wife's dealings with fraudster Peter Forster in a distorted fashion.

The original sentence (3)a has had its pronouns replaced in (3)b so that it "means" the same thing, but the result is a sentence that is awkward and harder to process. Since pronouns are so frequent, computers must be able to handle them if they are to communicate with human languages in a way that is useful to humans.

Unfortunately, life's not simple, and easy strategies for finding antecedents to pronouns don't work. Perhaps this is surprising, since people are very good at working out what a pronoun refers to, and are hardly even conscious of the quite complex reasoning that's involved. To see that things are more complicated than they first appear, let's consider what appears to be a simple and sensible strategy, and observe where it falls short. The simple strategy is the following: When you encounter a pronoun, take the following steps to find its antecedent.

1. Look back for an NP.

2. When you find one, check whether it refers to something of the same GENDER (masculine, feminine, or neuter) and NUMBER (singular or plural) as the pronoun.

3. If the number and gender information matches, then assume that the pronoun refers to this object. If they don't match, then go back to step 1 again, and repeat the process (i.e. find the next most recently mentioned NP).

This procedure already adds something to our grammar rule for dealing with pronouns; namely step 2 above. As we saw in section 10.2, the rule for pronouns we presented earlier allowed a pronoun like *he* to be identified with an antecedent like *bone*. Step 2 would block this from happening, because bones aren't masculine! The above procedure also encapsulates a preference for choosing most recently mentioned NPs as antecedents; our semantic rule for pronouns didn't express such a preference (or indeed, any preference).

Let's examine in detail how this procedure deals with example (1). In fact, things work out fine for this example. In (1), we encounter the word *he* in the second sentence. So we implement the above procedure for finding out what *he* refers to. The first NP we encounter as we look back in the text from *he* is *a bone*, but that refers to something neuter. So by the above procedure, we try again, looking for the next most recently mentioned NP. The next one is *Pip*. *Pip* is a masculine proper name, and so the gender is OK. Pip also refers to just one person (and not a group of people), so the number is OK too. So we fix the antecedent to *he* as Pip. This matches our intuitions. In contrast, our previous grammar rule would predict that there is a choice for what the pronoun *he* refers to: the bone, or to Pip.

But although this procedure fares better than our grammar rule did for example (1), it doesn't work in general. It makes the wrong predictions about the preferred interpretation of (2), for example, since the most recent NP prior to *he* is *Bill*, not *John*. And the situation gets even worse when we introduce things like NEGATION (that is, the word *not*) into the mix. Consider (4). We use "?" to indicate that the sentence sounds odd for some reason.

(4)   John doesn't own a car. ?It is red.

Intuitively, (4) is odd, because the pronoun *it* fails to refer to anything. But contrary to this intuition, the above procedure for finding an antecedent to a pronoun predicts that the pronoun does successfully refer to something. The first NP we encounter as we look back over the text is *a car*. This refers to something neuter and singular, and thus matches the gender and number of the pronoun. So by the above procedure, the antecedent to *it* is a car. But clearly, this isn't right. There is something about the fact that the first sentence asserts that something *isn't* the case that blocks the pronoun from referring to the car. Compare it with (5) which is more acceptable:

(5)   John owns a car. It is red.

In other words, there are LINGUISTIC CONSTRAINTS on finding an antecedent to a pronoun: the antecedents are somehow determined by the way information is presented in the preceding sentences; for example, (4) shows that one can't pick antecedents to pronouns that are within the scope of negation. The above simple procedure for identifying antecedents doesn't account for these effects of negation.

But what exactly are the linguistic constraints on identifying antecedents? We've already touched on one obvious one, which is that the gender and number of the pronoun must match that of the antecedent; (6)a is fine but (6)b and (6)c are odd because one shouldn't refer to *Etta* with *he* (wrong gender) or *they* (wrong number):

(6) a.   Etta found a bone. She barked.

     b.   Etta found a bone. ?He barked.

     c.   Etta found a bone. ?They barked.

We also saw in (4) that negation affects what a pronoun can refer to; it blocks certain NPs from being antecedents to subsequent pronouns. Overall, however, the linguistic constraints can get quite complex. Compare the sentences in (7):

(7) a.   A man loved Mary. He proposed to her.

     b.   No man loved Mary. ?He proposed to her.

     c.   Every man loved Mary. ?He proposed to her.

     d.   If a man loved Mary, he proposed to her.

Replacing the quantifier *a* in (7)a with *every* and *no*, as in (7)b and c, has blocked us from finding an antecedent to the pronoun *he*. On the other hand, putting the phrase *a man loved Mary* in the *if. . . ,then. . .* statement in (7)d has changed what *he* refers to, compared with (7)a. In (7)a, *he* refers to the man who loved Mary that is introduced in the first sentence; (7)a can be true when two men loved Mary, only one of whom proposed to her. But in contrast, (7)d expresses a regularity about men that loved Mary—they all proposed to her. The pronoun *he* in (7)d essentially refers to *every* man that loved Mary, and the sentence isn't true when two men love Mary, only one of whom proposed to her. So what precisely are the linguistic constraints on what a pronoun refers to? For a computer to deal successfully with these sentences, we must devise a systematic way of building their semantic representations and finding antecedents to pronouns, so that the difference in meaning between (7)a and (7)d is captured, and the fact that (7)a and d are better than (7)b and c is predicted.

Discourses (8) and (9) show that NONLINGUISTIC INFORMATION affects pronouns too.

(8)   If a baby hates cow's milk, boil it.

(9)   If an incendiary bomb falls near you, don't lose your head. Put it in a bucket and bury it in sand.

It could refer to the baby in (8) and your head in (9), but with unfortunate results; see Figures 14.1 and 14.2!

Intuitively, the general knowledge that one shouldn't boil the baby, or stick your head in the sand, influences our preferred interpretations of (8) and (9). When there's a choice of what a pronoun might refer to, we tend to prefer those choices that are "in tune" with general knowledge like *people don't boil babies*, to those choices that ignore such knowledge. We must therefore ensure that a computer that has to deal with pronouns uses general knowledge in this way. This is actually very difficult to do, given current state-of-the-art technology. Humans have a vast amount of knowledge about the world. But computers don't unless we tell them about these things. It is currently very difficult to encode even a tiny part of world knowledge in a manner that enables a computer to reason about its effects on text interpretation.

Figure 14.1
A bizarre interpretation of (8).

At any rate, it's important to stress that even if knowledge about the world makes it obvious which object the pronoun was *supposed* to refer to, the pronoun can still sound odd if the linguistic constraints (whatever they are!) aren't met. One sees many examples of pronouns being used in odd ways in newspapers, where text is written in a hurry. Journalists don't have enough time to check that the text "flows" fluently, and that computing the antecedents to pronouns will be "easy" for the reader. The following examples are all taken from *The Guardian*:

(10)   She was living with her husband when Wigan magistrates ordered her to be jailed unless she paid £5 per week, although <u>he</u> earned only £70 a week as a part-time postman.

(11)   The report by Touche Ross, administrators of Mr. Nadir's failed Polly Peck International empire, alleges that a large proportion of the £440,000 donations was from misappropriated Polly Peck funds and forms part of the £371 million <u>it</u> is claiming from Mr. Nadir. The party has always said the donations

Figure 14.2
A bizarre interpretation of (9).

would be returned if they were shown to have been stolen.

The underlined pronouns sound odd, even though our background knowledge about the world makes it obvious what object the pronoun is supposed to refer to (the husband in (10), and Touche Ross in (11)). These antecedents are clearly the ones that the author intended the reader to pick up. But even though background knowledge helps us guess that this was what was intended, the examples still sound a bit strange. So making the reference obvious through background information isn't always enough. The way information is presented in the context can either help, or hinder, finding the antecedents to pronouns. Note we can improve (10) by changing the way the information is presented, as in (12):

(12)   Wigan magistrates ordered her to be jailed unless she paid £5 per week, even though she was living with her husband and he earned only £70 a week.

Sentences (10) and (12) describe the same things, but do it in a different way. The *order* of presentation of information is changed in (12), making it easier to interpret *he*.

Ideally, we would want a machine to produce texts like (12) rather than (10), even though humans produce texts like (10) when they're in a hurry! If a computer could do this, then it would be a useful tool in assisting busy copy editors. It could spot the mistakes that journalists miss, and suggest improvements. But in order to get a computer to do this, it must be programmed with the appropriate linguistic constraints on antecedents to pronouns.

In this chapter, we'll address the following question: Can the way humans interpret pronouns be modeled in a mechanical way, so that we can get computers to do it? We'll approach this question by exploring how we might extend the grammar we constructed earlier in the book (see part III), to model what pronouns mean. We will show that the semantic representations of sentences we constructed earlier in the book encode information that we need in order to specify linguistic constraints on what a pronoun refers to, as illustrated in (6) and (7). We will demonstrate this by extending the grammar to account for what's happening in these examples. And we will discuss what kinds of mechanisms we would need, in order to rank the possible antecedents to pronouns on the basis of background knowledge, as shown in (8) and (9).

14.2   Linguistic Constraints on Pronouns

We saw in section 10.2 the "anaphora constraint," repeated here:

(13)   In constructing a DRS, a referent cannot appear more than once in the arguments to an atomic condition.

We saw that such a constraint was necessary to rule out co-reference in a number of cases. It models the fact that *he loved him* cannot mean he loved himself; one would have to say *he loved himself* if that was what was meant.

This constraint is *linguistic*: it seems to be part of the way English is organized. In this section, we'll consider a number of constraints of a similar nature, and these will go a considerable way toward solving the problems we observed in section 10.2.

Number and gender

Let's consider the sentences in (6) again. We want to extend the grammar, so that the analysis of the discourse (6)a "automatically" predicts that the person who barks is Etta—that is, *she* refers to Etta. On the other hand, we don't want to find antecedents to *he* or *they* in (6)b and (6)c at all. The grammar rule for pronouns that we outlined in earlier chapters allows *he* and *they* to refer to Etta. What we'll do here is refine this rule, so that we encode in the grammar that the antecedent to a pronoun must have the appropriate number and gender.

To do this, we must tell the grammar what the number and gender of the various pronouns are; for example, we must represent in the grammar that *she* is a SINGULAR, FEMININE PRONOUN. We must also convey information about the gender of the referents of nouns like *woman* (singular and feminine) and bone (singular and neuter). Moreover, we must leave room for some nouns to denote objects with an UNDERSPECIFIED gender (e.g. *neighbor, buyer, doctor,* and *client,* which can all refer to either masculine or feminine individuals).

Here's how we encode the necessary information in the grammar. First, we will continue to include a syntactic rule within the grammar that says that a pronoun is an NP:

(14)   NP $\longrightarrow$ PRO

In addition, we need to know which words are pronouns. So far, we have encoded this information as follows:

(15)   PRO $\longrightarrow$ he, him, she, her, it, they, them

But this doesn't record what kinds of things (i.e. singular or plural, masculine, feminine, or neuter) the pronouns can refer to. The simplest way to represent this information is to divide the category PRO into several classes, according to the number and gender of the thing referred to, as shown below (where "fem" stands for feminine, "masc" for masculine, and "neut" for neuter):

(16) a.   PRO $\begin{bmatrix} \text{num} & : & sing \\ \text{gender} & : & fem \end{bmatrix}$ $\longrightarrow$ *she, her*

b.   PRO $\begin{bmatrix} \text{num} & : & sing \\ \text{gender} & : & masc \end{bmatrix}$ $\longrightarrow$ *he, him*

c.   PRO $\begin{bmatrix} \text{num} & : & sing \\ \text{gender} & : & neut \end{bmatrix}$ $\longrightarrow$ *it*

d.   PRO $\begin{bmatrix} \text{num} & : & plur \end{bmatrix}$ $\longrightarrow$ *they, them*

We have added number and gender information to the syntactic category PRO, by stating it in square brackets as shown. For example, (17) stands for a pronoun that is singular and feminine:

(17)   PRO $\begin{bmatrix} \text{num} & : & sing \\ \text{gender} & : & fem \end{bmatrix}$

As shown in (16)a, we will include two such pronouns in our grammar: *she* and *her* (we're not including *herself*). We're also ignoring the syntactic distinction between *she* and *her* (i.e. nominative vs. accusative), and this means that our grammar will continue to predict, incorrectly, that *John loves she* is an acceptable sentence of English. But for simplicity, we ignore this problem here and focus instead on providing general principles for identifying antecedents to pronouns.

The texts (6) show that the antecedent to a feminine pronoun must refer to a female, the antecedent to a masculine pronoun must refer to a male, and so on. Strictly speaking, nouns in English aren't assigned gender (while French, German, and many other languages are different in this respect). However, for each noun, we need to mark in the grammar the genders of the pronouns that it can co-refer with. So for simplicity, we will approximate this by including an attribute gender on nouns as well. This is to be interpreted, however, as the gender of the pronouns that can co-refer with the noun. Thus we adopt the following rules in the grammar (and these replace the rules involving nouns from chapter 9; see p.224, for example):

(18) a.   N $\begin{bmatrix} \text{num} & : & sing \\ \text{gender} & : & fem \end{bmatrix}$ $\longrightarrow$ *woman, doctor, dog, ship,...*

b.   N $\begin{bmatrix} \text{num} & : & sing \\ \text{gender} & : & neut \end{bmatrix}$ $\longrightarrow$ *table, chair, house, ship, bone,...*

c.   N $\begin{bmatrix} \text{num} & : & sing \\ \text{gender} & : & masc \end{bmatrix}$ $\longrightarrow$ *John, man, doctor, boy, dog,...*

These rules reflect the fact that a pronoun that co-refers with *woman* and *Jane* must be singular and feminine, for *table* it must be neuter, for *man* it must be masculine, while for *ship* either a feminine or neuter pronoun is acceptable, and for *doctor* a masculine or feminine pronoun is acceptable.

In what follows, we'll ignore *they* and *them*, since computing antecedents to these plural pronouns is much more complex than for the singular pronouns. This is because you can "sum together" things in the context to form a plural group—this is what happens in (19), for example, where Jane and Mary are grouped together and *they* refers to both of them:

(19)   Jane went to the cinema. Mary went to the theater. They had
         a great time.

We don't want to discuss the constraints on this grouping process,
since they are very complex and not very well understood at present.
So instead, we'll concentrate on mechanizing the process of finding
antecedents to *he*, *him*, *she*, *her*, and *it*. We will also ignore INDEXICAL
pronouns like *I*, *me*, *you*, etc., and the DEICTIC use of pronouns like *he*
(e.g. you can successfully refer to something by using *he* and pointing to
the individual you intend to refer to).

We use the above rules to build the syntactic structure of sentences
involving pronouns, and then use that to construct the semantics. We
must represent the semantic contribution of using the rule (14). The
categories **PRO** and **N** are subdivided according to number and gender,
so that the grammar can use this information when calculating the
antecedents to pronouns. But this won't work unless information about
number and gender in syntax makes its way into the semantics—that is,
into the Discourse Representation Structure (DRS). So if the category
in the syntactic tree is (17), then the semantic representation must
state that the individual x that is taken to correspond to the individual
referred to by the pronoun is singular (written $sing(x)$) and feminine
(written $fem(x)$). Furthermore, we must record in the DRS that *she* on
its own doesn't tell us who's being talked about. We mark this with
$x =?$ (which you can think of as *Who is x?*). Taking all these things into
account we come up with the following translation rule for pronouns:

● Pronouns:

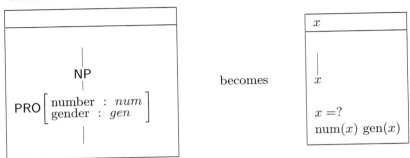

where x hasn't been used yet.

The condition $x =?$ is meant to state that we can't completely interpret the pronoun without the discourse context—that is, we can't work out what it refers to. This is a technical way of replacing the instruction that appeared in our previous semantic rule for pronouns, where it was stated that you had to reuse a discourse referent (note that the rule above uses a new discourse referent x, and we encode explicitly that we must work out who x is in the DRS conditions). The formula $x =?$ tells us that, even if there is something in the model that meets all the conditions in the DRS that are placed on x, that's no guarantee that the DRS is true, because the individual in the model that satisfies these conditions may not be the individual that the speaker of the sentence had in mind when he said *he*. We must therefore work out what individual the pronoun refers to, *before* we can assess whether the sentence is true or not (i.e. before we try to match the information in the DRS with information in the model).

There are in fact many expressions in English that are like pronouns, in that you can't work out who or what's being talked about without looking at the context in which the expression was uttered: *the one with the crazy dog, since then,* and *the above discussion* are just a few examples of such expressions. We will discuss how the mechanisms discussed here for interpreting pronouns can be extended to deal with some of these more complex expressions in chapter 15.

But for now, back to pronouns. The condition $x =?$ is an indication that we need more information before the DRS is of a kind that we can evaluate against a model to see if it's true; in particular, we need to identify x with some discourse referent that's already in the DRS. The condition $x =?$ can thus can be viewed as an *instruction* to find out, from the context, who x is. So $x =?$ is a bit different from the other conditions. The other conditions are things that you ultimately will check against the model, to see if the sentence is true or not—$\text{sing}(x)$ is true or false, for example. But $x =?$ isn't like this. You don't decide whether *Who is x?* is true or not. Rather, you have to answer the question.

Because $x =?$ has this different status to the other conditions on x, it's technically cleaner to demarcate it from those other conditions in some way. We'll do it by sticking it in a special place in the semantic representation. We will add a *third* box to DRSs, at the bottom, and we will call this additional box the INSTRUCTION BOX. So DRSs now have *three* parts: a list of discourse referents, a list of conditions on them, and a list of instructions. And the revised rule for pronouns is the following:

- Pronouns (Revised):

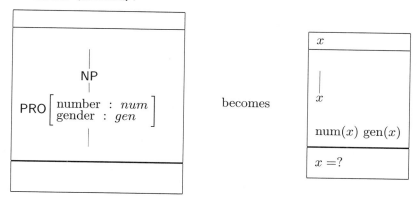

where x hasn't been used yet.

The box at the bottom contains instructions to do more processing. It's demarcated from the other elements of meaning. The fact that there is something in the instruction box for sentences involving pronouns reflects the intuition that *She barked* is uninterpretable—in the sense that we can't work out if it's true or not—until we work out who *she* is. When there's nothing in this instruction box, we don't need to do any more processing before evaluating the DRS against a model, to see if it's true or not.

We'll see how to replace the condition $x =?$ in the instruction box with more semantic information about x to appear in the conditions box shortly. The replacement of the instruction with a semantic condition will be highly dependent on the discourse context, since it will depend on what's in the DRS already. This reflects the heavy influence of context on the interpretation of pronouns. But first, let's illustrate how `Pronouns (Revised)` is used to *construct* the semantics of a sentence that has a pronoun in it. Consider sentence (20):

(20)   She barked.

The syntactic structure of this sentence is as follows:

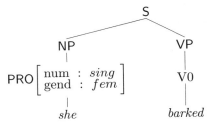

By the rule `Pronouns (Revised)`, we can form the following from this:

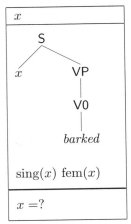

You can then reduce the rest of the syntactic tree to semantic information as we've done before (see chapter 10), so that the final semantic representation of (20) is (20′):

(20′)

x	
bark(x)	sing(x) fem(x)
$x =?$	

The DRS (20′) states there is just one thing talked about—x—where x is singular and feminine, and x barked, and we have to find out who x is.

Note that our extension to the syntax of the grammar has enabled us to explicitly encode the number and gender of discourse referents in the semantics. In the above example, this information is attached to the discourse referent x that was introduced when the bit of the tree containing PRO was translated into semantic information. And we'll use this to check which antecedents to this pronoun are acceptable.

We can check the number and gender of the discourse referent introduced by the pronoun against other discourse referents introduced by nouns, because these discourse referents will also have number and gender conditions on them. These number and gender conditions will be produced when the noun is converted into semantic information. We have subdivided the syntactic category N into several classes, according to number and gender. And the semantic rule for NPs containing N will change accordingly, so that this information appears in the semantic representation. For example, the rule for translating indefinites is just the same as before, except that the number and gender information gets added to the DRS:

- Indefinite Noun Phrases:

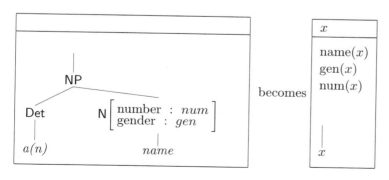

So, for example, *a bone* will produce a discourse referent y with the conditions bone(y), sing(y), and neut(y) in the DRS by the above rule. As we'll see, this information helps us to work out when the bone can be an antecedent to pronouns that appear subsequently in the text (if there are any), on the basis of whether its number and gender match that of the pronoun.

We must carry out the instruction $x =$? in (20'). That is, we must work out what x refers to. This involves stating rules that help us to identify x with a discourse referent y, where y has already been introduced into the DRS. One of the constraints on this identification procedure is that the properties of x and y are CONSISTENT. In other words, the things already said of x (including its number and gender) and those of y are such that we don't get a contradiction if we assume x and y refer to the same thing.

So let's illustrate how finding the antecedent to x in (20') works by means of an example:

(6) a.   Etta found a bone. She barked.

To build the DRS of an example like (6)a, we apply the following ALGORITHM. Steps 1–3 and 5 are procedures we've already assumed in the grammar for constructing DRSs from text (see section 10.2). Step 4 is the extension, and it tells us how (and when) to carry out instructions of the form $x =$?.

- **Algorithm for Constructing DRSs for Text:**

    1. Start by assuming that the first sentence of the text is the one currently being processed. Go to step 2.

    2. Use the grammar to construct a syntactic structure of the sentence currently being processed. Add it to the DRS being built. If there is more than one such syntactic structure, then construct a separate DRS for each of these analyses (to reflect the ambiguity), and continue with the steps in the algorithm for each of these DRSs. Go to step 3.

    3. Apply the rules that convert the syntactic structure in the DRS into semantic information. Go to step 4.

    4. Deal with instructions of the form $x =$?. Replace $x =$? in the instruction box with a condition of the form $x = y$, which is added to

the conditions box. This identity condition must meet the following:

  −y is a discourse referent in the DRS built already.

  −The choice of y is constrained by the **Consistency Constraint**, **Structural Constraint**, and **Knowledge Constraint**, which we will specify below.

If there's a choice of identity conditions, then each option is represented in a separate DRS (that is, the text is assumed to be ambiguous). If there's no choice at all, then the procedure for building a DRS for the sentence has failed, and so the sentence is predicted to be odd. If it succeeds, go to step 5.

5. Make the next sentence of the text, if there is one, the sentence that is currently being processed and go back to step 2. If there are no more sentences in the text, then stop.

The first constraint we assume for step 4 is the following:

- **The Consistency Constraint:**

$x =?$ can be replaced by $x = y$ only if the conditions on x and y are consistent; that is, $x = y$ must not lead to a contradiction, such as x is both masculine and feminine.

Given this consistency constraint, this algorithm at present looks like a convoluted way of stating the simple, and inadequate, mechanism for finding antecedents to pronouns that we discussed in section 1. But bear with it, because it won't remain like this. Crucially, we're going to add more constraints than just the Consistency Constraint. There will also be the Structural Constraint and the Knowledge Constraint, which we will describe below. According to step 4, these additional constraints will have to be taken into account when identifying x with a previous discourse referent. So these additional constraints will take us beyond what the earlier procedure could do.

But for now, let's apply this algorithm to (6)a.

(6) a.   Etta found a bone. She barked.

We start with step 1, and assume that the sentence we process now is the first one. We go onto step 2: working out its syntax. According to the grammar, its syntactic analysis is as follows:

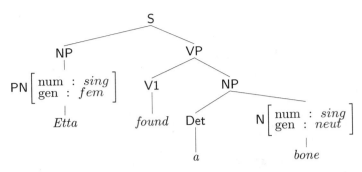

Now we go onto step 3. The above syntax produces the following semantic representation.

(21)

x, y		
Etta(x)	sing(x)	fem(x)
bone(y)	sing(y)	neut(y)
find(x, y)		

Note that so far, there is nothing in the instruction box; in other words, nothing in the first sentence requires us to go and find out more from preceding text, about what the sentence is about, before we can work out if it's true or not.

Now we go back to step 2 and process the second sentence. Note that the syntactic structure for the second sentence goes into the DRS you've built for the first one, reflecting the fact that it continues the discourse that the first sentence started. You should *not* start a new DRS!

(22)

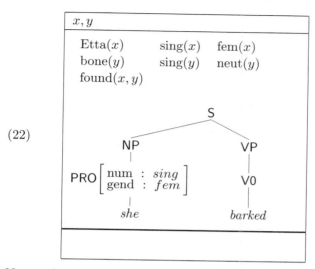

Now we're on step 3 again. Using the same rules as before, the above reduces to the following semantic information:

(23)

$$
\begin{array}{|l|}
\hline
x, y, z \\
\hline
\begin{array}{lll}
\mathrm{Etta}(x) & \mathrm{sing}(x) & \mathrm{fem}(x) \\
\mathrm{bone}(y) & \mathrm{sing}(y) & \mathrm{neut}(y) \\
\mathrm{find}(x, y) & & \\
 & \mathrm{sing}(z) & \mathrm{fem}(z) \\
\mathrm{bark}(z) & & \\
\end{array} \\
\hline
z =? \\
\hline
\end{array}
$$

Now we are on step 4. We have an instruction $z =?$ (z corresponds to *she*). We have to replace $z =?$ with an identity condition between z and some discourse referent already in the DRS. There are two such referents, x and y. By the **Consistency Constraint**, we can't assume $z = y$ because y is neuter and z is feminine. (This contrasts with the rule for pronouns given in earlier chapters). So we must assume $z = x$. So we remove $z =?$ from the instruction box (because we have carried out this instruction), and replace it with $z = x$ in the main semantic content:

$$
(24)\quad
\boxed{\begin{array}{l}
x, y, z \\
\hline
\begin{array}{lll}
\mathrm{Etta}(x) & \mathrm{sing}(x) & \mathrm{fem}(x) \\
\mathrm{bone}(y) & \mathrm{sing}(y) & \mathrm{neut}(y) \\
\mathrm{find}(x, y) & & \\
 & \mathrm{sing}(z) & \mathrm{fem}(z) \\
\mathrm{bark}(z) & & \\
z = x & &
\end{array} \\
\hline

\end{array}}
$$

Here, we see the advantage of explicitly marking the number and gender of pronouns and nouns in the semantics. If we didn't know the gender of x, y, and z in the DRS, then we wouldn't have known that identifying z with y would have been inconsistent.

The DRS (24) is equivalent to (25), where all occurrences of z are replaced with x, and we've removed $z = x$ from the conditions:

$$
(25)\quad
\boxed{\begin{array}{l}
x, y \\
\hline
\begin{array}{lll}
\mathrm{Etta}(x) & \mathrm{sing}(x) & \mathrm{fem}(x) \\
\mathrm{bone}(y) & \mathrm{sing}(y) & \mathrm{neut}(y) \\
\mathrm{find}(x, y) & & \\
\mathrm{bark}(x) & &
\end{array} \\
\hline

\end{array}}
$$

The DRS (25) asserts what intuitions would dictate is the meaning of sentence (6)a: There are two things we're talking about—x and y—where x is Etta, x found y, which is a bone, and x barked. There are no more sentences in (6)a, and so we stop there. (25) is the final representation of what (6)a means, and even though (6)a didn't *explicitly* say *Etta barked*, the DRS that represents its meaning has captured this.

Now we can see why (6)b is odd. Using the above algorithm, we get the semantic representation (6)b′.

$$\begin{array}{|l|}
\hline
x, y, z \\
\hline
\begin{array}{lll}
\text{Etta}(x) & \text{sing}(x) & \text{fem}(x) \\
\text{bone}(y) & \text{sing}(y) & \text{neut}(y) \\
\text{find}(x, y) & & \\
& \text{sing}(z) & \text{masc}(z) \\
\text{bark}(z) & &
\end{array} \\
\hline
z = ? \\
\hline
\end{array}$$

(6) b'.

There is no discourse referent that we can identify z with in (6)b′, because the candidates x and y all violate the Consistency Constraint (they're not masculine). So we can't do the instruction $z = ?$. So the text is found to be odd. Text (6)c is similar; there is nothing in the context that is plural in number, as *they* demands.[25]

Let's see what happens when we have two pronouns in a sentence:

(26)   Etta chased Pip. She caught him.

As we'll see, the above rule for analyzing pronouns means that the two pronouns *she* and *him* in (26) produce one instruction each. The analysis is as follows. First, we construct the DRS for the first sentence *Etta chased Pip*. Since we've done it many times before, we omit the sequence of steps, and simply give the final DRS for this sentence below:

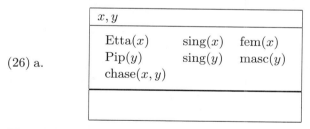

(26) a.

The conditions sing(x) and fem(x) are produced by the fact that *Etta* is classified as a singular feminine PN. Similarly for *Pip*. Now we deal with the second sentence. First, we add its syntactic structure to the DRS (26)a, to produce the DRS in Figure 14.3. We have a choice of rules that we could apply at this stage. We could either apply the pronouns rule to the NP under the S node (i.e. to *she*), or we could apply it to the NP under the VP node (i.e. to *him*). Here, we'll take the latter choice. This produces the DRS in Figure 14.4: Note that the pronouns rule

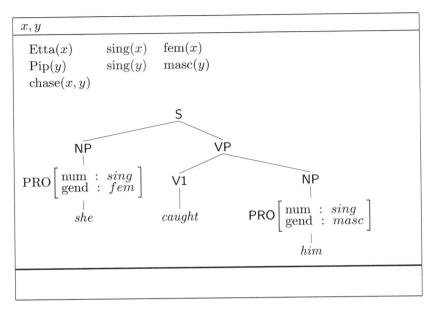

Figure 14.3
Adding a syntax tree to the DRS for (26).

has introduced something into the instruction box, and has added some number and gender conditions to the conditions box.

Now we have a choice of rules to apply again. We could still apply the pronouns rule to translate *she*, or we could use the rule for transitive verbs to translate the VP node. Here, we'll use the pronouns rule first, to produce the DRS in Figure 14.5. This second application of the pronouns rule has produced a second instruction into the instruction box. But we shouldn't carry out these instructions yet. We have to deal with the rest of the tree first. The only rule that we can apply at this stage is the one for translating transitive verbs. This produces the DRS in Figure 14.6. And now we apply the sentence rule. This tells us to substitute u with w to produce the DRS in Figure 14.7. We chose a particular order of application of semantic rules to arrive at this DRS, but we leave it as an exercise to the reader to demonstrate that the other orders of application would have yielded exactly the same DRS.

Now we have to empty the instruction box. There are two instructions we have to deal with. Step 4 in the algorithm for building DRSs doesn't

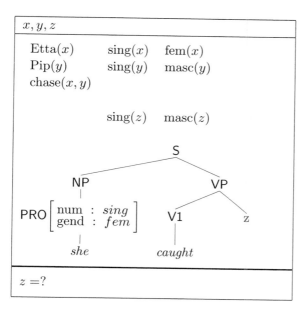

Figure 14.4
Applying the pronoun rule to the DRS for (26).

stipulate which instruction we should do first when there is a choice as there is here. So we could do the instructions in either order. We'll do $z =$? first. By the Consistency Constraint, $z = y$ is the only choice, because y is the only other discourse referent that's masculine. So we remove $z =$? from the instruction box, and add $z = y$ to the conditions box, to produce the DRS in Figure 14.8. Now we have just one instruction left. Again, by the Consistency Constraint, we should remove $w =$? from the instruction box and replace it with $w = x$ in the conditions box, because x is the only choice (it's the only other feminine discourse referent). This produces the DRS in Figure 14.9. Now the instruction box is empty. But we can do just one more thing: substitute all the zs for ys and all the ws for xs and get rid of the conditions $z = y$ and $w = x$. So the final representation of the text (26) is (26′):

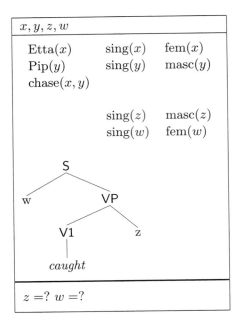

Figure 14.5
Applying the pronouns rule again to the DRS for (26).

(26′)

$$\begin{array}{|l|}
\hline
x, y \\
\hline
\begin{array}{lll}
\text{Etta}(x) & \text{sing}(x) & \text{fem}(x) \\
\text{Pip}(y) & \text{sing}(y) & \text{masc}(y) \\
\text{chase}(x, y) & & \\
\text{catch}(x, y) & & \\
\end{array} \\
\hline
 \\
\hline
\end{array}$$

So according to the DRS this text is about two things—x and y—where x is called Etta (and is singular and feminine), y is called Pip (and is singular and masculine), and x chased y, and x caught y.

Discourse structure

We've seen that number and gender can affect what a pronoun refers to, and we've shown how we can model this. But the discourses in (7) show that linguistic devices like determiners and connectives also affect what

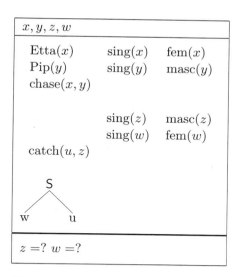

Figure 14.6
Applying the rule for transitive verbs to the DRS for (26).

a pronoun refers to.

(7) a.   A man loved Mary. He proposed to her.

     b.   No man loved Mary. ?He proposed to her.

     c.   Every man loved Mary. ?He proposed to her.

     d.   If a man loved Mary, he proposed to her.

How can we encode these effects in our grammar? Well, DRSs have STRUCTURE: there are boxes inside boxes. Inside each box, you get some information about objects that the discourse is about. And the particular box that a piece of semantic information appears in tells you something about how that information was presented in the natural language text. For example, if the semantic information is in the LHS box of a ⇒-condition (that is, it's in the LHS box of two boxes that are connected with ⇒), then you know that this information was presented either in a phrase containing *if* or in a noun phrase containing the determiner *every*.

It turns out that this structure can be used to *predict* which objects mentioned in the discourse are accessible as antecedents to pronouns. In other words, we can use the configuration of boxes to constrain

$$\boxed{\begin{array}{l} x, y, z, w \\ \hline \begin{array}{lll} \mathrm{Etta}(x) & \mathrm{sing}(x) & \mathrm{fem}(x) \\ \mathrm{Pip}(y) & \mathrm{sing}(y) & \mathrm{masc}(y) \\ \mathrm{chase}(x,y) & & \\ & \mathrm{sing}(z) & \mathrm{masc}(z) \\ & \mathrm{sing}(w) & \mathrm{fem}(w) \\ \mathrm{catch}(w,z) & & \end{array} \\ \hline z =? \ w =? \end{array}}$$

Figure 14.7
Applying the sentence rule to the DRS for (26).

$$\boxed{\begin{array}{l} x, y, z, w \\ \hline \begin{array}{lll} \mathrm{Etta}(x) & \mathrm{sing}(x) & \mathrm{fem}(x) \\ \mathrm{Pip}(y) & \mathrm{sing}(y) & \mathrm{masc}(y) \\ \mathrm{chase}(x,y) & & \\ & \mathrm{sing}(z) & \mathrm{masc}(z) \\ & \mathrm{sing}(w) & \mathrm{fem}(w) \\ \mathrm{catch}(w,z) & & \\ z = y & & \end{array} \\ \hline w =? \end{array}}$$

Figure 14.8
Carrying out the instructions in the DRS from Figure 14.7.

antecedents to pronouns. In a way, this isn't surprising. By looking at texts like those in (7), we have seen that the antecedents to pronouns are constrained by the way information is presented in a text—e.g. by factors like whether there is the word *if* or *every* in the context. And we have just seen that the configuration of boxes gives away clues about just these facts about presentation: i.e. whether there were words like *if* or *every* in the context. So we can "extract" the information we need from the configuration of boxes.

$$\boxed{\begin{array}{ll}
x, y, z, w & \\
\hline
\text{Etta}(x) \quad \text{sing}(x) \quad \text{fem}(x) & \\
\text{Pip}(y) \quad \text{sing}(y) \quad \text{masc}(y) & \\
\text{chase}(x, y) & \\
\\
\qquad\qquad \text{sing}(z) \quad \text{masc}(z) & \\
\qquad\qquad \text{sing}(w) \quad \text{fem}(w) & \\
\text{catch}(w, z) & \\
z = y, \ w = x & \\
\end{array}}$$

Figure 14.9
Carrying out the last instruction in the DRS for (26).

To clarify this, consider the semantic representations of the text in (7)a and (7)c. We give these below as (7)a′ and (7)c′, respectively. We've left out conditions like *man* is singular and masculine, *Mary* is singular and feminine, and the number and gender of the pronouns for the sake of simplicity. But bear in mind that the conditions are really there.

(7) a.   A man loved Mary. He proposed to her.

a′.

$$\boxed{\begin{array}{l}
w, x, y, z \\
\hline
\text{man}(w) \\
\text{Mary}(x) \\
\text{loved}(w, x) \\
\text{proposed}(y, z) \\
\hline
y = ? \\
z = ? \\
\end{array}}$$

(7) c.   Every man loved Mary. ?He proposed to her.

c′.

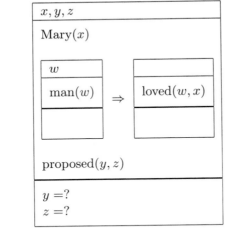

There are two things to note about (7)c′. First, the semantic conditions
arising from *He proposed to her* are in the biggest box. This is because
the syntactic tree for the sentence is introduced at this level, to reflect
the fact that it's not within the SCOPE of *every man*, which was in the
previous sentence.

Second, note that the object x that bears the name *Mary*, and the
condition Mary(x) have both been moved into the biggest box, rather
than appearing in the LHS box of the ⇒-condition. This is a refinement
of the rule for analyzing proper names that was given earlier in the
book (see section 10.2). We shall see why we make this refinement in
chapter 15. But briefly, the motivation for promoting x and Mary(x)
to the biggest box is the following. It reflects the fact that in *whatever
context* one uses the proper name, one asserts that someone exists who
bears that name. So, for example, the sentence *If Mary talks, she walks*
does not imply that Mary actually does walk, but it *does* imply that
Mary exists. If x and Mary(x) were in the LHS box of the ⇒-condition
for this sentence, as the grammar currently predicts, then the DRS would
fail to reflect this. This is because the DRS for the sentence can be true
even when all the things in the LHS of the ⇒-condition are false (cf. the
four card problem). By promoting the semantic representation of *Mary*
out of the LHS DRS of the ⇒-condition, and putting it into the biggest
box, we ensure that our analysis of the sentence captures the implication

that Mary exists. We'll see in detail how this promotion of the proper name to the biggest DRS occurs in chapter 15. But it's important to bear in mind now that this happens because we'll show below that it affects what a pronoun can refer to.

It is interesting to note that in (7)a′, the antecedents we want for the pronouns are both introduced in the same box as the instructions $y =?$ and $z =?$. Also, in (7)c, the antecedent for z that we want—namely x, who's Mary—is introduced in the same box as the instruction $z =?$. But the antecedent we want for y—namely w—is not. Rather, it's in a box embedded in this box. And in the natural language discourse (7)c, we can find an antecedent to *she* (Mary), but we fail to find an antecedent to *he*. So, let's assume that $x =?$ can be replaced with an identity condition $x = y$ when y is introduced at the same level, but not when y is introduced at an embedded level. Then this constraint captures our intuitions about (7)a and (7)c. It allows us to transform (7)a′ into (7)a″, and (7)c′ into (7)c″:

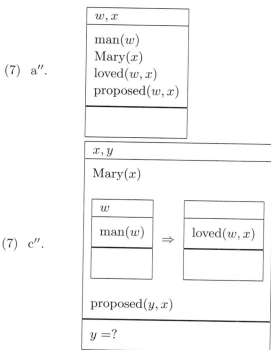

(7)a″ captures the natural interpretation of (7)a. In (7)c″, we can't successfully carry out the instruction $y =?$, because we can't identify y with w since w's introduced in an embedded box, and we can't identify it with x because it's the wrong gender, and there are no other possibilities. So we haven't managed to carry out all the instructions in the instruction box. Therefore, (7)c is correctly predicted to be odd; we can't interpret it.

We haven't talked about how to represent words like *no* in a DRS. We gloss over the details here. Just take it on account that, according to current thought in linguistics, the semantic representations of sentences containing *no* have similar structures to (7)c″; the DRSs look just like (7)c″, except that ⇒ is replaced with something else. So the above constraint, that ensures y can't be identified with w, also explains why (7)b is odd.

(7) b.   No man loved Mary. ?He proposed to her.

The above proposals about which antecedents are accessible are captured in the following constraint:

● **The Structural Constraint:**
You can replace $x =?$ with $x = y$ only if:

(a) $x =?$ is in a box that's (perhaps embedded in) the one where y is introduced; or

(b) $x =?$ is (perhaps embedded) in the RHS box of a ⇒-condition, and y is introduced in the LHS box of this condition.

This Structural Constraint basically states: objects in boxes embedded in the one you're in are inaccessible to pronouns, and so are objects in the RHS box, if you're in the LHS box.

The first of these conditions ensures that once you finish describing a certain package of information (by getting out of that box), you can't refer back to anything in it. So, for example, suppose you have a text of the form given in (27), where A_1, etc., are simple sentences:

(27) A_1. A_2. If A_3, then A_4. A_5.

Then the information *If A_3 then A_4* gets packaged up as embedded boxes connected by ⇒, to reflect the fact that unlike the rest of the text, this describes a hypothetical situation. Once you stop describing this hypothetical situation, you get out of these embedded boxes, and continue to add information to the biggest box again. The above Structural Constraint says that once you have done this, you cannot refer back to anything in the hypothetical situation. You would have to explicitly indicate in the subsequent text that you were talking about the hypothetical situation again, before you could use a pronoun to refer to things in it.

The condition (b) in The Structural Constraint captures the intuition that if you're in a LHS box, you can't refer to stuff in the RHS box, because in natural language discourse the stuff in the RHS box is usually said *after* the stuff in the LHS box, and you can't refer back to stuff you haven't said yet! Actually, there are very special circumstances where you can in fact use a pronoun *before* its antecedent is mentioned: this is a phenomenon known as cataphora. But for the sake of simplicity we'll ignore it here. Cataphora not withstanding, then, in a sentence of the form *If A then B*, *A* shouldn't contain pronouns that refer to individuals that are introduced in *B*. This would be different if you said, *B, if A*. But we're ignoring this ordering for the purposes of this book.

It's quite easy to identify which discourse referents the Structural Constraint allows you to use as antecedents to pronouns. You can use the following algorithm for "walking" through the DRS to work it out: Start in the box where the instruction $x =?$ that you want to resolve is. Then do the following: If you can move to a box immediately to your left, move to it; otherwise, if you can move up to a bigger box, move to that; otherwise, stop. This defines a path through the boxes in the DRS. Any discourse referent that is introduced in one of the boxes on this path is a possible antecedent to x. All the other discourse referents are ruled out.

The Structural Constraint makes the right predictions for (7)a, (7)b and (7)c. It also deals effectively with (7)d.

(7) d.   If a man loved Mary, he proposed to her.

The grammar produces the following representation of (7)d. First the semantic rule for *if* is applied to produce (7d′) (other semantic rules could have been applied first, such as the one for proper names or the one for indefinite noun phrases, and we leave it as an exercise to the reader to work out what the DRS would be).

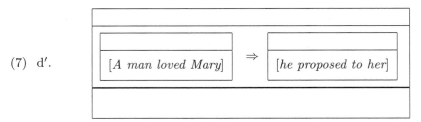

(7) d′.

Then the two sentences are reduced to semantic information in the usual way:

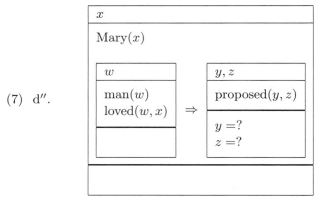

(7) d″.

The instructions $y =?$ and $z =?$ appear in an embedded RHS box, rather than in the biggest box, because of the place in the structure where *he proposed to her* is converted into semantic information. Mary(x) appears in the biggest box, because as we mentioned, proper names are always promoted to this level, regardless of where they appear in the syntax of the sentence.[26]

We must now carry out these instructions $z =?$ and $y =?$. $z =?$ can be replaced with $z = x$ because x is introduced in a box that *contains* the box where this instruction is, and so it meets the Structural Constraint. Moreover, replacing $y =?$ with $y = w$ also satisfies the Structural Constraint. And no other choices will do, because by the Consistency Constraint, the number and gender information on the antecedents and pronouns must match. Identifying the discourse referents this way produces the following:

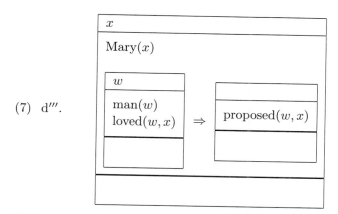

(7) d‴.

The DRS (7)d‴ is true only if the following holds: If a man w loved x, where x is Mary, then that man w proposed to x. Note that (7)d‴ is therefore false if it is uttered in a situation where there are two men that loved Mary, but only one of them proposed to her. This is in contrast to the conditions that make (7)a true. So the way information is presented—namely whether it's in an *if*-phrase or not, affects how to interpret the pronoun, and hence what the overall sentence means.

Exercise

Exercise 14.1: There is a scope ambiguity in sentence (7). Explain how the grammar captures this, and how it affects the interpretation of the pronoun.

Exercise 14.2: Do the Consistency Constraint and Structural Constraint explain the preferred interpretation of pronouns in (2)?

(2)   John met Bill. He asked him a question.

If so, how? If not, how could you extend the analysis to account for this example?

14.3   Non-Linguistic Constraints on Pronouns

Consider sentence (8):

(8)   If a baby hates cow's milk, boil it.

Neither consistency constraints nor structural constraints predict that we prefer an interpretation of (8) where the cow's milk, rather than the baby, is boiled! Our grammar produces the representation (8′):

(8′)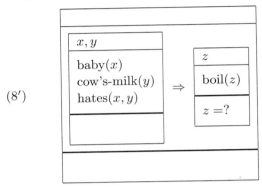

The Consistency Constraint is satisfied when z is identified with x (the baby), because it's consistent, if a little macabre, to boil the baby. The Structural Constraint is also satisfied. So these constraints don't distinguish the baby and the cow's milk as antecedents to the pronoun *it*. And yet, we prefer the reading where *it* is the cow's milk. Why?

Intuitively, the preference between the two possible antecedents to the pronoun *it* is grounded in knowledge about the way the world is—so called WORLD KNOWLEDGE or BACKGROUND KNOWLEDGE. We tend not to boil babies, whereas boiling milk is acceptable. Thus, (8) indicates that when there's a choice, we tend to disprefer interpretations of sentences that denote the "bizarre" (such as boiling babies) relative to the alternatives (such as an interpretation involving boiling milk, which according to world knowledge is not a bizarre occurrence). One can specify this constraint:

- **The Knowledge Constraint:**

If the **Consistency Constraint** and **Structural Constraint** supply a choice of identity conditions of the form $x = y$ with which to replace the instruction $x =?$, then prefer an identity condition which *doesn't* imply something which violates general world knowledge over the identity conditions that do.

This constraint is different from the other two. The other two don't rank choices when there is a choice, rather they tell you what the choices are.

But the Knowledge Constraint ranks choices. It says: Prefer readings that are in tune with world knowledge.

But as it stands, this constraint is specified in a very vague way. What precisely counts as something that violates general world knowledge? We've suggested that a situation in which a baby is boiled is one that violates such knowledge. But we need more general principles for making such decisions with arbitrary situations. What are those principles? These are open research questions.

The Knowledge Constraint uses concepts like those presented in chapter 4. There we described how humans reason about what usually happens, and what is about to happen, on the basis of partial information or uncertain knowledge. PROBABILITIES formed a vital ingredient in this reasoning. Here we see that this human ability to reason with uncertainty actually affects the way utterances are interpreted. In other words, this reasoning affects what's communicated. The Knowledge Constraint could be rephrased as follows: When the Consistency and Structural Constraints yield a choice of ways for interpreting a pronoun, prefer the interpretation that denotes a situation with the highest probability. But using probabilities here to specify the Knowledge Constraint begs questions. What is the relevant base rate information on which to evaluate the probabilities of the alternative readings of a sentence? How do we rank the probabilities of the alternative interpretations? And what should those probabilities be conditioned on (in other words, what factors in the discourse context should affect our probability calculations)? Further, how big a difference in probabilities do we need between the situations described by the alternative interpretations for humans to disambiguate the pronoun in favor of one interpretation over the other?

Another way of tackling the problem of formalizing the Knowledge Constraint is to use LOGIC rather than probabilistic reasoning. There are logics for reasoning with uncertainty that have been developed in AI to model how humans conclude things on the basis of incomplete evidence. These logics often model the same inference patterns as Probability Theory. However, they approach the problem in a different way. These logics exploit rules that symbolize the *meaning* of the various factors involved in the inference. They don't involve computation with numbers like probability theory does. Rather, these logics supply interpretations to rules such as (28), which are characterized by the fact that they have exceptions (e.g. penguins are an exception to this rule), and they provide the means to reason with these rules:

(28)   Birds fly.

Representing general knowledge like (28) in explicit ways, so that a computer can simulate the reasoning that humans do, has been a hot topic in AI for some years.

But the amount of knowledge a computer needs to know is vast; just think of the size of an encyclopedia, and that only states a small fraction of the kinds of things humans know. Encyclopedias don't include information such as people don't boil babies, which underlies the preferred interpretation of (8). Representing all general knowledge in a logical manner that a computer can understand is still very much an open research problem.

Furthermore, as we mentioned, even if one does know that people don't boil babies, it's still unclear exactly how this rule leads us to disprefer the reading of (8) where *it* is the baby. On what basis does this happen? Sentence (8) doesn't actually stipulate that someone boil a baby, even if *it* is interpreted as the baby (because *boil it* is in the consequent of a conditional, i.e. of an *if. . . ,then. . .* sentence). Clearly, reasoning about what the speaker *intended* to communicate, as well as reasoning with world knowledge, is important. Presumably, we conclude that there was a very small chance that the speaker meant *boil the baby*, even as a consequent of the conditional (and this assumption about what the speaker intended to communicate must be related to the fact about world knowledge that people don't boil babies); the chances that the speaker meant *boil the milk* are much higher. But how we reach such conclusions is as yet not very well understood because it involves reasoning about what the speaker was thinking, as well as reasoning about the world. Reasoning about what a person thinks is notoriously difficult, since we don't have direct access to this information, but rather must infer his or her thoughts through observing his or her behaviour. These problems are active research bizzare topics.

Encoding the knowledge one needs, together with the necessary inference mechanisms, in a way that would make the Knowledge Constraint an effective contributing factor to interpreting pronouns is beyond the current technology. But it is within our means to encode some   background information in simple ways, so that it can influence the interpretation of some very simple examples. We will look at some of this work in chapter 16. Statistical methods for interpreting pronouns are also proving to be an excellent way of approximating the complex reasoning over background knowledge that one would need to resolve anaphora. We give some references to this work in section 14.5.

14.4 Conclusion and Problems

People work out what pronouns denote on the basis of the context in which the pronoun is uttered. There are both linguistic and non-linguistic constraints on the process. If these constraints aren't met, then the pronoun sounds odd. We have suggested that there are (at least) three such constraints, in addition to the Anaphora Constraint that we introduced in chapter 10, and we've proposed how the grammar can be extended to encode the first two of them. Roughly speaking, these constraints express the following:

• **The Consistency Constraint:** One cannot pick an antecedent to a pronoun that results in a contradictory DRS.

• **The Structural Constraint:** One cannot pick up an antecedent from an embedded box, or from a RHS box when the pronoun is in the LHS box.

• **The Knowledge Constraint:** One prefers pronouns to have antecedents that create an overall interpretation of the text that is "in tune" with background information about the world, over those interpretations that describe something "bizarre."

It must be stressed that the process of finding antecedents to pronouns is in general much more complex than we've modeled here. The above constraints work for some simple texts, but they by no means model the task of interpreting pronouns in every case.

For example, our grammar can't explain what happens when a pronoun refers to something abstract, such as a fact or an event. This is partly because we haven't introduced discourse referents for abstract things like events in our grammar. So our grammar as it stands can't deal with texts like those in (29) from *The Wall Street Journal*:

(29) a.   Be careful what you wish...because wishes sometimes
            come true. <u>That</u>'s what the Semiconductor Industry As-
            sociation, which represents U.S. manufacturers, has been
            learning.

     b.   Well, a clerk told us, we'd need to hire a lawyer to make
            a petition—but <u>it</u> probably wouldn't be worth the effort.

     c.   As part of a corporate streamlining of programs, many
            companies are extending early-retirement packages to le-
            gions of senior managers. They see <u>it</u> as one relatively
            painless way to pare management ranks.

In (29)a, *that* refers to the *event* of wishes coming true. In (29)b, *it*
refers to the event of hiring a lawyer. And in (29)c, *it* refers to the event
of companies extending early-retirement programs. We don't currently
have discourse referents that refer to events in our grammar, and so we
can't identify *that* and *it* in (29) with events via the above procedure.
   One might think that we could solve these problems by refining our
DRSs so that they include more information, adding discourse referents
for the *events* that are talked about. But simply introducing discourse
referents for events into DRSs won't solve all our problems. Even if we
did this, the Structural Constraint would fail to predict that *it* in (30)
can refer to all three claims or just the third one, but not the second
claim to the exclusion of the other two:

(30) a.   One plaintiff had never received his full pay.

     b.   Another had been passed over for promotion three times.

     c.   Yet another had been denied a job because of his race.

     d.   But the jury didn't believe <u>it</u>.

The discourse structure should tell us that things in (30)b on their own
can't be referred to with a pronoun in (30)d. But given the way we've set
up the grammar, the structure for (30) is completely flat—we would just
get all the conditions in one big box, and we wouldn't have any embedded
boxes. So our Structural Constraint doesn't distinguish among the things
that *it* in (30)d could refer to, at least, it won't do it given the DRS that
would be constructed for this text.
   We'll return to this issue of discourse structure later in the book. We'll
suggest that the Structural Constraint itself is not at fault here. Rather,

the way in which we build DRSs is too simple. The DRSs we produce with our grammar are flatter than they should be. They leave out a lot of information that, in the case of (30), is important for constraining anaphora. In particular, our DRSs ignore the RHETORICAL CONNECTIONS between the sentences: The fact that the topic of conversation in (30) is the three claims made in court, and that (30)a–c describe the three claims individually. If you add this information to the semantic representation, then the structure changes, and thus the Structural Constraint will predict different things about the interpretation of pronouns.

Finally, our analysis of (7)d is inadequate in the general case.

(7) d.   If a man loved Mary, he proposed to her.

Our grammar currently predicts that *he* refers to *every* man that loved Mary. While this is the correct prediction for (7)d it's not the right prediction for other similar examples, e.g. (31):

(31)   If Pedro has a dime in his pocket, he'll stick <u>it</u> in the parking meter.

Because of our world knowledge about the way parking meters work, we don't interpret (31) as Pedro stuffing every dime he's got in his pocket into the meter. Rather, we assume that he puts just some of the dimes in. This contrasts with (7)d, where the pronoun *he* refers to all men that loved Mary. Given the way we've constructed the semantic representation of noun phrases such as *a dime* and *a man* when they're in an *if*-statement, we can't differentiate the interpretations of (7)d and (31). The natural interpretation of (31) is currently actually *blocked* by the grammar. And even if we were to specify the Knowledge Constraint more explicitly, we wouldn't be able to predict that Pedro puts only some dimes from his pocket in the meter, and not all of them, because the semantic representation blocks this from being a choice in the first place! Finding a way to solve this is currently an open research question.

Exercises

Exercise 14.3: There are many expressions in English that receive some of their meaning from the discourse context in which they appear.

Pronouns are just one example.

1. Write down four words or phrases that, like pronouns, require knowledge about the context for their interpretation.

2. Demonstrate that these words and phrases can mean different things in different contexts, by means of example texts.

3. Try to specify exactly what things in the context determine the meaning of these four expressions. What are the constraints on the effects that context can have on their meaning? Do they differ from the constraints we've given for pronouns? If so, how?

Exercise 14.4: The account of pronouns we've given here predicts that if an individual is introduced in a text by his proper name, then he can subsequently be referred to with a pronoun, *regardless* of the length and nature of the intervening material between the proper name and the pronoun. Explain why the account commits us to this. Do you think this prediction matches the facts about the way we use pronouns? If so, why? If not, why not?

14.5   Further Reading

The model of pronoun interpretation that we have presented here is largely based on that given in Kamp and Reyle (1993).

- Kamp, Hans and Uwe Reyle (1993). *From Discourse to Logic: Introduction to Modeltheoretic Semantics of Natural Language, Formal Logic, and Discourse Representation Theory*. Dordrecht: Kluwer Academic.

Chapter 5 of this book is devoted entirely to plural pronouns, something that we merely mentioned in section 14.2.

If you're interested in reading further on the subject of pronouns, then you may find the following references useful:

- Lyons, J. (1977a). *Semantics*, Volumes 1 and 2. Cambridge: Cambridge University Press.
- Lyons, J. (1977b). "Deixis and Anaphora," in T. Myers (ed.). *The Development of Conversation and Discourse*. Edinburgh: Edinburgh University Press.

These both contain discussions of the various ways in which pronouns can be interpreted. This research precedes some of the ideas that we presented here, however.

The following paper examines the problem of inferring what pronouns refer to, on the basis of needing to preserve DISCOURSE COHERENCE; that is, working out what the connections are between the various things mentioned in a discourse, in order to ensure that the discourse as a whole makes sense.

- Hobbs, J. R. (1979). "Coherence and Coreference," *Cognitive Science*, 3, 67–90.

This paper is using techniques that have been developed in artificial intelligence for natural language processing, including logics for reasoning on the face of incomplete evidence, which we mentioned in section 14.3. We will examine the issue of discourse coherence in chapter 16, although connecting it in detail to the account of pronouns discussed here is beyond the scope of this book.

In this chapter we used *features* and *values* to specify gender and number constraints on nouns and pronouns. Constraint-based grammars use these tools, in addition to operations known as inheritance and unification, to express partial constraints on the use of words. For a general introduction to constraint-based grammars, consult Sag and Wasow (1999).

- Sag, Ivan A., and Tom Wasow (1999). *Syntactic Theory: A Formal Introduction*. Stanford: CSLI.

We also mentioned in section 14.1 the role of commonsense reasoning in interpreting pronouns. There are many varieties of formal models of commonsense reasoning, some of which can be found in the following:

- Asher, Nicholas, and Michael Morreau (1991). "Commonsense Entailment," *Proceedings of the 12th International Joint Conference on Artificial Intelligence*, 387–392.
- Konolige, Kurt (1988). "Hierarchic Autoepistemic Logic for Nonmonotonic Reasoning," *Proceedings of the 7th National Conference on Artificial Intelligence*, 439–443.
- McCarthy, John (1980). "Circumscription—A Form of Nonmonotonic Reasoning," *Artificial Intelligence*, 13.1–2, 27–39.

- Pearl, Judea (1988). *Probabilistic Reasoning in Intelligent Systems: Networks of Plausible Inference.* San Mateo: Morgan Kaufmann.
- Reiter, Ray (1980). "A Logic for Default Reasoning," *Artificial Intelligence,* 13, 91–132.

The following papers use commonsense reasoning to predict what a pronoun refers to:

- Asher, Nicholas, and Alex Lascarides (2003). *Logics of Conversation.* Cambridge: Cambridge University Press.
- Grosz, Barbara, and Candy Sidner (1986). "Attention, Intentions, and the Structure of Discourse," *Computational Linguistics,* 12, 175–204.
- Hobbs, Jerry, et al. (1993). "Interpretation as Abduction," *Artificial Intelligence,* 63.1–2, 69–142.

The following book provides a good overview of many of the current techniques that are applied to the problem of pronoun resolution:

- Mitkov, Ruslan (2002). *Anaphora Resolution.* New York: Longman.

This includes an overview of linguistic work in this area, as well as corpus-based work involving machine learning and statistics. Unfortunately, we have not had space in this chapter to explore statistical approaches to pronoun resolution. Such approaches are designed to predict the preferred interpretation of pronouns in cases where several options are linguistically possible, for example the preferred interpretation of the pronouns in (2).

(2)   John met Bill. He asked him a question.

Centering Theory offers a very influential approach to predicting antecedents to pronouns, and the following is a seminal paper in computational linguistics on the interpretation of pronouns.

- Grosz, B., A. Joshi, and S. Weinstein (1995). "Centering: A Framework for Modeling the Local Coherence of Discourse," *Computational Linguistics,* 21.2, 203–226.

Centering Theory is an alternative rule-based account of pronouns to the one that we have described here. These two accounts have different strengths and weaknesses. For example, Centering Theory predicts the preferred interpretation of pronouns in (2) while our grammar does not; but Centering Theory does not offer an account at all of the pronouns in conditionals (e.g. (7)d) while our account does, albeit sometimes with the wrong predictions (e.g. (31)). It remains an open research question how the constraints on pronouns imposed by DRSs might be combined with the constraints described in Centering Theory.

15 Presuppositions

15.1 Presupposition vs. Entailment

There is a sense in which uttering the sentence (1), the speaker assumes that the hearer is prepared to take for granted the proposition that John has a wife:

(1)   John's wife took an aspirin.

In fact, one could go further, and argue that the sentence (1) would be entirely meaningless (rather than false) if John didn't have a wife. This contrasts with another proposition that's implied by (1), namely, that someone took an aspirin. If no one took an aspirin, then sentence (1) would be false rather than meaningless. Furthermore, observe the difference in status between the propositions that John has a wife and someone took an aspirin by negating the sentence (*John's wife didn't take an aspirin*). The negated sentence doesn't imply that someone took an aspirin, but it still implies that John has a wife.

These propositions that are presented in sentences as things that are to be "taken for granted" are called PRESUPPOSITIONS. So we say that the utterance (1) PRESUPPOSES that John has a wife. We may also say that *John's wife* presupposes that John has a wife. The things that trigger presuppositions, such as the possessive *'s* (e.g. *John's wife* presupposes John has a wife) and the DEFINITE ARTICLE *the* (e.g. *the man* presupposes there is a man) are known as PRESUPPOSITION TRIGGERS. How do we distinguish presuppositions from other propositions that are implied by utterances? And what role do presuppositions play in communication?

We have already contrasted two things that are implied by sentence (1): that John has a wife on the one hand, and that someone took an aspirin on the other. The latter proposition is an ENTAILMENT of the sentence (1). A necessary condition for being an entailment of a sentence is that it must be true, for the sentence is true. That someone took an aspirin must certainly be true for the sentence (1) to be true, for example. One of the uses for the grammar that we've been developing in this book is to compute in a rigorous manner the entailments of simple English texts; just delete some conditions in the DRS, and you have something that is entailed by the sentence. As an exercise, assure yourself that you know why this is so. Thinking simply about the truth conditions of the sentence, however, isn't sufficient for capturing what we see intuitively as a difference between the propositions that John has a wife and that someone took an aspirin in our example, since they both have the property that they must be true for the sentence (1) to be true.

Presuppositions are *different* from semantic entailments in two important ways. First, the most notable difference is their tendency to *project from embeddings*. What this means is: even if a presupposition trigger is within the syntactic scope of a conditional (i.e. it's preceded by an *if*-clause), a MODAL (i.e. it's preceded by a phrase like *it's possible that...*) or a negation (i.e. it's within the scope of *not*), the presupposed material can behave as if it was not within that scope at all, in that it's implied by the whole complex sentence. To use the terminology, the presupposition tends to have wide semantic scope over conditionals, modals, and negation even when its presupposition trigger had narrow syntactic scope. Semantic entailments don't project from embeddings in this way. For example, (1) entails *someone took an aspirin*. But adding the modal phrase *it's possible that...*, to produce (2) results in a sentence where this entailment doesn't survive: (2) doesn't entail *someone took an aspirin*.

(2)   It's possible that John's wife took an aspirin.

But it *does* still follow from (2) that John has a wife, just as it did from (1). Here we see a presupposition surviving the process of placing its trigger within the syntactic scope of a modal. Entailments don't survive in this way.

Here are further examples that serve to illustrate how presuppositions are different from entailments:

(3) a.   The king of France signed a peace treaty.

      b.   The king of France didn't sign a peace treaty.

      c.   If the king of France signed a peace treaty, then all disputes have been settled.

      d.   It's possible that the king of France signed a peace treaty.

The sentences in (3) all imply there is a king of France, but only (3)a implies that someone signed a peace treaty. That there is a king of France is presupposed because all these sentences imply it, even though *the king of France* is embedded in negation, a conditional, and a modal expression. That someone signed a peace treaty is a semantic entailment of (3)a: Observe how (3)b, c, and d don't entail that someone signed a peace treaty. So semantic entailments are distinguished from presuppositions in that the latter can be implied by the sentence even when the thing that triggers them is embedded, whereas entailments lack this "projection" property. Sentences can in fact have several presuppositions, induced by several triggers. In fact, sentence (1) presupposes that there is someone called John, as well as presupposing that John has a wife. (To convince yourself of this, observe that (2) implies that there is someone called John.) The proper name *John* is one presupposition trigger and the possessive marker *'s* is another.

The above observations about presuppositions may lead one to think that they are a kind of "super-entailment," able to survive as implications of a sentence however we modify it with negation, etc. But things aren't that simple. Sentence (3)e shows that presuppositions don't always survive.

(3) e.   The king of France didn't sign a peace treaty—there is no king of France.

Because of this, presupposition triggers such as *the king of France* are said to trigger POTENTIAL PRESUPPOSITIONS (this term is due to Gerald Gazdar; see section 15.7), and one of the tasks we must perform when interpreting discourse is to identify the subset of potential presuppositions that are *actual* presuppositions of the utterance.[27] In (3)e, the presupposition that there is a king of France is CANCELED (this term is also due to Gerald Gazdar and is re-used by other researchers such as David Beaver; see section 15.7). In fact, in a sense, the status of the proposition that there is a king of France with respect to the utterance (3)e suggests that the negation in (3)e is "metalinguistic" in some respect.

Semantic entailments cannot be canceled felicitously in the way that presuppositions can. Compare (3)e (which is acceptable) with the contradictory (3)f:

(3) f.   ?The king of France signed a peace treaty,
              but no one signed a peace treaty.

Another way in which a potential presupposition can fail to be an actual presupposition of an utterance is through what is known as FIL-TERING (again this term is coined by Gerald Gazdar and is subsequently used by many other researchers). Compare the examples (4)a and (4)b:

(4) a.   If baldness is hereditary, then John's son is bald.

     b.   If John has a son, then John's son is bald.

Both sentences contain the NP *John's son*, and thus they both potentially presuppose that John has a son (and that there is someone called John). However, in (4)a the potential presupposition that John has a son is an *actual* presupposition of the whole utterance, while in (4)b it is not. Both (4)a and (4)b presuppose that there is someone called John, however. We say that the potential presupposition that John has a son is FILTERED OUT in (4)b. Clearly, the semantic content of the *if*-phrase affects whether potential presuppositions that are triggered by expressions in the main clause are presupposed by the whole utterance or not.

The difference between canceling and filtering is that in the former the potential presupposition in question is implied to be false whereas in the latter it's not—(4)b doesn't imply that John has a son, nor that he hasn't. All these examples show that whether or not a potential presupposition is an actual presupposition is highly dependent on the content of the discourse context in which the sentence is uttered.

The preceding discussion begs a question, which is known as the PRO-JECTION PROBLEM. Suppose you have a complex sentence S, made up of simpler sentences via words like *or*, *and*, and *if..., then...* or via complement clauses (e.g. *John believes that his wife took an aspirin*) or adverbial clauses (e.g. *For John's wife to take an aspirin, she must have a headache*). Now suppose that these simpler sentences have presupposition triggers in them, which give rise to a set of potential presuppositions P (e.g. one of the simple sentences may contain the phrase *The king of France*, which is a presupposition trigger with corresponding potential presupposition *there is a king of France*, which would then be in the set P). Then the question is: Which elements in this set P survive as presuppositions of the sentence S itself? A solution to the Projection Problem must explain why the potential presupposition that there is a king of France is presupposed by (3)a, b, c, and d but not by (3)e. It should also explain why the potential presupposition that John has a son is a presupposed by (4)a, but not by (4)b. The differences between these sentences show that presupposition projection is heavily dependent on the content of the simple sentences that make up the complex sentence, their relation to each other, and their relation to each other's (potential) presuppositions. A solution to the Projection Problem must reflect these dependencies.

Presupposition triggers come in many guises. The following are just some examples:

(5)   *The:*
        The king of France is bald.
        (Presupposes there is a king of France).

(6)   *Proper Names:*
        John is bald.
        (Presupposes there is someone called John).

(7)   *Possessives:*
        All of John's children are bald.
        (Presupposes John has children).

(8)   *When:*
        The MPs were in revolt when Major started the investigation.
        (Presupposes Major started the investigation).

(9)   *Stop:*
        John stopped smoking.
        (Presupposes John smoked).

(10)   *It-Clefts:*
        It was John who ate the beans.
        (Presupposes someone ate the beans).

(11)   *Regret:*
        John regretted eating the beans.
        (Presupposes John ate the beans).

(12)   *Know:*
        John knows that Peter passed the exam.
        (Presupposes Peter passed the exam).

(13)   *Manage:*
        John managed to stop in time.
        (Presupposes it was difficult to stop in time, and that John

tried to stop in time).

You can carry out a simple test to confirm that these are presupposition triggers. Put the expression you're testing in a sentence, and see what it implies. Then put *not* in that sentence, to form a negated sentence. If the implication survives, then it's a presupposition,[28] and the expression you're testing is a presupposition trigger. Can you think of any other expressions, other than those above, that are presupposition triggers? Try testing some of your own examples.

Exercises

Exercise 15.1: Write down which expressions in the following sentences are presupposition triggers, and also what they presuppose:

- John knows when Bill arrived at the party.
- John managed to forget the keys to his car again.

Hint: List propositions that are implied by these sentences (e.g. John forgetting to do something implies that John intended to do it), and test whether this proposition is implied by the negated form of the sentence as well.

Exercise 15.2: Do the same exercise on example sentences from a newspaper editorial or scientific article. To what extent do you think that the author is exploiting presuppositions to get his or her point across?

Modeling presuppositions

We must model the way presupposition triggers like *the* and *manage* affect meaning. In particular, we must capture the fact that presupposition triggers make certain propositions into potential presuppositions, and we must classify which of these potential presuppositions are actual presuppositions in a way that does justice to the influences of the discourse context.

People can use presuppositions to good effect in communication. First, people can save time through using them, because they allow you to get a message across, even when part of that message is left unsaid. So, for example, you can say (7) instead of the more cumbersome (14):

(7)   All of John's children are bald.

(14)   There is someone called John, and he has children, all of whom are bald.

Secondly, politicians and lawyers exploit presuppositions all the time in order to convey what might be quite controversial as if it were taken for granted (and hence not controversial at all). A senator asking (15) to Alan Greenspan rather than (16) is using language to much greater effect:

(15)   When did you realize that you had screwed up the economy?

(16)   Did you screw up the economy?

When is a presupposition trigger, and so (15) presupposes (17). Indeed, *realize* is a presupposition trigger, too. (17) presupposes (18), and so both (17) and (18) are presuppositions of (15):

(17)   You realized that you had screwed up the economy.

(18)   You screwed up the economy.

So (15) "takes for granted" that Greenspan screwed up the economy and realized this, in contrast to (16). Greenspan is put on the defensive if he is to refute the presuppositions in (15), where a response like (19) would be necessary:

(19)   But I haven't screwed up the economy.

Presupposition triggers are ubiquitous in communication. Just pick a sentence in a newspaper article, and count the number of presupposition triggers and corresponding presuppositions! You will probably get more than one of them in every sentence that you pick. Think about the following sentence:

(20)   Luke Skywalker regretted finding out that Darth Vadar was his father.

This sentence has five presupposition triggers in it, yielding five potential presuppositions, which in fact all turn out to be actual presuppositions when (20) is uttered as the first sentence of a discourse. Can you find them? Try the above test involving negation, to assess whether a given expression in (20) is a presupposition trigger.[29] The presuppositions in (20) add up to virtually all of (20)'s meaning. The fact that people interpret sentences like (20) with ease shows how good they are at dealing with presuppositions. To get computers to handle human languages, we must program them to deal with presuppositions, too.

We have, in fact, already seen an analysis of a presupposition trigger in our grammar. In earlier chapters of this book, we provided the syntax and semantic rules for translating NPs of the form *the N* (e.g. *the dog*) into the DRS notation (see p.251). But we also saw that this analysis had shortcomings. It allowed you to build a DRS for the discourse (21) where John denotes the same individual as the dog, leading to an implausible interpretation of (21), in this context at least:[30]

(21)   John ran. The dog barked.

Having now discussed the fact that *the N* is a presupposition trigger, we can point at a few more shortcomings in this analysis. First, this analysis doesn't explain on its own why the presupposition associated with *the dog* (i.e. that there is a dog) projects from embeddings (i.e. the presupposition survives when a *not* is added to the sentence, or when you precede the sentence with an *if*-clause). Secondly, the analysis fails to capture the intuition that the speaker assumes that the hearer is prepared to take for granted that there is a dog. Rather it treats this information and the information that something barked in exactly the same manner. To rectify this, we're going to think again about how one might analyze *the dog* in our grammar, and try to improve on the existing analysis. We'll look at some simple proposals first, and see where they fall short. This will give us clues on how to rectify the analysis, which will be done in section 15.4. The analysis of *the N* given there will not only block the above implausible interpretation of (21), but it will also explain why presuppositions project from embeddings.

15.2   Russell's Simple Proposal for Dealing with *The*

One of the earliest theories for the semantics of the presupposition trigger *the* is by the philosopher Bertrand Russell. He suggests that "the N" means there's something that's an N, and it's unique. He provided a formula in FIRST ORDER LOGIC that specifies this. Basically, the formula states: there is an object x that's an N, and for all objects y, if that object y is an N, then y is in fact the very same object as x.

So consider sentence (3)a again.

(3) a.   The king of France signed the proclamation.

This means that there is an object x that's a king of France. It's in fact the only object (in the world) that is a king of France. Similarly, there is an object y that's a proclamation, and it's the only object (in the world) that's a proclamation. And x signed y. Intuitively, there is something compelling about viewing *the king of France* as meaning, *there is a unique king of France*. But this can't quite be right. We already see problems in (3)a with this kind of semantics for *the*, because surely (3)a *doesn't* mean that there's one and only one proclamation in the whole world.

Things get worse when we consider definite descriptions like *the man*. According to Russell's semantics, (22) is true only if the world contains just one man, and just one store, and that man walked to that store.

(22)   The man walked to the store.

But (22) in practice doesn't mean that there's only one man in the whole world. If this is what it was supposed to mean, we would never be able to say *the man* truthfully!

The problem with Russell's proposal lies in the fact that he has divorced the semantic content of definite descriptions like *the man* from the context in which they're uttered. Consider text (23), for example.

(23)   Two men walked in the park.
         One was fat and one was thin.
         The fat man told the thin one a joke.

In this context, the definite description *the fat man* doesn't mean there is a unique fat man in the whole world, as Russell's analysis would predict. Rather, this description serves to refer back to one of the men mentioned earlier. The unique aspect of the meaning of *the fat man* isn't that a fat man is unique *in the whole world*; rather, we must try to specify that it's unique in the relevant situation. In this case, there is only one man introduced into the discourse context that can be described as fat.

These examples show that we must modify Russell's semantics so that definite descriptions are linked in the right way to objects that have already been mentioned in the context. Sometimes we must ensure that the definite description refers to an object that was referred to earlier. The rule for analyzing *the* that we gave earlier in the book did this (see p.251). But as we mentioned, we must change this rule, because it gives the wrong analysis of several kinds of texts. We must automatically predict in any given discourse context when a definite description refers to something already mentioned, and when it introduces something new. We need to do this in a systematic way so that a computer can do it. This is a prerequisite to a computer understanding texts that have definite descriptions in them.

In the next section, we'll propose how one might modify the semantics of definite descriptions so that they link to context correctly. We discuss a proposal made by Rob van der Sandt (see section 15.7 for the full citation) that presuppositions behave like PRONOUNS. Since the semantics of pronouns are inextricably linked to the context in which they're uttered, presuppositions will be, too. So viewing presuppositions this way could conceivably solve the problems that Russell's analysis is up against.

15.3   Presuppositions Behave like Pronouns

We saw in chapter 14 how one can model pronouns binding to antecedents in the discourse context. The following examples indicate that presuppositions behave a lot like pronouns, because replacing the presupposition trigger with a relevant pronoun doesn't change the overall meaning:

(24) a.   Jack has children and all of $\left\{ \begin{array}{c} Jack's\ children \\ them \end{array} \right\}$ are bald.

   b.   If Jack has children, then all of $\left\{ \begin{array}{c} Jack's\ children \\ them \end{array} \right\}$ are bald.

   c.   Either Jack has no children, or all of $\left\{ \begin{array}{c} Jack's\ children \\ them \end{array} \right\}$ are bald.

(25) a. John failed his exams, and he regretted
$$\left\{ \begin{array}{c} \textit{that he failed his exams} \\ \textit{it} \end{array} \right\}.$$

b. If John failed his exams, then he regretted
$$\left\{ \begin{array}{c} \textit{that he failed his exams} \\ \textit{it} \end{array} \right\}.$$

c. Either John didn't fail his exams, or he regretted
$$\left\{ \begin{array}{c} \textit{that he failed his exams} \\ \textit{it} \end{array} \right\}.$$

One proposal in the literature is the following: Presuppositions are like pronouns, but they have more SEMANTIC CONTENT. In other words, just as we have to find antecedents to pronouns, we should also find antecedents to presuppositions. The difference is that whereas something like *them* tells us very little about what is being referred to (merely that whatever it is is plural), something like *Jack's children* gives a lot more information (what's being referred to are human non-adults, offspring of some adult male called *Jack*, and so on). When one can't find an antecedent to a pronoun in the discourse context, the utterance sounds odd:

(26)   ?All of them are bald.

In contrast, presuppositions can be felicitous even when there is no suitable antecedent for it in the context. In such cases, language users simply add the appropriate content to the context. So, for example, suppose that the hearer of (1) doesn't know that John has a wife:

(1)   John's wife took an aspirin.

The hearer doesn't get confused because the speaker, in using (1), has presented the proposition that John has a wife as if it is to be taken for granted. Rather, the hearer infers that the speaker assumes he knows or will accept that John has a wife. Accordingly, he adds the information that John has a wife to the context, and then processes the semantic information that she took an aspirin in the usual way. This process of adding information to the context so as to ensure that an utterance is felicitous is known as ACCOMMODATION.

Intuitively, accommodation is a way of giving the speaker the benefit of the doubt; the hearer adds what's necessary to the context to ensure that what the speaker uttered "made sense," or isn't odd in any way. Of course, there will be occasions when the hearer cannot do this because it would conflict with knowledge he already has. For example, he cannot accommodate the presupposition that John has a wife if he already knows that John is unmarried. In this case, accommodation would fail, and the hearer may use his next turn in the conversation to indicate this; e.g. by uttering something like *But John doesn't have a wife.* In general, accommodating antecedents to pronouns isn't possible. One might speculate that this is largely because pronouns don't carry enough semantic content for the hearer to really know what he is supposed to add to his model of the world. Accommodation is thus what differentiates presuppositions from pronouns. And their similarity lies in the fact that in both cases one attempts to bind them to antecedents in the context.

The similarities and differences between presuppositions and pronouns aren't surprising when one thinks of the phenomena in terms of GIVEN INFORMATION and NEW INFORMATION. The given information is stuff that isn't up for negotiation. The new information is the stuff under discussion. When one says something like *he is bald*, one is assuming that the information about who *he* refers to is "given;" the new information is that whoever that is is bald. Similarly, a sentence carrying a presupposition, such as *the man is bald* carries "given" information that there is a man, and "new" information that he is bald. When conversing, people enter a Given-New Contract: The speaker agrees to try to construct the given and new information of each utterance in context so that

(a)   the listener is able to compute from memory the unique antecedent that was intended for the given information; and

(b)   he will not already have the new information attached to that antecedent (because otherwise it wouldn't be new!).

So processing given information—in other words, processing pronouns and presuppositions—becomes a matter of finding a unique antecedent.

One can see how this explains the way *the fat man* is used in (23). A unique fat man exists in the context already. And so the description *the fat man* can bind to this. This is very different from Russell's proposed semantics of *the fat man*, which would commit us to (23) being true only if there was a unique fat man in the whole world. Here, we need only find a unique antecedent in the context. There may be millions of fat men in the world, but the constraint according to this proposal is that only one of them is taken to be relevant in the context.

As already mentioned, if there's no antecedent that a presupposition can bind to, then we add it to the context of utterance, subject to certain constraints being met. One of these constraints is that the result of adding the presupposition should be consistent. If adding the presupposition would produce a contradiction, then accommodation fails and the sentence carrying the presupposition cannot be interpreted. For example, the discourse (27) sounds odd because the speaker at one and the same time takes for granted that John has a wife, and asserts that he doesn't:

(27)   ?John is single. John's wife is bald.

When the hearer processes the second sentence of (27), he can't accommodate the information that John has a wife to the context (which contains *John is single*), because there is no way of adding this without producing a contradiction (that John is single and John has a wife).

How does viewing presuppositions like pronouns with semantic content help solve the Projection Problem? In (24) and (25), the potential presuppositions (that Jack has children and that John failed his exams, respectively) are not presupposed by the sentences as a whole. Observe, also, that in each of these cases, one can replace the presupposition trigger with a construction containing a pronoun: in (24) *Jack's children* is felicitously replaced with *them* and in (25) *regretted that he failed his exams* is felicitously replaced with *regretted it*. The fact that we can paraphrase using pronouns is evidence that there is a suitable antecedent in the context for the potential presupposition to bind to. In other words, all these sentences are ones where an antecedent is found without accommodating anything. Thus, the context of interpretation of the presupposition trigger doesn't change, and the potential presupposition doesn't project out, to be presupposed by the whole sentence.

In contrast, when we utter (28) in isolation of such a discourse context, we need to *accommodate* the presupposition:

(28)   All of Jack's children are bald.

That is, we need to add the information that Jack has children to the context, before we process the information that all of them are bald. Compare this with (26), where referring to Jack's children with a pronoun doesn't work because there isn't a suitable antecedent.

These observations about substituting presuppositions for pronouns suggests the following *informal* solution to the Projection Problem. To test whether a potential presupposition is presupposed by the sentence or not, investigate what happens when the relevant phrase containing the presupposition trigger is replaced with a pronoun (as we do in (24) and (25)). If the resulting sentence containing the pronoun is felicitous, then the potential presupposition is *not* presupposed by the sentence. Otherwise, the resulting sentence containing the pronoun is not felicitous and the potential presupposition is a presupposition of the whole sentence. So none of the sentences in (24) presuppose that Jack has children, even though they feature the presupposition trigger *Jack's children*. Similarly, none of the sentences in (25) presuppose that John failed his exams, even though they feature the presupposition trigger *regret* that potentially presupposes that John failed his exams (since this is the sentential complement to *regret*). But (28) does presuppose Jack has children, because (26) is odd.

This procedure for identifying the presuppositions of a sentence is not a fully precise solution to the Projection Problem. It certainly isn't a solution that is stated in a way that would help a computer process presuppositions, since the procedure relies heavily on *human* intuitions about paraphrases (Does the sentence containing the potential presupposition mean the same thing as the sentence containing the pronoun?), and human intuitions about whether the sentence containing the pronoun is felicitous or not.

We will, however, develop below a more formally precise model of presuppositions that builds on these informal observations about their behavior. That is, the formal model will exploit the close relationship, and the differences, between presuppositions and pronouns that are exhibited in the above linguistic data.

15.4   Modeling Presuppositions Systematically

Handling presuppositions is essential for several applications concerning natural language technology. For certain applications, it would be important for a computer to deny that the presuppositions of the user's sentences are true in appropriate cases. Such applications would include, for example, tutorial dialogue systems and database query systems. Recall the list of language technology applications from chapter 12, and think about which of these need a proper treatment of presuppositions. You will find that some of them do and some of them (e.g. machine translation) do not.

Since the grammar we have been developing has mechanisms for working out antecedents to pronouns, it should be possible to re-use these mechanisms as a component in the model of presuppositions. After all, we're claiming that presuppositions behave like pronouns and we intend our model of them to exploit the similarities. Presuppositions will thus be identified with antecedents, if they can, just as pronouns are so identified. The process of binding a presupposition to an antecedent, however, clearly can't simply be a case of using an old discourse referent, as our old rule for *the*, given in previous chapters, would have it. This allows co-reference where we don't want it. So we must spell out exactly when a presupposition can bind to an antecedent, in terms of the content of the presupposition, and the content of the antecedent. We can, at least in part, use the existing mechanisms for pronouns to capture this.

But like we've said, presuppositions are different from pronouns, in that when you can't bind it, you can add it. So we have to extend the grammar before it can deal with presuppositions completely. We must add mechanisms for ACCOMMODATION. That is, when there isn't an antecedent that the presupposition can be identified with, we must encode in the grammar how we *add* the presupposition to the DRS. What do we add? And in what bit of the DRS (i.e. in which box) do we put it?

First, let's review how pronouns contributed to the overall semantics of a sentence. Recall that pronouns triggered an INSTRUCTION: identify the discourse referent with another one already in the DRS. Our conjecture is that presuppositions behave like pronouns. So presuppositions triggers must do something similar. They will also trigger an instruction to identify the presupposed material with stuff that's already in the DRS. But in addition, if this isn't possible, then we must accommodate the presupposition in the DRS. We must represent this instruction in our grammar rules for converting syntactic information into semantic content.

Let's take a specific presupposition trigger: the word *the*, which is known as the DEFINITE ARTICLE. We're going to provide a new semantic rule for NPs containing *the* in our grammar, which takes account of the fact that it will introduce an instruction, as all presupposition triggers do. We'll first review its syntax, and then indicate how we can represent its semantic content, including the relevant instruction. We have already seen the following rules in syntax:

(29)   NP $\longrightarrow$ DET N

(30)   DET $\longrightarrow$ *the*

These ensure that a phrase like *the man* is an NP, assuming that *man* is classified as an N, of course! The syntax will remain the same in this new analysis.

But our semantic rule for *the* will be different from what we offered before. We have suggested that a phrase such as *the man* triggers a (potential) presupposition that there is a man. In fact, as we've mentioned, it's also presupposed that this man is unique in some sense. For the sake of simplicity we will largely ignore this uniqueness aspect of the meaning of *the* for now, and return to it later in this section, and in section 15.5. For now, we will concentrate simply on the problem of binding, or accommodating, the (potentially) presupposed information that there is a man.

We argued above that if a (potential) presupposition can be bound to an antecedent in the DRS, it will be. Otherwise, you add it. So the instruction a presupposition trigger introduces into a DRS must amount to the following:

- **Instructions for Presuppositions:**

    1. Identify the presupposition with something of the same content that's already in the DRS, if you possibly can. That is, like pronouns, the antecedent must meet the Consistency Constraint and the Structural Constraint (see chapter 14).

    2. If you can't bind it, then add it. Make sure you add it in a place in the DRS that meets the Consistency Constraint (i.e. the result of adding it isn't a contradiction), and the Structural Constraint (i.e. it's not added to an embedded box or RHS box when you're in the LHS one).

We have made this instruction for presuppositions subject to the same constraints as pronouns given in chapter 14 because presuppositions behave like pronouns.[31]

The DRS (31) means that there is a man.

(31)
$$\boxed{\begin{array}{l} x \\ \hline man(x) \end{array}}$$

This is the content of the potential presupposition triggered by *the man*. So we represent the above Instructions for Presuppositions for *the man* by preceding (31) with a question mark, thus:

(32)
$?\boxed{\begin{array}{l} x \\ \hline man(x) \end{array}}$

In other words, the "instruction" (32) means try to bind the x in the DRS (31) to an antecedent discourse referent y that has the same conditions imposed on it already (i.e. man(y)); otherwise, if no such y exists, add x and the condition man(x) to the DRS.

The grammar must ensure that processing *the man* results in the instruction (32) being inserted in the instruction box. This is different from the original rule for translating *the* that we had in our grammar (see p.251). Recall that this rule told you to re-use a discourse referent if you could, and if you couldn't, to add a new one. But this old rule allowed you to re-use a discourse referent that lacked the condition that the individual denoted by it was a man. That's why it gave the wrong analysis of (21). This new rule for *the man* fixes this: You have to bind *all* of the content of the presupposition to an antecedent. That is, with respect to (32), the presupposition will bind to an antecedent y only if man(y) is already in the DRS. So this new semantic rule for *the* will refine the old one, because the instruction constrains the re-use of discourse referents in a better way.[32] Furthermore, as we'll shortly see, the instruction also tells you exactly what to add (and where in the DRS to add it) when you can't re-use a discourse referent.

We're now in a position to state in detail the rule that converts NPs containing *the* into semantic information. This rule triggers an instruction to find an object with appropriate content (that is, which satisfies the property described by *name*) in the context, and failing that, to add one:

● The:

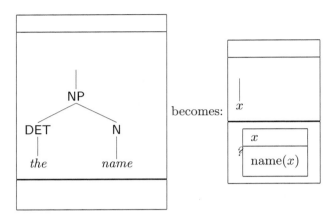

becomes:

Where x hasn't been used yet, and name is the translation of *name*.

This rule is best explained by means of an example. Consider the sentence (33):

(33)   The man talked.

Its syntactic structure is the following:

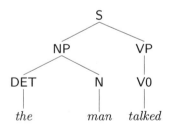

Using The, this produces (33′):

(33′)

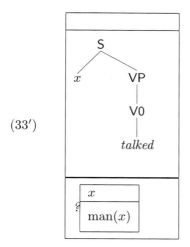

So using the rules for converting intransitive verbs to semantic information, and then using the S rule given in chapter 10, we end up with the
following semantic representation of (33):

(33″)

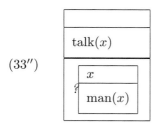

This DRS states: x talked, and we must find an object y in the context
such that man(y), and identify this y with x. Failing that, we must add
the object x (and its condition man(x)) to the context. This matches our
intuitions: (33″) states that a man talked, and if there's already been a
man mentioned then it's that man that's doing the talking, and if not,
then it's a new man we're talking about. Intuitively, that's what (33)
should mean. Contrast this with what (34) means.

(34)   A man talked.

Because (34) doesn't induce an instruction like that in (33″) to identify
the talking man with a man already mentioned in the discourse, the
man in (34) could be a completely new man, even if we've already been
talking about men. This isn't so for (33), because of the content of *the*.

Compare the rule The with the one for converting pronouns to semantic information. With pronouns, we introduced an instruction $x =?$, which meant: identify x with a discourse referent already in the context. So both the Pronoun and The rules introduce instructions. Both instructions involve identifying the thing being talked about with something already in the context. But the difference is that with presuppositions, if this identification (or binding) procedure fails, then accommodation is possible for the instruction to be carried out successfully. This option isn't available for pronouns.

We need to say more about how one fulfils the instruction in $(33'')$. To do this, we consider what happens when (33) is part of a longer text, such as (35):

(35) a.   A man walked.

     b.   A woman walked.

     c.   The man talked.

The grammar rules that we've given so far deal with the first two sentences (35)a and b to yield the DRS given in (36):

(36)
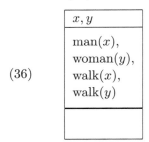

We now add the syntactic representation of (35)c to this to obtain (37):

(37)

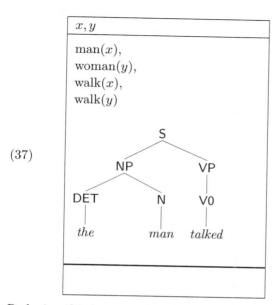

Reducing this to semantic information as we did above, via the rule **The**, we obtain the following semantic representation of the text (35):

(38)

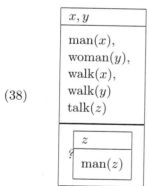

The analysis isn't complete yet, because we have to carry out the instruction expressed in (38). Strictly speaking, given the uniqueness aspect of the meaning of *the* that we mentioned earlier, this instruction amounts to the following: Try to identify z with a unique object in the DRS that's a man; and failing that, add z to the list of discourse referents of the DRS and man(z) to its conditions. In this example, we do have an object in the DRS that's a man, namely x. Moreover, it's the only man in the DRS. So we can identify z with x; x is the only option—it's a *unique antecedent* in this respect. Thus we successfully carry out the instruction by binding z to x—this means that we replace all occurrences of z with the discourse referent x, and we remove the instruction from the instruction box (to indicate that we've completed this instruction). The result is the following final semantic representation of (35):

(39)

$$
\begin{array}{|l|}
\hline
x, y \\
\hline
\text{man}(x), \\
\text{woman}(y), \\
\text{walk}(x), \\
\text{walk}(y) \\
\text{talk}(x) \\
\hline
 \\
\hline
\end{array}
$$

Since there are no more instructions left, we're done. We can now work out whether (35) is true or not. According to its truth conditions, (39) is true if and only if there are two objects—denoted by x and y—where x is a man that walks and talks, and y is a woman that walks. It's important to note that (39) *doesn't* imply that there is a unique man in the universe. This is what Russell's analysis would be committed to. Rather, the uniqueness condition was placed in the instruction; we had to find a unique antecedent (as suggested earlier in the discussion of given and new information), and failing that, we had to add one.

Treating presuppositions like pronouns allows us to work out systematically when a presupposition is canceled. On at least one interpretation of the sentence (40), the (potential) presupposition that there is a man is canceled in because of (40)'s *if*-phrase.

(40)   If a man walked, then the man talked.

We capture this in our analysis, by the fact that the presupposition triggered by the phrase *the man* is BOUND to the man in the *if*-phrase, and we don't have to accommodate it. Here's the analysis in detail. There is in fact a choice of three semantic rules that we can apply first to the syntactic structure of the sentence (40): the one for indefinite NPs (to *a man*), the one for definite NPs (to *the man*), or the one for *if*. We will give the details here of the analysis of (40) where we apply the rule for *if* first. This yields the DRS (41) (where to save space we have omitted the syntax trees on the two constituent sentences).

(41)

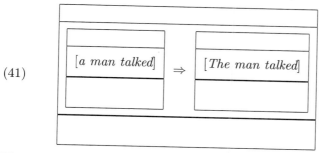

Then we can convert these two constituent sentences to semantic information in the usual way:

(42)

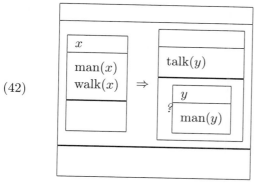

The instruction to find a man appears in the RHS box of the ⇒, rather than in the instruction for the biggest box, because of the places in the structure where the sentence *the man talked* is converted to semantic information, as shown in (41). We now have to carry out this instruction. We must identify it to a man in the same way that we would a pronoun, and if we can't do that, we must add it. In this case, we can identify it with the man x in the box on the LHS of the ⇒. Note that this is permitted, because the discourse referent x meets the Structural Constraint for finding antecedents that we introduced in chapter 14 when we analyzed pronouns. So the final representation is:

(43)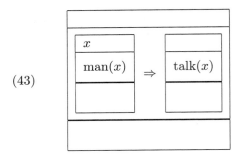

Note that our analysis correctly predicts that (40) doesn't presuppose
there is a man; the potential presupposition that is triggered by *the man*
doesn't reach the status of an actual presupposition in the context of the
if-phrase of (40). Because the instruction is carried out via binding, the
semantic information that there is a man is never accommodated into the
discourse context, and in particular is not added to the DRS outside the
scope of the implication, in the biggest box. Viewing presuppositions
as pronouns has helped here. Analyzing them this way has correctly
predicted that the whole sentence (40) *doesn't* imply there was a man.

Exercise

Exercise 15.3: Work out the alternative analysis of sentence (40)
that's allowed by the grammar, where the semantic rule for indefinite
NPs is applied before the semantic rule for *if*. In what ways does this
affect binding and accommodation? And does the result presuppose that
there's a man?

   Now consider a more complex example where there are several presuppositions, some of which end up getting bound, and others which end
up getting accommodated:

(44)   If the king of France comes to the party, then the party will
         get press coverage.

As for (40), we first convert the words "if...,then..." to semantic information (as before, there are other semantic rules we could have applied
first, but we will investigate this order of application in detail here).

(45)

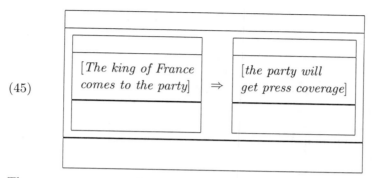

Then we can convert the two simpler sentences to semantic information in the usual way:

(46)

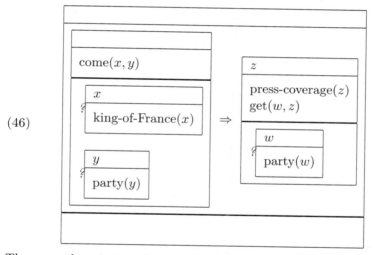

There are three instructions resulting from the three occurrences of the presupposition trigger *the*. We have to decide on the *order* in which we carry out these instructions. We will assume the following: Carry out instructions in the embedded boxes before doing those in the biggest box, and carry out instructions in the box on the LHS of a ⇒-condition before doing those in the box on the RHS. The first part of the ordering constraint reflects the fact that embedded information is caused by simple sentences that form part of the complex sentence represented by the biggest box, and the complex sentence should always be interpreted in the light of what the simpler sentences that form it mean. The second ordering constraint stems from the fact that as humans we process information *incrementally* (cf. the discussion in section 13.1 about the way humans disambiguate words before they get to the end of the sentence). That is, we work out what the words and phrases mean as we hear them. And so we process S_1 in a sentence of the form *If S_1, then S_2* before we process S_2, because we hear S_1 first![33]

This ordering constraint means that we have to deal first with the instruction to find an antecedent for x—the king of France—and the instruction to find an antecedent for y—the party. Then, having carried out these instructions, we will deal with the instruction to find an antecedent for w—the party.

So let's deal with the king of France first. There is no suitable antecedent discourse referent to which the king of France x can be bound. Therefore, this discourse referent and its conditions (i.e. king-of-France(x)) must be added to an accessible place in the structure, as defined by the Structural Constraint given in chapter 14. According to this constraint, there are two accessible places to which we could add the king of France. We can add it to the biggest box, or to the box where the instruction is (i.e. the LHS box of the ⇒-condition). If we were to add the king of France to the RHS box of the ⇒-condition (i.e. where the information on z is), it would be inaccessible to x according to the Structural Constraint, and so we can't add it there. It has been argued (by van der Sandt—see section 15.7 for details about the relevant articles) that there is a preference for adding information in the biggest box possible. But this preference is constrained. In particular, the Consistency Constraint must be satisfied by the addition of the presupposed information to the DRS. That is, the result of adding the presupposition to the DRS should be a consistent DRS. In this case, it is indeed consistent to add to x and king-of-France(x) to the biggest box; there is nothing in the context that implies that this information is false. So accordingly, we add x and king-of-France(x) to the biggest box to produce the following:

(47)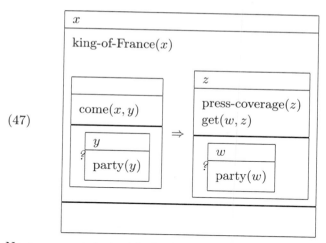

Next we must deal with the instruction to find an antecedent to y—the party. As before, there is no discourse referent we can identify with y (x won't do because x is the king of France and not a party!), so we add it in a similar way as before to produce:

(48)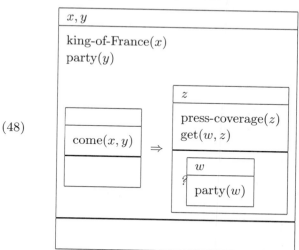

Finally, we deal with the instruction in the consequent box: to find an antecedent to w—the party. Now we have one in (47): y. Note that the Structural Constraint makes y accessible to w, because w is in a box embedded in the one where y is introduced. So we identify w with y, replacing all occurrences of w with y. So the final representation of the meaning of (44) is:

(49)

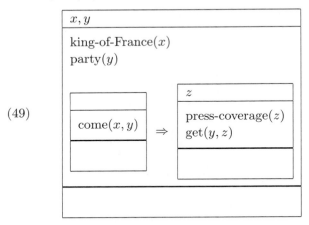

There are no more instructions, and so we're done. The DRS (49) is true with respect to a model if there are individuals a and b in the model that are a king of France and a party, respectively, and if a comes to b, then b will get press coverage. This matches our intuitions about what (44) means. Note that even though (44) featured two NPs of the form *the party*, we still capture in the semantics that the sentence is about only one party (which happened to be mentioned twice). Also note that (49) can be true even if there is more than one party and more than one king of France in the world. The important thing for processing this sentence was that *the king of France* referred to a unique object *in the context*.

Our analysis of (44) also indicates why presuppositions tend to "project out" from linguistic constructions, such as conditionals, to be presupposed (and hence implied) by the whole sentence. When an instruction appearing in an embedded box has been dealt with via accommodation, the material ends up in the biggest box (so long as its consistent for it to be there). The result, then, is a DRS that is true only if the presupposed material is true. This is what happened in (44). *The king of France* and *the party* were in an *if*-phrase, and stuff in an *if*-phrase isn't necessarily true (rather it describes a hypothetical situation). But nevertheless, that there is a king of France and that there is a party is ultimately implied to be true because these things finally appear in the biggest box, and not in the antecedent (or LHS) box. In other words, these things projected

Proper Names (Revised):

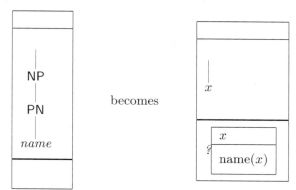

becomes

Where x hasn't been used yet and name is the translation of *name*.

Figure 15.1
The revised rule for proper names.

out from the conditional because they had to be accommodated.

Proper names are presupposition triggers, too. And our theory predicts that presuppositions project out of embeddings to feature as conditions in the biggest box. This means that we can now justify why we assumed in chapter 14 that proper names such as *Mary* yield semantic conditions in the biggest box, regardless of which box in the DRS the syntactic analysis of the proper name was converted into semantic information via the semantic rule for proper names.

So let's look now at the semantics of proper names. The analysis for proper names we had before didn't deal with the presupposition. The revised rule in Figure 15.1 rectifies this. This new semantic rule explains why generally, x and Mary(x) end up in the biggest box. It also explains why repeated mentions of *Mary* in a text are assumed to refer to the same person. Proper Names (Revised) captures this, because the instruction triggered by the first *Mary* is accommodated in the DRS, and all subsequent instructions triggered by subsequent mentions of *Mary* will bind to it. Finally, this rule rectifies our analysis of (50). The old rule for proper names told us to re-use a discourse referent if we could, *regardless* of whether or not that old discourse referent had a condition on it already that it was the bearer of the relevant proper name. So the old rule for proper names got the wrong analysis of (50), in that it allowed you to build a DRS where Pip and Etta were one and the same person.

(50)   Etta chased a bird. Pip caught it.

The final representation of (50) is (50′) with our revised rule for proper names. Compare this with the representation (50″) that we got with the old rule:

(50′)

x, y, z
$\text{Etta}(x)$
$\text{bird}(y)$
$\text{chase}(x, y)$
$\text{Pip}(z)$
$\text{catch}(z, y)$

(50″)

x, y
$\text{Etta}(x)$
$\text{bird}(y)$
$\text{chase}(x, y)$
$\text{Pip}(x)$
$\text{catch}(x, y)$

Exercise

Exercise 15.4: Does the grammar make the correct predictions about the interpretation of the proper name and definite description in the discourse *Tony Blair announced the election. The prime minister will resign after he has secured a third term for his government*? If not, why not, and what can be done to improve the analysis?

We haven't given a detailed semantic analysis of words like *not* and phrases like *it's possible that* in our grammar. And so it's beyond the scope of this book to show in detail that presuppositions project from embeddings in the general case. However, we can go some way towards showing what would happen in the grammar. First, we must translate sentences of the form *It's possible that S* into DRSs. We don't want a sentence like this to entail that *S* is actually true. *S* need only be possible. We capture this by introducing an embedded box that is labeled *Possible* in the semantic representation of *It's possible that S*:

(51)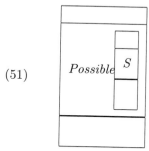

In other words, (51) is true if *S* is possible. And so (51) could be true even when *S* is false.

Using this semantic representation of *it's possible that...* together with the existing semantic rules in the grammar, we obtain the logical form (52') of (52).

(52)   It's possible that the king of France signed a proclamation.

(52')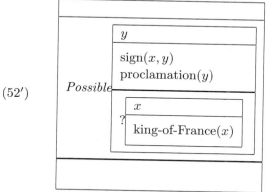

The instruction triggered by *the king of France* is in the embedded box, because this is where the sentence containing it is reduced into semantic conditions.

We can't bind the presupposition, so it must be accommodated. When a presupposition in an embedded box has to be accommodated, it will typically end up in the biggest box because of the preference for

accommodating presuppositions at as high a level in the structure as
possible (subject to the resulting DRS being consistent). Because of this,
the presupposition is implied to be true, unlike the rest of the material
that remains embedded. In particular, (52′) becomes (52″):

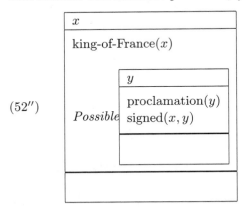

(52″)

This DRS states there is a king of France (x), and it's possible that
there is a proclamation (y) that x signed. So, we have modelled the
contrast between presuppositions and semantic entailments with regard
to projection from embeddings via the mechanism of accommodation.

15.5   Garden Paths

Now consider the so-called garden path sentence (53):

(53)   The horse raced past the barn fell.

In section 13.2 we discussed the ease (or lack of it!) with which we
parse sentences like (53). This is a grammatical sentence that can be
paraphrased as: *The horse, which was raced past the barn, fell.* But there
is a feeling of "stumbling" when we hit the word *fell.* This is because
upon reading the word *raced* in (53), we—as human speakers of English—
typically understand that word to be the start of the VP of the sentence
(and not part of the subject NP). We should, in fact, have interpreted
it as a verb that forms part of a relative clause (RC) in the subject NP,
but we didn't. This problem isn't exposed until we hear the word *fell,*
and at that point we can't undo the analysis we've constructed so far.

Crain and Steedman (1985) (see section 15.7 for detailed references) did psychological experiments on how humans disambiguate the categories of words as they parse sentences. They showed that this disambiguation process is influenced by the discourse context in which the sentence is uttered. Indeed, they showed that by preceding the "garden path" sentence with an appropriate discourse, human subjects had no problem at all in parsing it. It ceased to be a garden path sentence. In other words, with certain discourse contexts human subjects understand the word *raced* in (53) in the right way (i.e. as a verb that forms part of the subject NP), *as they hear this word*. They therefore don't encounter any processing difficulty, even at the point where they hear the word *fell*.

But what do these special discourse contexts, which make (53) easier to process, look like? Crain and Steedman suggest that if there are two horses already mentioned, one of which is known to have been raced past the barn, and the other which isn't, then we parse (53) easily:

(54)   There were two horses in the stables that day. One of them had to rest for the whole afternoon. But the other was raced around the farm and past the barn.
The horse raced past the barn fell.

If, on the other hand, there are no previous mentions of horses, or if only one horse has been mentioned, then we are led down the "garden path."

Garden path effects arise because we interpret sentences on a "word by word" basis. Sometimes when we hear a word we make a guess as to what it will contribute to the meaning of the whole sentence, and we don't wait to find out what else is said in the sentence before coming to decisions about this word (see for example the discussion about Mike Tanenhaus' experiments on human sentence processing in chapter 13). This is a necessary strategy because of limited memory resources and the utility of rapid comprehension of what's being communicated. But it's also a risky strategy because sometimes, as the rest of the sentence is uttered, we realize that we made the wrong choices, and we have to undo things we've already done, which is costly. Crain and Steedman's experiments were designed to investigate the circumstances when we make the wrong choice.

Sentences (55)a and b are the garden path sentences discussed in section 13.2. And they all behave the same way as (53), in that you can ameliorate the garden path effect by preceding them with an appropriate discourse (compare (55)a with (56)):

(55) a.   The cotton shirts are made from grows in Mississippi.

   b.   The man who hunts ducks out on weekends.

(56)   There are two types of cotton that are grown in the States. One
          of them is typically used to make shirts; the other is typically
          used to make skirts.
          The cotton shirts are made from grows in Mississippi.

One can now restate these ideas about how the interpretation of words
like *raced* in (53) is affected by context by using our model of the way
presuppositions behave. Sentence (53) includes the word *the*, and this
introduces an instruction as we've shown in the rule The. What goes in
the instruction box depends on the semantic content of the NP. But as
we parse (53) word by word, we have a choice about where to attach the
word *raced*: (a) it can either be a verb that forms part of a relative clause
in the NP; or (b) it can be a verb that is part of the sentence's VP (i.e.,
the NP is just *the horse* and nothing more). The choice at this point will
affect the instruction about what kind of antecedent we must find in the
context. If we go for choice (a), then the instruction becomes: Find an
antecedent discourse referent that is a horse that was raced past the barn,
and this antecedent must be unique (because recall *the* presupposes that
the object described is unique in the context). If we go for choice (b) then
the instruction is: Find an antecedent discourse referent that is a horse,
and this antecedent must be unique. If the instruction corresponded to
option (b), and there were two horses in the context, then we wouldn't
be able to carry out that instruction successfully because the uniqueness
condition would be violated. However, if one of the horses was known to
have been raced past the barn, and the other wasn't, then the instruction
corresponding to option (a) would be carried out successfully. So the way
we interpret *raced* in (53) is intimately connected with whether or not
the presupposition triggered by *the* can be processed successfully.

So we can predict the way humans parse (53) via the following constraint:

• **Parsing Constraint:**
Suppose you encounter a word that can attach at two alternative points
to the syntactic tree given so far. Suppose furthermore that this choice of
attachments affects an instruction. Then choose between these syntactic

alternatives *at this point in parsing* according to the following constraint:

—If the material you have so far in the instruction box does *not* enable you to carry out the instruction successfully, then attach the word to the syntax tree so that the content of the instruction changes.

—Otherwise, attach the word to the syntax tree so that the instruction doesn't change.

This constraint amounts to: if it ain't broke, don't fix it. More specifically, it encapsulates the intuition that if we can deal with the presupposition without changing the instruction, we do so and attach new words so that the content of the presupposition (and hence the instruction) remains unaltered. Intuitively, this is a strategy for minimizing the chances of getting presupposition failure because you deal with the instruction at the point when you know you can succeed.

So consider parsing (53) in a discourse context where no horse has been mentioned. Then having parsed *the horse*, we end up with a semantic representation that looks like (57): $y, z, \ldots$ are discourse referents introduced by the context (but we know none of them satisfy the condition that they are a horse); Q must be filled in with VP stuff still to be parsed, and P will be filled in with stuff if we add more things to the NP *the horse* to make a bigger NP, but otherwise it will be void of content:

(57)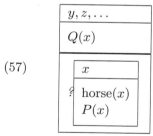

Now we parse *raced*, and we have a choice: We can attach this to the NP or VP; that is, it can fill out $P(x)$ in the instruction, or it can fill out $Q(x)$. So we check whether we can successfully carry out the instruction in (57) as it stands: That is, we try to bind x to an existing, unique horse; and if that fails we try to accommodate it uniquely. In this case, we can't bind x to anything, but we can accommodate it. So the instruction as it stands can be dealt with successfully. Hence, by the above Parsing Constraint, we attach *raced* to the VP so that the content of the instruction doesn't ultimately change. (Note that if we attached *raced* to the NP, then the content of the instruction would change because we would have to find an antecedent that's a horse that's been raced, rather than an antecedent that's just a horse). Making *raced* part of the VP turns out to be the wrong choice, but we don't realize this until we reach the last word *fell* of (53), because the phrase *raced past the barn* is a perfectly good VP. Hence the Parsing Constraint predicts correctly that we garden path in this context. Also note that we would have made the same choice for *raced* if there had been exactly one horse y in the context; in this case the horse x would have been bound to y. Hence the Parsing Constraint predicts correctly that we garden path in this context as well; it predicts that when we read *raced*, we'll assume it's part of the sentence's VP.

Now consider a situation where two horses have been mentioned, only one of which has raced past a barn. Then at the point at which we've parsed the words *the horse*, the semantic content is as in (58): Again Q is to be filled in by VP information, the two horses y and z are those already mentioned in the discourse context, and P may be filled in with more content if we end up adding more to the NP *the horse* to make a bigger NP:

(58)

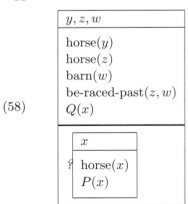

As before, we now parse *raced*, and we have a choice: We can attach this to the NP (thereby filling out $P(x)$) or to the VP (thereby filling out $Q(x)$). So we check whether we can successfully carry out the instruction in (58) as it stands. In contrast to (57), we *can't* successfully carry out the instruction in this context because there is a choice of two horses to which we can bind x to—y and z—and no way currently of differentiating which horse we should prefer. So the uniqueness condition on the antecedent isn't met. Furthermore, we can't add a horse to the context and uniquely identify x with that added horse either; the uniqueness condition is violated again because we still can't differentiate which horse x is. So as it stands, we can't carry out the instruction. Hence according to the above Parsing Constraint, we assume that *raced* is part of the NP, so that the content of the instruction changes. This makes *past the barn* part of the NP, too (because this completes the relative clause and cannot start the VP). So the semantic content becomes the following at this stage (note that *the barn* produced its own instruction):

(59)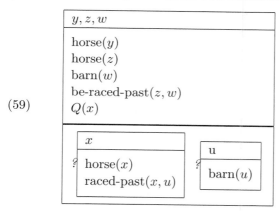

Now we need to identify x and u with (unique) things in the context. This time, we can do it. We can identify the barn u with the barn w. The horse x can't be identified with the horse y because y isn't asserted to have been raced past the barn w. But z has done this, and so the content on z matches that on x: They are both horses that have been raced past the barn w. Therefore, we can identify x with z uniquely. That is, through adding the relative clause to the NP, we have managed to differentiate which horse from the two already mentioned in the context we are talking about in the sentence (53). So the resulting semantic representation becomes (60):

(60)

y, z, w
horse(y)
horse(z)
barn(w)
raced-past(z, w)
$Q(z)$

Now we must parse the word *fell*. And we still have a VP to be filled in (with the corresponding semantic content $Q(z)$ to be filled in), which *fell* can do, to produce the following:

(61)

y, z, w
horse(y)
horse(z)
barn(w)
raced-past(z, w)
fell(z)

So we don't garden path; that is, we don't make a mistake when we parse *raced*.

The above Parsing Constraint can also explain why (55)a is easier to parse in the context of (56). Without this context, the instruction triggered by *the cotton* can be carried out successfully, but the next word (*shirts*) can't start a VP. So suppose we assume that the subject NP is now *the cotton shirts*. The instruction triggered by this can be done successfully, too (we accommodate a cotton shirt into the context). And so the next word (*are*), which can be interpreted as starting the VP, is taken to do that, so that the content of the presupposition doesn't change. This was the wrong choice.

In the context provided by (56), however, the instruction triggered by *the cotton* can't be carried out successfully, because we can't bind it to a unique antecedent (there are two types of cotton in the context). On the other hand, if *shirts are made from* is treated as a relative clause, then the resulting presupposition (there is cotton that shirts are made from) binds to a unique antecedent. This contrasts with what would happen if the subject NP were taken to be *the cotton shirts*, and one chose to parse *are* as the start of the sentence's VP. In this case, the corresponding presupposition would have to be accommodated (because we've mentioned shirts in the context, but not *cotton* shirts). We've assumed in this chapter that binding presuppositions is preferred to accommodating them. We can refine our Parsing Constraint to reflect this by adding to it that you prefer to parse things so that the instruction triggered by a presupposition trigger is bound rather than accommodated. This predicts that in the context of (56), *shirts are made from* will be parsed as a relative clause *as and when the interpreter hears it*, and so he won't be led up the garden path, in contrast to (55)a.

This matches the psychological data in Crain and Steedman's experiments on human sentence processing. So this is evidence that the above Parsing Constraint is psychologically plausible.

The Parsing Constraint is a first step toward providing principles on how the grammar can be parsed so that it matches the way humans process language. But the constraint is controversial, partly because Crain and Steedman's results on which it is based are controversial. And at any rate, it only solves a very small part of the larger problem of specifying how humans parse sentences.

Exercise

Exercise 15.5: What impact does the Parsing Constraint have on the debate about the degree of modularity in human sentence processing?

15.6   Conclusion

Presuppositions are different from semantic entailments in two important respects. First, they typically project from embeddings in phrases like *It's possible that*, *if*, and *not*. They don't always project though; see (4)a where the (potential) presupposition does project out from the condition vs. (4)b where it doesn't:

(4) a.   If baldness is hereditary, then John's son is bald.

     b.   If John has a son, then John's son is bald.

This indicates that the status of a presupposition in a discourse is dependent on the content of the presupposition, and the content of the discourse context. This isn't so for semantic entailments. The second difference is that presuppositions can be canceled (to use Gerald Gazdar's terminology) or "denied" as shown in (3)e (and repeated below). In contrast, attempting to deny a semantic entailment simply yields a contradiction, making the sentence sound odd, as shown in (3)f.

(3) e.   The king of France didn't sign a peace treaty—there is no
               king of France.

     f.   ?The king of France signed a peace treaty,
               but no one signed a peace treaty.

Presuppositions are used to great effect in communication. They can put your adversary in a debate on the defensive. They can help you keep your utterances brief and concise, while still getting across a rich array of information. Presupposition triggers are commonplace in communication. Just pick a sentence of English at random from a novel, a textbook, or a newspaper article, and it will almost always have at least one presupposition trigger in it. So it's really important that we work out how to deal with them in systematic ways. If we don't, computers won't be able to communicate with human languages like English in the way that we want them to. Nor will we have a good understanding of how humans use them.

We argued that presuppositions behave like pronouns in that in both cases one searches for something in the context that can act as an antecedent. But presuppositions are different from pronouns in that when such an antecedent can't be found, we can *add* it to the context so long as adding doesn't yield a contradiction (which is why (27) is odd). This difference stems from the fact that presuppositions have much more semantic content than pronouns, and so we have good clues about what the antecedent should be if there isn't one already there. We don't have such clues in the case of pronouns because the semantic content of pronouns is almost nil; we just have information about number and gender.

We showed how our grammar can be extended to model presupposition triggers. We looked at the trigger *the* in detail. We showed that treating presuppositions like pronouns enabled us to systematically predict when a potential presupposition is in fact presupposed by the whole text and when it isn't. The mechanisms for accommodating presuppositions also explain why presuppositions *project from embeddings*; that is, they tend to be implied by a text even when the presupposition trigger was syntactically within the scope of a word like *not* or *if* or a phrase like *it's possible that*.

But the mechanisms encoded in the grammar model just some of the aspects of the phenomena. It can only handle some simple texts, and more complicated mechanisms are necessary for dealing systematically with presuppositions in general. This is a very active research area in philosophy, linguistics (especially formal semantics), and cognitive science.

One huge gap in the above analysis is that we don't account for the inference in (62) and (63), that the engine is part of the car:

(62)   John took his car for a test drive. The engine was making a weird noise.

(63)   If John has a car, then the engine will be at least two litres.

Our above analysis is one where because there is no previous mention of an engine, we accommodate an engine into the biggest DRS in both cases. But this addition of the engine is too simplistic; we should relate it to what's already in the context. This might not seem to matter for the analysis of (62)—the DRS for this sentence simply misses information about the relation between the car and its engine. But the analysis of (62) is just plain wrong. Here, the engine is added to the biggest box since its relation to the car that appears in the RHS box of a conditional is missed, and thus we incorrectly predict that (63) implies there is an engine.

Human language processors use background information to infer connections between objects mentioned in a text. In the case of (62) and (63), they would use the world knowledge that cars have engines to infer that the engine mentioned in the second sentence is part of the car that was mentioned in the first sentence (and so in (63), the engine should be accommodated into the RHS box of the conditional, where the car is introduced). Our attempts to mechanize the way presuppositions are dealt with doesn't account for this because accommodation as we have modeled it in the grammar isn't affected by background information at all. Rather, the car and the engine are treated as separate, unrelated entities in our grammar. And this misses a very important aspect of the meaning of (62) and (63), in the latter case capturing the wrong meaning altogether.

No one as yet has a satisfactory account of accommodation that is systematic and that allows background information to influence the process. But this is what we need to deal with texts like (62) and (63). However, extending the treatment of presuppositions so as to predict inferences such as those in (62) about the relation between the car and the engine is currently an active area of research. Arguably, the reason why no one as yet has come up with a satisfactory explanation of how to model this is precisely because it involves recourse to encyclopedic knowledge. As we've discussed before, it is currently very difficult to mechanize processes that involve this type of knowledge. Currently, the best models to date are essentially engineering solutions that approximate this knowledge via statistical models that are learned from online linguistic data.

Exercises

Exercise 15.6: The following text exhibits the bridging phenomenon.

(64)   John was murdered yesterday. The knife lay nearby.

1. Say what *the knife* presupposes.

2. Specify what information people infer from the expression *the knife* in (64) (clue: Clark gives a specification of this in the paper).

3. How does what people infer differ from our account of what gets accommodated in (64), in our formal model of communication? In other words, what information is missing in this model?

Exercise 15.7: Imagine a world where people couldn't accommodate presuppositions in the way Lewis describes. Then for each of the sentences (65–67) below, write down what people would have to say prior to uttering these sentences, in order to make them acceptable:

(65)   The king of France is bald.

(66)   John regretted that he didn't stop beating his wife.

(67)   Alex forgot to lock her Alfa Spider again.

Clue: The relevant discourse that would replace the man is bald *would be* There is a man. He is bald.

Exercise 15.8: Think up three linguistic texts where a presupposition cannot be bound or accommodated, making the text sound odd. Try to list the factors that contribute to the text sounding bad.

Exercise 15.9: Consider the following discourse:

Every chess set has a spare pawn. I bought a chess set yesterday and it was taped to the top of the box.

Explain how the grammar rule for pronouns, and in particular the constraints on which antecedents are accessible, makes the wrong predictions about the interpretation of *it* in this example. Now consider the following "paraphrase" of the above discourse:

Every chess set has a spare pawn. I bought a chess set yesterday and the spare pawn was taped to the top of the box.

Is the definite noun phrase *the spare pawn* bound or accommodated during discourse processing? In light of your answer to this question, what conclusions do you draw about the antecedent to the pronoun in the first discourse?

15.7   Further Reading

David Lewis wrote one of the seminal papers on presuppositions and accommodation:

• Lewis, David (1979). "Scorekeeping in a Language Game," *Journal of Philosophical Logic*, 8, 339–359.

In it, he claims the following. Presuppositions can be created or destroyed in the course of a conversation. But it's actually not that easy to say something that will be unacceptable for lack of the required presuppositions. This is because if you say something that requires a missing presupposition, then straight away, that presupposition springs into existence, making what you said acceptable after all. This is what has come to be known as accommodation.

The formal model of presuppositions we have examined here is largely inspired by the model developed by Rob van der Sandt:

• Van der Sandt, R. (1992). "Presupposition Projection as Anaphora Resolution," *Journal of Semantics*, 9, 333–377. Oxford: Oxford University Press.

This is the first paper where the proposal that presuppositions behave like pronouns is discussed.

Scott Soames has worked extensively on presuppositions. An accessible account of his work appears in the following:

• Soames, S. (1982). "How Presuppositions Are Inherited: A Solution to the Projection Problem," *Linguistic Inquiry*, 13, 483–545.

In it, he suggests that a person presupposes a proposition at a given point in a conversation just in case he believes that proposition to be one that the conversational participants already accept as part of the shared background information against which the conversation takes place.

Exercise

Exercise 15.10: 1. How do you think accommodation fits into Soames' view on presuppositions? Do you think it's compatible with it?

2. In defining presuppositions this way, Soames is emphasizing that they are intertwined with pragmatic and conversational information. Why does he do this? Explain your answer by giving examples where the speaker's and hearer's beliefs play a part in interpreting the presuppositions in a conversation, and examples where the context of the conversation affects what's presupposed.

Robert Stalnaker has also written seminal work on presuppositions:

• Stalnaker, R. C. (1974). "Pragmatic Presuppositions," in M. K. Munitz and Peter. K. Unger (eds.). *Semantics and Philosophy*. New York: New York University Press.

He argues in this paper that efficient communication requires the participants to have common ground; that is, they must share beliefs, and know that they do so.

Exercise

Exercise 15.11: What impact do shared beliefs have on communication? Why is it easier to communicate when the participants share beliefs than when they don't? How does this relate to the Shannon and Weaver model of communication? And if we need shared beliefs to communicate, then what impact is this going to have on the efficient communication between computers and humans?

If you want to find out more about bridging (e.g. the thing that goes on in (62)), then the following contains a very accessible discussion of the issues involved:

- Clark, H. (1975). "Bridging," in R. C. Schank and B. L. Nash-Webber (eds.). *Theoretical Issues in Natural Language Processing.* Cambridge: MIT Press.

In this article, Clark argues that accommodating a presupposition involves more than just *adding* its content to the context. Rather, we try and *relate* that added content to what's already there in the context.

In addition to the above articles on presupposition, the interested reader can find out more about presuppositions from the following sources.

- Beaver, D. (1997). "Presupposition," in J. van Benthen and A. ter Meulen (eds.). *The Handbook of Logic and Language.* Amsterdam: Eslevier, 939–1008.
- Gazdar, G. (1979). *Pragmatics: Implicature, Presupposition, and Logical Form.* New York: Academic Press.
- Karttunen, L. (1974). "Presupposition and Linguistic Context," *Theoretical Linguistics*, 1, 181–194.
- Levinson, S. (1983). *Pragmatics*, chapter 4. Cambridge: Cambridge University Press.
- Russell, B. (1967). "On Denoting," in I. M. Copi, J. A. Gould (eds.). *Contemporary Readings in Logical Theory.* 93–105. New York: Macmillan. Reprinted from *Mind*, Vol. 14, 1905.
- Crain, S., and Steedman, M. (1985). "On Not Being Led up the Garden Path: The Use of Context by the Psychological Syntax Processor," in David R. Dowty, Lauri Karttunen, Arnold M. Zwicky (eds.). *Natural Language Parsing: Psychological, Computational, and Theoretical*

Perspectives. 320–358. Cambridge: Cambridge University Press.

Beaver (1997) provides an excellent overview of all the different analyses of presupposition to be found in the literature, including a comparison of van der Sandt's analysis with the influential accounts proposed by Gazdar (1979) and Karttunen (1974). Levinson (1983) contains an overview of the way presuppositions behave, but its publication precedes the theories that treat presuppositions like pronouns. Russell (1967) proposes the semantics of definite descriptions that we described in section 15.2, and that is refuted by Stalnaker (1974).

I include the reference to Crain and Steedman (1985) here simply because we refer to it in section 15.5. Strictly speaking, it's not a paper about presuppositions *per se*, but it does discuss how humans parse sentences like (53) and presupposition triggers like *the* in particular (see chapter 13).

In section 15.1, we mentioned how negated sentences which feature a presupposition can be followed by a clause that "denies" the presupposition. This kind of phenomenon is discussed in Horn (1985, 1989), where he examines something known as "metalinguistic negation."

- Horn, Larry (1985). "Metalinguistic Negation and Pragmatic Ambiguity," *Language*, 61, 121–174.
- Horn, Larry (1989). *A Natural History of Negation*. Chicago: University of Chicago Press.

16 Juxtaposing Sentences

16.1   Juxtaposing Sentences Adds Meaning

When you juxtapose sentences you must have a reason to do it. You don't just take a random selection of sentences that you think are true, and say them one after the other. Rather, you juxtapose sentences to form connected text where a certain point of view is argued, or a narrative story is told, etc. There are any number of reasons why you may say one sentence and follow it with another. But there is always a reason. Otherwise, your utterances will just sound odd.

So when speakers juxtapose sentences, they rely on the assumption that the hearers will reason about *why* they did this. Hearers come up with all kinds of reasons about why things in a text are said one after the other. This is why a simple text like (1) can be enough to tell the hearers that Keith drives Alex to drink.

(1)   Alex drinks a bottle of whisky a day. Keith is her boss.

The speaker didn't explicitly say this, but the hearers can infer it anyway. They do this by using general knowledge about the speaker, language, and the world, to try to get a meaningful link between the two facts *Alex drinks a bottle of whisky a day* and *Keith is (Alex's) boss*. The hearers do this in order to assure themselves that there was a reason for saying these things together. If the hearers can't work out why the sentences are juxtaposed, then it sounds odd or "incoherent":

(2)   ?John entered the room. Mary's hair is black.

There have been extensive studies of how one computes more meaning from text than is revealed by the grammar. From Philosophy, Grice defines a set of principles that encode how we use language in conversation. These principles specify things like: avoid obscurity, be truthful, be informative, be relevant, be orderly, avoid ambiguity, and so on. In particular, the above inferences concerning the semantic content of (1) are arguably justified on the basis of the principle *be relevant*. The hearers must establish the relevance between the contents of the two individual sentences if they are to be justified in assuming that the speaker was following the principle *be relevant*. One possible connection between the events that would ensure the relevance of the second sentence to the first would be that Keith being Alex's boss *caused* her to drink a bottle of whisky a day. Thus the interpreters of (1) might *accommodate* this causal link into their interpretation of (1) (recall the notion of accommodation, which we used to interpret presuppositions in chapter 15), so as to ensure that their interpretation of the text is compatible with the assumption that the speaker adhered to the principle *Be Relevant*. Accommodating the causal link as part of the interpretation of (1) is made possible by the fact that it's entirely plausible for one's boss to drive one to drink! But in contrast to (1), the hearers can't compute any relevance between the facts in (2): Assuming a causal relation between the events seems untenable because there's no background information that would support such an assumption. On that basis, the hearers can't accommodate a relevant link between the sentences, and the text sounds odd.

Grice suggests that the above principles, which he argues govern the way conversation is produced and interpreted, follow from assuming the conversational agents are RATIONAL (i.e. they are not prepared to believe contradictions) and COOPERATIVE (i.e. they typically help other people to achieve their goals). He did not, however, demonstrate this formally, nor did he offer a formal model of rationality and cooperativity. Indeed, this remains a big challenge in the study of pragmatics. An alternative perspective one might take on these principles (although this wasn't Grice's perspective), is to view them as a "contract" between the speaker and hearer: They encapsulate rules for communicating effectively. Think about how you follow such rules when writing an essay, for example.

To get computers to converse in the way humans do, the computer must know about and reason effectively with these conversational principles. For example, we want a computer to produce the text (3) rather than (4):

(3)   The year 1993 will start with the world in a pessimistic frame of mind. The gloom should soon dispel itself. A clear economic recovery is under way. Though it will be hesitant at first, it will last the longer for being so. If you are sitting in one of the world's blackspots, this prediction will seem hopelessly optimistic. But next year's wealth won't return to yesteryear's winners; these middle-aged rich people need to look over their

(4)   shoulders to the younger world that is closing in on them.
The year 1993 will start with the world in a pessimistic frame of mind. A clear economic recovery is under way. That gloom should soon dispel itself. These middle-aged rich people need to look over their shoulders to the younger world that is closing in on them. But next year's wealth won't return to yesteryear's winners; it will last the longer for being so. If you are sitting in one of the world's blackspots, though it will be hesitant at first, this prediction will seem hopelessly optimistic.

Texts (3) and (4) consist of the same clauses, but in a different order. Because they consist of the same clauses, they introduce the same events and individuals; in a way, they are about the same thing. But text (3) is acceptable whereas (4) is distinctly odd. This difference in acceptability is evidence that the order in which things are described affects the overall coherence or fluency of a text. Obviously, some of the sources of incoherence in (4) stem from the lack of ease with which to find antecedents to pronouns and other kinds of anaphoric expressions (recall the analysis of pronouns from chapter 14). But this cannot be the only source of incoherence. The first two sentences of (4) do not contain anaphoric expressions that cannot be interpreted, for example, and yet this sequence of sentences sounds odd (in this context, at least):

(5)   The year 1993 will start with the world in a pessimistic frame of mind. A clear economic recovery is under way.

The demand that there be a meaningful connection between the clauses, as predicted by the principle *be relevant*, would predict this: Why should the world be pessimistic if an economic recovery is under way? The two statements appear to be contradictory, and we do not expect the writer to believe both of them. (Observe how the text improves if you add the cue phrase *But* to the beginning of the second sentence in (5).)

A computer will avoid producing texts like (2) or (5) only if it has a model of when two clauses can be juxtaposed and when they can't. Conversely, a computer will *interpret* texts like humans do only if, like humans, it identifies the semantic consequences of juxtaposing the sentences, thereby extending beyond the semantic information that's yielded by the grammar. Modeling this aspect of text processing is a major challenge in computational linguistics today. There are a number of approaches that are currently being explored. At one extreme, researchers have explored the use of THEOREM PROVERS—which are automated systems for performing logical inferences—accompanied by rich representations of language (both its syntax and semantics) and of background knowledge (about the world, the dialogue agents, and so on). At the other extreme, researchers have explored the use of machine learning and statistics, using online linguistic resources such as newspaper articles and parsers as training material for the machine learning process. Neither of these approaches appear to be ideal when used on their own. The former approach tends to be "brittle" in that for many kinds of linguistic data it fails to give any analysis at all. The latter approach degrades more gracefully, but it generally fails to supply the kinds of detailed analyses of the semantic content of texts that only come with carefully handcrafted models of language.

Grice suggests that principles like *be relevant* govern inferences about what conversations mean. But clearly, such principles don't work in isolation. They interact with other knowledge sources that contribute to the interpretation of discourse: knowledge about the world, and the beliefs and desires of the speaker and/or the hearer. Their (relative) social status, culture, and conventions also all play a central role. We observed this when discussing the semantics of pronouns in chapter 14. We argued in section 14.1 that a computer model for processing pronouns must encapsulate information about world knowledge to understand pronouns correctly. Similarly, in text (1), we use the world knowledge that certain events can make a person crave a drink (or even a lot of drink) to help us infer a plausible connection between the facts described in (1). So we must tell computers how to use knowledge about the world when dealing with multisentence text, where the connections or relevance between juxtaposed sentences must be computed.

In this chapter, we will study Grice's principles for using language in conversation. We'll show that some of them can be represented in a sufficiently precise manner in which one can model how one "automatically" infers their consequences when interpreting (or producing) text. These principles help to guide decisions about how to interpret the current sentence on the basis of the interpretation of the sentences that preceded it. These principles together with the vast array of other information sources that we mentioned above help language users to augment the content of the clause that is extracted from the grammar. Thus the syntax of sentences becomes just one source among many to contribute towards the content of the utterance.

So far, we have explored how one can represent the relationship between the form of a sentence and its meaning in a very precise fashion. In fact, using DRSs has already brought in some interaction between the discourse context and the current clause; observe how the results of carrying out instructions in the instruction box are dependent on what's in the DRS already (both for pronouns and for presuppositions). Now we want to extend these techniques for modeling the information flow between context and the content of the current utterance even further. We would like to also model how world knowledge, Grice's principles of conversation, and other factors influence the content of a discourse.

In particular, we will show in an informal, but systematic, fashion how one can model the principles that allow us to detect the difference in meaning between the simple texts (6) (where the textual order of events matches temporal order) and (7) (where there is mismatch), in spite of the fact that the sentences in these texts have exactly the same syntax.

(6)   Max stood up. John greeted him.

(7)   Max fell. John pushed him.

The prediction that (6) and (7) mean different things will stem from representing in a principled fashion some aspects of the nonlinguistic information that contributes to the way people interpret language in conversation. The form-meaning relation in (6) is the same as in (7) because the sentences involved have the same syntax. But their interpretations are different because other factors influence their overall meaning.

As we've mentioned, programming computers to take account of these other "nonlinguistic" factors that influence meaning remains a major challenge in computational linguistics. Although there has been dramatic progress over the last decade, both representing such rich knowledge resources and reasoning with them effectively is currently beyond the state of the art. So what we offer here is a very simple taste of how to build a systematic procedure for building a semantic representation of very simple texts, which goes beyond the semantics generated by the grammar. Giving any formal detail would go beyond the scope of this book. However, the simple account we present here of principles for interpreting conversation are formalizable in logics that are designed to model COMMON SENSE reasoning; these logics have been developed within the field of Artificial Intelligence (AI) to address problems in knowledge representation and inference.

We'll first discuss Grice's principles of conversation in more detail. We'll then give a taste of how some aspects of these principles, together with things like world knowledge, can be represented and exploited in computing what a text means. We will concentrate on the task of inferring how events described in a text are connected with part/whole and causal relations, even when those relations aren't part of the semantic representation that's generated by the grammar, as we observed in texts (1), (6), and (7).

16.2   Grice's Maxims of Interpretation

We now describe Grice's PRAGMATIC MAXIMS in more detail. Grice aimed to demonstrate that discourse interpretation is governed by principles of rationality and cooperativity, making it systematic and predictable. He proposed certain conversational principles (known as Gricean maxims or pragmatic maxims), which form the basis for reconstructing the speaker's conversational goals. Grice's own theory centers on a Cooperative Principle:

- **The Cooperative Principle**

Make your contribution such as is required, at the stage at which it occurs, by the accepted purpose or direction of the talk exchange in which you are engaged.

This doesn't mean very much unless we spell out what is required and how we work out the purposes or direction of communication at the various stages of the exchange. Accordingly, Grice states four pragmatic maxims, and these four maxims encapsulate the Cooperative Principle in more detail. These are given below:

- **The Maxim of Quality**

Try to make your contribution one that is true, specifically:

(i)   Do not say anything you think is false.

(ii)   Do not say anything for which you lack adequate evidence.

- **The Maxim of Quantity**

Make your contribution as informative as is required for the current purposes of the exchange, and no more.

- **The Maxim of Relevance**

Make your contributions relevant.

- **The Maxim of Manner**

Be perspicuous, and specifically:

(i)   Avoid obscurity.

(ii)   Avoid ambiguity.

(iii)   Be brief.

(iv)   Be orderly.

16.3   The Maxims at Work

Let's clarify how these maxims affect interpretation by examining some simple examples. Consider the dialogue in (8). The maxims can be used to infer a partial answer to A's question; namely, that whatever time it is, it's after the time that the milkman usually arrives.

(8)   A: Can you tell me the time?
           B: Well, the milkman has come.

Conversing according to the maxims helps prevent B from having to say (8′) instead of (8).

(8′)   B: No, I don't know the exact time of the present moment, but
           I can provide some information from which you may be able to
           deduce the approximate time; namely, the milkman has come.

Here's why. According to Grice's maxims, B's response in (8) must *be relevant* to the question. The questioner A, knowing this, decides to compute what makes it relevant. He concludes that the relevance is this: It must be that whatever time it is, it's after the milkman comes. There seems to be no other plausible connection between the question and B's response. Moreover, A can infer from (8) that B doesn't know the exact time (and so we've included this in (8′)). This is because if B did, then he would have been bound, via the Maxim of Quantity (be as informative as is required by the purposes of the current exchange), to tell A the exact time. Note that because of the Maxim of Quality, B can't just make a time up and say it just because an exact time is required for the current purposes! So the fact that B doesn't stipulate an exact time indicates to A that he didn't know the exact time. So Grice's maxims can be used to infer things from what's *not* said, as well as infer things from what is said. In this case, A uses the maxims to work out that B really meant $(8')$ when he gave his response (8) to the question. Moreover, B actually *shouldn't* say $(8')$ instead of (8), because if he did, he would be violating the Maxim of Manner—specifically, *be brief*!

Grice's way of articulating this kind of reasoning, from his maxims to the content of conversation, in fact used the notion of what one must assume to be the case to ensure that what looks like a *violation* of a maxim isn't in fact a violation at all. In other words, he talked about the *apparent violations* of maxims contributing to the meaning of conversation. In the above example, the fact that B doesn't give an exact time *appears* to violate the Maxim of Quantity. However, this violation is apparent rather than real, so long as one assumes that B doesn't know the exact time. (If he did know it, then he would really be violating the Maxim of Quantity by not saying it.)

The fact that we can convey the information in $(8')$ with the much more concise (8) shows how powerful making assumptions (as allowed by certain constraints and principles) can be during communication. We must make sure computers can follow the instructions in the contract on how to converse with language in the same way that humans do, so that computers can produce the much more natural (8) instead of $(8')$.

Now consider again text (6).

(6)   Max stood up. John greeted him.

Text (6) means Max stood up *and then* John greeted him, even though this temporal order isn't explicitly stated in the text. The hearer concludes that (6) must mean this, because otherwise the speaker wasn't following Grice's principles of communication. The relevant principle is the Maxim of Manner, which stipulates that one should be orderly. This can be interpreted as: describe events in the order in which they occur. So when a speaker doesn't indicate otherwise, the hearer can assume that she's describing the events in this order. This dovetails with a default strategy in writing narrative fiction, which is to describe things in the order in which the protagonist sees them.

This begs the question as to why (7) is different from (6).

(7)   Max fell. John pushed him.

Why doesn't *be orderly* ensure that for (7) we infer that the falling preceded the pushing? Well, in contrast to (6), we have some relevant knowledge about the world in (7), about the way pushings and fallings are normally connected, if they're connected at all. The knowledge is: if a falling and pushing are connected in a causal or part/whole relation, then normally the connection is that the pushing caused the falling. We don't have similar causal knowledge for standing ups and greetings. Instead, we must rely solely on the order in which the events are described for clues as to the order in which they happen in the world, because this is the only clue we've got. The presence of the causal knowledge for (7) and its absence for (6) will ultimately influence the overall interpretation of these texts, and explain the differences between them. We'll examine this in detail shortly. It is important to stress, however, that Grice doesn't model how the various pragmatic maxims interact with each other and with other information sources such as world knowledge during discourse interpretation. Modeling the differences between (6) and (7) requires one to predict how causal knowledge about pushings and fallings on the one hand interacts with principles such as *be orderly* on the other. One would have to expand Grice's theory accordingly.

More generally, it is important to stress that you don't have to meet all of the maxims all of the time. For example, there are texts that are perfectly acceptable, but they *don't* describe events in the order in which they occur, and therefore don't, strictly speaking, adhere to the principle *be orderly*. Compare (9) with (10):

(9)   The lone ranger jumped on his horse. He rode into the sunset.
(10)   Before the lone ranger rode into the sunset,
        he jumped on his horse in a reckless fashion.

In (10), the order in which the events are described doesn't match the order in which they occur. But there are explicit linguistic clues for this (specifically, the word *before*). Thus, one way to view the maxim *be orderly* is as a *default* clue about how to interpret text (this is not how Grice put it since he talked about apparent violations of the maxims, but an alternative view of them as default rules seems entirely plausible).

To put it another way, the maxims are principles that predict what a text means *in the absence of information to the contrary*.[34] If there is linguistic information that conflicts with the clue about temporal order given by *be orderly*, then this default principle doesn't affect the overall interpretation because there is an indication in the text that it wasn't being followed.

In (6), we used Grice's heuristic *be orderly* to infer that the textual order of events matches temporal order.

(6)   Max stood up. John greeted him.

(7)   Max fell. John pushed him.

But in (7) there is conflicting world knowledge that when a pushing and falling are connected, then normally the pushing caused the falling (and so preceded it). This wins over Grice's *be orderly* in the final interpretation; i.e. we interpret (7), at least in this context, as the textual order mismatching temporal order. Text (11) is similar.

(11)   Max ate a huge meal last night.
          He devoured lots of salmon.

Text (11) consists of two sentences that describe events. So Grice's principle of orderliness suggests a temporal order for its events, just as it did in our analysis of the earlier texts. In this case, it predicts that first, Max ate the meal, *and then* he devoured the salmon. But another clue comes from world knowledge: If eating a meal and devouring salmon are connected somehow in a causal or part/whole relation, then normally, devouring the salmon is part of eating the meal. This world knowledge allows us to choose a preference among all the ways that two events can be connected: the latter was part of the former. This clue conflicts with *be orderly*, because an event that is part of another event cannot happen after it. So as in (7), the default world knowledge wins over the conflicting default rule *be orderly*.

This discussion of (6), (7), and (11) begs a question. We've suggested that the rules that govern how information beyond the grammar augments the content of a text overall are not hard and fast rules. Indeed, they sometimes give conflicting clues about what to infer. So the question is: when such conflict occurs, how do we resolve the conflict? Grice didn't address this question.

We'll show that we can explain in a systematic fashion these prioritizations among conflicting clues by using technology from artificial intelligence (AI) that has been developed to reason with partial evidence. An integral part of this enterprise is the notion that you abide by rules that admit exceptions. Grice articulated an account of meaning where one assumes whatever content one needs to in order to ensure that what might look like a violation of a maxim isn't in fact a violation at all. But this doesn't account for the content of discourse situations where it is logically impossible for two maxims to be followed simultaneously. In other words, he doesn't fully predict which texts are exceptions to which maxims (such as (7) being an exception to *be orderly*). We will propose how one can use techniques from AI to construct such an explanation, dropping the talk of apparent violation of maxims. In essence, we will be using a tool from AI to make precise an ongoing discussion in Philosophy about the rules that govern the way humans converse.

16.4 What Syntax Tells Us About Meaning

Before we explain how to encode Grice's maxims formally, and model their role in interpreting discourse, we must review the way we extract meaning from the syntax of the sentences. We have been developing a grammar that does this, but we haven't represented anything to do with TIME in this grammar. Since we're going to concentrate on examples like (6) and (7), where the temporal order of the events is central to their meaning, we must make some assumptions about what the syntax tells us about time in the semantics. Clearly, we must learn something about time from the tense used, for example. Changing the tense of a sentence from past tense to future tense results in a corresponding change in meaning.

We assume the form-meaning relation records the following semantic information:

1. What our grammar has encoded so far.
2. Tense Information:

    - the event described occurs before the time of speech, if the event-description is in the past tense (e.g. *Max fell*);
    - the event described occurs at the time of speech, if the event-

description is in the present tense (e.g. *Max falls/is falling*);

- the event described occurs after the time of speech, if the event-description is in the future tense (e.g. *Max will fall*).

3. The fact that two adjacent sentences describe events that are connected in some way, either in a causal relation (e.g. as in (7)), or a part/whole relation (e.g. as in (11)).

In addition, we assume that discourse interpretation keeps track of the *order* in which events were described. Indeed, this assumption is necessary for the above item three to make sense. We have to record this information somewhere for the principle *be orderly* to have the appropriate effects on discourse interpretation. So far, the DRSs generated by the grammar don't record information about the textual order of the events. But this order is implicit in the way the DRS is *constructed*: One processes the sentences one at a time, in the order in which they are uttered. So it should be clear that it's possible to encode—either in the DRS or elsewhere—the order in which the events are described. We'll assume that this information is recorded somewhere (it should be clear that recording this information in the DRS itself isn't necessary for the principle *be orderly* to access and use the information, although clearly recording it there would be sufficient).

Item three above, on what syntax tells us about meaning, amounts to an instruction that we must compute the relevance of juxtaposing the sentences (as demanded by the Gricean maxim *be relevant*). As we saw at the beginning of this chapter, a coherent text must enable one to work out the connections between the juxtaposed sentences. So item three amounts to an assumption that the text we're interpreting is coherent.

It is important to note, however, that the assumptions we have made about the semantics we can retrieve from the syntax of the sentences, and their juxtaposition in text, *excludes* any information about the exact nature of the connection between the events described. Indeed, the above items 1 to 3 tell us nothing about the order in which the events occur in the world. This information will be computed on the basis of default rules that influence the way conversation is interpreted. Language users don't simply compute what syntax reveals about meaning; they use Grice's maxims and knowledge of the world as well.

We must represent the influence of these things on meaning somehow. To do this, we must represent the maxims and world knowledge. The way we represent these information sources must respect the fact that they are rules that have exceptions. For example, the principle *be orderly* is a rule that admits exceptions; (7) is an exception to it.

So over and above the rules we already have for turning syntactic information into semantic content, we also have a representation of background knowledge in the form of rules that admit exceptions. These rules can be thought of as the principles that underlie discourse interpretation. Gricean maxims form part of this.

We must also have a logic for performing inferences with these rules. This logic will then be the "engine" that yields the semantic representation of a text, augmenting the information already given by the grammar. For example, in (6), the principles that apply must be such that the logic working over them predicts that the standing up precedes the greeting. The form-meaning relation doesn't specify this aspect of meaning. Rather, it only specifies that the events are connected somehow. But we nevertheless compute this additional meaning via reasoning with nonlinguistic information, as specified by the rules that admit exceptions and a logic that allows us to reason with these rules.

The rules that admit exceptions are known in AI as DEFAULT RULES, and the logics that tell us how to reason with such rules are known as DEFAULT LOGICS or NONMONOTONIC LOGICS. In the next section, we will discuss how one might use these logics to explain in a systematic fashion why we infer a lot more than what's explicitly said in text.

16.5 Reasoning with Rules that Have Exceptions

The above texts suggest that we should think of the rule *be orderly* as a default rule. That's because sometimes there are other conflicting clues about what the text means, which win over the rule *be orderly*, thus producing texts that have a different meaning to that predicted by the rule *be orderly*. (In other words, the textual order doesn't match temporal order.)

How do we represent *be orderly*? And how does it interact with other default rules? We must ensure that we have a logic for reasoning with default rules that resolves conflict among the various clues about what a text means "automatically." We don't want to have to resolve conflict manually every time it arises, because we want the computer to be able to work out the final meaning of a text on its own.

The patterns of inference

Let's think about rules that admit exceptions for a bit. We must think about how humans reason with such rules, since we must make sure that we don't assume some weird kind of reasoning process when dealing with the task of using such rules to extract more meaning from a text.

Birds fly is a default rule—or a rule that admits exceptions—because there are dead birds, glass birds, birds with broken wings, penguins, and so on. However, if we know that birds fly, and that Tweety is a bird, and that's *all* we know, then we conclude that Tweety flies:

Defeasible Modus Ponens
> Birds fly
>
> Tweety is a bird
> _____
>
> So: Tweety flies

We call this pattern of inference **Defeasible Modus Ponens**. We may retract the conclusion if we find out more about Tweety; this is **Defeat of Defeasible Modus Ponens**:

Defeat of Defeasible Modus Ponens
> Birds fly
>
> Tweety is a bird
>
> Tweety doesn't fly
> _____
>
> So: Tweety doesn't fly

This example exhibits an important characteristic of default reasoning: One never draws default conclusions that contradict the premises. This example also illustrates why the logics that model this kind of inference are called nonmonotonic logics: Unlike classical logic, it's *not* the case that as you add to the premises of the inference, the number of conclusions you can draw can only get bigger.

In the above, we had just one default rule that applied. But we have argued that sometimes background knowledge gives *conflicting* default clues about what a text means, and that conflict must be resolved whenever possible. In other words, we must think about the way humans reason when there are several default rules that are pertinent, which give conflicting clues about a particular fact. Which default, if any, wins in such cases?

An example of this is known as **The Penguin Principle** in the AI literature. It is exemplified as follows:

The Penguin Principle
All penguins are birds
Birds fly
Penguins don't fly
Tweety is a penguin
So: Tweety doesn't fly

In the above, there are two default rules that are relevant for working out whether Tweety can fly or not. First, Tweety is a penguin, and we know that (by default) penguins don't fly. Second, since Tweety is a penguin, he's also a bird. And we know that (by default) birds do fly. So can Tweety fly or not? Do we prefer to think of Tweety as a normal penguin and an abnormal bird, or as a normal bird and an abnormal penguin? It should be clear that intuitively, we prefer the former. That is, we assume that he is a normal penguin (and hence an abnormal bird), and so he can't fly.

Why? Well, Tweety being a penguin is *more specific information* than his being a bird, because all penguins are birds. So when there are several default rules that apply, and the consequences of these default rules conflict, we prefer the default that stems from the most specific information. Intuitively, this amounts to never ignoring any information that might be pertinent to working out whether something is true or not. In the above, we don't ignore the crucial information that Tweety is a penguin, and not just any old bird, when working out whether he can fly. Of course, the above conclusion may be retracted if we find out more about Tweety. We may find out later that he's a rocket-powered penguin. In this case, an even more specific default than *penguins don't fly* becomes relevant (namely, *rocket-powered penguins fly*), and so, as above, the more specific default will win, and we'll conclude that Tweety can fly after all.

But it's not always the case that conflict among the defaults is resolvable. Consider the following case: Suppose that Quakers are pacifists, but Republicans aren't. Suppose, furthermore, that *all* we know about Nixon is that he's both a Quaker and a Republican. Then what can we conclude about whether he's a pacifist? Nothing, unless we find out some more stuff about Nixon, or about the relationship between Quakers and

Republicans. This amounts to the pattern of inference that's known in AI as **The Nixon Diamond**:

> ### The Nixon Diamond
> Quakers are pacifists
> Republicans are hawks
> Nixon is a Quaker
> Nixon is a Republican
> _____
> So: We conclude nothing about whether
> Nixon is a pacifist or not

The Nixon Diamond is like the Penguin Principle in that there are default rules that apply and conflict. The difference is that in the Nixon Diamond the default rules aren't ordered in terms of the specificity of information. The result is that we can't decide which default to prefer, and so we come to no conclusions.

In the next section, we'll show how these inference patterns can be used to work out how background knowledge affects the meaning of a text.

Using default rules to extract meaning from text

We have suggested that communication is governed by a number of rules that admit exceptions. In particular, Grice's maxims are default rules. The easiest is *be orderly*. This is stated in `Be Orderly`:

- `Be Orderly`:

If the event e_1 is described in a text just before the event e_2 is described, then normally e_1 occurs before e_2 in the world.

The force of the word *normally* in `Be Orderly` is to capture the fact that it is a rule that allows exceptions. To see its relation to rules like *Birds fly*, simply paraphrase this rule as *If something is a bird, then normally it flies*.

We also represent some causal knowledge as default rules because causal knowledge like "pushings cause fallings" (if the pushing and falling are related at all) admit exceptions. First, note that as a consequence of Grice's Maxim of Relevance, we must find connections between events that are described in juxtaposing sentences. For if they're not connected in causal or part/whole relations, then we have failed to see the relevance of saying them together, and the *be relevant* rule isn't observed. This was why we included the fact that the events in juxtaposed sentences are related in our assumptions about the meaning of text that we extract from syntax (see item 3. above). This means that we can assume, from syntax, that if the event e_1 is described in a text just before the event e_2, then they're connected in a causal or part/whole relation. In view of this, the following Push Law states a piece of default causal knowledge:

- **Push Law:**

If the event e_1 is described in a text just before the event e_2, and moreover, e_1 is an x falling event, and e_2 is a y pushing x event, then normally e_2 caused e_1.

This law seems very "local" or "specific" since it talks about pushings and fallings in particular. It could be generalized to say something like e_1 describes movement and e_2 describes a force that can cause movement, for example. Then the law would apply when e_1 is described by the sentence *Max stumbled, Max tripped, Max moved*, etc.; and e_2 is described by *John shoved Max, John bumped into Max*, etc. Actually, getting exactly the right form to this law, so that it applies in as many cases as is plausible, is a task that no one has solved as yet. One attempt is given below:

- **Generalized Law:**

If the event e_1 is described in a text just before the event e_2, and moreover, e_1 is an event where x undergoes a change along some dimension (movement, creation/destruction, mental change), and e_2 is an event where y causes a change to x along the *same* dimension as e_1, then normally e_2 causes e_1.

This Generalized Law will apply to (7) and to a lot of other examples where the words are semantically similar to *push* and *fall*, such as those in (12).

(12) a.   Max tripped. John shoved him.

    b.   Max stumbled. John banged into him.

    c.   Max moved to the right. John gave him a big push.

That's because we'll see from the lexicon or dictionary that all these words cause change or describe change in movement. The above law would also account for the causal connection in (13)a (the destruction dimension) and (13)c (the dimension of mental change):

(13) a.   John broke the vase. He dropped it.

   b.   John believes that he is tall. Max convinced him that
             anyone who is five feet tall is tall.

This is a very sketchy discussion of one particular way in which you can
get a more general rule about causation than the `Push Law`. We won't go
further than this here, because solving this problem is not important for
our purposes. The important thing to note here is the *structure* of the
law. It's a default rule, and has as part of its antecedent the statement
that e_1 is described before e_2 and that e_1 and e_2 are events, which is
exactly the content of the antecedent of `Be Orderly`. This is important
when we look at the way it interacts with this law as text is interpreted.

We also have indefeasible causal knowledge, such as `Causes Precede
Effects`:

- `Causes Precede Effects`:

If e_2 causes e_1, then (without exception), e_2 precedes e_1.

Note the relationship between `Be Orderly` and `Push Law`. The conclusions
of these rules conflict, because of `Causes Precede Effects`. However, `Push
Law` is more specific than `Be Orderly`, because it contains the additional
information that the events concerned are a falling and a pushing (`Be
Orderly` applies to events in general). Hence if both rules were to apply,
`Push Law` would win over `Be Orderly`, via the Penguin Principle. This
relationship between the default rules will prove very important when
we analyze (7).

We can now use these rules, via inference patterns like Defeasible
Modus Ponens and the Penguin Principle, to extract more meaning from
a text than syntax alone gives us. These rules will give additional information about the temporal relationships between the events described
in the text.

First consider text (6). The rules in the grammar for converting
syntactic to semantic information yield that the standing up is an event,
the greeting is an event, they both occurred in the past, they were
described in that order in the text, and they're connected somehow.
This means that only one of the above default rules has its antecedent
verified: `Be Orderly`. Intuitively, we can't decide on the basis of world

knowledge alone which kind of connection between the standing up and greeting we prefer. So `Be Orderly` is the only clue. The consequent of `Be Orderly` is consistent with the other things that are known (at least, this is true in the context where (6) starts the text, and the hearer doesn't know anything already about the temporal order of these events). So by Defeasible Modus Ponens, the reader infers that the standing up precedes the greeting, as intuitions would dictate.

It should be stressed, however, that in a different context, the reader (or the computer) may come to a different conclusion about the temporal order between the standing up and the greeting. For example, if one already knows that the greeting preceded the standing up, then Defeat of Defeasible Modus Ponens, rather than Defeasible Modus Ponens, will be the relevant pattern of inference. And so we *won't* infer from (6) that the standing up precedes the greeting.

Now compare (6) with (7):

(7)   Max fell. John pushed him.

The syntax of the sentences in (7) are the same as those for (6). Consequently, the rules of the grammar yield similar semantic content from that syntax. The semantic representation of (7) ensures that *two* of the above default rules are verified: `Be Orderly` and `Push Law` (because e_1 is a Max falling event, and e_2 is a John pushing Max event).[35] As we've already stated, when both these rules apply, the `Push Law` wins over `Be Orderly` by the Penguin Principle. Thus, we infer its consequent: e_2 causes e_1. In other words, the pushing causes the falling, and so precedes it by `Causes Precede Effects`.

Again, it must be stressed that the default inferences could change when (7) is uttered in a different context, such as (14):

(14)   John and Max were at the edge of a cliff. John applied a sharp blow to the back of Max's head. Max fell. John pushed him. Max fell over the edge of the cliff.

In (14), the falling precedes the pushing, rather than the other way round. We would account for this via other default rules that conflict with `Push Law`, and are more specific than it, which would be verified by the semantic information in (14), but not by (7) in isolation of the discourse context provided by (14).

Now consider text (11).

(11)   Max ate a lovely meal. He devoured lots of salmon.

We have the following background knowledge that's relevant:

- **The Meal Law:**
If an event e_1 is described just before the event e_2, where e_1 is the event of x eating a meal, and e_2 is the event of x devouring something, then normally (i) e_2 is part of the event e_1, and (ii) the thing that was devoured was part of the meal.

The Meal Law conflicts with Be Orderly, because an event e_2 can't be part of e_1 and precede it at the same time. The Meal Law is more specific, however. And both laws apply in the analysis of (11). So by the Penguin Principle, The Meal Law wins, and we interpret the events in (11) as connected in a part/whole relation, rather than one of temporal precedence.

Now consider a text that sounds odd, or like a joke:

(15)   ?Max ate a gourmet meal. He devoured a rubber tire.

The default laws Be Orderly and The Meal Law both apply in this case, just as they did with (11). But in addition to this there is world knowledge that normally a rubber tire is *not* part of a gourmet meal. We specify this knowledge in Rubber Tyre:

- **Rubber Tyre:**
If x is a gourmet meal and y is a rubber tyre, then normally y is not part of x.

This rule applies and conflicts with The Meal Law. But Rubber Tyre and The Meal Law are not in a specificity relation to each other. On the one hand, The Meal Law talks about eatings and devourings and Rubber Tyre doesn't. On the other, Rubber Tyre talks about rubber tyres, and The Meal Law doesn't. There is an important difference between Rubber Tyre and the other background knowledge we have represented. It doesn't say that e_1 and e_2 were described in sentences that are juxtaposed in a text. This is to reflect the fact that rubber tyres aren't part of gourmet meals, *regardless* of whether they are described in juxtaposed sentences or not.

So there are three default rules that apply: `Be Orderly`, `The Meal Law`, and `Rubber Tyre`. `The Meal Law` conflicts with `Be Orderly` and is more specific than it, and so by the Penguin Principle it deems `Be Orderly` as irrelevant. But `The Meal Law` and `Rubber Tyre` conflict, too. And these laws aren't in a specificity ordering. So we have a Nixon Diamond: There is irresolvable conflict between the default rules that apply. Hence, we *fail* to conclude the precise nature of the connection between the events. The fact that we don't have enough information to infer what the connection is makes the text odd, or like a joke. This "joke" has arisen here from the fact that there is irresolvable conflict among the various sources of information that provide clues about how the sentences connect together. Thus, certain kinds of jokes seem to be caused by irresolvable conflict about how to interpret something.

Indeed, this irresolvable conflict among principles for interpretation seems to be the basis of word puns like (16):

(16)   John likes mustard on his thighs, but Bill prefers suntan lotion.

One the one hand, the background information about what mustard is used for favors interpreting *thighs* as *chicken thighs*. On the other, the background information about what suntan lotion is used for favors interpreting *thighs* as *human thighs*. We can't resolve these conflicting clues about how to interpret *thighs*. There's a Nixon Diamond here because two default rules apply, but neither one is more specific than the other. (There's nothing about mustard that makes it more specific than suntan lotion, or vice versa.) So we can't decide which clue about the interpretation of *thighs* should take precedence—the one about mustard, or the one about suntan lotion. This produces a word pun effect.

16.6   Some Concluding Remarks

When sentences are juxtaposed to form a text, people reason about why the facts described are grouped together. Consequently, they infer a lot more content than that which is revealed by the syntax of its sentences. As well as syntax being a source of information about meaning, people also use background knowledge, such as knowledge about causation and action, their beliefs about the speaker, rules about how language is used in conversation, and so on.

Some aspects of this background knowledge can be represented as default rules; that is, rules that have exceptions. These rules sometimes give conflicting clues about what a text means, and so we need to provide a logic that resolves this conflict "automatically" when it is appropriate to do so. In recent years, there have been interesting developments in AI about how to mechanize reasoning with default rules. Some researchers use these AI techniques to systematically model ideas from philosophy and linguistics about how language is used in conversation. These theories use inference patterns like the Penguin Principle and the Nixon Diamond to encode how default rules affect the meaning of a text. Roughly speaking, the Penguin Principle captures the intuition that you never ignore information that's relevant to working out what a text means. The Nixon Diamond, on the other hand, forms the basis for explaining when a text sounds odd, or like a joke.

But there is still a very long way to go! Current theories of text meaning can only deal with very simple texts and very simple aspects of the way background knowledge affects what we think a text means. The crucial difficulty is that there is a very delicate balance between the way the various default clues are represented and the way these clues interact in the logic. If we want one clue to have precedence over another, then making it more specific guarantees this. But knowing when we want this prioritization is difficult to evaluate. And so representing the background knowledge in the right way is a very complex task. Clearly, encoding rules that are as specific as Push Law wouldn't be practical if we were building an automated natural language understanding system. There would have to be many, many rules like it! We would also be in danger of encoding the rules so that the logic generates unwanted inferences.

It has so far proved impossible (and some would argue is impossible *in principle*) to manually specify all the rules needed to process text in a robust manner. One needs automated support for acquiring the rules that encode our background knowledge. There is just too much of it for us to do it manually, and so researchers have begun to explore whether we can acquire the necessary knowledge automatically, through machine learning. MACHINE LEARNING statistical models have proved successful in other research areas where knowledge-rich information sources are needed to perform particular tasks; the statistics is one way of approximating such knowledge, thereby avoiding the need to handcraft it. In particular, machine learning has been used very successfully to learn grammars for various languages, such as English. And the machine learning techniques themselves are improving all the time, as well as being applied in novel ways to various tasks in language processing.

However, while machine learning in natural language processing has revolutionized the whole research field in areas such as parsing and lexical processing, there is still much to be learned about how it might apply in the area of *pragmatic* interpretation of discourse. One problem that currently hampers progress in this area is that typically machine learning has to be trained on linguistic data that contains the target information (this is known as SUPERVISED LEARNING). In the realm of discourse interpretation, then, the texts in the training data would have to be annotated with representations of their pragmatic interpretation—these representations would go beyond the content supplied by any grammar. Manually annotating natural language texts with such rich semantic information is prohibitively expensive—at least, for the quantity of texts that are required for effective training. So to date, this richly annotated semantic data (e.g. texts that are annotated with part/whole and causal relations between events that are linguistically implicit) simply doesn't exist.

We therefore need to explore ways of learning pragmatic models from *unsupervised learning*—for example, by exploiting surface syntactic cues in the training data to estimate paraphrases. An alternative is to *semiautomatically* generate training data for the supervised learning of models of discourse interpretation. Linguistic models that are represented as rules can help here: The human annotator and the system that implements the language model can work in tandem, with the user suggesting or replacing the semantic representations that are predicted by the system when appropriate. The system can then even learn from the annotations done so far, so that it converges on the correct output. This process, of a human annotator and machine learner working in tandem, is known as active learning. And there are currently a number of research efforts that explore how active learning might contribute to the enterprise of machine learning statistical models of discourse interpretation.

This chapter has focused only on the way *adjacent* sentences are related or connected. Sometimes, however, a sentence in a text doesn't connect to the previous sentence; rather, it connects to one much earlier than that. (17) is an example of this:

(17) a.   I have several hobbies.

b.   I collect classic cars.

c.   My favorite car is a 1968 Alfa Romeo Spider.

d.   I also take lindy hop classes.

Sentence (17)d is related to the segment consisting of (17)a and b rather than to (17)c. Note that (17)c and d on their own make a very strange text:

(17) c.   My favorite car is a 1968 Alfa Romeo Spider.

d.   ?I also take lindy hop classes.

Also, we could remove (17)c and the text would still make sense:

(17) a.   I have several hobbies.

b.   I collect classic cars.

d.   I also take lindy hop classes.

Intuitively, this is because (17)d *elaborates* the hobbies I have, rather than being connected with my owning an Alfa Spider directly. One could represent the connections in (17) with the following picture:

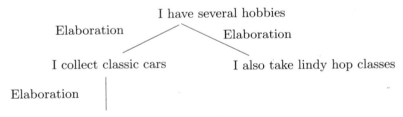

The above representation provides a much richer discourse structure than the ones we've been building with our simple grammar. The elaborations get subordinated, for example, whereas in our simple grammar they would not be in an embedded box. Recall the problems with constraining antecedents to pronouns that we mentioned in chapter 14. We showed that the structure of DRSs, and its role in the Structural Con-

straint, in fact overgenerate the possible antecedents to anaphora in some
cases. Structuring the discourse using rhetorical connections produces a
richer structure than DRSs do. And some people have argued that this
added structure provides at least part of what's needed to improve the
constraints on anaphora provided by structure.

To illustrate this, consider (17) again. Its DRS structure lacks any
embedded DRSs since no words like *if* or *every* are present. This means
that the Structural Constraint as it stands would predict that any of the
discourse referents introduced by any of the NPs is a possible antecedent
to subsequent anaphora. But the following continuation (17)e of (17)
indicates that this is the wrong prediction:

(17) e.   I drive in one of them to the lindy hop class.

Contrary to the theory we've developed so far in this book, it appears
that *them* cannot refer to the classic cars and (17)e sounds odd. Now
suppose that we modify the Structural Constraint to the following: The
antecedent to a pronoun must not be introduced in an embedded part of
the *rhetorical structure* of the context. Then at the point where (17)e is
interpreted, *classic cars* in (17)b is not available as an antecedent since
(17)b is in an embedded part of the rhetorical structure.

Investigating the interaction between these richer discourse structures
and pronouns any further would take us beyond the scope of this book.
The important thing to note here is that (17)d has been connected to
(17)a and not (17)c. This phenomenon of "getting back" to something
you were talking about earlier, after you've had a little digression, is
known as DISCOURSE POPPING.[36] The fact that people can cope with
digressions in conversation and then perform a "discourse pop" and go
back to an earlier topic of conversation considerably complicates the
models of language and of language use. Discourse interpretation involves not only identifying the rhetorical connections between utterances, but also identifying exactly *which* utterances in the text are so
connected. Clearly, these two tasks are heavily dependent on one another, and the suite of default rules that we introduced earlier don't
address the problem of how one decides which sentences in a text are
connected. They would have to be extended accordingly.

The problem of constructing the rhetorical structure of a text is
an ongoing research area in AI, computational linguistics, and formal
semantics, and researchers are beginning to take advantage of recent

developments in formal models of reasoning with partial information or uncertainty—such as default logic, probability theory, and statistics—to get some interesting results for modeling systematically how to interpret conversation.

Exercises

Exercise 16.1: 1. Can you think of principles other than Grice's pragmatic maxims that guide the way we use language in conversation?

2. Can the principles you just stated be seen to follow from Grice's principles? If so, how? If not, what consequences does this have for Grice's theory?

Exercise 16.2: Is there any redundancy in Grice's list of maxims? That is, could any of the principles that Grice gives be deleted without affecting the predictions of how language is used in conversation?
Clue: Can you come up with an argument that some aspects of the Maxim of Quantity are covered by the Maxim of Relevance? Are there any other redundancies?

Exercise 16.3:
We infer a lot more from sentence (18) than the content that's derivable from the meaning of its words and its syntax alone. Describe what this sentence implies.

(18)   John wrote a series of sentences corresponding closely to a description of the "problem" known as *the Projection Problem*.

Try to explain how Grice's maxims predict these implications.
   Clue: Use "be brief" and the Maxim of Quality. Think also about the content that's conveyed by putting something in scare quotes. Do Grice's maxims have a bearing on our choice as to whether we express something with scare quotes or not?

16.7   Further Reading

A general overview of Grice's maxims can be found in the following:

- Levinson, S. (1983). *Pragmatics*, chapter 3. Cambridge: Cambridge University Press.

Chapter 6 in this same book discusses CONVERSATIONAL STRUCTURE, which is the study of the general structure of different types of conversations (phone conversations, narrative fiction, and so on). Unfortunately, investigating the differences among different types of conversations and text genres is beyond the scope of this book.

The original paper in which Grice describes the maxims is:

- Grice, H. P. (1975). "Logic and Conversation," in P. Cole and J. L. Morgan (eds.). *Syntax and Semantics*. 59–82. New York: Academic Press. Reprinted in H. P. Grice (1989). *Studies in the Way of Words*. Cambridge: Harvard University Press.

Jay Atlas adds further maxims to Grice's list; Sperber and Wilson offer a criticism of Grice's model, arguing that the maxims are epiphenomenal on a general principle of Relevance:

- Atlas, Jay (1989). *Philosophy without Ambiguity*. Oxford: Clarendon Press.

- Sperber, Deirdre, and Dan Wilson (1986). *Relevance*. Oxford: Blackwells.

If you're interested in the technical details of how one can use default rules to infer more from text than what's actually said, then the following references discuss these issues:

- Asher, Nicholas, and Alex Lascarides (2003). *Logics of Conversation*. Cambridge: Cambridge University Press.

- Grosz, Barbara, and Candy Sidner (1990). "Plans for Discourse," in P. R. Cohen, J. Morgan, and M. Pollack (eds.). *Intentions in Communication*, 365–388. Cambridge: MIT Press.

- Hobbs, J. R., et al. (1985). "Interpretation as Abduction," *Artificial Intelligence*, 63, 69–142.

- Joshi, A., B. Webber, and R. Weischedel (1984). "Default Reasoning in Interaction," *Proceedings of the Non-Monotonic Reasoning Workshop*, AAAI, New York, 144–150.

- Lascarides, A., and N. Asher (1991). "Discourse Relations and Defeasible Knowledge," *Proceedings of the 29th Annual Meeting of the Asso-*

ciation for Computational Linguistics, Berkeley, Ca., 55–62.

- Lascarides, A., and J. Oberlander (1993). "Temporal Coherence and Defeasible Knowledge," *Theoretical Linguistics*, 19, 1–37.

- Litman, Diane, and James Allen (1990). "Discourse Processing and Commonsense Plans," in P. R. Cohen, J. Morgan and M. Pollack (eds.). *Intentions in Communication*. 365–388. Cambridge: MIT Press.

- Perrault, Ray (1990). "An Application of Default Logic to Speech Act Theory," in P. R. Cohen, J. Morgan and M. Pollack (eds.). *Intentions in Communication*, 161–186. Cambridge: MIT Press.

Many of the above papers (e.g. Asher and Lascarides (2003), Grosz and Sidner (1990), Hobbs et al. (1993)) take the position that the interpretation of discourse depends on a discourse structure that is determined by *discourse coherence* (see section 16.6 for discussion), a point that was first discussed in Hobbs (1979):

- Hobbs, J. R. (1979). "Coherence and Coreference," *Cognitive Science*, 3, 67-90.

The following articles offer various logics for reasoning with default rules:

- Asher, Nicholas, and Michael Morreau (1991). "Commonsense Entailment," *Proceedings of the 12th International Joint Conference on Artificial Intelligence*, 387–392.

- Konolige, Kurt (1988). "Hierarchic Autoepistemic Logic for Nonmonotonic Reasoning," *Proceedings of the 7th National Conference on Artificial Intelligence*, 439–443.

- McCarthy, John (1980). "Circumscription—A Form of Nonmonotonic Reasoning," *Artificial Intelligence*, 13.1–2, 27–39.

- Pearl, Judea (1988). *Probabilistic Reasoning in Intelligent Systems: Networks of Plausible Inference*. San Mateo: Morgan Kaufmann.

- Reiter, Ray (1980). "A Logic for Default Reasoning," *Artificial Intelligence*, 13, 91–132.

Following Grosz and Sidner (1990), Litman and Allen (1990), and Perrault (1990), mentioned above, the following paper uses reasoning with intentions to interpret multisentence text:

- Cohen, Philip, and Hector Levesque (1990). "Rational Interaction as the Basis for Communication," in P. R. Cohen, J. Morgan and M. Pollack (eds.). *Intentions in Communication*, 221–255. Cambridge: MIT Press.

Finally, for reasons of space, we have not covered in this chapter corpus-based methods for automatically acquiring a model of discourse interpretation. The following papers are just two examples of the work in this area:

- Stolcke, Andreas, et al. (2000). "Dialogue Act Modeling for Automatic Tagging and Recognition of Conversational Speech," *Computational Linguistics*, 26.3, 339–374.
- Marcu, Daniel, and A. Echihabi (2002). "An Unsupervised Approach to Recognizing Discourse Relations," *Proceedings of the 40th Annual Meeting of the Association for Computational Linguistics*, 368–375, Philadelphia.

17 Processing Dialogue

17.1   The Problem

The preceding chapters of part IV have focused mainly on the content of MONOLOGUE (that is, talk where only one person does the speaking). In chapter 16, we described theories of discourse interpretation that assume that interpretation processes are governed not only by the syntax of the language, but also by reasoning based on BELIEFS about the world, the speaker, and the way language is used in conversation. In DIALOGUE, things are much more complex. DESIRES and INTENTIONS to perform actions, as well as beliefs, play a central role. For example, just responding with *yes* to the question (1) can be unhelpful.

(1)   Can you pass the salt?

The utterance (1) is not simply a question about the hearer's ability to pass the salt; competent language users infer that asking this question is evidence that the speaker *wants* the salt, and as such the question is (also) a REQUEST to pass the salt. An appropriate response to this question, therefore, is to actually pass the salt; not simply to answer the question with *yes*.

   More generally, our responses in dialogue are in part determined by what the other speakers in the dialogue want and intend to do, as well as what they believe. We infer these beliefs, desires, and intentions on the basis of observing their behavior and in particular, on the basis of their utterances. Things can go horribly wrong when people don't understand what the questioner wanted. For example, offering someone a cup of coffee by asking *coffee?* does not have the desired effect if the response is *yeah, that would be my guess too!*

   People are very good at recognizing the underlying purpose of an utterance. If *B* answers *A*'s question (2)a with (2)c or (2)d instead of (2)b, then he's not being particularly helpful:

(2) a.   A: I was wondering whether I could buy two of the best
              seats in the house for the opera on Saturday.

    b.   B: I'm afraid we don't have two available seats together
              in the highest price range. The closest two seats are sep-
              arated by three rows. I could give you two seats together
              at the rear of the stall.

    c.   B: But we don't sell furniture, only tickets to the opera.

    d.   B: Oh, really? I was wondering whether I could have a
              512MB memory upgrade.

In (2)b, *B* offers a piece of information *A* didn't even ask for: that *A*
could buy two adjacent tickets at the rear of the stalls. He does this
because he has identified why *A* asked the question in the first place: he
wants to go to the opera on Saturday with a companion. Sentences (2)c
and (2)d sound funny to us precisely because as competent participants
in conversation we can work out what *A* wanted on the basis of what he
said in (2)a. But computers, in this sense at least, are stupid. They can't
work out why questions are asked unless we tell them these things in
explicit programming languages. If we don't, then a computer is just as
likely to answer (2)a with (2)d or (2)c as it is with (2)b. But computers
must anticipate the user's needs in the manner illustrated in (2)b, if they
are to engage in conversation with human users in a natural way.

Like the examples we discussed in chapter 16, the utterances in (1) and
(2) show that people often intend to convey information that goes beyond the content of the utterance that's derivable from its syntax alone.
Further, responses take this "added" information into account when deciding how to respond. Modeling these aspects of communication involves complex reasoning about how what we say affects and is affected
by what we desire (e.g. wanting the salt) and what actions we intend
are carried out (e.g. passing the salt). We will examine how language,
intentions, and desires connect in the context of simple dialogues involving questions and answers. Examining examples like (1) sheds light on
how information flows between language and thought during dialogue.

17.2   Speech Act Theory

John Austin and John Searle are among the first philosophers to emphasize that utterances are things we *do* (see section 17.4). To emphasize
that utterances are actions, they view each utterance as the author or
speaker performing a particular SPEECH ACT. There are several speech
acts in the taxonomy; in fact, there is no general agreement as to what
kinds of speech acts should be in a speech act taxonomy, but we will
study several fairly uncontroversial examples of speech acts in this chapter. Each speech act has a so-called ILLOCUTIONARY FORCE; roughly put,
this is the the author's or speaker's purpose behind it.

Austin and Searle both argue that communicative intentions are the
basis for distinguishing speech acts in the taxonomy. For example, issuing
a request is distinct from asking a question because their underlying
purposes are distinct: The goal of a question is to know an answer,
and the goal of a request is that the action described in the request be
performed. This intentional analysis of speech acts reveals that Searle's
famous example (1) is a request, even though the sentence mood is
evidence that it's a question as well. So in line with Grice and others
(see chapter 16), both Austin and Searle defend the hypothesis that the
speaker communicates to the hearer more content than is revealed by
syntax, thanks to general reasoning with shared background information,
both linguistic and nonlinguistic.

Unlike Grice, however, Searle emphasizes the fact that the connections
between an utterance and its illocutionary force are typically a matter
of linguistic convention. For instance, they're encoded within sentence
mood: interrogatives (e.g. (3)) express questions, declaratives (e.g. (4))
express assertions, and imperatives (e.g. (5)) express requests.

(3)   Is your name Anakin?

(4)   Your name is Anakin.

(5)   Avoid the dark side of the force!

But this link between linguistic form and the speech act performed—
as determined by its illocutionary force or "purpose"—raises puzzles.
Sentence (1) reveals that things get complex. Sentence (6) is similar in
this respect:

(6)   I was wondering whether you could pass the salt.

Its linguistic form indicates that it's an ASSERTION. It conveys a proposition that can be true or false (it's true if I was indeed wondering whether you could pass the salt, and false if I wasn't). Intuitively, however, much more is going on. The utterance (6) plausibly has a different purpose. It's a request, where the speaker's goal is for the interpreter to pass the salt. This and (1) are thus classified as an INDIRECT SPEECH ACT, which Searle defines to be an utterance in which one speech act is performed indirectly by performing another. With (6), requesting that the hearer pass the salt is performed indirectly by performing another communicative act—telling the hearer that the speaker was wondering whether the hearer could perform this action. Similarly, (1) is an indirect speech act; here the speaker makes a request by performing the (distinct) speech act of asking a question.

There are many ways of requesting a person to pass the salt. (7)a is arguably the "direct" way of doing it. But (1), (6), and (7)b–d are also perfectly valid ways of doing it, and these latter utterances are all examples of indirect speech acts because in each case the request is performed by performing an act of a different type (either asserting or questioning).

(7) a.   I request that you pass me the salt.

     b.   May I have the salt please?

     c.   Is it possible for you to pass the salt to me?

     d.   If it's not too much trouble, I would like the salt.

Studying indirect speech acts raises many questions. One of the most pressing is the following: Is there a systematic relation between the "direct" speech act (i.e. the one indicated by linguistic form) and the indirect speech act? Looking at the indirect speech acts (1), (6), and (7)b–d, one might think not. There seems to be a very loose connection between the meaning of (7)d that's derivable from its linguistic form (via the grammar), and its intended meaning (which is equivalent to (7)a), for example. (7)d is an assertion that features an *if*-phrase. In contrast, (7)a is a request. It's not an assertion, because it can't be said to be false; the action of uttering it is "self-fulfilling"—I make the request by uttering it. It's also different from (7)d in that it doesn't feature an *if*-phrase. (7)a talks about *passing* the salt, and (7)d doesn't. Just about the only thing (7)a and (7)d have in common is that they both have something to do with the salt!

But the meaning derived from grammar and the intended meaning cannot be totally independent. This is because the phenomenon is PRODUCTIVE. That is, sentences of the form *If it's not too much trouble, I would like you to X* can always be interpreted as having the indirect speech act *I request you to X*, regardless of what *X* is. We must capture this generalization, and this requires us to encode a systematic relationship between sentences of these two forms.

There are at least two potential solutions to this puzzle. The first is to assume that all indirect speech acts are IDIOMATIC. This means that they aren't analyzed in terms of the individual words they consist of, the way they're put together and what effects this construction has on meaning, in contrast to the grammatical analysis of sentences that we described in chapters 9–15. Rather, they appear as indivisible "wholes" in the LEXICON. For example, *Can you X?* has the same relation to *I request that you X* as *kick the bucket* has to *die*. So the relation between the literal and nonliteral meaning of *Can you X?* is encoded in a very direct way; we don't relate them on the basis of the individual words that are used. Rather, we just encode in the lexicon something like: *Can you X?* is a polite way of saying *I request that you X*. Note that this doesn't analyze *Can you X?* in terms of the meaning of *Can*, *you*, and *X*. It's in this sense that it's like an idiom; the relation between *kick the bucket* and *die* is not expressed in terms of the meanings of the words *kick*, *the*, and *bucket*.

But there are problems with this view of indirect speech acts. One of the main problems with this view is that we can create a very large number of indirect speech acts in systematic ways. For example, as well as *Can you X?* standing in for *I request that you X*, we have the following:

(8) a.   Please, can you *X*?

     b.   If it's not too much trouble, please can you *X*?

     c.   If it's not too much trouble, I was wondering whether please, can you *X*?

One could go on almost indefinitely in this way, adding linguistic modifiers to *Can you X?* while ensuring that the result is still a request. Under the idiom story, we fail to provide a systematic relationship between these various ways of requesting *X* because we treat all of them as unanalyzable. Since there are an indefinite number of "polite" ways of requesting X, we would have an indefinite number of things in our lexicon that behave like idioms. And this misses generalizations about indirect speech acts.

The second main problem with treating indirect speech acts as idioms is that sometimes *both* the direct speech act (as indicated by linguistic form) and the indirect speech act are equally relevant to the purposes of the dialogue:

(9)   Can you get that suitcase down for me?

The person asking (9) may genuinely not know if the addressee can get the suitcase down. If this is the case, then it was not only a genuine yes/no question, but also a request to pass the suitcase, if the answer to the question is *yes*. In other words, it conveys a conditional request: if you can get the suitcase down for me, please do it. If indirect speech acts were idiomatic, then it would be irreducible and (9) couldn't have both meanings simultaneously, much like *kick the bucket* can't mean literally to kick the bucket and to die simultaneously.

The second way of addressing the puzzle of encoding the relation between the literal force of an utterance and its indirect speech act is to study the *inferences* that people undertake when listening to utterances in dialogue. These inferences involve reasoning not only about the meaning of the sentence that's derived from its syntax, but also the situation in which it's uttered. For example, *Can you X?* conveys a question, according to the grammar. But you can also infer that it has the indirect force of a request by taking into account the context in which the question is uttered. These inferences that interpreters makes about the force of a sentence s are designed to answer two questions. First, why did the speaker S utter s? And second, given that, what is the hearer H supposed to do? Believe something, or do something (such as pass the salt)?

To model such inferences, we need a theory that links what people want to what they say. When someone wants something done, sometimes the best way to achieve the goal is to communicate with somebody in a dialogue. How do we link goals to things that are said in a dialogue? Do we use something like Grice's maxims of conversation (see chapter 16) to model the link? Or is something else more appropriate?

Certainly, Grice's maxims of conversation help us to infer what's wanted from what's said in dialogue, even if it's not the whole story. Take (10) as an example.

(10)   Can you close the door?

The hearer H of (10) can conclude that this was an indirect speech act, and amounted to a *request* to shut the door rather than simply a yes/no question, by reasoning along the following lines. Note the use of Grice's maxims in what follows, together with the knowledge of the background situation in which (10) is uttered:

1. Why did S utter (10)? (Recall from chapter 16 that all Gricean predictions about the content of an utterance start with this question).

2. The utterance (10) would be conversationally inadequate if all he wanted to know was the answer to this question, and wanted to know nothing more. This is because the BACKGROUND SITUATION of this utterance is one where both S and H know that H can close the door. So S already knows the answer to the question before she utters it. So by Grice's maxim of QUANTITY—which stipulates that S must utter things of just the right informativeness for the current purposes of the dialogue—the answer to the *yes/no*-question (10) would not be informative enough. So the maxim of Quantity renders the purpose of (10) pointless, if it was really intended to be just a *yes/no*-question in this context.

3. So what else is S after? What else is (10) supposed to mean, so that it doesn't violate the maxim of Quantity?

4. S must be interested in the status of the proposition *the door is closed*.

5. So assume that S *wants* this proposition to be true.

6. So (10) is a *request* for H to make this proposition true because wanting this proposition to be true is by Searle's definition of speech acts the illocutionary force of the request.

7. So H's response to it should be to engage in an action of closing the door, rather than simply uttering *yes*. Otherwise, H will violate Grice's maxim of Quantity too!

Note that in the above line of inference we started with the meaning of (10) that's derivable from its syntax and considered what S and H believe (e.g. the fact that they both believe that H has the physical ability to close the door). We used these premises to come to some conclusions about what *S wants* (i.e. via reasoning which involved an apparent violation of the maxim of Quantity), and this in turn led to an *intention* on the part of *H* to engage in a particular action. This is because given that the purpose of *S*'s utterance was to get the door shut, any other response would violate Grice's maxim of Quantity. In sum, this simple example shows that engaging in dialogue involves linking beliefs, desires, and intentions with the content of utterances.

So in modeling the link between the meaning of an utterance conveyed by grammar and its intended meaning (including cases where the intended meaning is one of an indirect speech act), we start with the meaning given by the grammar, and we perform inferences about why a sentence with that meaning was said in this context. This leads to inferences about the *intended* meaning of the utterance, and the intended meaning often augments the meaning revealed by grammar. This is analogous to the discussion in chapter 16 about inferring more about content than what's revealed by its syntax in monologue.

Inferring more than what's said in dialogue is just as pervasive as it is in monologue. Take (11) as a simple example.

(11) a.   A: How can I get to the treasure?

     b.   B: It's at the secret valley.

     c.   A: But I don't know how to get there.

In the context of (11)a, (11)b means (11)b′:

(11) b′.   B: The treasure is at the secret valley,
              and I assume you know how to get to the secret valley.

The inference that (11)b means (11)b′ in this context is quite complex. First, on the basis that *A* asked (11)a, we assume he wants to get to the treasure. We also infer that *A* believes that there's some response to (11)a that will help him achieve this. For otherwise *A* wouldn't think that asking the question would help achieve his goal. So *B*'s response must enable *A* to get to the treasure, assuming that *B* is trying to be as helpful as possible. So first, *A* must be able to compute an answer to (11)a from (11)b—that is, he must be able to compute a way of getting to the treasure from (11)b. Using knowledge of geometry and causation, he can do this; he can get to the treasure *by going to the secret valley*. Second, since *B* is trying to be helpful (and the maxim of Quantity demands that he be helpful), B must think that once A knows this, he can achieve his goal of getting to the treasure. So, B must believe that A knows how to get to the secret valley. If he didn't believe this, he would have given A directions for the secret valley—he would have been bound to do this via the maxim of Quantity. Thus, once again we use what a person says—in this case, B saying (11)b—to come to some conclusions about what he thinks—in this case, B thinks A knows how to get to the secret valley. This is then part of what (11)b means, as stated in (11)b$'$.

More generally, people can learn quite a bit about what people think by talking to them, even when they're not talking about themselves directly. Here, A and B learn that (11)b means (11)b$'$. B learns about A's goals. A learns about what B thinks A can do.

Sometimes participants in a dialogue make the wrong assumptions about each other. These wrong assumptions can then be addressed in the dialogue itself. In (11), A can conclude that B was making the false assumption that A can get to the secret valley. He can do this because he uses the Gricean inferences we have just described to conclude that the meaning of (11)b can be paraphrased as (11)b$'$. His utterance (11)c is designed to expose this misunderstanding to B. Note that the word *but* is used to indicate a discrepancy in their beliefs and expectations. The use of *but* in (11)a, b, and c$'$ is odd precisely because (11)c$'$ doesn't violate expectations about what B and A think, arising from reasoning about what the utterances (11)a and b mean.

(11) c$'$.   A: ?But I know how to get there.

The above discussion about the simple dialogue (11) gives some indication about how complicated processing dialogue can get. Reasoning flows from the content of sentences that's determined by their linguistic form, to what people think, and then back again to what the utterances meant, in the light of what people think. For example in (11), the meaning of *but* is dependent on the content of (11)b in the context of (11)a. Its content is (11)b$'$ in this context; the added meaning is an inference about what B thinks A thinks, which we obtain from the fact that he responded to A's question in the way he did. It is this *added* meaning that makes the use of *but*—which signals that some expectation is violated—an acceptable use. This reasoning links meaning, beliefs, desires, and intentions to perform action. As yet, the puzzle as to how one can model in a formally precise way the interactions among cognitive states and the content of utterances is not very well understood.

17.3   Conclusion

When engaging in dialogue, people have to think about what the other participants in the dialogue believe, want, and intend to do. All these things affect the way we should interpret utterances, and the way we should respond to them. If we come to the wrong conclusions about why someone said something, then we may respond in inappropriate ways, as illustrated in (2)a and d:

(2) a.   A: I was wondering whether I could buy two of the best seats in the house for the opera on Saturday.

     d.   B: Oh, really? I was wondering whether I could have a 512MB memory upgrade.

According to syntax and its link with meaning, sentence (2)a is an assertion; it's either true or false that A is wondering whether he can buy two seats to the opera. But that's clearly not all that (2)a means in this context. It's also a *request* to buy two seats to the opera. Since the request is performed via a distinct speech act from requesting—that of asserting—this is an example of an indirect speech act.

The relationship between the meaning of an utterance as revealed by its linguistic form and its intended meaning is highly complex and needs to be modeled via a reasoning system that stipulates how the content of utterances, and the beliefs, desires, and intentions of the dialogue agents all interact. The pragmatic maxims that Grice suggests may provide some informal beginnings of the rules that such a system must obey. But as yet no one has a solid theory of how all of these factors in communication relate to one another. In spite of the current lack of consensus, there has nevertheless been dramatic progress in this area of linguistic analysis over the last twenty years or so; for some examples see section 17.4.

Using beliefs, desires, and intentions to compute the meaning that the speaker intended to convey in her utterance poses many challenges. One of the main challenges is that one generally doesn't have direct access to information about cognitive states. A speaker very rarely says *I want...* explicitly. Rather, we have to make an educated guess as to what a speaker is thinking, based on observing her behavior and actions (including her utterances). Drawing conclusions about cognitive states from the agent's actions can be modeled by default rules, in line with the strategy used in chapter 16. But devising the appropriate default rules about how we infer what a person thinks, and how that affects our interpretation of what she says, is a very complex task. At present, we don't know how to do it effectively. In essence, we need a systematic way of inferring the motivation behind each utterance. But this is just a specific example of a more general problem that should be addressed in cognitive science. We need a theory that connects goals with actions more generally—not just the action of uttering things in conversation, but all kinds of actions. For example, why do I turn the doorknob? Why do I press my foot on the gas pedal? I undertake these actions because of what I want and because of what I believe these actions will cause. But how do we model this link between action, belief, and desire? If we had a theory of this, then we could explain why people behave the way they do in conversation and elsewhere.

Exercises

Exercise 17.1: Some of the ideas presented in this chapter are taken from the following seminal paper on indirect speech acts:

- Searle, J. (1975). "Indirect Speech Acts," in P. Cole and J. L. Morgan (eds.). *Syntax and Semantics*, 59–82. New York: Academic Press.

In this paper, Searle discusses the following dialogue:

(1)   Student X: Let's go to the movies tonight.
(2)   Student Y: I have to study for an exam.

This is in a section entitled "A Sample Case." Read this section (it's only about two pages.) Can you see any connections between Searle's discussion of utterance (2) in the context of (1), and what Grice would say about what's implicated by utterance (2) in this context? In other words, do Grice's maxims help us infer from (2) that Y is rejecting X's proposal, and if so, how?

Exercise 17.2: Herb Clark has done a lot of work on the way people respond in dialogues:

- Clark, H. (1979). "Responding to Indirect Speech Acts," *Cognitive Psychology*, 11, 430–477. New York: Academic Press.

Clark gives *Uh—it's six* and *Let me see–it's six* as possible responses to the question *What time is it?* He says that *Uh* and *Let me see* are not necessary parts of the expected response. So why do you think people say things like *Uh, Umm,* and *Er?*

Exercise 17.3: Give two reasons why a person might use an indirect speech act rather than a direct one to get what he wants.

17.4   Further Reading

The work by Austin and Searle mentioned above can be found here:

- Austin, John L. (1962). *How to Do Things with Words*. Cambridge: Harvard University Press.
- Searle, J. R. (1962). "Meaning and Speech Acts," *Philosophical Review*, 71, 423–432.
- Searle, J. R. (1965). "What is a Speech Act?" in M. Black (ed.). *Philosophy in America*. 615–628, Ithaca: Cornell University Press.
- Searle, J. R. (1968). "Austin on Locutionary and Illocutionary Acts," *Philosophical Review*, 77, 405–424.
- Searle, J. R. (1969). *Speech Acts*. Cambridge: Cambridge University Press.
- Searle, J. R. (1975). "Indirect Speech Acts," P. Cole and J. L. Morgan (eds.). *Syntax and Semantics, Vol. 3: Speech Acts*. 59–82. New York: Academic Press.

Chapter 5 of the following book contains a survey of the literature on speech acts.

- Levinson, S. (1983). *Pragmatics*. Cambridge: Cambridge University Press.

One of the exercises in the previous section mentions the following paper, which investigates indirect speech acts through psychological experimentation and corpus study:

- Clark, H. (1979). "Responding to Indirect Speech Acts," *Cognitive Psychology*, 11, 430–477.

Many researchers have studied in a logical setting the relationship between dialogue content and cognitive states. Here are some examples of this work:

- Allen, J., and D. Litman (1987). "A Plan Recognition Model for Subdialogues in Conversations," *Cognitive Science*, 11.2, 163-200.
- Allen, J., and C. Raymond Perrault (1980). "Analyzing Intention in Utterances," *Artificial Intelligence*, 15, 143–178.
- Asher, N., and A. Lascarides (1998). "Questions in Dialogue," *Linguistics and Philosophy*, 23.3, 237–309.
- Asher, N., and A. Lascarides (2001). "Indirect Speech Acts," *Synthese*, 128.1–2, 183–228.
- Asher, N., and A. Lascarides (2003). *Logics of Conversation*. Cambridge: Cambridge University Press.
- Cohen, P. R., and H. J. Levesque (1990). "Rational Interaction as the Basis for Communication," in P. R. Cohen, J. L. Morgan, and M. Pollack (eds.). *Intentions in Communication*, 221–255. Cambridge: MIT Press.
- Cohen, P. R., and C. Raymond Perrault (1979). "Elements of a Plan-Based Theory of Speech Acts," *Cognitive Science*, 3, 177–212.
- Litman, D., and J. Allen (1990). "Discourse Processing and Commonsense Plans," in P. R. Cohen J. L. Morgan, and M. Pollack (eds.). *Intentions in Communication*, 365–388, Cambridge: MIT Press.
- Perrault, R. (1990). "An Application of Default Logic to Speech Act Theory," in P. R. Cohen and J. L. Morgan and M. Pollack (eds.). *Intentions in Communication*, 161–186, Cambridge: MIT Press.

Unfortunately, we have been unable to focus in this chapter on theories of dialogue processing that stem from psychology. The following offer seminal—and opposing—psychological models of dialogue processing:

- Clark, Herb (1996). *Using Language*. Cambridge: Cambridge University Press.

• Garrod, Simon, and Tony Sanford (1998). "The Role of Scenario Mapping in Text Comprehension," *Discourse Processes*, 26, 159–190.

V GRAPHICAL COMMUNICATION

18 Graphical Communication

18.1 Introduction

So far this book has been heavily focused on communication in language. The beginning of the book dealt generally with the cognitive approach to understanding communication in terms of information and computation, but even there most of the examples were linguistic—reasoning in Wason's selection task, solving Tversky's puzzles, analyzing how we remember the gist of texts. The central portion of the book was devoted to formalizing linguistic communication, even if one of its aims was to show how much more than language is involved. But now we turn to consider communication in MODALITIES other than language, and we will pay most attention to diagrams.

Communication in the "wild," even when language is the main vehicle, is rarely language alone. With speech between participants present (not over the telephone) there is facial expression, body language, and the immediately perceivable surrounding environment. Speakers point at things, and this plays a role in their communication. Even when they don't point, the visually sensed presence of objects and people can be used in communicating. The written and printed word is often accompanied by pictures, maps, graphs, diagrams, etc. Communication would often be virtually impossible without these nonlinguistic supports—imagine an atlas without maps, or a maintenance manual without diagrams. On the other hand, graphics without any words at all are rather unusual. Raymond Briggs' picture story *The Snowman* is one of the very few books with no words. Instructions for assembling flat-packed furniture are notorious examples of attempts to dispense with language in favor of diagrams (to save producing multiple language editions), but they are often quite hard to understand.

So one of our interests in looking at graphics is to give an antidote to the idea that all communication is linguistic. It is also useful to compare what we find with what we have observed about language. Diagrams give some "distance" to stand back from language so we can see what is unique and what is shared. A third reason for including non-linguistic communication is that there is a technological revolution going on that is making available media, and combinations of media, that have never been used before. *Multimedia* (or maybe *multimeejah?*) is the buzz word of the times. Information superhighways are burrowing through the streets of Edinburgh to deliver us megabits of up-to-the-minute digital hype. We are sometimes told that education is to be revolutionized, and more prosaically, that all but a few lecturers will be redundant as information is opticfibred into every home.

Combinations of media that have never been used before offer opportunities for better-than-ever communication, but, as you will have observed, they also offer opportunities for worse communication than ever before. There is a great need to understand, even at a craft level, how to use these media. There is also a need, at a more theoretical level, to extend our theories of meaning from language in order to be able to control them in machines. This actually opens up opportunities to come to a better understanding of some venerable questions about means of communicating that have been around at least since Euclid scratched his first diagram in the sand, and perhaps to understand something about the mind's internal representations.

So what are we going to consider under the terms "graphic" and "diagram?" A range of representations all the way from photographs, through line drawings, diagrams, maps, graphs, tables, cartoon strips, videos, and animations have been included under the term "graphics." Even the old division between still and moving images is beginning to break down under the influence of new technology, which has also increased the scope for interactive graphics and virtual reality displays. Sharp definitions are hard to come by. Very roughly, graphics are planar displays of information that use the distribution of shapes, patterns, and annotations and the relations between them to convey information. So we use the term more inclusively than some practitioners. We will take diagrams and graphs as our paradigm instances. One of our main points will be to come to a deeper understanding of the different possible meanings of "diagram." We do this because one of our main purposes is to compare and contrast graphics with language, and it is easiest to do this in the domain of diagrams. Much of what we have to say can arguably be extended to a broader range of graphics, but this is a wide field and we do not pretend to comprehensiveness.

Modern newspapers are full of tables, maps, diagrams, histograms, line graphs, pie charts. Often these occur in combinations—what have come to be called infographics. There are graphic designers whose profession

Table 18.1
Output of molasses (metric kilotonnes) by region for the years 1880–82.

Regions	'80	'81	'82
Bavaria	27	41	63
Bohemia	42	36	83
Bulgaria	8	88	8

consists of the design of these information displays, and they have developed considerable understandings of what works and when. (A wonderful introduction to this world is Tufte [1992]). This approach to graphical communication is analogous to stylistics and rhetoric (the study of how best to communicate in language), which contrast with descriptive linguistics. This is not a bad starting place for our more theoretical approach to graphical semantics (that can be thought of as analogous to linguistics' theoretical approach to language).

To give a flavor of the generalizations that have been discovered, let us look at a table of information and some alternative graphical presentations of it.

Supposing we are writing our thesis on the middle-ish-European treacle industry in the late nineteenth century and we need to display the information in the table. How should we best do that? Well, we could leave it in the table. Or we could turn the table into text. But we could also use either the histogram, the pie chart, or the line graph. We will call this class of graphics for representing relational data *matrix* graphics. There are other kinds of matrix graphics we could use. Notice that there are two kinds of questions here. First, how do we choose what *kind* of graphic? And second, how do we design the best example of its kind?

What is to choose between table, histogram, line graph, and pie chart? The question turns to what are we trying to do? Tables have the virtue (and the vice) that the numbers entered are absolute quantities. If we want to know absolute quantities, for whatever reason, then tables are good. But if we are less interested in absolutes, but want to know about relative trends (Was Bohemia on the up relative to Bulgaria? Did Bohemia ever get above Bavaria? Which was the bumper-year for molasses?) then a histogram or a line graph is better than a table. We can work it out from the table. All the same information is there. But we have to work.

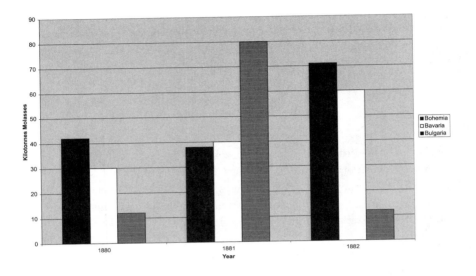

Figure 18.1
A histogram showing molasses output.

There are some relational questions that are still not easy from the histogram or the line graph. Suppose we want to emphasize the relative importance of the regions in a year, but are uninterested in the absolute levels? We can read the relations off a line graph or histogram, but if there are more regions than three this can become hard and a pie chart makes this relational information easier to process. The pie chart represents magnitudes by angular proportions of a fixed 360 degrees, and so removes all but relational information. It has something like the effect of citing proportions as percentages because, like percentages, it provides a standardized unit.

These are only some rather crude examples of the kinds of rules that are fairly well established for choosing the best kinds of graphic for displaying information, relative to the purpose of communication. What about the question how to design a specific graphic within one of these kinds?

One approach is to observe the design decisions that have gone into

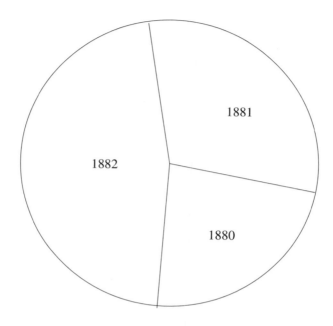

Figure 18.2
A pie chart showing treacle output in the Bavarian region for the years 1880–82.

the examples just used. The histogram (Figure 18.1) has a vertical axis marked kilotonnes, the horizontal axis as years, and three different kinds of bars for the three regions. It has a *legend*, but we could have labeled the bars to show which corresponded to which regions. There are a huge number of implicit alternatives, some pretty nutty. Why put the years on the horizontal axis? And the tonnage on the vertical? Why assign the regions to lines in the line graph and kinds of bars in the histogram? To be really bizarre, we could have broken the kilotonnage range into bands (1–30, 31–60, 61–90) and assigned the three bands to three points on the vertical axis, or used the legend to assign them to different lines in the line graph, or to different textured bars in the bar graph in Figure 18.1. This would mean that the regions and the years would have to be assigned to the two axes. Try it—it produces a pretty hard graphic to read.

To be less bizarre, but still odd, we could have put the years on the vertical and the tonnages on the horizontal axes (in horizontal

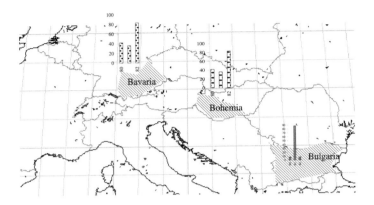

Figure 18.3
An "infographic" relating molasses output and location. The map in the
background was provided by the Xerox PARC Map viewer.

histograms this is common; in a line graph it is not so common—the
vertical is usually reserved for some "dependent" variable quantity (such
as output, rainfall, . . .), and time is generally on the horizontal. We are
accustomed to looking at the increases and decreases in the quantity we
are focusing on reflected as rises and falls through time that is portrayed
as flowing from left to right horizontally across the page. Choosing what
the quantity is that we want to focus on is, of course, the central choice in
designing these graphics. Lots more is known about the craft of selecting
kinds of graphic and designing specific examples. These design issues are
much better treated by authors such as Tufte than we have room or skill
for here.

We turn to more fundamental questions—as usual questions whose
answers may seem extremely obvious but that repay explicitness. How
is it that a table, a histogram, a pie chart, and a line graph convey
information at all? Tables are a good place to start. Tables are a nice
halfway house between graphics and language, but they certainly qualify
as graphics under our crude definition because they use spatial relations
between annotations to determine their meanings.

The top left cell of Table 18.1 contains the numeral 27. In order to
interpret what this 27 means we have to use the spatial relations between
annotations in the table and combine them with information from the
caption. How the numeral stands for the number "twenty-seven" we leave

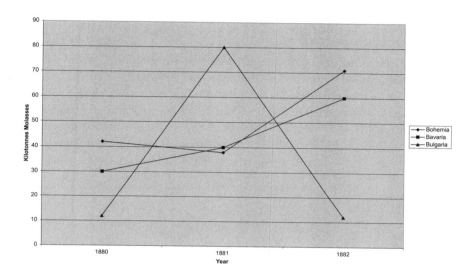

Figure 18.4
A line graph showing the evolution of molasses output over time.

to familiar linguistic semantics to define. But what does the number in the table mean? Well, it is associated with a region (Bavaria) because it is in the row labeled Bavaria, which is in turn in the column labeled *regions*. It is associated with a year (1880) because it is in the column headed '80, which is the row of years (which we can interpret by using the information in the caption). So the number 27 has some relation to the region Bavaria and the year 1880, and this tripartite relation is that 27 is the number of metric kilotonnes of molasses produced in that region in that year (the latter again from the caption). Spatial relations between places-on-the-page of number, annotation, and caption combine to yield sentences of English. Try designing an algorithm for turning the table into text made up of such sentences.

This diagrammatic combination of meaningful elements occurs in quite an intuitively different way than in paragraphs of written language. The thoughtful reader will notice a problem lurking behind this intuition. While we may feel there is an obvious difference between the way spatial relations are interpreted in the diagram and the way they are interpreted in text, nothing we have said explains the basis of this difference. Running through the definition of a graphic (remember: "planar displays of information that use the distribution of shapes, patterns, and annotations and the relations between them to convey information") shows that it fits text just as well as diagrams. Printed texts (this one included) just are "planar displays of information that use the distribution of shapes, patterns, and annotations and the relations between them...." Printed words are surely shapes and their spatial relations on the page are used in conveying their information. So what's the difference?

The difference is so obvious as to remain largely unremarked. This intuition that diagrams use space on the page quite differently than language uses space on the page (or time in spoken language) is correct, but so far not captured. The critical differentiating feature is the layering of linguistic structure. As we have seen in earlier chapters, sentential languages are made up of words *concatenated* together in essentially one-dimensional space or time. The links in this spatial chain do not have fixed meanings directly interpreted. Instead the chains are interpreted as having a syntax (represented usually as a tree, or by parentheses, in the ways now familiar), and it is only these much richer syntactic relations that can be semantically interpreted. The meaning-relation between a noun and a following verb is quite different than the meaning-relation between a verb and a following noun. But their spatial relation as links in the chain are identical. If languages did not have this abstract syntax, and the single concatenation with a single meaning-relation was all there was to interpret, they would be able to say little indeed. Think back to the finite state machines of chapter 6 that had no abstract syntax. All this is just to reprise what was said about logical languages in chapter 5 and developed into great detail in the central parts of the book. It is so obvious as to be invisible.

We will speak of this interpolation of syntax between the surface of a representation and its meaning as INDIRECT interpretation. The spatial relations between elements (here words) in an indirect representation cannot be interpreted until a syntactic structure is assigned on the basis of the concatenation and the identity and category of the words concatenated.

Diagrams, in contrast, are interpreted DIRECTLY. They usually interpret more than a single spatial relation, but they interpret these relations without *any intervening concatenation or abstract syntax*. We can see this in the line graph in Figure 18.4. The vertical distance relations between ○ (and the other markers) and the x-axis are interpreted in terms of size of tonnage; the horizontal distance relation between ○ and the y-axis is interpreted in terms of year. Both are directly interpreted—distance means time (or distance means weight). There is no syntax. True, the diagram incorporates verbal annotations in the legend. These are lists in our example, but they could be sentences. But all they do in terms of the main graphical field is to define the meaning of the graphical icon ○. This particular diagram has three dimensions directly interpreted—year, tonnage, and region. The first two are simple spatial relations and the third is defined by a set of unordered icon shapes. Of course we could add more dimensions—perhaps the hue of the ○-icon could indicate the market price in that year in that region, and so on. But each dimension is directly interpreted.

These diagrams are limited in the number of dimensions that they could use. A large number of dimensions for a diagram (say five or six) is still trivial compared with the number of combinations of words and syntactic relations that can be packed into a paragraph of text each having a distinct semantic interpretation. Diagrams and language derive their respective strengths and weaknesses from these fundamentally different ways of meaning—direct interpretation vs. indirect interpretation. To see how these far-reaching implications follow, consider the issue of what information is required to draw a diagram.

It is an immediate consequence of the directness of interpretation of diagrams that this kind of representation demands a certain sort of completeness in the set of information to be portrayed. If we only know that in 1880 *some* region produced 45 kilotonnes of molasses, we cannot enter this fact into the table at all. Only if we know the year, the identity of the region, and the size of the output can we represent the fact. Tables are not quite totally coercive of completeness. We do not have to have an output figure for every year in order to represent a region in the table, though if we don't then we have to have a convention that "empty cells" mean unknown quantities. If we want to allow even this minimal amount of ignorance for a line graph, then we have to have some fairly unnatural convention such as a "spurious points" icon for each point that is in fact unknown. This "coercion" of completeness

by the kind of representation chosen is one of the critically important
functional properties of images, graphics, and especially diagrams. We
came across this concept of information enforcement in chapter 7 in
studying the properties of our mental representations of the gist of texts.
In this respect, those mental representations appear to share a centrally
important property with diagrams.

How does this coercion of completeness of representation follow from
the directness of interpretation of graphics? Well, every point within
the field of a line graph has coordinates on both axes, and so any
point represents values on both axes. And lines that pass through levels
on an axis automatically represent values on that axis. So although
every table/histogram/line graph generates a text (or many texts), the
reverse is not so. Many texts have no corresponding graphic. The texts
that do not have corresponding graphics are abstract with regard to
determining some data on some dimension(s). Language can leave out
what information it will; graphics is compelled to include.

Presently, we will see how this basic contrast between modes of meaning plays a fundamental role in determining the cognitive properties of
these different kinds of representations. But first we need to look at some
apparent counterexamples to our generalizations described so far. These
are graphical representations that are capable of expressing abstractions
rather in the same way that sentential languages do. They will lead us
to a refinement of what we mean by "diagram."

We take as our examples NODE-AND-LINK FORMALISMS. Graphically
these consist of nodes (possibly of various shapes, with various attached
linguistic annotations), joined by links (which may be symmetrical lines
or asymmetrical arrows, with heads and tails). This class of graphics
is extremely widespread. It is interesting because the same graphical
ingredients are interpreted in many different ways. Some interpretations
are concrete in much the same way as the kinds of graphics that we
have been discussing so far. For example, the nodes may be interpreted
as kinds of components in an electronic circuit (perhaps with different
shapes for capacitors, resistors, transistors, etc., and numbers to express
values of capacitance, resistance, etc.) The links are then interpreted as
wires connecting components.

Semantically, such a circuit diagram is rather like a map. Often the map
only represents the circuit's topology (its connections; not its shape), but
nevertheless its semantics is fully direct. For example, if two nodes are

shown in different places, then they represent distinct components, even if they may be of the same type. If two components are not connected by a wire, then the nodes that represent them in the diagram will have no joining link. And vice versa, if there is no link in the diagram, then there is no wire. We cannot draw a picture of one wire that goes to one component or another. Information is enforced as is usual in diagrams. So far, everything is just as we have described in diagrammatic semantics. However, the same kind of graphic can be interpreted in different ways that are not simply diagrammatic. Figure 18.5 gives an example.

Consider the node-and-link graphic in Figure 18.5. The style of interpretation of the right-hand figure (of these very same graphical node-and-link formalisms) is essentially linguistic, and is capable of expressing abstractions just like linguistic representations generally. Such interpretations are common in computer science where they often underlie so-called "visual programming" languages. This righthand diagram is a simple example of what is called an entity-relationship diagram in computer science. We interpret each node as denoting the person who is named by its label, and we interpret the graphical arrow relation as indicating that the person denoted by the node at an arrow's root loves the person denoted by the node at its tip. So the diagram can be "read" as indicating that Pavel loves Sue. Sue loves John. Pavel loves Sarah. Sarah loves John. The usual kind of tangle.

How does this kind of graphic compare with the matrix graphics for molasses that we discussed above? Does it demand completeness? This question has to be taken at several levels, and raises questions at each. Asked about just the nodes first, the question at first seems that they do completely determine the identity relations of the people they denote. But this is only because we tend to assume that Sue is not Sarah and Pavel not John. If we assume that the nodes determine all identity relations, then we can rule these complexities out. If we look at the use of such diagrams, say in specifying databases, then this assumption is not so clearly universally true. If we have some nodes in a hotel database labeled "room booker," "room occupant", and "bill payer", it may indeed be indeterminate whether or not these roles are filled by the same or different people (or companies) on the same occasion.

When we turn to the arrows we find similar problems. The interpretation of the ones that are in the diagram may be straightforward enough once we have decided who the nodes denote. But what about the ones

A vocabulary of symbols:

P, Q, R, ...

&, ∨, ...

(,), ...

Some rules of combination:

If P is a sentence, and Q is a sentence, then P & Q is a sentence.

To be strict, rules of combination are about a spatial relation
(concatenation) and how it forms strings of symbols. If a "frown" (⌢)
is used to denote concatenation then a complex formula might look like
the example below. If it continued over a line break, the concatenation
relation would have to be defined to take this into account.

(⌢P⌢&⌢Q⌢)⌢∨⌢R

Some rules of interpretation that operate on syntactic structures:

P & Q is true just in case P is true and Q is true.

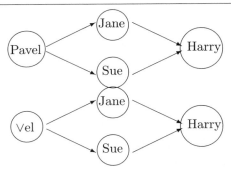

Graphical semantics is sometimes similar and sometimes different to
linguistic semantics. In the left-hand network the spatial relation is
directly interpreted and has a uniform meaning. But in the right-hand
network the links between the logical operator *vel* and the other nodes
have a different semantic significance. So again, it is an abstract syntax
that is being interpreted in this second case.

Figure 18.5
Sentential and graphical semantics compared.

that aren't in the diagram? Do we know that Sarah does not love Sue because there is no arrow between their nodes? Do we know that Pavel does not love himself because there is no arrow from his node to itself? Such problems are compounded when we consider the other diagram in Figure 18.5 in which the node labeled *vel* stands for disjunction (*vel* is the Latin name for ∨). It is quite common to have different kinds of nodes in these diagrams, some standing for concrete entities and some for abstract logical functions, and to interpret the arrows differently according what kinds of nodes they join. If arrows from a *vel* node point to the arguments of the logical function, then we can read our graphic as saying that "either Sue loves John or Sarah loves John"—a possibly less tangled situation.

The question these examples are designed to raise is whether these graphics are more like the molasses diagrams or more like sentential languages? In fact, their semantics is more like sentential language than that of directly interpreted diagrams. The *vel* example is the one in which this is clearest. In that diagram, the arrow is working like concatenation in sentences. There is nothing semantically in common between the meaning of the arrow that connects *vel* to Sue, and the identical arrow that connects Sue to John. It is their *syntax* that distinguishes their different meanings. There is an abstract syntax defined on a concatenation relation—their semantics is *indirect*. True, concatenation in this diagram is not exactly like concatenation in a sentence—it is not linear, but branching. But it still has the hallmark of a concatenation relation: It does not have any semantics independent of its syntactic type.

The kinds of incompleteness of the graphics in Figure 18.5 stem from the same source as that of the ability of language to leave matters incomplete. For example, we cannot know from the absence of an arrow from Jane to Sue whether Jane loves Sue, just as we cannot tell from the absence of a statement to that effect in a story that there is an absence of the relevant love. In chapter 6 we saw that a large part of our comprehension of stories, such as the one about Napoleon, consisted in specifying the relations between descriptions that the language left vague. We can now see that that process consists of deriving something further towards an image in the rather more precise terms we now have for thinking of images and diagrams. The mental representations of gist appear to be direct in our technical sense.

The very same node-and-link graphics permit different kinds of interpretation, some of which, like the circuit diagram, may be directly interpreted just like our earlier example diagrams, and some of which are indirectly interpreted just like sentential languages. This at least has the clear moral that it is always the interpretation of the diagram that determines its semantic properties. No amount of staring at the ink on the paper alone will tell us which kind of interpretation is intended. The latter kind of indirect "linguistic" interpretation of graphics is practically important because there are many attempts to use these kinds of formalisms in computer science and elsewhere. Their use is often justified on the grounds that they are visual and therefore make things clearer. But if it is the kind of interpretation that determines whether they make things clearer we have seen reason to believe these abstractly interpreted diagrams should perform more like texts.

Directness vs. indirectness is a fundamantal distinction in the way that different kinds of representations take their meaning. We will argue that this distinction plays a crucial role in determining the cognitive properties of representations. If fact, we will argue that it is this distinction between direct and indirect representations that is the essential difference that distinguishes language and image. In what follows we will use the term "diagram" only for graphics that are directly interpreted, leaving "graphics" as a more general term for the larger set of representations, some of which are indirectly interpreted.

In summary, we have seen that there is a craft to the design of graphical communications just as there is skill in presenting ideas in text. There are general rules that can guide us in their design, though there is also much that is difficult to make explicit. Turning to the more fundamental questions about how graphics convey meaning at all, we saw that there was a tendency for graphics to coerce completeness of representation and that this meant that though graphics could always be turned into language, language could not always be turned into graphics. The root cause is the demand for completeness of information for graphical display and we saw that this followed from the directness of the semantic interpretation of graphics as opposed to the indirect interpretation of language being syntactically mediated. Finally, node-and-link formalisms are an example that show that the same graphic can in fact receive both direct and indirect interpretations. We now set about making this semantic distinction do some cognitive work.

The very general scientific question that we will focus on next we

will call the media/modality assignment problem (definitions of those
M words presently). The media assignment problem asks what are the
cognitive effects on the consumer of expressing the same information in
different media or modalities? To caricature: "Which picture is worth
which thousand words?" And we can add "for which user, with what
background knowledge, doing what task, in what context?"

Take for a very simple example, the choice between a text, a table, and
a map. We can write a text about the distances between three cities:

C is five miles from B. B is two miles from A. A is four miles from C.

But we can also present various tables, or maps.

	Alphabetical Table				Long./Lat. Table				Map	
	A	B	C			B	A	C			
A	0	2	4		C	5	4	0			C
B	2	0	5		B	0	2	5		B	
C	4	5	0		A	2	0	4			A

These two tables are organized on different principles (perhaps for
different purposes). The longitude and latitude table is in fact logically
close to being a map (of a certain granularity)—the zeros in the table
become the cities in the map.

Needless to say, even within the textual modality, there is enormous
scope for different information presentations with very different cognitive
properties. A not very helpful author might start off presenting the same
information as follows:

The northernmost city is five miles from the city that is neither most northern
nor most southern. The town that is neither most eastern nor most western
is two miles from the town that is on average furthest from the other two. . . .

All these sentences are well-formed, but the paragraph is, to say
the least, unhelpful. This serves to remind us that while linguistics
has much to say about what is *possible* in language, it has had less
to say about what design of language constitutes skilled or optimal
communication. That is left to rhetoric and stylistics. This issue how

to optimize communication comes to the fore with our question about media/modality assignment.

In the current examples of paragraphs, tables, and maps, the same information is presented in several different ways. What is the consequence for the reader? What tasks will these expressions facilitate, and which will they retard? And why? This last question is the scientist's question. It seeks an explanation. It is not satisfied with obvious "truth." For some people it is obvious that graphical interfaces for computers are best, and it is obvious that that is because they are graphical. But for other people, linguistically driven interfaces are obviously best. The only thing that is obvious to the scientist is that what is obvious may or may not be true, and even if true, we may or may not have an explanation for why it is true.

The approach we will take to this question is, as with most of the examples in this book, to look in depth at a rather simple example. The example we will take is the use of diagrams in teaching very elementary logic. We choose this domain, as usual, for many reasons. First, it is one in which we can assess accurately what information is expressed by alternative diagrammatic and linguistic expressions. If we are to study alternative expressions of the same information, then it had better be the same information. Second, teaching/learning logic is a difficult kind of communication (for both teacher and learner), and so provides something more than a toy example. Third, this is a domain in which there has been strong controversy within the teaching profession for several centuries—the disputes between those in favor of using diagrams and those against sometimes feel like a microcosm of the wars over the religious use of imagery. Fourth, logic is the discipline that has contributed most to an understanding of sentential semantics, and so it provides a useful place to branch out into the study of the meaning of other representations. And finally, elementary logic has much to offer to an understanding of communication, and so relates back to several other parts of this book—conditional reasoning, logic and computation, theories of discourse, conversational implicature, and so on. As usual, we are skinning several cats.

Our plan is as follows. In the next section we define some of the terms involved—particularly *media* and *modality*. In section 18.3, we introduce the teaching of syllogistic logic as an example domain that can be taught using diagrams. First, we describe what it is that has to be learned in learning the logical "game" in terms of two components of communication, *exposition* and *derivation*. We then define the particular fragment of logic that is the syllogism. In the following subsections we present some alternative graphical methods for solving syllogisms. In section 18.4, we use the logic teaching example to illustrate some differences between diagrammatic semantics and the semantics of sentential language. Finally, in section 18.4 we present some results of experiments on the effects of diagrammatic and nondiagrammatic teaching, and use the differences in the semantics to explain what differences the media make in teaching and learning, and discuss how these differences may generalize to other domains.

18.2   Media and Modalities

There is a terminological problem that pervades the study of multimedia that stems from the different disciplines that contribute. Computer scientists use the term MEDIA to describe the physical modes of input and output of information to computer systems. VDU screens, printers, graph plotters, and loudspeakers are *output* media; keyboard, mouse, microphone, and scanner are *input* media. Notice that these terms take the perspective of the machine. Tape and disk may serve for both input and output. Logicians and computer scientists, in contrast, use the term *modality* to talk about representations with common *styles of semantic interpretation*. So language (the prime example) is a unified modality that can be presented in many media, dominantly speech and writing, and has a common interpretation across those media. Diagrams are another example of a modality that can be presented in different media, for example, as visual patterns (the same *medium* as printed language), or as tactile patterns on embossed paper for the blind—the same *medium* as braille-printed language. Diagrams cannot easily be presented acoustically, though it is possible to represent some spatial relations by sounds using our ability to detect the direction of sound sources. To the extent that diagrams in different media (visual and tactile) have certain features of their style of interpretation in common, they are a modality that crosses different media. Visual diagrams and written language can be presented in many different physical media (paper, VDU screen, projection screen, smoke writing in the sky...).

These physical presentations form a family of media all grouped under the abstract category "visual media." They have in common that we perceive them by eye.

But this is where the terminological problems begin. Psychologists use the term *modality* for sensory modalities: sight, hearing, smell, touch, etc. And so psychologists' modalities are closely related to what computer scientists call "media." The physics of the computer scientists' medium determines which of the psychologists' modalities can perceive them. Psychology does not have a systematic term for what is common to language across media, or common to diagrams across media, because psychology has not concerned itself with the systematic study of semantics. Since this aspect of semantic interpretation is our main focus, we will retain the term *modality* in the logic/computer science sense. Just remember that psychologists often use it to mean sensory modality. Figure 18.6 is intended to help you remember what these two terms mean through examples. As usual, these terminological issues prove to be rather important when discussing the "facts." For example, when it is claimed that "visual" computer languages are good because they are visual, it is obvious that the "visual" cannot mean perceived through the eye, since text is read through the eye and is exactly what is contrasted with "visual languages." Probing for just what *is* meant by visual helps to get nearer to well-defined empirical questions.

18.3   An Example Domain: Teaching Logic

The reason for choosing to explore a single example of graphical communication in depth rather than surveying a wide range of diagram use is that the cognitive consequences of using diagrams or sentences depends heavily on what task we are doing in what context and with what prior knowledge. A single example where we can examine these issues in depth is more illuminating than a lot of superficial cases where these issues remain implicit.

What is there to be communicated in this domain?

Teaching and learning logic is clearly a case of communication. In chapter 5 you experienced an attempt to communicate linguistically the basics of logic through the example of propositional calculus (though

Modality Contrast

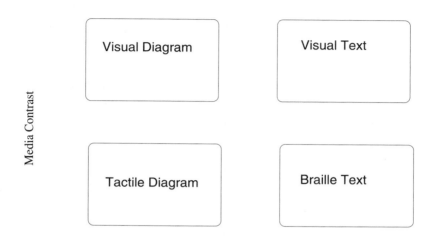

Figure 18.6
The concepts of *medium* and *modality* applied to tactile and visual diagrams and to printed and Braille texts.

tables were also used). We suspect you found it hard to grasp these ideas that are at once too familiar and too abstract. We certainly found the writing of the chapter a nontrivial task. But just what was it that was communicated? If we are to consider what effects communicating through diagrams has, compared with communicating without them, then we first have to consider what it is that has to be communicated.

This is a more than usually interesting question in the domain of logic. On one view of the matter, there is nothing to teach, and the very idea of *learning logic* is paradoxical. English-speaking students know what *if, and, not, all, some, none*, and *some. . . not* mean long before they get in a logic class. So what is there to learn? Along with this way of thinking about the problem goes the answer that what there is to learn is the technical details of whatever fragment of logical formalism is taught—facts like $P, P \rightarrow Q \models Q$, and how to interpret them. This is the logic-as-Ps-and-Qs view. Along with this view often goes the conclusion that logic is not of much interest or use outside the practice of logic. This is not the view we took in chapter 5. There we argued that what we were teaching was an explicit grasp of things that were previously familiar but only known implicitly—such as the concepts of validity, consequence, etc.—and that learning to make these concepts explicit had important effects on reasoning and learning. Here we develop that view in terms of learning about kinds of discourse—what we will call EXPOSITION and DERIVATION.

So what are exposition and derivation?

They are fundamentally social relations in communication. Exposition is communication where one participant (the speaker) knows something, and the other (the listener) adopts a credulous attitude, and where both understand that this is the relation between them. So there is an *asymmetry of authority for information*. The speaker has authority for the information and utters some sentences on the basis of which the hearer tries to construct the model of the sentences that the speaker intends. If all goes well and the hearer constructs the right model, the hearer then knows what it was that only the speaker knew before. This is the credulous attitude to discourse described in chapter 5 and modeled there by default logic. This attitude was contrasted to a skeptical attitude adopted in argument and modeled in classical logic. The Map Task (p. 333) where both parties have identical maps is a fairly pure case of exposition in communication. When sender and receiver begin, they do not share the knowledge of the route; by the end, if all goes well, they have established the route as a common assumption.

Note that it is not really important from the point of view of a theory of communication whether the speaker really does *know* or even *believe* what she says, nor that the hearer know or believe it afterwards. They may both treat it as the telling of a fictional story. Indeed, there is no place that actually corresponds to the map used in the Map Task experiments. What is important here is that there is asymmetry of authority for the information—that the speaker knows and the hearer doesn't and both accept this understanding (or pretense) of the state of affairs. If the hearer suddenly, in midstream, announces that she disagrees and won't accept something said, then exposition has broken down. The hearer is then asserting *symmetrical* authority and a skeptical attitude, and some negotiation will have to take place to restore the earlier situation before exposition can be resumed.

But much more actually goes on in communication, even in the Map Task. The participants establish a *language* with a mutual interpretation,

albeit a very local language, which they did not share at the outset. This
establishment of a common local language is what especially involves
derivation. Derivation, in contrast to exposition, is a mode of communication in which authority for information is *symmetrical* between participants. They share a set of *assumptions* with regard to which they have
equal authority. The business of derivation is to represent some part of
this shared set of assumptions in a novel form. The most sustained cases
of pure derivation occur in mathematics where proofs may proceed for
many thousands of lines. In less formalized cases, derivation frequently
goes on interspersed between bouts of exposition. Just as with exposition, it is generally not important whether the assumptions are in fact
true. What is important is that they are *shared*—that all participants
are on an equal footing with regard to the base assumptions. Remember what you learned about the difference between truth and validity in
chapter 5.

If a previously undetected disparity between participant's assumptions
emerges during a derivation, then repair is necessary. A "fact" may be
checked (thus appealing to some authority for a piece of exposition). But
sometimes one participant simply agrees to change their assumption of
the offending item *for the sake of argument*. Without agreement about
the assumptions that are going to operate (and the consequent symmetry
of authority), derivation cannot proceed.

Exposition is about passing contingent knowledge from one communicator to another. Derivation is about exploring the necessary consequences of shared assumptions. The former is all about getting *new*
information to the receiver. In the latter, if any information emerges
as *new*, then something has gone wrong. Derivation produces only new
forms for old information *content*. Of course, derivation may lead to new
surprising conclusions. But what is new is that the new conclusion re-
represents some aspect of our old assumptions in a new way. The newness
is at a meta-level—we realize that something is a consequence of what
we already knew—not some new assumption at the object-level given us
in exposition. This re-representation of shared knowledge is important
in learning abstract concepts and establishing mutual languages because
often our only way of ensuring that we have the same interpretation for
our language is to ensure that we make the same inferences from the
same assumptions.

The whole goal of communication is to arrive at a community of

people who share assumptions and interpretations, and represent them
in common forms. But there is a tendency to think of communication
on the expository model (neglecting the importance of derivation), and
we will see presently that there is good evidence that that is what
students tend to do in many psychological experiments on reasoning.
Students may have a sophisticated ability to conduct communications
including both exposition and derivation without an explicit grasp of
the difference between the two modes. This is analogous to the way they
have a sophisticated mastery of the syntax of their native language, but
do not explicitly know about the rules. Much of logic teaching has to do
with making implicit knowledge explicit. And succeeding in doing that
changes peoples' abilities to do things—explicit knowledge generalizes
in ways that implicit knowledge does not.

This is our model of what has to be learned about components of
discourse in learning logic. In fact, it is our model of what happened
when you learned the fragment of logic in chapter 5. We now turn to
look at the details of a particular logical fragment. We will return to this
distinction between exposition and derivation when we have looked at
some of the differences between graphical and sentential semantics.

Problems in interpreting quantifiers

We already saw in chapter 3 student subjects struggling to understand
what experimenters meant by the instructions for reasoning tasks such
as Wason's selection task. For example, some students interpreted an
"if ..., then..." sentence to mean "if and only if ..., then...." We
argued that these interpretational struggles arose from conflicts between
the students' understanding of the task and the sentences used. Similar
problems arise in even simpler tasks than the selection task. For example,
if undergraduate subjects are given the sentence "All As are Bs" and
asked whether it follows that "All Bs are As" a substantial number say
that it does follow. This pattern of inference is known as the "illicit
conversion" of the conditional and has been well known to logic teachers
since classical times as a fallacy. It is generally assumed that this is
always an error of reasoning. Certainly it is a fallacy in classical logic.
Again we will argue that this and other errors arise from students'
interpretations of what they are being asked to do.

For another example, the philosopher Paul Grice, whose conversational
maxims you have heard about in chapter 16, was originally inspired to

develop his view of the relation between logic and communication by his observations of problems experienced by his students learning logic. For example, told to assume that *Some As are Bs* they would show evidence of inferring that *Some As are not Bs*, and when challenged they would justify themselves by reasoning as follows:

"Some As are Bs must imply that *Some As are not Bs* because otherwise the speaker would have said *All As are Bs"*.

This prompted Grice to formulate his conversational maxims as presented in chapter 16. Grice noticed that this pattern of inference is based on an assumption of the speaker's cooperativeness. The hearer assumes that the speaker is cooperating by saying just the things that will allow the hearer to guess the particular model that the speaker has in mind. The hearer does *not* take the stance of trying to find a model that will defeat the speaker's statements as they would in adversarial communication. In terms of our discussion in the previous section, the student, quite reasonably, adopts an expositional model of communication rather than a derivational one. In other words, there is a misunderstanding between student and teacher about the meaning of "follows" just as there were many misunderstandings in the selection task. The teacher meant *logically follows*, but the students interpreted the question as *conversationally follows*. And of course it doesn't help merely clarifying the task by saying "logically follows" because before learning logic the distinction between logical consequence and conversational consequence is not explicitly available. And even after learning logic, one needs to specify in which logic something does or doesn't follow.

Although Grice (and subsequent discussions) focused on cooperation, it is also worth noting that the hearer appears to make a further assumption, namely that the speaker is *omniscient* (regarding the matters at hand at least). If the speaker didn't *know* whether all As are Bs, he might well say just *Some As are Bs* for that reason. The making of the inference to all As are Bs appears to indicate that the hearer thinks of the speaker as omniscient. Perhaps the way to think of this is in terms of the "omniscience" of the narrator of a story?

These examples of "errors" in reasoning (illicit conversion and conversational implicatures) are sins of *commission*—inferences that should not have been made according to the experimenter's competence model *are* made. But careful investigation of students' interpretations of simple quantified sentences also reveals sins of *omission*. An example is

FAILURE TO CONVERT sentences that do logically allow conversion. For example, given the premise *Some As are Bs* the reasoner fails to conclude that *Some Bs are As*. These errors are important for what they can tell us about what students have to learn about logic. An explanation is given below in terms of what we will call information packaging, and INFORMATION PACKAGING is one feature of language that sets it off from diagrams.

Even more important than finding unnoticed errors is that by looking at the full range of errors of ommission and commission we observe highly systematic individual patterns of error across quantifiers. For example, students who make the first error (illicit conversion), rarely make the second (failure to convert), and *vice versa*. There are "styles" of interpretation of these sentences that cross particular inferences. We do not yet know the full basis of these styles, but they appear to be related to the graphical/linguistic preferences that we describe below.

These problems we have described are problems that students have with interpreting quantifiers in a classical logical way before learning logic. So if these problems are evidence about what has to be learned about logic, how can we study the cognitive processes involved in learning logic with and without diagrams? We now describe a study of some very simple logic learning designed to do just that. First, we describe syllogistic logic and different ways of teaching it, before reporting the results of a study of the effects of different assignments of modalities in its presentation.

What are syllogisms?

We choose syllogisms as a fragment of logic for several reasons. We could take the propositional calculus that appeared in chapter 5. But we only know of one graphical method of teaching it (namely, Peirce Diagrams) and that method uses indirectly interpreted graphics and therefore does not permit the contrast in modalities we want to explore. The syllogism has the great advantage that there are several graphical systems and we can compare them, both amongst themselves as well as with a sentential method. Besides, learning another logic is helpful for comparison purposes, too.

Syllogisms are historically important as one of the first fragments of logic for which there was a real logical theory—developed by Aristotle. Syllogisms are logic problems in which two premises about relations between two *end* terms and a shared *middle* term license conclusions about the relation between the two end terms. For example, in the syllogism shown here,

(1)   All artists are botanists.
        All botanists are chemists.

(2)   Therefore, all artists are chemists.

artists and *chemists* are end terms and *botanists* is the middle term. Syllogistic premises and conclusions have one of four quantifiers: *all, some, none,* and *some... not.*

Syllogisms are about *types* of individuals defined by combinations of three properties designated by the terms A, B, and C. *Maximal* types are described by combinations of all three predicates of a syllogism. Taking $\neg A$ to mean that the type does not have property A, there are eight such types:

(3)   ABC
        $AB\neg C$
        $A\neg BC$
        $A\neg B\neg C$
        $\neg ABC$
        $\neg AB\neg C$
        $\neg A\neg BC$
        $\neg A\neg B\neg C$

Interpretations of the syllogism consist of sets of these maximal types of individual. So for example, in a "world" in which there are just two types of individual, say, the first and the last from our list of eight, the premises of the example syllogism above are both true, and it can be seen that the conclusion is indeed also true *in that world.* Moreover, this pattern holds up no matter which world we take defined by a set of types from the list of eight. Either at least one of the premises is false, or the conclusion is true. So remembering what was said in chapter 5, this pattern of argument is valid.

Since syllogisms are just about whether there are or aren't things of these eight types, there are obviously 2^8 or 256 possible syllogistic worlds. That is just all combinations of presence or absence of the eight types. The reader can check for our example syllogism that indeed the conclusion is true whenever the premises are true in *all* 256 possible worlds. Laborious?

If we take an example like

(4)   All As are Bs.
         All Cs are Bs.
         Therefore, all As are Cs.

we find that there is no valid conclusion. For *any* of the eight possible candidate conclusions, we can exhibit a counterexample world in which the premises are true and the conclusion false. The world where there are just two things, one ¬ABC, and the other AB¬C, is such a world. Thinking about these two example syllogisms should be enough to make it clear that exhaustive searching of this space of models is an arduous way of deciding whether a proposition is a valid conclusion of a syllogism, or whether a syllogism has any valid conclusions. What we have presented here is what logicians call the "model theory" of the syllogism—its most fundamental semantics. What we need is some less arduous way of computing valid conclusions. It's even clear that we must have some intuitive method of solving some of these problems because we don't need to search through the 256 models to check that the first (very easy) example is valid.

Before going on, it is worth comparing this (your second logic) with the propositional calculus (PC) described in chapter 5. The model theory for the syllogism that has just been described is like truth tables for propositional logic—a way of examining all possible worlds. The methods we are about to look at for solving syllogisms are like the natural deduction rules (proof theory) we gave for the propositional calculus, except that some of the methods use diagrams instead of sentential rules. The main difference between the two logics is that syllogisms analyze the truth of sentences in terms of individuals that have properties, whereas propositional calculus never analyzes below the level of whole atomic sentences.

Finally, it is worth solving a few syllogisms for yourself to get a feel for the processes involved. What if anything follows from each of these examples?

- *All Bs are As. All Bs are Cs.*

- *All As are Bs. Some Cs are not Bs.*
- *Some As are Bs. Some Bs are Cs.*
- *All As are Bs. All Cs are Bs.*
- *No As are Bs. No Bs are Cs.*
- *No As are Bs. Some Bs are not Cs.*

Some methods for teaching syllogisms

What we will present here are three methods of solving syllogisms—of finding valid conclusions from pairs of syllogistic premises (if there are any). The first is a sort of sentential baseline—a method that uses no diagrams. The second method, Euler's circles, will be the diagrammatic system that we will consider in the most depth. In the third method, we will briefly describe Venn Diagrams, chiefly as a contrast with Euler's Circles.

Each of these methods of solving syllogisms can be the basis for many different methods of *teaching* people how to solve them. We will not go into the fine grain detail of possible teaching interventions based on the methods. But when we have described the methods we will return to the question about how they relate to the more general learning about exposition and derivation that was stressed in the previous subsection.

A sentential method

We begin with some terminology. UNIVERSAL PREMISES are ones that generalize about a set, i.e. those with *all* and *no* quantifiers. EXISTENTIAL PREMISES are ones that say something particular about a set i.e. those with *some* and *some. . . not* quantifiers.

The method of solving syllogisms used here chooses a SOURCE PREMISE and uses it as a basis for constructing a representation of the whole syllogism that we call the *identifying description* (ID) because it identifies a critical type of individual fully specified in terms of having, or not having, the properties A, B, and C. From the ID, conclusions (if there are any) can be read off. Finally, *modus ponens* (MP) is the rule that allows us to conclude from *if A then B* and *A* that *B*. *Modus tollens* (MT) allows us to conclude from *if A then B* and $\neg B$ that $\neg A$ (see chapter 5).

Figure 18.9 shows how this many-to-many mapping can be simplified to a one-to-one mapping by using a × annotation to distinguish subregions that *must be non-empty* from ones that might be empty.

Figure 18.7 presents a method of solving syllogisms that makes no reference to diagrams, but solves them by entirely sentential means. We present it here mainly as a baseline for you to compare with the graphical methods.

Euler's Circles

There are several diagrammatic systems for logical reasoning that rely on the analogy between spatial inclusion and set inclusion. Two of the best known are the eighteenth-century system known as Euler's Circles, and the system as later modified by Venn. Euler had the job of teaching logic to a Russian princess and found that her difficulties were much alleviated by the following diagrammatic method.

Euler's method of solving syllogisms requires strategies for:

- choosing premise representations,
- unifying premise representations,
- deciding whether there are valid conclusions, and
- formulating valid conclusions.

Figure 18.8 shows a primitive method for encoding syllogistic premises in Euler diagrams. If we simply map sentences onto diagrams of which they can be true, we get the illustrated many-to-many mapping. Because the semantics of Euler's Circles are direct, they force us to distinguish cases that are abstracted over by the linguistic quantifiers.

1. Seek a unique existential premise:

    (a)If there are two, then respond NVC.

    (b)If there are none, then go to 2.

    (c)If there is a unique one, make it the source premise and go to 3.

2. Seek a unique universal-premise with a subject end-term:

    (a)If there are none, choose an arbitrary source premise. Go to 3.

    (b)If there are none, conclude NVC.

    (c)If there are two, reverse a "No" premise.

    (d)If there is now a unique one, choose its premise as the source premise and go to 3.

3. If the source premise is an existential premise, then take its two terms as the first two clauses of the ID. If the source premise is universal, assume its antecedent. Apply MP and conjoin the consequent to the antecedent to make the first two clauses of the ID.

4. Compare middle terms:

    (a)If a source middle term matches (with regard to negation) the antecedent middle term of the conditional premise, apply MP, and conjoin consequent term to ID. Go to 5.

    (b)If the source middle term mismatches (with regard to negation) with the conditional consequent middle term, apply MT to the conditional premise, and conjoin consequent term to ID. Go to 5.

    (c)otherwise conclude NVC and quit.

5. ID is now complete.

6. Draw abstract conclusion from ID:

    (a)Delete B conjunct from ID. Quantify with existential for a conclusion (reordering any positive conjunct into subject position).

    (b)If clause (2c) was satisfied, then there is a universal conclusion with the source premise end-term as subject.

Figure 18.7
A "sentential" method based on the process of constructing an *individual description* (ID) by conjoining terms for each predicate or its negation ("no valid conclusion" is abbreviated NVC).

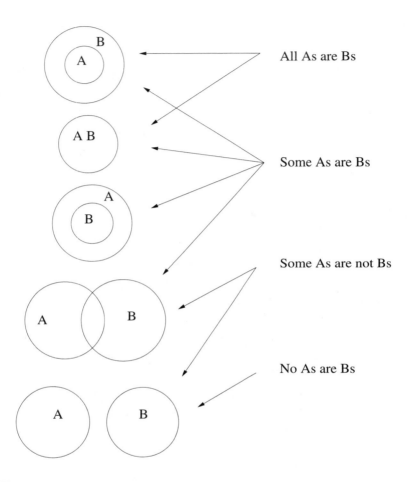

Figure 18.8
A primitive encoding of premises in Euler's Circles.

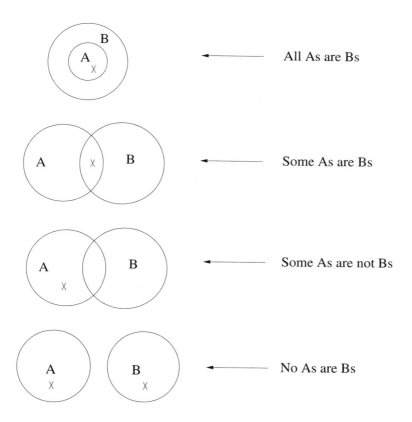

Figure 18.9
An encoding of premises in unique Euler's Circles by marking non-empty subregions with crosses.

Using the one-to-one encoding method gives us a single diagram for each premise and a composite of the two diagrams for each syllogism. We unify the two by making the B circles coincide. In doing so we must choose a relation between the A and C. We always choose the arrangement that has *the most subregions consistent with the premises*. We then look to see if subregions containing crosses have been cut in this unification process. If they have been cut, then their × is removed.

There is now a simple way of drawing any valid conclusions. If there are any remaining ×s, then there is a valid conclusion. If not, then there is no valid conclusion.[37]

We can formulate any valid permitted existential conclusion by describing the type of individual corresponding to the ×-marked region, and dropping the middle term from the description. If the ×-marked region is circular, then we can draw a universal conclusion with the circle's label as the subject term—positive if the circle is inside the other, negative if it is outside. An example will illustrate the method.

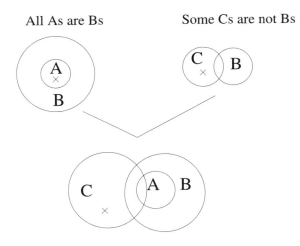

Therefore, some Cs are not As

Figure 18.10
An example of the graphical algorithm applied to the syllogism *All As are Bs. Some Cs are not Bs.*

Figure 18.10 illustrates the method applied to the syllogism *All As are Bs. Some Cs are not Bs.* Each premise is first represented by its diagram from Figure 18.9. The two premise diagrams are then "registered"— their B circles superimposed and their A and C circles arranged to form the maximum number of regions consistent with both premises. The $\times$ from the universal premise does not survive registration because its region is bisected. The $\times$ from the existential premise survives because its region is not bisected. This remaining $\times$ marks the minimal model of the conjunction of the two premises. Having found a $\times$-marked region, corresponding to the type $C\neg A\neg B$, we can conclude that *Some Cs are not As*, and so solve our example.

This graphical algorithm is summarized in Figure 18.11. This completes our description of Euler's system. You should spend a little thought on why the rules are as they are. For example, why are crosses removed if their regions are intersected? Why are the premise-diagrams registered so as to have the maximum number of regions consistent with the premises?

Venn Diagrams

We introduce Venn Diagrams briefly for comparative purposes. They are both very similar and yet semantically quite different from Euler's Circles. Venn's system uses only one diagram, the eight-subregion diagram that represents all possible types (see the right-hand subfigure of Figure 18.12). The background of the diagram serves as one subregion in this accounting and represents the type $\neg A\neg B\neg C$. The system augments this with annotations that distinguish the status of the type of individual corresponding to the annotated region. Whereas Euler expresses the fact that a type cannot exist by having no subregion corresponding to it, Venn uses an explicit mark (here a zero) in the corresponding subregion to denote its emptiness. In fact, Venn Diagrams are merely tables with eight cells in an unconventional layout. In contrast, Euler's system uses geometrical constraints to express combinations of (possible) types of individual.

Figure 18.12 illustrates a syllogism solved by Euler's Circles and by Venn Diagrams. Venn's system is used with a single static arrangement of circles to which notations are added. As with Euler's Circles, a $\times$ denotes the non-emptiness of its subregion. In addition, Venn uses two other notational devices, zeros and question marks. Zeros indicate the

1. Draw the characteristic diagram for each premise;

2. Register B circles of the two characteristic diagrams of the premises and arrange A and C circles with most types consistent with the premises.

3. If a region containing a cross in a premise diagram is cut in two during this registration process, delete the cross.

4. If no crosses remain after registration, then exit with No Valid Conclusion response. The remaining crosses mark the *critical* region(s).

5. If such a region does exist, but both premises are negative, then exit with a No Conventional Valid Conclusion response. (If task permits, conclude that *Some non-As are not Cs*).

6. Formulate conclusion:

    (a)Take the description of the individual type represented by the critical region of the diagram (e.g. $A\neg BC$).

    (b)Eliminate the B term from this description.

    (c)Existentially quantify the remaining description for an existential response.

    (d)Is the critical region circular?

        i.If so, it is the subject term of a universal conclusion.

        ii.If not, there is no universal conclusion.

Figure 18.11
Summary of a graphical algorithm for solving syllogisms using Euler's Circles.

emptiness of the minimal region in which they appear. Question marks appear on the borders between pairs of minimal subregions and indicate that one or another of the bordering subregions are non-empty. Unlike subregions without annotation in Euler's system, a subregion without annotations in a Venn Diagram indicates nothing about the status of its corresponding type.

One possible sequence of construction for the example Venn diagram is as follows. The universal premise is represented by placing zeros in the two subregions representing As that are not Bs. The existential premise is represented by a question mark placed on the border between the two

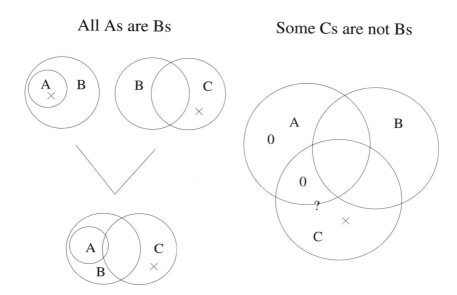

All As are Bs

Some Cs are not Bs

Therefore, some Cs are not As

Figure 18.12
An example syllogism solved by Euler and Venn systems.

subregions that represent Cs that are not B. The further inference can be
made that since there is nothing in the zero-marked region representing
As that are Cs that are not Bs, the question mark can be replaced by a
× in the subregion representing the Cs that are neither As nor Bs. The
existence of Cs that are neither As or Bs (marked by the ×) enables us
to conclude that *some Cs are not As*. On the one hand Venn's system is
very like Euler's, but in other respects it is very different. Some further
differences emerge below.

18.4   Contrasting Sentences and Diagrams

Having spent some time on what has to be communicated in teaching
logic, and having set up graphical and sentential methods of communicating the same thing, in this section we pause to consider what our theories about graphics and langauge can say about the differences between

the example systems. The reader, especially the reader of an empirical temperament, might feel we should get on and do the experiment, and then see whether we can interpret it. But it is important to consider beforehand what theory predicts. It is all too easy to feel that in hindsight we can interpret what happened.

Graphics and conventions

A common belief is that it is obvious what is special about diagrammatic semantics. On this view, diagrams are transparent—depictions look like what they depict and so there isn't the problem that we have with words of connecting graphical signs to their denotations. $\triangle$ looks like a triangle, so there isn't the same problem with an image with understanding what $\triangle$ means that there is with understanding how "triangle" gets its meaning. In contrast, word meaning is almost wholly conventional (remember the discussion of Locke in chapter 7 and the discussion of conventions and abritrariness in sections 4.2 and 10.1). It is almost wholly arbitrary what meaning is attached to what word-sound. Of course, this view, if correct, would have strong implications for learning. On this view that image meaning is transparent, there is nothing about diagrammatic meanings to learn.

We saw in those earlier discussions that the main problem with the transparency of meaning of diagrammatic elements is with *just seeing* the role they play in their system of diagrammatic representations. Just what does the diagram $\triangle$ mean? Does it mean the same as the diagram $\triangledown$, for example? The answer of course is that you (and I) can't tell until we specify what system of diagrammatic meaning we intend to analyze. If you think this is just a semantician being clever, the following true anecdote is worth telling. After explaining what a triangle was to a geometry class of eight-year-olds using a diagram rather like $\triangle$, a teacher found that a number of the children would reject $\triangledown$ as an example of a triangle. It turned out from her inquiries that the children had got the idea that triangles always had a base horizontal to the base of the paper—a generalization that happened to be true of all of the examples she had used. Diagrams are not quite so transparent.

The reason for describing both Euler's and Venn's methods is that they provide another example of the nontransparency of diagrammatic semantics. First, they clearly don't look like what they represent— syllogisms, which is one good reason for taking an abstract domain like logic. Second, the differences between two systems that look so similar is a warning against illusions of transparency of meaning. For example, the presence of an unannotated region in Venn means nothing, whereas in Euler it means that its type of individual *may* exist. So there is very definitely something to learn when we learn these diagrammatic systems. Diagram semantics may not be transparent, but that does not mean it is identical to sentence semantics. Let us consider some real differences.

Self-consistency

It is easy to construct sets of sentences that are inconsistent, as we all know at our cost. An inconsistent set of sentences describes nothing, or, in logical parlance *has no model*. Subsets of its sentences may describe things because they may be consistent, but there is nothing that is a model of the whole set. For example, the pair of sentences *All As are Bs, Some As are not Bs* has no model.

A remarkable property of Euler diagrams is that there are no diagrams that correspond in what they express to inconsistent sets of sentences. It is impossible to construct an inconsistent Euler diagram. For example, try representing the pair of inconsistent sentences quoted in the previous paragraph in Euler diagrams. We can define this property of representational systems as SELF-CONSISTENCY. A self-consistent representational system cannot represent inconsistent sets of propositions.

What underlies this difference between sentences and Euler's Circles? We might be tempted to argue that all diagrams are self-consistent. We can't draw a picture of a square circle although we have no trouble producing the singleton set of sentences: *There is a square circle*. Maybe this *is* the fundamental semantic property that distinguishes diagrams from sentential languages. We could even have a slogan: "The diagram never lies, or at least if it does, it always tells a good story."

But we don't have to go far to find that this is not the simple essence of diagrammatic representation. We have only to look at Venn. In this system it is easy to represent inconsistent sets of sentences. If there is a × and a zero in the same subregion, then the diagram is inconsistent.

Now one might try to rescue Venn by introducing some formal rule that ruled out all such diagrams as "ill-formed," thus leaving well-formed Venn diagrams as self-consistent. But to do so would be to miss the fundamental. Euler's system does not have the resources for expressing inconsistencies. The topology of three circles, plus the mechanism of marking individual regions for non-emptiness, just will not express inconsistency. Euler uses only topology to express the emptiness of categories (through the absence of subregions). Venn's system has the required means of expressing inconsistency because it does not use topology, but an arbitrary placeable mark to express emptiness. One can introduce conventions to prevent inconsistency (such as "don't put two marks in one minimal region," but these are not graphical constraints).

Self-consistency is a property of some diagrams but not others, and adding certain expressive powers of arbitrary notation appears to be what leads to its breakdown. Later we will return to consider what cognitive effects this property might have, but here we turn to another related semantic property—expressiveness.

Expressiveness—concreteness and abstraction

EXPRESSIVENESS is a technical term from logic that denotes the power of a representation system to express abstractions. In general, natural languages such as English are highly expressive—there may be no abstraction they cannot express. In general, diagrams are less expressive, often extremely so. To take a very simple but crucial example, suppose we want to express the abstraction that there is an evening star and a morning star but it is not known whether they are the same or not (if you cannot handle this degree of astronomical ignorance, then think of Mr. Ortcutt and my bank manager. I assure you they both exist, and you don't know whether they are the same or not). In language, expressing these abstractions is easy. We can say: *There is an evening star and there is a morning star.* If we want to be absolutely sure to avoid confusion, we may explicitly say we don't know whether they are the same or not.

But now try drawing a diagram with both the evening star and the morning star in it, but without resolving whether or not they are one and the same. Maybe, if you are resourceful enough, you can find some way of conveying this particular abstraction, but in general you have to resort to some very *ad hoc* tricks. Most diagrammatic systems *force* the representation of identity relations. They cannot abstract over these relations, as was dicussed in the context of mental imagery in chapter 7.

This is another side to the $\triangle \neq triangle$ problem we discussed under conventionality. The more we treat $\triangle$ like a conventional symbol, the more it takes on the powers of a word to abstract over details of the particular triangle drawn. But the more we treat $\triangle$ as a picture of a triangle, the more its meaning fails to abstract over details like the exact values of angles. We cannot draw a triangle without completely fixing the ratios of its sides. We can fiddle with whether or not our diagrammatic system *interprets* (treats as significant) the details, but we cannot avoid them being there.

As we saw with Euler's system, the introduction of abstraction "tricks" like $\times$ can make all the difference between a usable and an unusable system. We call them "tricks" not because there is anything underhand about them, but because they tend to be local, idiosyncratic and not easily transferred from one diagrammatic system to the next. Most diagrammatic systems employ such tricks, but they are idosyncratic from system to system. Without using $\times$, Euler's system needs to present four fully specific diagrams in order to represent a single sentence *Some As are Bs*. But this trick does not allow the system to express all possible abstractions over its domain. It just happens to express all the abstractions that are ever needed in solving syllogisms.

There is a close relation between the power of a system to express abstractions and the complexity of making inferences in the system. In general, the more expressive a system, the more complex the inferences in it become. To understand what this means, imagine a large set of statements like the evening star/morning star example, about a small number of things, but formulated so the identities are at least locally undetermined. Making inferences within such a system will require lengthy inferences about identities. We saw an example earlier in this chapter in our discussion of tables of inter-city distances, maps, and texts describing them. Compare a text requiring complex identity inferences to a situation in which these facts are represented in a diagram that has to resolve all the identity relations because it is not expressive enough to leave them undetermined. Inference in the diagrammatic system will be relatively simple. This observation leads to the hypothesis that perhaps diagrams are useful (when they are useful) because they are inexpressive (when they are inexpressive).

Another earlier topic that touches on these differences was our dicussion in chapter 6 of the processing of the text about Napoleon's dramatic entrance. The text did not explicitly mark many of the identity relations between its descriptions, yet to understand the text required resolution of these identities. We can now see that this was a case of processing a representation in a highly expressive language, and deriving a representation for its gist in a much less expressive language, which was thereby more like an image system of representation.

Evidently, it will depend on what task is at hand what inferences are required. If the diagrammatic system (say perhaps Euler without the ×) is too weak to express the abstract proposition that some As are Bs, and the task at hand requires this abstraction (or is at least made much easier by having it), then the diagrammatic system will be a hindrance, and a sentential system preferable. But if these abstractions are not required, then the weak diagrammatic system will make inference easier. If this is right, then we should expect modality assignment to be a question of horses for courses. We would need to analyze carefully what abstractions are really useful for the task, and which representations can express them. Going back to syllogisms, Euler (with crosses) is sufficient for expressing all the abstractions necessary for syllogisms in a single diagram for each problem. So we might expect this system to be effective.

Information packaging in sentences

Our last contrast between diagrammatic and sentential semantics has to do with features of sentential semantics that do not have any corresponding features in diagrammatic systems. Language allows us to present the same information in many different ways. In speech (at least in English), intonation and stress (the rising and falling pitch and loudness) plays a part in what linguists call INFORMATION PACKAGING. In writing, these same distinctions are expressed syntactically by changes in the structure of the sentence. For example, a simple indicative statement such as *The pipes are rusty* normally bears main stress on *rusty* and the end of the sentence has a falling intonation. Such a pronunciation of the sentence is roughly what would be typical if it was uttered as an answer to the question: *What's the matter with the pipes? The pipes are* **rusty** (boldface crudely marks main stress). In contrast, if the same sentence were uttered in answer to a different question, it receives different stress and intonation: *What's rusty? Its the* **pipes** *that are rusty.* (Note the change in syntactic organization that might go along with this—the sentence is now a *cleft* structure beginning with an *it is* clause). Different question contexts can give rise to yet different renderings: *Is it the taps that are rusty? No, the rusty ones are the* **pipes**. Here the stress would be contrastive and rather more pronounced than in the previous example.

Speech tends to use PROSODIC information to mark these distinctions. Written language cannot, so it must use syntax. Spoken language can use syntax, too. Different languages use different resources for expressing the distinctions. But what are these distinctions? They are not completely understood, and are quite subtle. They do not obviously involve differences in the proposition expressed. In each case, the proposition is just that the taps are rusty and the truth values of the proposition do not seem to be affected. One important part of what is different from one packaging to another is the distinction between *new* and *old* information. Take our first example: *What's the matter with the pipes?* Answer: *They are rusty.* The answerer assumes on the basis of the questioner's mention of *the* pipes, that the pipes are already known to her—they are *old information.* What is unknown to the questioner is the rust—this is the *new information.*

In very simple sentences like these, the syntactic subject tends to be *old information*, the syntactic *predicate* new *information*. Even in a monologue, speakers structure their sentences so that they use subjects that are old information and predicates for new information. Of course, once information has been introduced as new, it becomes immediately old. In the archetypal story where nothing is old information at the very beginning, a special form is chosen that ensures that the only new information is in predicate position: *Once upon a time there was a cat. The cat was a tabby.* We see that whereas the cat is new information in the first sentence, that even by the second sentence, the cat is already old (informationally). If you want to expose information packaging and its power to control communication, take a simple newspaper story, and starting at the end rearrange the syntax of each sentence so that it expresses the same proposition, but the new/old information packaging is changed. Then try reading the story. It usually becomes profoundly incomprehensible. Another context in which we may notice these structures is in the speech of young children who may not be completely adept at understanding the knowledge state of others, and especially of strangers.

Even from this crude description of information packaging, it is evident that information packaging is tailored to the expositional model of communication. In derivation, since all assumptions are shared, all information is technically old. In actual practice, matters may be more complex, especially in a lengthy derivation, but there is a clear link between the categories of information packaging and the expositional model of communication. In exposition, *Some As are Bs* is not equivalent to *Some Bs are As*. But we have to learn that in derivation these *are* equivalent. This is our explanation of why some students refuse to conclude *Some Bs are As* given the premise that *Some As are Bs*. These two sentences are not "conversationally" equivalent even though they are logically equivalent in classical logic, and these students haven't yet differentiated the two types of equivalence.

Notice that diagrams simply do not have anything corresponding to information packaging. The Euler diagrams for these two existential statements are identical. In fact, there is a general correspondence between diagrammatic symmetry and logical symmetry. The two logically symmetrical syllogistic premises *Some As are Bs* and *No As are Bs* are represented by diagrams in which the two terms A and B are diagrammatically symmetrical: the two logically asymmetrical premises *All As are Bs* and *Some As are not Bs* are represented by diagrams in which the two terms A and B are diagrammatically asymmetrical.

The reason is that in an indirectly interpreted sentential language with a concatenation relation and an abstract syntax, the concatenation of elements sometimes has semantic significance and sometimes only information packaging significance. In a directly interpreted diagrammatic system without a concatenation relation, a given diagrammatic relation is either always or never semantically interpreted.

If part of what has to be learned when learning logic is how to recognize propositional invariants amid variable information packagings, then this difference between languages and diagrams might be expected to have significant effects on logic learning.

We have reviewed some differences between diagrams and languages that might be expected to have implications for their usefulness in teaching logic. Now to experiment.

The facts?

What actually happens when these different systems for presenting syllogistic logic are actually used in teaching? There have been remarkably few careful studies of teaching methods in action. But some things are known. One of them is that there tend to be large individual differences between students in whether they learn best from graphical or from sentential teaching. Remember our discussion of individual differences in reasoning in chapter 3. One study showed that it is possible to divide students into two groups on the basis of tests of thinking style, and that one group will benefit greatly from graphical methods where the other will do better without the graphics. (It is as well to remember that the diagrams are always accompanied by lots of words!) That study also showed that it is the student's facility at using graphical tricks (like the × in Euler diagrams) that determines whether they find graphics useful. This study was done with students taking a whole semester course in predicate logic, and is too complicated to present here. Instead we present a smaller study of the learning of syllogistic logic.

In the previous section the Euler method of solving syllogisms was presented along with a sentential method. These two specifications are easy to turn into methods of teaching syllogisms. In the study (Monaghan and Stenning 1998), twenty first-year Edinburgh students were randomly assigned to groups tutored using Euler's method and the sentential equivalent. All students did some pretest practice problems to give a baseline and to get them into thinking about the domain, and all did several subsequent posttest problems after the teaching session to assess their performance in the domain after teaching.

Because it seemed likely from earlier studies that individual differences in learning styles would prove important in understanding the results, some psychometric tests were given before the teaching to assess learning styles. The one we report here is the GRADUATE RECORD EXAM ANALYTICAL REASONING SCALE (GRE). The tutor (and the students, for that matter) was "blind" with regard to the psychometric pretest results. All the tutoring sessions were videotaped, and were subsequently analyzed to assess teaching/learning effectiveness. The two measures focused on here are number of errors made by the student, and number of interventions made by the tutor. The first result was that the two methods of teaching worked exactly as well as each other overall.

The question at hand is, of course, whether this overall similarity masked the same differences in learning styles as had been found before in more realistic studies of logic learning.

We analyzed the results using the GRE as our criterion of individuals' learning styles. The analysis separated the reasoning process into three phases: translating into the formalism (graphical or sentential) from English, manipulating the formalism, and translating back into English. Because of the theoretical equivalence of the methods, it was possible to make the same division into stages of reasoning for both teaching methods. Here we present results only for the manipulation phase though similar effects are observed in the other two phases.

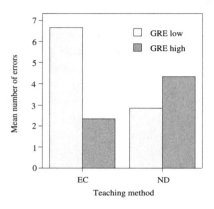

Figure 18.13
Number of reasoning errors at manipulation phase by GRE score and by teaching method.

The results for the reasoning style differences involving the GRE are shown in Figures 18.13 and 18.14, and are rather clear. Students scoring high on the GRE pretest, as opposed to their classmates scoring low, reacted differently to the two teaching methods—graphical and sentential. Students scoring high on the GRE test made fewer errors and required fewer interventions by the tutor when taught using Euler diagrams than their peers who scored lower on this test. But when taught the sentential method this effect was reversed—students scoring low on the tests made *fewer* errors and required *fewer* teaching interventions than their higher scoring peers. This is what is called, in educational research, an APTITUDE/TREATMENT INTERACTION. Students with one aptitude (doing well or badly on the GRE) learn differently under different teaching "treatments"—with or without diagrams.

The symmetry of these individual differences is particularly striking. There are cases where *higher* test scorers show *poorer* performance with a teaching method, and cases where *lower* test scorers show *better* performance. This means that there is more here than merely the

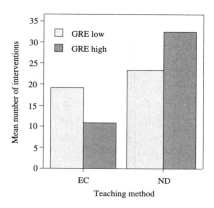

Figure 18.14
Number of tutor interventions at manipulation phase by GRE score and by teaching method.

tendency of any psychometric test to test "general aptitude" or, worse still, "general test savvy." These are real stylistic differences. Some methods suit some people better than others.

None of our discussions here of the differences between graphical and sentential semantics have so far indicated why one should find these individual differences. Sometimes psychologists tell simplistic stories that some people use images a lot (visualizers) and others prefer words (verbalizers), and claim that this explains these individual differences. We can already show that matters are considerably more subtle than that. The students in our study who do well with diagrams actually use *less* diagrams. What they are really good at is translating *between* diagrams and sentences, and knowing when it is useful avoid diagrams. They are also adept at using the abstraction tricks such as the ×-notation to solve problems. The difference is not just one of preferences for representations. Can our theory about the directness of interpretation of diagrams and the indirectness of interpretation of language provide a better analysis?

Different students have different ways of interpreting the syllogistic premises in the interpretation studies described earlier, and these differences can be traced to differences in how they conceive of the experimenter's intentions with regard to the language used—whether they adopt an expositional or a derivational model. We have seen that information packaging is tuned to operation in expositional language. For students who adopt these expositional interpretations we might expect diagrams to be useful in learning to distinguish proposition from information packaging and conversational consequence from logical consequence. For example, students who refuse to conclude *Some Bs are As* given *Some As are Bs* tend to benefit from the symmetry of the Euler diagram for these propositions. The symmetry is a result of the directness of interpretation of these diagrams. Other students with different interpretation patterns learn better from sentential methods, perhaps because these methods stress the justification of each inference step by rules. Stenning (2002) gives the argument that directness gives a better account of the cognitive processes than intuitive notions of transparency.

We hope to have illustrated something of what is involved in coming to grips with that seemingly innocent question "Which picture is worth which thousand words?" We have at least shown that the answer depends critically on what task is being undertaken and what learning style the user has. In presenting the argument we have illustrated something of the kind of detail required in understanding what concepts are being communicated, in equating the diagrammatic and linguistic presentations, and in analyzing subjects' performances.

In summary, diagrammatic representation systems can be studied by extensions of the kinds of semantic techniques that have taught us so much about the way that languages work. At a craft level, much can be said about how to draw a good graphic rather in the way that much can be said about how to write a good text. At a more theoretical level, we asked what distinguished language from diagrams and proposed the answer that modalities such as language and diagrams are distinguished by the way they take their meanings—directly, or indirectly, through an interpolated syntax. Attending carefully to the semantics shows that some graphics are directly interpreted but some are not.

This distinction was then taken into the classroom "laboratory" and used to analyse the details of some very elementary logic learning. What emerged is that the semantic theory can serve as a basis for understanding distinct styles of learning. In principle analyses of individual differences in communicating with diagrams could also be extended to analyses of individual differences in language use, though research on that topic is only just beginning.

This brings us to the end of the section of the book that deals with the details of communication. In the remainder we are going to look at some high level philosophical issues about the whole cognitive/computational approach to the mind.

Exercises

Exercise 18.1: Diagrams can be turned into texts, but texts can't always be turned into diagrams. Illustrate this with a useful example diagram and paragraph showing how this follows from the inexpressiveness of diagrams.

Exercise 18.2: Find a diagrammatic system that uses abstraction tricks, comparable to the crosses on Euler's sytems described here, to express more than one possible model in a single diagram.

Exercise 18.3: Which of the two learning styles described here do you think fits your own study methods most closely? Say why you think this may be so.

18.5   Further Reading

- Chandrasekaran, B. and J. Glasgow (eds.) (1995). *Diagrammatic Reasoning: Cognitive and Computational Perspectives on Problem Solving with Diagrams.* Cambridge: MIT Press.
- Stenning, K. (2002). *Seeing Reason: Language and Image in Learning to Think.* Oxford: Oxford University Press.

VI SCIENCE APPLIED TO THE SUBJECTIVE?

19 Where Have All the Qualia Gone?

Part I reviewed some examples of easily observed phenomena that arise as people take in and transform information. Part II gave an introduction to the computational foundations of the cognitive science approach to understanding these phenomena. Part III introduced methods of modeling language, and Part IV looked at the background of assumptions that are very much involved in communication. Part V compared linguistic and graphical communication. None of these parts could be more than a sketch. But rather than continuing fleshing out the skeleton, we turn now to consider whether it shouldn't just be buried.

Discussing burial will no doubt seem premature to many of my colleagues. How can students assess the viability of this research program with no more introduction to it than a few mere gestures? But this response is misguided. Our own mental experiences are the most intimate part of life, so familiar yet so elusive. This is an area where even the least philosophical souls among us are prone to raise objections to the very possibility of some sorts of understandings. These objections are essentially philosophical arguments. If these doubts are already to the fore, asking to postpone them until the scientific details are fleshed out is only inviting deepening incomprehension. An explicit consideration of these puzzles at the earliest opportunity offers the possibility of an early informed choice of whether the cognitive science research program is the place to invest your time. Mental processes are extremely elusive, and fundamental arguments about the kinds of approach that will yield progress are one way of understanding what they are all about. So the final chapter will review two prominent arguments against the very possibility of computational theories of mind.

19.1 Some objections to cognitive science

Two current lines of sustained criticism of cognitive science's approach to understanding the mind are worth reviewing for what they clarify about the approach this book has taken. These criticisms are more commonly aimed at AI rather than at cognitive science. But they are aimed at the very idea of a computational theory of mind, and so they are arguments against cognitive science as much as AI. We feel that even an introduction owes its readers a review of, and a response to, these arguments.

The first criticism is due to John Searle. It is essentially an argument that computationally based theories cannot give an adequate account of consciousness and the qualities of subjective experience that are constitutive of the human mind. The second criticism is Roger Penrose's argument that human mathematical abilities are demonstrably not implementable in a computing device (in Turing's sense), and that therefore the mind must be understood as a quantum phenomenon. Although these two arguments appear to start from quite different assumptions, it is interesting that they both turn out to be driven strongly by the intuition that conscious experience is inherently beyond the grasp of computational approaches. While we agree that there are aspects of conscious experience that are currently baffling for all known approaches, both these arguments strengthen our belief in computational theories properly understood, and that computational and informational analyses are the only hopeful basis for explaining the mind (and consciousness).

One can but have great sympathy for the intuition that human conscious experience is an elusive creature. Faced with the crudity of our tools of pursuit, and the extreme mobility of the quarry, discouraged by the less than stunning results obtained so far, anyone could be forgiven for rejecting current computationally-based theories of tiny fragments of the mind as justifying the promise of an eventually complete computational theory. But Searle's and Penrose's arguments are arguments *in principle*. According to these arguments it is obvious that the whole program is as wrongly conceived as the phlogiston theory of fire, metempsychosis, yogic flying, or the tarot. Furthermore, both critics gesture toward alternative research programs, as indeed they must. Who is going to take seriously a criticism of physics that it is totally misconceived unless some alternative way of understanding some physical phenomena is proposed?

The situation is not unlike the situation that faced Darwin's proposal that evolution is to be understood by the operation of selection on random variation. It was 'obvious' to many in Darwin's day that this was an idea flawed *in principle*. It was *just obvious* to them that life was a *spirit* that transcended the bodily mechanism, and that all creatures were created by God on a day in the first week, possibly with minor revisions later. We still cannot construct even the simplest critter from scratch, but few scientists now argue against the view that Darwin and his heirs in modern biology won the *in principle* argument. Of course there are huge controversies about exactly how evolution works, but the range of possibilities entertained generally fall within the area of Darwin's proposals. Cognitive science's argument that some aspects of the mind can be understood as computational processes is a similar argument in principle. It will be won or lost not when we can produce artificial human beings with minds from scratch, but when the arguments persuade scientists that they are much more plausible than the alternatives.

Another analogy from biology may be helpful at the outset. Outsiders like Searle and Penrose often complain about psychology and cognitive science that they give no treatment of consciousness, even though consciousness is surely one of the defining phenomena of what is mental. This complaint is rather strongly analogous to a complaint about biology that it gives no account of life, even though life is constitutive of what biology is about. In an introductory course on biology one typically hears the word "life" during the first lecture definition of the topic, and very little thereafter. In this respect, "consciousness" in cognitive studies is very like "life" in biology—the whole subject is about approaches to understanding it, but it gets rather little explicit mention. For example, cognitive psychological analyses of perception start out from analyses of discrepancies between the physical stimulus and the perceiving subject's awareness—say explaining visual illusions. Computational analyses of learning investigate the discrepancies between what subjects have gained information about and what they are conscious of having learned—witness the discussion of implicit and explicit processes in chapter 4. Every topic in psychology is about consciousness, even if the term often disappears from the proposed accounts.

This is not to suggest that current explanations of consciousness are in as good shape as current explanations of life. Nor that consciousness does not present any conceptual questions that challenge current cognitive science. Nor even that it is a bad thing to confront head-on from time to time this disappearence of the term consciousness from scientific theory. Consciousness and our conceptual confusions about it are far too important to be left to the experts. Searle's and Penrose's arguments are productive in clarifying the state of the art. But it is a great mistake to think that current cognitive science says nothing about consciousness just because it barely uses the word.

Searle plays homunculus

Searle's critique starts from his "Chinese Room" argument. Briefly, Searle hypothesizes a Chinese room (think of it as a black box), that receives through its letterbox questions written on slips of papers in Chinese ideograms and returns out through its letterbox answers written in Chinese ideograms. It is, in AI parlance, a Chinese question answering system. Black though the box is, it happens that a fair amount is known about its internal structure, because a brash neuroscientist one day opened the lid and discovered that there inside was Searle himself. Observing the room in operation, the neuroscientist saw the following. Searle had a large look-up table of rules for transforming Chinese symbols, just as a more orthodox computational implementation of a Chinese question answering system might have. When a question arrived, Searle was observed to match the symbols against the antecedents of rules, and to write down symbols as they occur in the consequents. This is, in computational terms, an *expert system*. Searle was merely a strange computational implementation running the "software" in the room. Eventually, as long as the question has a computable answer, the room halts by Searle pushing a piece of paper out of its letterbox, which bears the system's answer in Chinese ideograms.

By hypothesis, the Chinese room implements a system that can answer all the Chinese questions that a Chinese reading human being can answer—let us assume the Chinese mastermind champion. Given this hypothesis, Searle's objection to computational theories of mind are as follows. The room is, *ex hypothesi*, a complete and veridical implementation of a computational account of Chinese question understanding and answering. It passes the *Turing test*, for example. That is, we cannot in principle tell whether the room we are dealing with by input and output is an expert system simulation (based on Searle's rule rewriting), or merely contains a Chinese-reading and question-answering human being.

But, goes the argument, he, Searle, does not understand Chinese characters because he does not know any Chinese. All he can do is recognise formal identities of ideograms. Since the process is computational, all processing is done with respect only of the *form* of the symbols on the paper that arrives through the chute, and of the *form* of the rules in the look-up table. He, Searle, *is* (part of) the system, but he has no understanding of the meaning of any of the processes that go on in it, so the room may be an implementation of question-answering but it simulates none of the experiences of a human Chinese question-answerer. It has no consciousness beyond Searle's completely insulated American one. So no computational simulation can have consciousness. All computational simulations (even robots that can move around and act in the world) are *zombies*—individuals that can perfectly simulate all human outward behavior, but have no feelings or mental experiences within.

Searle has greatly amplified this argument in subsequent papers and there is an industry of commentary on it. In fact, in the early paper little emphasis is placed on the failure to recreate conscious experience in a perfect computational simulation. But it is clear from the way the argument develops that this intuition of computers as zombies is close to the heart of the philosophical intuition that computational approaches cannot embrace conscious experience. No one, least of all cognitive scientists, dispute that this is a powerful *intuition*. But it was a close to universal intuition that human beings could not possibly have evolved by blind chance processes, or that life could be the consequence of biochemicals, up until a century ago. Now, those intuitions are held strongly by practically all scientists. Intuitions are important but highly changeable, and not enough for an argument.

Interestingly, Searle is *not* necessarily opposed to a MATERIALIST view of human beings. He is prepared to accept that he may be nothing more than a collection of cells made up of nothing more than a collection of molecules all assembled just thus and so. But he strongly believes that the particularities of his chemical implementation are absolutely constitutive of his human mental life. Silicon and electricity just can't replace the exact jelly that we are, without leading to a fundamental lack of conscious experience. Even if some mad cognitive scientist (or more likely mad interdisciplinary team of them) could make a robot that he, Searle, could not in principle distinguish from a real human being by any behavioral test, the discovery that it worked by a quite different physical implementation would mean that Searle would have to reject that its experience was human experience. Presumably if some race we had always accepted as humans were found to have a different biochemistry, they would thereby be exposed as imposters? This invites the question just how different can the jelly be, and why is the jelly what's important?

Just think a minute about what it means to pass all such tests. This robot would have to have a sense of humor (especially with Searle asking it questions designed to prove its inhumanity all day). It would have to be able to produce all outward empathetic behavior, crack its own jokes in appropriate contexts, and generally keep up the outward appearances of humanity at which we all have to work so hard.

A possibly misleading issue that should be disposed of here is the limitation to communicating with the room through written slips of paper. Although this limitation is critical for Searle's argument because it is assumed to establish the formal character of the internal processes of the room, it is a mistake to think that it really limits what can be demanded of the room's abilities to simulate Chinese question-answerers. For example, for Searle's hypothesis, the room will need to simulate an aesthetic appreciation of novel Chinese poetry as evidenced in questions and answers about Chinese poems, just as much as an ability to look up bus times. Remember, Searle is accepting that this simulation can be done as the hypothesis in his argument.

You should also remember that this is not a judgment that *in fact* Searle would always actually be able to tell it was a robot. After all, Searle is human and can make mistakes. This is an *in principle* argument that the simulation could pass *all conceivable* behavioral tests and still it wouldn't satisfy Searle.

Many responses to Searle's argument have appeared, and interesting clarifications of both sides have been achieved. It has been pointed out that there is a real problem about "grounding" the meaning of symbols in systems that are only coupled to their environment by the input and output of symbols on paper. A robot that moves through an environment thus controlling aspects of its own sensorimotor loops, is the minimal sort of coupling that might be expected to yield an interesting simulation. A system being embedded in the physics of its environment in this kind of feedback loop has immense implications for what sort of functions it has to compute.

Rather trivially, one might observe that Searle is going to have to be a pretty nifty symbol shuffler to keep the robot off the deck. Current robotic systems use huge processing power to establish these sensorimotor loops. This need for processing power is partly due to the inelegance of the definitions of the problem we have been able to invent. But there is also reasonable evidence that the nervous system *does* do a lot of computation.

More seriously, one can observe what this means for the *kinds* of functions that need to be computed. Time will be an absolutely critical feature of the specification of these functions. If robot "muscle twitches" (whatever they are implemented by), don't happen in breathtaking coordination with the relevant "sensory impulses" (whatever they are implemented by) then our robot is going to have a truly rough day. It is a striking fact about Turing's model of computation, as it is usually conceived, that time is *not* part of the specification of the functions computed. The function "+" is defined as a set of triples of numbers $< 1, 1, 2; 1, 2, 3; 2, 2, 4; \ldots >$, in which the first two elements are the arguments, and the last is the value. But suppose we define a function as having the arguments $< 1, 1 >$ and the value of the function is $< 2within7seconds >$, which is interpreted as the symbol 2 output within 7 seconds. Similarly, the arguments $< 1, 2 >$ for this function have the value $< 3within7seconds >$, interpreted as meaning the value 3 output within 7 seconds, and so on. Some implementations of "+" are going to also be implementations of this function, but others are not.

Notice that the problem is not one of *representing* time. It is easy to include representations of time in the specifications of what is computed, say, in terms of a number of seconds. But what is not easy to include is the idea that the time of execution of the computation of the function is interpreted as part of the specification of the function. We cannot insist that time represents time without diverging from Turing's abstraction. The speed of execution is a matter of the implementation, not of the function implemented.

It is pretty obvious that many of the functions that we have to interpret human beings as implementing do have this characteristic of incorporating aspects of their implementation in their specification. Human question-answering, for example, has to be simulated on a timescale commensurate with human life or it cannot be said to be an adequate simulation of human question-answering.

If cognitive science ever claimed that the implementation of cognitively interesting functions was completely irrelevant to understanding the mind, then here would be a real problem with cognitive science's computational models of mind. It may be that some early claims were legitimately interpreted to be of this kind. Early treatments of the importance of the abstraction of computation over different implementations stressed the need for abstraction. Perhaps in so doing they neglected the fact that the mind is embedded in a physical world and interacts with a physical world, and so implementation cannot be a matter of complete indifference. Nevertheless, much of the need for abstraction survives, as indeed we argued in section 6.2.

So what computations can simulate minds is constrained by the physical embedding of body in world, just because the specification of the functions we count as constitutive of minds include at least some specifications of the time things take to execute. Does this mean that the computations that constitute the mind must be made by the exact jelly we are composed of for us to be conscious? Searle appears to believe so. He likens consciousness to the process of digestion—just another biochemical process constituted by the biochemicals that we are. But this loses all insight about the differences between information and food.

One cure for the idea that some perfect zombie might be the only end product of the AI program of research is neuron replacement therapy (NB., just in case there is any doubt, the following *thought experiment* is a philosophical joke, though a perfectly serious joke, for all that.).

The neuron replacement therapy you are invited to imagine works from the inside out. Remember the purpose is to try to analyze what lies behind Searle's claim that it is the chemical composition of our jelly that is crucial to consciousness. Our thought experiment starts with the simple idea that neurons compute by taking a function of the input signals on their synapses and outputting a value signal down their axons (see section 6.2 for the introduction of how neural systems compute). This much is easy to implement in silicon and electricity instead of ectoplasm and electrochemical depolarizations. Suppose for a moment that our neuroscience collaborator succeeds in replacing all neurons with semi-conductors suitably deposited on the synapses of a human brain. But after some research, we find that our Mark I android doesn't run well at all. We find that what the implementation doesn't implement is the variable length of the axon connections. Unlike slow electrochemical signals that travel at speeds that are functions of the synapse diameter, electricity has a nearly constant, much higher speed. So Mark II is equipped with delay lines between synapse and synapse that produce electrical delays exactly mimicking the delays in the dendrites and axons. Mark II now runs a bit better, but still does not report the right feelings at all, and his qualia are just deplorably pale.

The problem is traced to the fact that there are several ion channels in the synapse that control the refractory periods of the neuron after firing (don't worry if this is neuroscience mumbo jumbo—the details aren't what's important—only the concept of gradual approximation of the implementation). It's not just a single signal, but a set of parallel signals, each with slightly different delay characteristics. The functioning of the mind depends on these waves of signal remaining in reliable phase relations. Having fixed this glitch, Mark IV begins to report the normal roughness shortly after getting up, but qualia reports are severely distorted. The problem turns out to be due to the fact that human neurons learn—they change their resistance to signals as a function of the temporal association of signals on their input synapses. Once this plasticity of resistance is achieved by eighth-generation gallium arsenide technology, Mark V really is beginning to look more promising—some qualia reports sound just like the qualia reports in his philosophy tutor's papers.

And so on. Laying aside facetiousness for the moment, let us suppose that we can successively approximate the information processing of the neuron in our semiconductor technologies. Remember, this is an argument in principle, not an estimation of the prudence in investing your life savings in some new technology. The points I want to make are two. What could we look to to explain remaining divergences between human and robot Mark N other than the information processing capacities of the neuron replacements? Of course we might turn out to be wrong that the brain is really what plays the main role in controlling behavior—maybe it's really the fluid computer in the kidneys. And certainly it will be the embodied brain that we have to account for rather than the version in the vat. But short of such revelations, controlling behavior is just computation (implemented within some important constraints of time), and so if Mark N isn't quite right, then we must have got some aspect of the signal processing of neurons wrong. Of course we could also be wrong about the physical implementation, and it could all turn out to depend on quantum phenomena in the mitochondria (we'll come back to this when we discuss Penrose later). But then we will just have to go back to the bench and replace *that* information processing with some other brand.

Of course, it might turn out that when we have pursued the development of neuron replacement therapy for many years, and we have

a thorough understanding of what information processing needs to be
replaced, we *might* actually be able to show that the current physical
implementation of the human computer is the *only possible* one—it really does have to be the exact jelly. But if we ever reached that point,
then we would have a theory that explained exactly what kind of computation was required, and proved that only one physical device could
implement it. This would surely be an ultimate victory for the computational paradigm—a peculiarly strong one, and highly unlikely.

The second point to be made about this thought experiment is also
about specification, but this time not about the specification of what
computations have to be performed by neurons, but rather the specification of what behavior Mark N must perform to pass the test of
implementing human consciousness. Critics ofstrong AI like Searle tend
to vastly underestimate the subtlety of the specification of what has to
be simulated in human behavior to pass as a perfect simulation. They
talk about it as if outward behavior could be specified in some specification of what our robot must be able to do, without specifying anything
about the coherence of whole patterns of behavior that express subjective feelings. They perhaps forget that verbal reports of inner experiences, as well as nonverbal expressions of feeling (like dancing) are overt
behavior and often external representations, and will therefore have to
be simulated in exact coherence with all other behavior. The argument
always runs as if the specification comes complete, and at the beginning of the research program. But of course it does not. Each successive
Mark N may fail some behavioral test that we had not even thought of
when we started out, because in carrying out the program of research
we would learn an immense amount about what does allow people to
detect zombies, and the mistakes they would undoubtedly often make.
Any differences in internal experience between human and zombie would
have to be in principle *inexpressible* to be in principle *unimplementable*.
Most cognitive scientists would be quite happy to leave the *in principle inexpressible* feelings and experiences to the theology department, at
least for now.

This argument from the immense subtlety that a full implementation
of human behavior would require will undoubtedly reinforce your belief
that the strong AI program is in fact pie-in-the-sky. That is exactly
our own estimation of the situation—the full realization of the program
is pie-in-the-sky. Most AI researchers would be happy to accept that

description of the program's likelihood of success even in the indefinite future. But that is not what is at issue in the philosophical and scientific argument. Such scientific or philosophical programs do not have their impact by complete realization. Most AI researchers believe that their strong program of research has already deepened understanding of many aspects of human behavior immeasurably because conceiving mental process as computations is basically right. Remember the analogy of Darwin's biology as an explanation of life—we may believe we will never actually be able to create critters from scratch, but Darwin has won the *in principle* argument. We don't accept materialist accounts of physiology because we can *in fact* build bodies out of chemicals. We can't even build the simplest virus. Most biologists would predict that we will *never* be able to build a mammal from atoms. That does not diminish the argument that life is based on chemicals one bit.

The real value of the program is that it will lead us to understand much more fully just how much would be involved in specifying what has to be computed by a conscious creature, and in understanding how that specification is implemented in us.

Penrose's argument

Penrose argues in *The Emperor's New Mind* that it is *in principle* impossible that human behavior is to be understood in terms of Turing computation. His argument, at least in its outer form, is quite different from Searle's argument, though there is some evidence that it is driven by some of the same philosophical intuitions, and that at bottom it rests on the belief that human consciousness is what Turing computation cannot encompass.

The argument hinges on Gödel's proof of the incompleteness of arithmetic, described in section 6.1. The theorem is technically demanding and its complete cognitive significance is far from clear seventy-odd years after its proof. The outline of Penrose' argument, however, does not rest on the technicalities, and it is possible to get something of the nature of Penrose's illuminating objections without resorting to the full technicalities.

Penrose's argument goes, in outline, like this. Gödel's theorem shows that the program of capturing all of mathematics (even all of number theory) in a formal system (and therefore in a Turing computer) is impossible. Penrose's second premise is that human mathematicians can, *in principle*, encompass all mathematical reasoning. Penrose concludes that therefore human mathematical ability is an ability that is not a computational phenomenon. It is a nice irony that human mathematical abilities should be the domain that provides the example of the mental phenomenon that are argued to be not encompassable in computation.

The extremely brief exposition of logic in sections 5.2 and 6.1 mentioned that certain functions are incomputable. Turing proved, under a certain set of assumptions, that the Halting Problem—whether a program will run to completion rather than cycle in endless loops—was not generally computable. Similarly, many logics are not decidable—there is no algorithm for computing whether or not an arbitrary sentence of the logic is a theorem of the system.

Penrose takes Gödel's results as showing what computers cannot do, and wants to contrast these shortcomings with what human's can do, in order to conclude that human capacities cannot be explained as Turing computations. So Penrose argues that in principle, human beings can comprehend or prove any mathematical truth, and he argues that Gödel's results show that computers cannot.

In fact, Penrose wants to go further and propose that there are kinds of computation that exceed Turing computation, in particular quantum computation, and that therefore the human must be understood as a quantum device.

This is all rather technical and the details are well beyond this author's grasp. But as so often, it is not clear that the technical details are all necessary to assess the arguments. There are several things to say about the outlines of the argument. First, in claiming that quantum computation is the right basis for understanding the mind, Penrose in a sense concedes everything the cognitive scientist needs for the argument that the mind is to be understood computationally. Few cognitive scientists would be much alarmed to find that our concepts of computation need to be modified. Such conceptual revolutions are what every scientist should expect. It might be that cognitive science would have to consider different kinds of simulations within a quantum framework, but the main point that mind is first and foremost an informational phenomenon is cognitive science's whole argument. Quantum informational? Whoever denied it? Thus far, Penrose might be taken to be attempting at least to refine cognitive science rather than demolish it (his title strongly hints at the latter intent).

Second, Penrose' argument misinterprets Gödel's results. Here, the disagreement is important and substantial. Gödel's incompleteness result is a demonstration that some truths that can be seen by human beings to be true by considering a system from *outside*, metalogically, cannot be proven to be true *internally* within a computational formalization of the system. Gödel's result does not show that there is a particular conclusion that cannot be derived formally—only that it is not possible to derive *all* semantically valid inferences about the domain of number theory within a single formal system.

There is a dynamism to Gödel's result. The result is not about a single formal system and its deficiency. Gödel starts by taking a particular formalization of number theory and showing that some truths of number theory cannot be theorems in this system. But he goes on to show that it is possible to generate a new system in which the unprovable but true proposition can be proved, but only at the expense of generating a new true but unprovable proposition in the new system, and so on *ad infinitum*. What the result shows is that it is not possible to capture *all* the semantic consequences within a *single* syntactic system.

The simplest explanation of how human's can comprehend truths which are not provable within a system is that they can encompass them in another system at a meta-level relative to the initial one. There is of course, nothing to stop computers from also doing this. The only thing that Gödel's result rules out is that there is a *single* formal system that encompasses all the truths of number theory. So what we should conclude is that *if* human minds can potentially apprehend all the truths of number theory *and* they are made up of computational systems, then they are not made up of *a single, complete, homogeneous, and consistent system.*

This is surely not news. As we have stressed at a number of points in this book, careful analysis of the simplest cognitive functions suggests that they are as much about metaprocesses of interpreting, constructing, or choosing representational systems as about operating inferences within systems. That is precisely one of the big gains of using our understanding of computation to understand minds—an insight into the many levels that cannot all be collapsed into a single level. And we have not been offered any alternative to understanding these metaprocesses other than as computational processes (even if Penrose prefers to speculate that they are *quantum* computational processes). So we conclude that the really important cognitive consequence of Gödel's result is that it teaches us that if human beings are really capable of apprehending all mathematical truths (and we remain agnostic on whether they can, jolly clever as they no doubt are), then that must be because they can construct multiple systems for that apprehension.

Searle and Penrose both help us to deepen our appreciation of the role computation plays in understanding minds. Throughout this book there have been a number of points at which we have responded to criticisms of computational theories of mind by being careful to adopt weak and abstract concepts of what we mean by computation. An important example was our preserving the notion of mental representation (in chapter 6) by being careful to deny some overstrong assumptions about what representations had to be like—say whether they are localized, symbolic, and enumerable by the experiences they represent. The studiously weak notion of mental representation that resulted might strike some as innocuous—but useless. We regard it as innocuous but vital, and we presented some arguments to that effect. In truth, we believe that the claim that mind must be understood computationally, in informational terms, is a very weak claim—almost true by definition, once we have suitably abstract notions of information and computation. Weak it may be, but an indispensable conceptual foundation nonetheless.

For the practicing cognitive scientist, the question must be which program of research promises to throw most light on what mathematicians (and human language users, and so on) can and cannot do, and how informational analysis can capture these abilities. Both Searle and Penrose are strangers to the business of painstakingly specifying just what people do and do not do in what situations. The great illusion of these attacks is that they assume that we *know* what people do, and what they experience but we just need to understand the implementation. Of course, the real problem is that we don't know what people do or experience in the first place—we don't have the specification. Studying the specification and the implementation and how they interact is the only real program of research one can offer.

If this book has generated a little wonder at the extent of our ignorance about what people do, and given some idea about some current methods of analyzing and understanding the cognitive phenomena of communication, then it will already have succeeded in its most important aim.

19.2   Further Reading

• Searle, J. R. (1980). Minds, Brains and Programs. *Behavioral and Brain Sciences*, 3, 417–24.

• Penrose, R. (1989). *The Emperor's New Mind: Concerning Computers, Minds, and the Laws of Physics*. Oxford : Oxford University Press.

Notes

[1]Anthropologists use the term "primitive" to describe cultures that lack the highly differentiated division of labor that "developed" cultures exhibit. This is an important technical distinction and one that should not be assumed to necessarily carry any moral prejudice with it. In fact, one might (and some anthropologists do) regard "primitive" culture as in some ways morally superior to "developed" cultures.

[2]Even their pronouncements about witchcraft-substance being found in the bellies of witches at *post mortem* chimes rather accurately with our tabloid press's pronouncements about the evil inherent in this week's target—even if we may more often localize the evil substance in the brain than in the belly.

[3]If you are among the 5% who made Wason's designated choice, you are even more likely to accept Wason's model answer.

[4]The drunk who knows he lost his keys when he fell in the ditch nevertheless perseveres in searching beneath the lamp post. When asked why, he replies that the light is far better there.

[5]In fact there are many deontic relations—how we *intend* the world to be; how we *want* the world to be; how we *fear* the world may be etc. Nothing about these differences between varieties of deontics is particularly crucial here.

[6]Hint: the commonest interpretation in our culture should strictly be stated "If a person eats red meat and drinks wine, then they drink red wine." ie. it is not false merely because people often eat red meat without drinking any wine.

[7]Except students might be failed for failing to wonder how the 1932 paper could precede Wason's publication by 34 years?

[8]The technique of thinking of extreme cases is a handy technique for understanding many unintuitive results.

[9]We have already come across a related problem with the ravens in the previous chapter. Whether the student stood to learn anything from searching the lab for nonblack objects to see if they were ravens depended on some rather subtle things about his previous knowledge.

[10]Strictly speaking, one would need predicate calculus, the logic that

analyzes propositions into terms and predicates, in order to encode Wason's rule, because it is about four cards, but predicate calculus has the same conditional connective and so we need not introduce its extra-complexities here.

[11]If you are not prone to visual imagery of this kind, you have perhaps nevertheless had the experience of seeing a picture of a long-acquainted radio personality and feeling that their visual appearance was not what you had "imagined." You had filled in visual details on the evidence of voice, but in some way "got it wrong."

[12]We simply observed in chapter 2 that the sentences of English, or any other natural language, aren't listable, and so modeling the transmission of information in English with a Shannon and Weaver approach to information is overly simple.

[13]This is so particularly if you note that a good translation of this sentence is something like *Gaul is divided into three parts in all.*

[14]To start off with, we will limit ourselves to atomic conditions in DRSs. That's to say, only conditions that state either a property of a single individual, or a relationship between two or more individuals, will be allowed. Later in section 10.2, we will extend this to allow "implications" in DRSs.

[15]This is a technical use of this word, and you should be careful to distinguish it from our more general use of "model" to mean a scientific theory.

[16] As we'll see later there are other words of category Det; *a* and *the* are also known as the definite and indefinite ARTICLES.

[17]As with the arithmetic grammar, words separated by commas on the right-hand side of a rule indicate that any one of the words is possible.

[18]Here we've used the convention of writing a triangle above the words *the bird*, on the assumption that either you know what the analysis of the constituent is, or that it's unimportant for the current discussion.

[19]We would need to have another rule for dealing with the so-called DEICTIC use of *he*, where the speaker actually points to somebody when he says *he*, his intention being that *he* refer to the person to whom he's pointing.

[20]There are words that violate the constraint as stated here, most notably REFLEXIVE PRONOUNS, such as *myself, herself, himself,* .... To

cater for these, we could revise the condition to read:

In constructing a DRS, a referent cannot appear more than once in the arguments to an atomic condition, unless one occurrence of the referent was introduced in the semantic rule for reflexive pronouns, in which case you *must* identify that occurrence with another argument.

This would allow us to generate sentences such as

i. Etta loved herself.
ii. ?Herself loved Etta.

while not permitting referents to be identified in the following cases:

i. Etta loved her.
ii. she loved Etta.

As we will not extend the grammar to cover such pronouns, we won't pursue this topic here.

[21] In fact, strictly speaking we're over-simplying here. Pronouns can appear in the first sentence, so long as that sentence is of the form *If sentence-1, sentence-2*, and the pronoun appears in *sentence-2*. But since we haven't yet introduced the semantic rule for sentences containing the word *if*, we ignore this for now.

[22] In fact, this example makes it easy to see why these ambiguities are called scope ambiguities: Here the choice is to interpret the indefinite article *a* either within the scope of the conditional, or outside it.

[23] In case you're wondering, there are better ways of designing parsers than we discuss here. For example, by recording parts of analyses, one can avoid repeating work done for one analysis that can be used by another. This technique can lead to a dramatic reduction in the amount of time required to do syntactic analysis. In this case, we can still make the argument we wish to make here, but we would have to phrase it in the following terms. If you have a syntactic processor that computes all analyses, then it will take the later stages of processing (e.g. the application of semantic rules) a time exponential in the length of the sentence to create each interpretation of a sentence. In the production line analogy (see below), all we have done is shift the bottleneck—that is, the point at which we have too much work to do—from the syntactic

to the semantic processor.

[24]See http://www.hcrc.ed.ac.uk/dialogue/maptask.html.

[25]Actually, you can sometimes *create* plural objects for pronouns to refer to, from those that are introduced in the context by singular devices. But this doesn't happen in (6)c, because the objects *Etta* and *bone* are of distinct sorts (where by "sort" we mean the set of attributes such as number, gender, animacy, etc. that these words have), and they can't be grouped together to form a plural object coherently.

[26]We'll see why this happens in chapter 15, when we look at presuppositions.

[27]There is, in fact, a lot of controversy in the literature on presuppositions as to whether they are properties of sentences or of utterances, and this is partly why in this informal discussion of the phenomena we are using either the term "sentence" or the term "utterance" according to convenience. Ultimately, we will see that in extending our DRSs to analysis of presuppositions the contextual effects on what is presupposed are captured without having to make the distinction between sentence and utterance clear anyway.

[28]Actually, testing for presuppositions is a matter of controversy, and there is not even a universally agreed upon technical definition of presuppositions within the literature. But to keep matters simple, we will assume that this test is always reliable enough to distinguish those implications that are presupposed from those that are not.

[29]Answer: (a) *Luke Skywalker* (presupposes there's someone called Luke Skywalker), (b) *regret* (presupposes that Luke Skywalker found out that Darth Vadar was his father), (c) *find out* (presupposes that Darth Vadar was his father, (d) *Darth Vadar* (presupposes there is someone called Darth Vadar), and (e) *his father* (presupposes Luke Skywalker has a father).

[30]Note that if there is background knowledge to suggest that the definite description denotes an individual with the proper name in question then our intuitions change in this respect; e.g. *Tony Blair fumed. The prime minister was angry at the ministers' rebellion.*

[31]As a matter of fact, it may be more appropriate to think of pronouns as behaving like presuppositions, since using a pronoun presupposes that the hearer will be able to determine a likely antecedent for it.

[32]However, the analysis falls short on texts like *Tony Blair fumed. The prime minister was angry at the ministers' rebellion.* It will fail to bind *the prime minister* to the discourse referent introduced by the noun phrase *Tony Blair.* In essence, our constraint on binding a presupposition is too strict, and fails to allow for the fact that domain knowledge can be sufficient for identifying two discourse referents in the DRS. We'll ignore this for now though.

[33]For the sake of simplicity, we're ignoring utterances like S_2, *if* S_1 here.

[34]We introduced the notion of default rules, or rules that have exceptions, in chapter 4. There, we considered the way humans reason with generalisations.

[35]This assumes that the pronoun *him* is resolved to co-refer with *Max*, using the rules for finding antecedents to pronouns that we discussed in chapter 14. We have omitted details here.

[36]This term is due to Barbara Grosz, and draws on analogies about popping elements off a stack from computer science.

[37]As an exercise you should try finding the interesting exceptions to this rule. Hint: The conclusions are of a different form than any of the four kinds of premise Aristotle allowed viz. *Some not-As are not Cs.* There are interesting historical reasons why these conclusions were not admitted by Aristotle.

VII APPENDIXES

A Appendix: Bibliographical Notes and Further Reading

A.1 General Introductions to Cognitive Science

There are several introductory textbooks for cognitive science. Neil Stillings et al.'s *Cognitive Science: An Introduction*, Cambridge: MIT Press (1995), is probably the most widely used, and you should be well-equipped to approach all of the material in that volume. The collection edited by Michael Posner, *Foundations of Cognitive Science*, Cambridge: MIT Press (1989), is rather more advanced than the Stillings volume. *The Computer and the Mind* by Philip Johnson-Laird, Cambridge: Harvard University Press (1988) represents an accessible, rather personal view of the field.

Johnson-Laird and Wason's *Thinking: Readings in Cognitive Science*, Cambridge: Cambridge University Press (1977), is a very useful collection of classic articles.

Howard Gardner describes the history of cognitive science up to 1986 in *The Mind's New Science: A History of the Cognitive Revolution*, New York: Basic Books (1987). Even though we don't investigate questions of visual perception and processing in detail in this course, David Marr's volume, *Vision: A Computational Investigation into the Human Representation and Processing of Visual Information*, New York: W.H. Freeman (1982), is highly recommmended both for its readability and informativeness, as well as for its influence in shaping the methodology of cognitive science. Jay Garfield edited a further collection of readings in *Foundations of Cognitive Science: The Essential Readings*, New York: Paragon House (1990).

Douglas Hofstadter's book *Gödel, Escher, Bach: An Eternal Golden Braid*, Hassocks: Harvester Press (1979), presents material from many areas touched on by the course in an entertaining and enlightening way.

Barbara Von Eckardt's *What Is Cognitive Science?*, Cambridge: A Bradford Book MIT Press, (1995) attempts to give a modern definition of the field.

Peter Baumgartner and Sabine Payr have recently edited *Speaking Minds: Interviews with Twenty Eminent Cognitive Scientists*, Princeton: Princeton University Press (1995).

The Oxford Companion to the Mind, edited by Richard Gregory, Oxford: Oxford University Press (1987), provides generally useful, short discussions of topics and areas.

A.2   Chapters 1–7

John R. Pierce, in *Symbols, Signals, and Noise: The Nature and Process of Communication*, London: Hutchinson (1962), offers a readable, mathematically thorough overview of the Shannon and Weaver model of communication.

Thomas Gilovich's book *How We Know What Isn't So: The Fallibility of Human Reason in Everyday Life*, New York: The Free Press (1991), is an accessible, generalist introduction to human reasoning.

Two of the key volumes in the investigation of neural-like computation are those by David Rumelhart and James McClelland *Parallel Distributed Processing: Explorations in the Microstructure of Cognition* Vol. 1 *Foundations* and Vol. 2 *Psychological and Biological Models*, London: MIT Press (1986).

Patricia Churchland is one of the most famous advocates of the view that understanding neural processing is the key to understanding mind. See her books *Neurophilosophy: Toward a Unified Science of the Mind-Brain*, Cambridge: MIT Press (1986), and (with Terrence Sejnowski) *The Computational Brain*, London: MIT Press (1992).

A.3   Chapters 8–13

An excellent introduction to many of the areas covered in this section of the course is Steven Pinker's *The Language Instinct*, New York: W. Morrow and Co. (1994). It's also very readable. The book argues for a strongly modular view of language and language processing. Relative to the presentation of the course, this book has a lot to say about syntactic rules, but relatively little about semantics. We've been using a relatively simplified form of syntactic rule derived in spirit from the work of Gazdar et al., *Generalized Phrase Structure Grammar*, Oxford: Blackwell (1985). (That book is rather hard going for nonlinguists.)

Discourse representation theory was invented by Hans Kamp in the early 1980s. Irene Heim was responsible for very similar, independent developments. The presentation of semantic rules is adapted from Hans

Kamp and Uwe Reyle's *From Discourse to Logic*, Boston: Kluwer (1993). This is a good, but advanced, textbook introduction. We have simplified the presentation omitting a lot of the more complicated maths and relying on a more intuitive understanding of how semantic rules apply and the relationship between a DRS and its models.

There are a number of good introductions to general linguistics. For example, Akmajian et al.'s *Linguistics: An Introduction to Language and Communication*, Cambridge: MIT Press (1990), gives a thorough grounding in most areas of linguistics. John Lyons' *Language and Linguistics*, Cambridge: Cambridge University Press (1981), covers similar ground in somewhat less detail.

One of the classic texts on ambiguity is William Empson's *Seven types of ambiguity*, London: Chatto and Windus (1930), which takes a very literary perspective on the issue of ambiguity.

Ways of getting computers to process syntax, semantics, and (to some extent) pragmatics are discussed in Gazdar and Mellish's *Natural Language Processing in Prolog*, Reading: Addison-Wesley (1989).

Chapter 11 of the Stillings volume offers a survey of human language processing and the debates over modularity and parallelism. Survey articles on the human processing of language are: Merrill Garrett "Sentence Processing" and Ken Forster "Lexical Processing" in Osherson and Lasnik (eds.) *An Invitation to Cognitive Science*, Vol. 1 *Language*, Cambridge: MIT Press (1990).

Specific notes

The material in section 8.4 is based on distinctions best articulated in Noam Chomsky's *Aspects of the Theory of Syntax*, Cambridge: MIT Press (1965), pp.1–9. Chomsky's arguments are primarily to do with the description of syntax. In chapter 1 of Gennaro Chierchia and Sally McConnell-Ginet, *Meaning and Grammar: An Introduction to Semantics*, Cambridge: MIT Press (1990), similar arguments are applied to the study of semantics.

There is a lot of technical material on the kinds of syntactic rules we develop in chapter 9 onwards. Gazdar and Mellish give further information and readings. Some arguments for the inadequacy of such rules for describing human language were famously proposed by Chomsky in *Syntactic Structures*, The Hague: Mouton (1957).

The engineering argument for modularity (section 12.3) is proposed by Herb Simon in *The Sciences of the Artificial*, Cambridge: MIT Press (1981). The idea that modularity might be an organizing principle of the human mind is advanced by Jerry Fodor in *The Modularity of Mind: An Essay on Faculty Psychology*, Cambridge: MIT Press (1983). The idea is discussed by a number of contributors to the volume edited by Jay Garfield, *Modularity in Knowledge Representation and Natural-Language Understanding*, London: MIT Press (1987).

The eye-tracking experiment discussed in section 13.4 is very recent. It was presented by Mike Tanenhaus, "Using Eye Movements to Study Spoken Language Comprehension: Evidence for Incremental Interpretation," invited lecture at the *34th Annual Meeting of the Association for Computational Linguistics*, Santa Cruz, 23–28 June 1996. Related research is reported in Spivey-Knowlton, et al., "Eye movements Accompanying Language and Action in a Visual Context: Evidence against Modularity," *Proceedings of the 17th Annual Conference of the Cognitive Science Society*, Pittsburgh, 22–25 July 1995, pp.25–30.

A.4   Chapters 14–17

See the "further reading" sections of the above chapters for detailed references to the literature. One of the standard textbooks on pragmatics is Stephen C. Levinson's *Pragmatics*, Cambridge: Cambridge University Press (1983).

A.5   Chapter 19

Bibliographical details for Edward R. Tufte's book *Envisioning information* are Cheshire: Graphics Press (1992).

A key collection of readings in Artificial Intelligence up to 1980 is John Haugeland's *Mind Design: Philosophy, Psychology, Artificial Intelligence* Cambridge: MIT Press (1981). Haugeland himself produced a critique of aspects of AI in *Artificial Intelligence: The Very Idea* London: MIT Press (1989).

Roger Penrose's objections to the idea of Artificial Intelligence are presented in his *The Emperor's New Mind: Concerning Computers, Minds, and the Laws of Physics*, London: Vintage (1990). More recently he has attempted to answer critics of the earlier work in *Shadows of the*

Mind, New York: Oxford University Press (1994).

There is a lively debate between John Searle and Patricia and Paul Churchland in "Minds and Brains" *Scientific American*, Sept. 1992 (Special Issue) Vol. 267.

The relationship between computer technology and humanity is discussed in Joseph Weizenbaum's book *Computer Power and Human Reason: From Judgment to Calculation*, Harmondsworth: Penguin (1984).

B Appendix: Consolidated Grammars

This document shows all of the grammar rules used in this book.

B.1 General Conventions for Semantic Rules

Unless otherwise stated, the appearance of a discourse referent (e.g. x) in the DRS on the RHS of a rule that did not appear in the LHS of the semantic rule, indicates that a new referent (that is, one that is not already used in the DRS) should be chosen. The only exceptions are in the rules for *the*, proper names and pronouns in grammar 1. There, you are instructed to "reuse a referent," i.e. to identify an existing referent to substitute for the referent in the rule.

Often in the rules below, the symbol *name* appears at the leaf of a tree in the LHS of the rule, and there is a corresponding symbol "name" in the DRS on the RHS of the rule. This means that you should take the condition "name" in the DRS to be the predicate symbol for the word *name* in the tree. For example, *Etta* in the tree will be represented by the predicate symbol "Etta" in the DRS. Likewise for *chased* and "chase." See example derivations for more examples.

B.2 Grammar 1

This grammar is used in part III of this book.

Syntactic rules

S → NP VP	V1 → *chased, caught, ate, loved* ...
NP → PRO	V0 → *barked, slept, walked, ran,* ...
NP → PN	Det → *a, an, every, the,* ...
NP → Det N	N → *cat, dog, bird, woman, man,* ...
VP → V0	PN → *Etta, Pip, Mac,* ...
VP → V1 NP	PRO → *she, he, it, her,* ...
S → *if* S S	

A discourse consists of one or more sentences each terminated by a full stop.

Semantic Rules

Grammar 1: Proper names (PN)

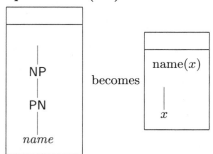

Reuse a referent, if you can. Otherwise introduce the referent at the top of the box.

Grammar 1: pronouns (PRO)

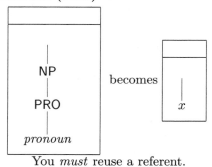

You *must* reuse a referent.

Grammar 1: intransitive verbs (V0)

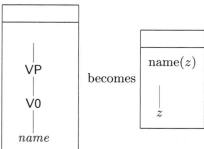

Grammar 1: transitive verbs (V1)

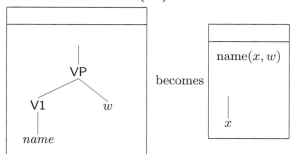

Grammar 1: the indefinite article (*a*)

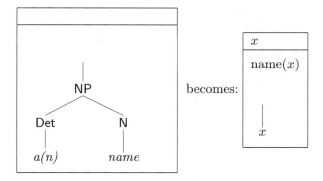

Grammar 1: the definite article (*the*)

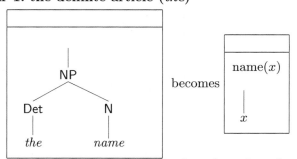

Reuse a referent, if you can. Otherwise introduce the referent at the top of the box.

Grammar 1: *every*

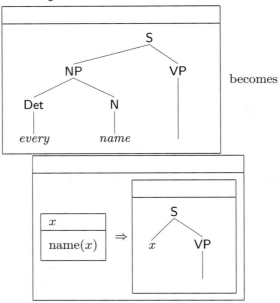

becomes

Grammar 1: *if*

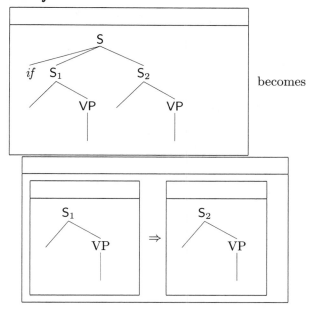

Grammar 1: the sentence rule

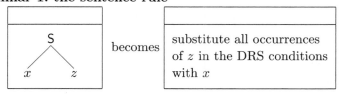

The anaphora constraint governs the reuse of referents:

In constructing a DRS, a referent cannot appear more than once in the arguments to an atomic condition.

In processing a discourse, process the first sentence inside a box. Then process any subsequent sentences *inside the same box.*

B.3   Grammar 2

This grammar is used in Part IV of this book. The difference between the syntax rules and those for grammar 1 is the introduction of features to indicate number and gender information. The semantic rules for this grammar are shown in section B.3 The main differences between these semantic rules and those for grammar 1 are the instruction box, changes to the way one decides which discourse referent to use (e.g. for pronouns, *the*, and proper names), and the representation of number and gender information in the logical form.

Syntactic rules for grammar 2

S → NP VP
NP → PRO
NP → PN
NP → Det N
VP → V0
VP → V1 NP
V1 → *chased, caught, ate, loved, . . .*
V0 → *slept, barked, walked, ran, . . .*
S → *if* S S
Det → *a, an, every, the, . . .*

$N\begin{bmatrix} \text{num} & : & sing \\ \text{gender} & : & neut \end{bmatrix}$ → *bird, stick, dog . . .*

$N\begin{bmatrix} \text{num} & : & sing \\ \text{gender} & : & fem \end{bmatrix}$ → *lawyer, dog, cat, girl, woman, . . .*

$N\begin{bmatrix} \text{num} & : & sing \\ \text{gender} & : & masc \end{bmatrix}$ → *lawyer, dog, cat, boy, man, . . .*

$PRO\begin{bmatrix} \text{num} & : & sing \\ \text{gender} & : & neut \end{bmatrix}$ → *it*

$PRO\begin{bmatrix} \text{num} & : & sing \\ \text{gender} & : & fem \end{bmatrix}$ → *she, her*

$PRO\begin{bmatrix} \text{num} & : & sing \\ \text{gender} & : & masc \end{bmatrix}$ → *he, him*

$PN\begin{bmatrix} \text{num} & : & sing \\ \text{gender} & : & fem \end{bmatrix}$ → *Etta, Nina, . . .*

$PN\begin{bmatrix} \text{num} & : & sing \\ \text{gender} & : & masc \end{bmatrix}$ → *Pip, Mac, . . .*

The rule for discourses is as before.

Semantic rules for grammar 2

Grammar 2: proper names (PN)

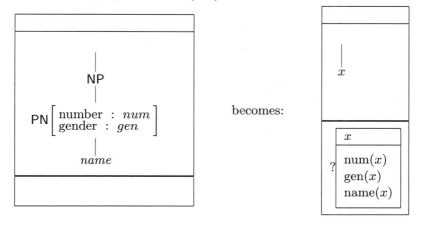

becomes:

Grammar 2: pronouns (PRO)

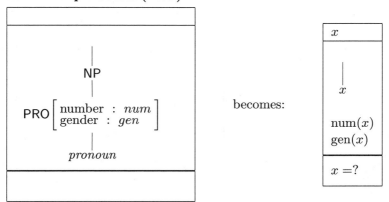

becomes:

Grammar 2: intransitive verbs (**V0**)

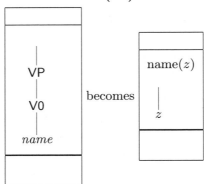

Grammar 2: transitive verbs (**V1**)

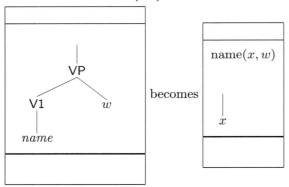

Grammar 2: the indefinite article (*a*)

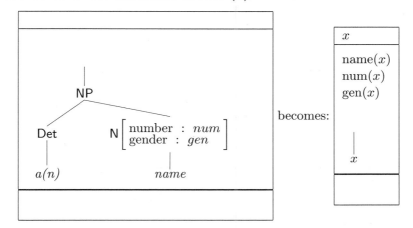

Grammar 2: the definite article (*the*)

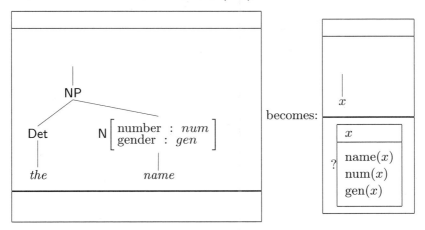

Grammar 2: *every*

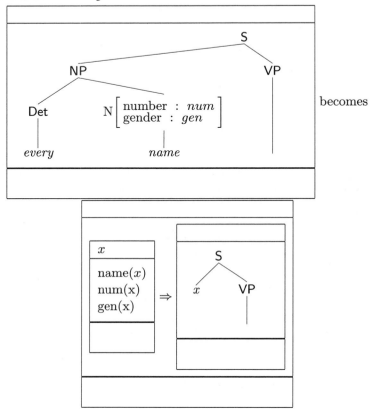

Grammar 2: *if*

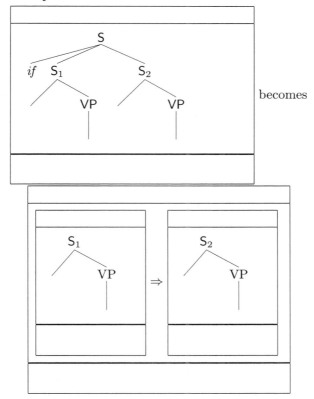

Grammar 2: the sentence rule

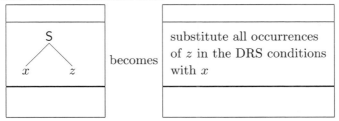

The rule for discourses is as before. The interpretation of pronouns is governed by the Anaphora Constraint, and by the Consistency Constraint, the Structural Constraint, and the Knowledge Constraint.

C Appendix: Glossary

Jargon is always a problem and more than ever so when we deal with several disciplines. We try to minimize it, but some is unavoidable, and learning the jargon is sometimes inseparable from learning what it's all about. A piece of general advice: Try to see if you can extract from the context what meaning of a word is intended. Check the index for other occurrences of the same term and see whether your understanding of the term makes sense.

Below, a word or phrase in **boldface** within a definition refers to another glossary entry. We have provided definitions only where we think them useful. We have omitted definitions in some cases where the first index entry refers to a page where a definition of the term appears. Various definitions below have been adapted from other sources.

Symbols

* notation for ungrammaticality 194

? notation for when a discourse or sentence sounds odd, or is uninterpretable 341

A

a priori 12

accommodation This term refers to a component in the interpretation of **presuppositions**. If the presupposition isn't already present in the context of the conversation, then you can add it. This process of addition is called accommodation. . 84, 393, 395, 397, 402, 404, 410, 413, 417, 420, 424

algorithm A mechanically applicable method guaranteed to reach a solution in finitely many steps. In other words an explicit procedure that a computer can follow. . 128, 300, 301, 354

ambiguity Having more than one possible interpretation. 279, 429

analogue Varying continuously. The notes give the example of voltage. Similarly, musi-cal pitch can vary continuously: the sound of a siren is a smooth progression. See also **quantization, discrete**. 19

analysis The analysis of a sequence of words is the tree (or trees) associated with that sequence of words. More generally, a theory of some phenomenon, e.g. Russell's theory of definite descriptions as discussed on p. 390. . . 11, 227, 307

anaphora Reference to something that has already been introduced in the discourse context, e.g., the use of **pronouns** (in particular) to refer to individuals in a discourse. 187, 339

anecdotalism A policy of translating generalities into particularities. 86

antecedent

1. An object in the context with which a subsequent expression in the discourse—such as a pronoun—is identified. So, for example, in *Bill owns a company. He is rich*, *Bill* is an antecedent to the pronoun *he*, because *he* is identified as being Bill.

2. The left hand side of a **conditional** sentence or formula.
131, 339, 344, 346, 347, 349, 354, 355, 363, 368, 372, 392–394, 397, 398, 404, 405, 408, 409, 416, 418, 420, 422, 431

l'arbitraire du signe The phenomenon that the link between a word and its meaning is arbitrary. 232

arbitrary A relationship not governed by any laws or principles. 7, 231

article See **definite article, indefinite article** and **determiner**. 542

Artificial Intelligence Abbreviated as AI, the field which seeks to build intelligent systems. 12

aspect The classification of sentences into events, processes and states. 274

assertion A condition in a **discourse representation structure** relating individuals. An atomic condition consists of a **predicate symbol** and a sequence of discourse referents as its arguments. See also **implication**. 462

availability The ease with which one may create a pattern distinct from other patterns. 79

axon A long fibre that is part of the brain. 151

B

background information See **background knowledge**. 90, 345, 374, 375

background knowledge Background knowledge is the knowledge people have that helps them interpret communication. It includes knowledge about the world; knowledge about the participants in the dialogue; knowledge about the situation in which the dialogue is taking place; knowledge about heuristics of the way language is used in conversation; and more. This is also sometimes referred to as **background information**. 372

background situation A background situation is a description of the situation in which a dialogue is taking place. This could be a description of the **map task**, for example. 465

backtracking Describes a processor which, when faced with a choice of rules in some situation, chooses one of them and remembers other possible choices. If the processor later detects a problem, the processor can revisit a particular choice and examine the consequences of one of the other rules.   . . 303, 304, 311, 322

base rate information   In probability theory, how likely some outcome is, regardless of any more specific information about a situation.   79

behaviorism   A movement in psychology which sought to eliminate reference to the mind in favour of functions from stimuli to responses.   10, 11, 152

belief   A belief is something you think is true.   .   43, 45, 338, 465, 466, 468

biconditional   A logical connective defined in classical logic as the conjunction of a conditional and the conditional derived by exchanging antecedent and consequent; e.g. $(P \Rightarrow Q) \wedge (Q \Rightarrow P)$, read as "If and only if" in English.   40

bind   **Pronouns** and **presuppositions** bind to **antecedents**.   394, 395, 397–399, 402, 404, 406, 411, 413, 417, 419, 420

bit   The smallest possible unit of information. One bit of information can serve to distin-

guish two states or two messages ("yes" and "no" or 0 and 1).   20–22

body language   A non-verbal form of communication, often subconscious, involving movements and posture of the body.   475

bottom-up   operating in terms of the features present in some input to be processed, e.g. I can combine these two words into a larger unit. See also **top-down**.   304

branches   Part of a **tree**   . 226

brittle   A generalisation is brittle if a single instance which doesn't fit it is sufficient to falsify it. In contrast, a generalisation is robust if some exceptions to it don't falsify it.   44, 50

C

category   In syntax, the kind of unit to which some sequence of words is assigned.   . . 223, 347

center embedding   273

central processor unit   The "mill" of a modern computer which is the active part that processes data retrieved from passive memory and writes

out the results to memory.
e.g. the head in a Turing machine. 150

channel A component in Shannon and Weaver's model of communication. 19

classical logic The most taught kind of logic which has just two truth values (true and false), and **truth functional semantics**. See also **first order logic** and **logic**. . . . 30, 117

clause A clause is a sentence that forms part of a bigger sentence. For example, in *If it's raining, then I'll take my umbrella, it's raining* and *I'll take my umbrella* are both clauses. Also used in logic, in the sense of one or more formulas joined by **logical connectives**. 122

co-reference The phenomenon of two expressions in a sentence or discourse that refer to the same individual; e.g. *John* and *he* co-refer in *John entered the room. He sat down.* 256, 259, 346

common sense The term given to the kind of reasoning one does with default rules; i.e. rules that admit exceptions. 434

competence One's knowledge (in particular of language) abstracted away from how that knowledge is used. See also **performance**. 194

competence theory An idealized theory specifying what it is to know a language as opposed to a **performance** theory explaining how the language is actually processed by users. The term is also use more broadly outside linguistics to contrast abstract theories of a task (such as drawing inferences), as opposed to a reasoning mechanism. . . 30

complement sets In the set of integers, the sets of even and odd numbers are complements, i.e. they share no elements and, taken together, they constitute the set of all integers. Likewise, the set of vowels {a, e, ...} and that of consonants {b, c, ...} are complements of each other with respect to the set of all letters. 47

completeness A property of some logics: any formula that is valid has a proof. 127

compositionality A system is compositional if the meaning of a sequence of words is determined by the meaning of the individual words and how they're put together.   .   234

conclusion In logic, a conclusion is something which logically follows from a set of **premises**. 119

conditional In natural language, conditionals are sentences of the form *if . . . , then . . .* (the *then* is optional). In logic, a conditional is a formula of the form $A \Rightarrow B$.   28, 41, 45, 46, 262, 384, 411, 462

conjunction In English, conjunction amounts to the word *and*; in logic, it corresponds to the logical connective $\wedge$.   61, 130

connective Connectives are words that link sentences to make bigger sentences: e.g., *and, or, if . . . then, but, because,* and so on. Also used in a similar sense in logic. 362

consequent The right hand side of a **conditional** sentence or formula. 131

consistency A set of sentences is consistent if it is possible for them all to be true simultaneously. 354

content Easiest to define as complementary to **form**. Consider a sentence such as "if a letter is sealed, it must have a

first-class stamp". This sentence has the form of a conditional. On the other hand, its content has to do with regularities about letters and stamps. It is reasonable to equate form in this sense with the consequences of **syntactic rules**, and at least the literal part of content with the consequences of **semantic rules**.   64, 107, 118, 357, 391, 394, 395, 397–399, 401, 416–420, 422, 427, 441, 446, 447, 467

context Refers to the situation in which a sentence is uttered, and consists in particular of the content of the prior sentences in the discourse, as well as **background knowledge**. 253

context free Of grammar, whether it allows general **rewriting** rules of the form

$$A \Rightarrow C_1 \ldots C_n$$

where $C_1 \ldots C_n$ can consist of **terminal** or **nonterminal** **symbols**. Languages whose sentences can all be described with a context free grammar are called context free languages. 155

context sensitive Of a grammar, whether it allows general

rewriting rules of the form

$$A_1 \ldots A_n \Rightarrow C_1 \ldots C_n$$

where $A_1 \ldots A_n$ and $C_1 \ldots C_n$ can consist of **terminal** or **nonterminal symbols**. Languages whose sentences can all be described with a context sensitive grammar are called context sensitive languages. 155

convention A regularity that could be otherwise. . . . 101

cooperative communication In cooperative communication, speaker and hearer engage in the task of constructing the same intended model of the discourse. See also **adversarial communication.** . . 50

creativity The ability of humans to produce or understand an effectively unlimited number of sentences, and similar abilities in other fields, e.g. vision, thought. 24

credulous A hearer with a credulous attitude to the discourse attempts to find the speaker's intended interpretation. See also **skeptical.** 138

Creutzfeldt-Jakob disease A human brain disease. . . . 87

cross-modal priming An experimental paradigm in psy-

chology, where data is presented in more than one modality to the subject, and some aspects of the data in the two modalities are related. . . 319

D

daughter See **tree**. 226

decidability Of a formal system, whether there exists an **algorithm** for proving whether a **formula** is true or false, given a set of **premises**. 128

declarative A sentence is declarative if it can be true or false. Alternatives are instructions (imperatives) and questions (interrogatives). 111

declarative knowledge Knowledge of facts as contrasted with procedural knowledge of how to do something. . 111

deduction The application of logical laws to arrive at a conclusion, for example:

If A then B

A
___

B

I.e. if you know that the formula "above" the line are truth, then you know the formula "below" the line is true as well. To be contrasted with **induction** and **abduction**.

. . . . 37, 47

default reasoning   Default rules are rules that have exceptions. For example, *birds fly* is a default rule, because it's generally true, but there are exceptions: penguins, dead birds, birds with broken wings etc. Default reasoning is the reasoning we do with such rules. See page 442 for some intuitively compelling patterns of default reasoning, involving default rules.   437, 441, 444, 450, 454, 469

definite article   The definite article is the word *the*.   . . 250, 383, 398

definite description   A definite description is a NP which starts with *the*; e.g. *the dog*. 336

dendrite   A part of neuron cells in the brain. 151

deontic   Deontic logic reasons about how things should be (according to some prescription) rather than how they are. Legal laws are obvious examples of deontic statements. 50

derivation   A syntactic and semantic analysis of a sentence or discourse through the application of rules in a gram-

mar. 204

descriptive   Aiming to describe how things are, rather than how they ought to be. See also **normative**.   . 12, 13, 29, 32, 50, 77, 192, 196

desire   Desires are things that you want. 338, 459, 460, 466, 467, 469

determiner   A syntactic **category** that goes in a noun phrase, and precedes a noun: e.g. *a, some, the, every, most, few, many*, and so on. See also **definite article** and **indefinite article**. 223, 362

deterministic   A system is deterministic if it operates mechanically and all the operations it makes are fully predictable, and not subject in any way to random chance. The parsing model sketched on 303 is deterministic, for example. 149

dialogue   Dialogue is a conversation between two or more people. 459

digital   Varying discretely. See also **analogue**. 19

discourse   A sequence of utterances, perhaps involving more than one speaker. . . 23, 37, 210, 251

discourse coherence Discourse coherence is the term given to the ease with which you can make sense of a discourse (i.e. a multisentence piece of communication). If a discourse is coherent, then you can make sense of what is being communicated quickly, efficiently, and easily. If it is incoherent, then you can't understand what the speaker is trying to convey. This is to be contrasted with the situation when sentences are ungrammatical. The sentences in a coherent discourse may be grammatical, but the discourse may be incoherent because you can't work out why the sentences were juxtaposed, for example. So whereas grammaticality is a syntactic notion, coherence is a pragmatic one. 195, 379

discourse popping This is the phenomenon of "getting back" to something you were talking about earlier, after a digression. 453

discourse referents These are the variables that form part of a **discourse representation structure**, which keep track of what's being talked about. 214, 353

discrete Operating in terms of a fixed number of elements. For example, the Western musical scale picks out twelve points from the continuous range of pitch. A digital computer operates in terms of **bits**. See also **analogue**, **digital**, and **quantization**. 19

domain The set of things that one can talk about. . . . 121

E

elimination rule A logical rule of inference which eliminates from the conclusion a connective which appears in the premises; e.g. $P, P \Rightarrow Q \vdash Q$ 126

empiricist Empiricism is "the thesis that all knowledge is based on experience" (Pan *Dictionary of Philosophy*). Empiricism denies in particular that humans arrive in the world with innate knowledge about, say, the organization of the world as an environment or the organization of human language. 315

end term The A and C terms of a **syllogism** which occur in only one of the two premises, as opposed to the middle term which occurs in both. . 499

entailment An entailment from a group of sentences or **premises** is something that must be true if the premises are true. For example, "A and B" entails A and it entails B. 383

epicycle From Ptolemaic astrology, an epicycle is the motion of celestial bodies on spheres. 42

equivocation An error in an argument in which different occurrences of a word are interpreted differently. 135

ethnomethodology The study of interpersonal aspects of language. 197

Euler's circles 502

expansion How a syntactic **category** may be **rewritten**. 226

expert system An AI program which captures expert knowledge of some domain, usually in a rule-system. 528

eye tracker A device for identifying where a person is looking. 325

F

failure to convert In human reasoning, the phenomenon that subjects fail to convert sentences that do logically allow conversion; e.g. failing to convert $A \Rightarrow B$ to $\neg B \Rightarrow \neg A$. 497

falsification The idea that theories should be tested by attempting to disprove them, rather than attempting to find justification for them. This idea is then extended as a way of characterizing some aspects of human reasoning. See also **verification**. 41

fast-and-frugal 85

filtered out In the sentence *If John has a son, then John's son is bald*, the potential **presupposition** that John has a son, which is triggered by *John's son*, is filtered out, and is not presupposed by the sentence. This contrasts with the situation where a presupposition is **cancelled**; in this latter case the potential presupposition is denied. 386

finite state machine A machine which has a finite number of internal states and transitions between them, with no memory for how it arrived at the present state. . 153, 273

first order logic A special kind of **logic**, where you can count individuals, but you can't count properties or other more abstract concepts. 390

form To do with elements and arrangement. For an example, see **conditional**. See also **content** and **formal**. In a linguistic context, this has the additional meaning: to do with the words involved and their syntactic arrangement. 64, 118, 222

form-meaning relation The relation between a sentence's syntactic structure and its meaning. 338

formal Operating purely in terms of **form**. Our grammar and our rules for checking truth in a model are formal: they operate only in terms of the symbols we use and we don't have to bring anything else to bear. 206

Freudianism In psychology, the theories of Sigmund Freud. 42

G

gambler's fallacy A pattern of reasoning where subjects ignore the independence in likelihood of the outcome of a sequence of events. 75

game theory An area of math-

ematics, studying the origin and deployment of **conventions**. 102

garden path sentences Sentences which cause the hearer to "stumble" when processing them. 321

gender Gender is a linguistic property given to nouns, proper names, and pronouns. They can be masculine, feminine, or neuter. 341

generate To produce (perhaps automatically) a sequence of words from a set of **syntactic rules**. 224

"good English" English which abides by rules (perhaps written down somewhere) that dictate what counts as a well-formed sentence of English. For example, the rule that one doesn't put prepositions at the end of a sentence might be one of the rules one must abide by. 189

grammar A grammar is a system which relates **form** and **meaning**. 194, 231

grammaticality A judgement as to whether a sentence, say, of English, adheres to or violates the rules of language that we as speakers know. . 194

Gricean Maxims Gricean Maxims of conversation are rules about the way language is used in conversation. There are four of them: Quality, Quantity, Relevance and Manner. Grice claims that these are derivable from the fact that agents are **rational** and **cooperative**. 432, 434, 435, 440, 444, 454, 465, 467

grounding The process of coming to a mutual agreement about the meaning of some expression. 530

H

Halting Problem The problem of answering the following question: Is there a way of computing from the descriptions of programs and their data whether or not they will terminate? 148, 536

head In grammar, the head is the 'most important' element in a constituent. e.g. in a noun phrase, the noun is the head, similarly for verb phrases and verbs. In a Turing machine, the head is a component of the machine. 272

homunculus A notional person-within-a-person, posited to perform mental actions such as perceiving internal representations; an explanation

prone to vicious regress arguments. 145

human computer interaction The field which applies psychological and sociological insights to the understanding and design of interactions between humans and computers (abbreviated as HCI or CHI). 143, 146, 147

hybrid Involving knowledge both of a formal, symbolic kind, and of a statistical, nonsymbolic kind. 315

I

idealization A scientific field studies a phenomenon under an idealization which defines which aspects of the data will be treated in theories, and which ignored. For example, classical mechanics idealized away from friction in its theories of motion. 13

ideational communication To do with the communication of **propositions** rather than with the reinforcement of social groupings. See also **phatic communication**. 3

idioms An idiom is a phrase which has an established meaning that is quite different from its literal meaning. For exam-

information In terms of the Shannon and Weaver model, information may be conveyed as a message via some medium (or "channel"). Particular messages may contain more or less information according to the likelihood of a particular message and amount of **redundancy** in the message. .. 9

information packaging The partition of information in a sentence, often indicated by the pitch and stress in speech. 498, 514

information theory See **information**. 20

input In the context of processing language, the input is the speech stream, or sequence of words. 300

instruction An instruction is something that goes in the **instruction box** of a DRS or **discourse representation structure**. With pronouns, the instruction is to identify an **antecedent** for the pronoun. For presuppositions, the instruction is to identify an antecedent for the presupposed content, and failing that, to add that content to the context (see also **accommodation**). 397

instruction box The part of a **discourse representation structure** where **instructions** are inserted through the application of semantic rules in a grammar. 351

intention An intention is the will to do an action. 338, 459

interpretation The meaning of a sentence, perhaps above and beyond its **literal meaning**. 119, 205

introduction rule A logical rule which introduces a connective into the conclusion which does not appear in the premises; e.g. $A, B \vdash A \wedge B$. ... 126

intuit To establish on the basis of introspection and reflection. 10

invalid From logic, a sentence is invalid if it is false with respect to every model. . 119

L

lexicon A dictionary. 233, 463

linguistic constraints A constraint on some aspect of communication that arises from the way information is presented; in other words, from the choice of words and the syntactic forms used. .. 342

literal meaning The meaning

of sentence purely in virtue of the words it contains and how they are organized. . . 211

logic A mathematical system that models reasoning and **inference**. There are many different kinds of logics, each designed to capture different sets of valid arguments. For example, propositional logic represents inferences involving logical connectives such as conjunction and negation. **First order logic** allows you to capture inferences from propositional logic as well as those that involve quantifiers. The term "classical logic" is used to refer to these two logics. By contract, **nonmonotonic** logic or default logics are nonclassical: these capture valid inferences of common sense reasoning, including those involving rules with exceptions. 119, 373

logical connective A vocabulary item which syntactically can be applied to one or more sentences to make compound sentences, and which is semantically interpreted as a **truth function** from the values of the components to the truth value of the complex. Examples of logical connectives are conjunction ($\wedge$), material con-

ditional ($\Rightarrow$), negation ($\neg$) and disjunction ($\vee$). 61, 122

logical form The form abstracted away from the content of a sentence which determines its inferential behavior in arguments. The same sentence may be analyzed into different forms required to capture its part in different arguments e.g. propositional and predicate level. 49, 238

M

map task The map task is a task widely used to gain some experimenter control over the meanings which speakers have to express. "Sender" and "receiver" each have a map but cannot see the others'. The sender has to describe a route marked on the map so that the receiver can draw it. 334

materialism The idea that matter is the only kind of stuff there is: anything non-material, like spirit, angels, ... is a fiction. 529

materialist One who holds the philosophical position that the universe contains nothing but matter. 529

media Various physical implementations of communication

systems; e.g. speech, writing, or tactile diagrams.... . 491

metalanguage A language in which you express properties of another language. .. 126

metalogic 147

middle term The B term of a **syllogism** which occurs in both premises, each time with different **end terms**. . 499

minimal pair A pair of distinct linguistic entities (words, sentences,...) which differ by the identity of only one unit (phoneme, word, ... 108

modality The type of medium of communication; e.g. language and graphics are both modalities. 475, 491

modularity The extent to which a system is broken down into smaller components with limited communication between those components. 308

modus ponens A rule of inference (called $\Rightarrow$-elimination in modern logic) of the form $P, P \Rightarrow Q \vdash Q$ 134, 501

modus tollens The rule of inference $P \Rightarrow Q \vdash \neg Q \Rightarrow \neg P$. 501

monologue A sequence of sentences that are spoken or written by one person. ... 459

monotonic A property of logical systems in which adding a premise never invalidates a conclusion which is already valid. Classical logic is monotonic. See also **nonmonotonic**. 134

morpheme The smallest linguistic unit with meaning. 233

morphology The study of how the form of a word may vary according to its syntactic context. 198

mother See **tree**. 226

multimedia A type of communication, which takes place in more than one medium. 476

N

natural deduction A style of **proof-theory** in which rules are given for the introduction and elimination of each logical vocabulary item, as contrasted with axiom systems. 126

negation In natural language, negation is the term given to negative expressions such as *not* and *no*, and to phenomena involving such words. In logic, negation is the logical operator $\neg$. .. 123, 341, 384

neuron A brain is composed of

cells called neurons. . . 151

new variant CJD A variant of CJD believed to have arisen by humans contracting BSE. 93

nodes See **tree**. 226

noise Information may be conveyed in 'noisy' environments, i.e. as well as hearing someone speak, we also hear all the other noises around. Relative to what a hearer is trying to extract from what s/he hears, the noise is just random variation. More explicitly, **Information theory** states that every channel will be more or less noisy. See also **redundancy**. 21, 22

non-zero-sum game A game where the normalized total payoffs for all the players does not sum to zero—that is, it depends on the play, what this total will be. 103

nondeterminism 280, 303

nonlinguistic communication 475

nonlinguistic information Another term for **background knowledge**. It's information that influences the way we interpret language, but it's not part of the language itself. 343

nonsymbolic Not operating in terms of explicit symbols, e.g. statistical models of language processing. 313

nonterminal symbols . . . 203

normative (Or "prescriptive".) In contrast to **descriptive** activities, a normative statement says how things ought to be. . . 12, 29, 32, 77, 189

noun A syntactic **category**. 224

noun phrase A syntactic **category** representing a **phrase** containing a noun. . . . 224

number A property that pronouns, nouns, proper names and verbs have. They can be singular or plural. 341

O

object A noun phrase appearing immediately within a verb phrase. 227

object language A usually formal language in which derivations (proofs) are conducted. The properties of an object language may then be studied by reasoning about it in a **metalanguage**. 126

object-level The level at which a logical system models proof by inference steps within the system, as opposed to the meta-level at which the system is studied from outside and statement are made about it which are not derivable in the system. 99

omniscience An agent is omniscient if he can perform all possible inferences over a given set of premises. . 497

onomatopoeia Words that sound like the sound they describe; e.g. *miaow.* . . . 232

optimizing In this case, improving how good an organism is, by the process of natural selection. 13

order The order of words in a sentence or other unit. 223

oronym Another term for phonetic ambiguity. 293

P

paradigm In Kuhn's philosophy of science, a paradigm is a collection of beliefs which define a particular approach to some subject. Researchers can either accept those beliefs, and so carry on 'normal science', or opt to change paradigms. 42, 43, 209

paradox A seemingly absurd statement or conclusion that is or may be true. 48

parallel 152, 304

parallel computation Computation in which subprocesses proceed at the same time. Most conventional computers give an appearance of "multitasking" but only by computing serially at high speed. 152

parity bit A way of recording **redundant** information about a message which can be used to improve the accuracy of transmission. 22

parser An algorithm for computing the **tree**(s) associated with a sequence of words. 303

parsing The action of assigning a **tree** to a sequence of words. 301

payoff-matrix A matrix which specifies the payoff outcome of a play of a game for each player. 103

performance Aspects of linguistic behavior that derive from the fact that speakers (and hearers) are real-time processors of language. Actually occurring speech and text will be full of errors of various kinds, e.g. false starts, typos, corrections, which we assume don't reflect one's knowledge of language. See also **competence.** 194

phatic communication Communication which contributes towards the establishment, maintenance, or dissolution of a community of communicators (of any size from pairs to the global community). . . 3

phonetics The study of the vocal tract, how it may be used in the production of speech sounds and the resulting acoustic effects. 198

phonology The study of the patterning of sounds in language. 198

Platonism The philosophy due to Plato: forms (here, especially mathematical forms) constitute an abstract realm of their own, independent of the world of particulars. Cognitive scientists' distinction between an abstract computational level and an implementational level echoes some of Plato's position. . . . 148

population The whole class of cases relevant to a statistical analysis, from which samples are drawn. 75

potential presuppositions 385

pragmatic maxims See **Gricean maxims**. 434

pragmatics The study of the influence of non-linguistic in-

formation, such as people's **beliefs** and **desires**, on the meaning conveyed in discourse. 333

predicate Used in school-style grammars to refer to what we call a verb phrase. . . . 227

predicate symbols In **predicate calculus**, a predicate symbol is a symbol which denotes a property, defined semantically by its extension set. e.g. The 'F' of 'Fa', which denotes the set of things in the domain that are F. If the thing denoted by "a" is in the set of things denoted by "F" then the sentence Fa is true. 234

premise An assumption which defines a proof. E.g. in the proof of $Q, (P \wedge Q) \Rightarrow R \vdash P \Rightarrow R$, Q and $(P \wedge Q) \Rightarrow R \vdash P \Rightarrow R$ are premises. . 119

prescriptive See **normative**. 192

presupposition Presuppositions are bits of content that are conveyed as if they were given information or mutually known by the speaker and hearer. The test for a presupposition is to negate the sentence, and examine whether the presupposition is still implied. 383

presupposition trigger Phrases

that introduce potential **pre-suppositions**. Some examples are *the, again, when, stop,* and *regret*. There are many more! 383

procedural knowledge Knowledge of how to do something e.g. prove a theorem or ride a bike. 111

productive When there is a particular phenomenon that applies to a large class of linguistic items, that phenomenon is known as productive. . 463

pronouns In English, the pronouns are *he, she, it, her, him, they, them, himself, herself, itself*. They refer by binding to descriptions of entities in the discourse context. . 339, 392

proof theory In logic, a system of rewrite rules which allow one to write a sequence of formulae, where the current formula is a consequence of the previous ones in the sequence. 126

proper name A name which may appear as a noun phrase on its own, typically referring to people, animals, countries, planets and so on. 224, 248

propositional calculus A simple logic which analyses arguments based on **logical con-nectives** but does not further analyse sentences or the propositions they express. It is also sometimes called propositional logic. 122

propositions The bearers of truth values in an interpreted language, generally corresponding to sentences that express them. 6, 123

proprioceptive Using an internal feedback mechanism. For example, when we speak, we make use of a system of nerves which tell us where our tongue is relative to the mouth as a whole. 144

prosodic Prosodic information is information about the 'tune' in speech; i.e. changes in pitch and intensity. 515

Q

qualia (Adapted from Gregory). Qualitative aspects of our perception, like the smell of ground coffee, or the thrill of a sunset. We can't easily describe what it's like to have such an experience, but we know what such experiences are like and we are relatively confident that our experience of them is not significantly different from how other humans experience them. 532

quantifier A quantifier in logic allows one to state that a particular statement is true for some individual (existential quantification) or for all individuals (universal quantification). The natural language correlate of this can be seen in **determiners**, e.g. *a, every.* 499

universal 501

quantization The action of dividing a continuous, **analogue** scale into a finite number of **discrete** steps. For example, a digital watch with a readout in hours and minutes quantizes time into 1440 discrete units. 19

R

random access memory A kind of computer memory in which all stored items can be accessed equally quickly. . 151

rationalist Rationalism is the idea that there exist absolute systems of, for example, logic or grammar, that are distinct from humans' use of such systems. 315

receiver A component in Shannon and Weaver's model of communication. 19

recursive definition A particu-lar kind of definition which involves the use of a concept in its own definition, but in a way which does not lead to regress. For example, an even number is either 2, or a number attained by adding an even number to 2, but no other number. 122, 227

reduction The action of explaining a phenomena in simpler terms. We maintain here an "antireductionist" stance, which says that not all cognitive phenomena can be insightfully explained in terms, say, of the physical state of the brain. 23

redundancy In **information theory**, a message contains redundancy if part of the message can be obliterated or altered, but the original message can still be recovered. . . 22

referring In contrast to artificial cases (e.g. programming languages), sentences in human languages often refer to individuals "in the world". 217

reflexive pronoun The pronouns *himself, herself* and *itself.* 542

representativeness The degree to which a sample from a population accurately reflects the properties of that population. 75, 79, 82

resonance Physical systems vibrate with a natural resonant frequency. 5

responses In a **behaviourist** psychological model, the mechanical reaction provoked by some **stimulus**. 153

rewriting The act of replacing one symbol with a sequence of other symbols. In this context, the act of replacing a label for a syntactic categories with its constituents. 226

rhetorical connections Links between sentences in a text or dialogue; e.g. elaboration, explanation, and contrast.   377

robust

> 1. In logic, a conditional is interpreted robustly if it may remain true despite some exceptions. See also **brittle**.

> 2. In natural language processing, robust NLP is a system which degrades gracefully in the face of ungrammatical or ill-formed linguistic expressions.
> 44

root See **tree**. 226

S

scenario In this context a hypothesis that might account for the descriptions in one of Tversky's experiments. . 80, 84

scope Cf. *Every man loves a woman*. According to the order in which the semantic rules for *every* and *a* are applied, the corresponding quantifiers receive different "scopes." In one case (the one in which there is at least one woman for every man), the semantic representation of *a* appears within one of the smaller boxes. In the jargon, *every* takes scope over *a*. In the case where there's a single woman that all men love, the semantic representation of *a* takes place first; *a* then takes scope over *every*. See also **quantifier**. 366

selection task A task due to Peter Wason in which subjects have to select cases to decide whether a rule is true. . . 28

self-consistency A property of a representation system whereby it cannot express inconsistent specifications. 511

semantic To do with **meaning**.
. . . . 120

semantic content The semantic content of a sentence is its **meaning**. 393

sender A component in Shannon and Weaver's model of communication. 19

sense ambiguity An ambiguity where a word or phrase has more than one meaning; e.g. *bank* can mean "financial institution" or "river bank." 283

sequence A token sequence is a particular concrete sequence of events, whereas a type of sequence is a kind of sequence e.g. a sequence of six tosses containing at least three heads. 75

serial Of a computational model, able to operate on only one task at any one time. See also **parallel computation**. 304

signal A component in Shannon and Weaver's model of communication. 19

signal detection theory A statistical method of analysing repeated attempts to detect perceptual targets, in which false positives and false negatives are counted and used to calculate a measure of discriminability, and a bias in favour of error-type. . . . 80

skeptical A skeptical attitude toward understanding a discourse seeks counterexamples in some possible interpretation of the speaker's utterances. See also **credulous**. 138

socratic tutoring A method of teaching by asking students questions which lead them to discovery. 52

sound See **soundness**. . . 127

soundness A metaproperty of a logical system, that no false conclusion can be derived within the system from true premises. 127

source premise The **premise** of a **syllogism**, if any, which establishes the existence of the fully-specified kind of individual whose existence justifies a valid conclusion. 501

stimulus A psychological concept: the information which the environment (often dominated by the experimenter) presents to an animal, and to which the animal responds. 153

structure As the term is used here, this refers to a property of **discourse representation structures**. The structure of a **discourse representation structure** is the configuration of boxes inside boxes. 203, 363

subject

1. the observed participant in a psychological experiment.

2. a noun phrase appearing immediately within a sentence.
.... 27, 227

supervised learning Learning in which the learner receives feedback about the correctness of judgements during the course of learning. 451

syllogism A fragment of logic, where each inference pattern consists of two premises and one conclusion. The premises relate A and B, and B and C, respectively. The conclusion relates A and C. .. 498

synapse A part of the brain. 151

syntactic form The way that the words group together in a sentence to form larger constituents. See also **trees** and **constituency**. 337

syntactic rules Rules which state **order** and **constituency**. 223

T

tape A component of a Turing machine. 149

tense The form of a verb indicating whether the event described happens in the past, present or future. 274

terminal symbols A vocabulary item which can appear in a sentence output by a grammar (as opposed to an **nonterminal symbol** which only appears in the generation of a sentence at stages prior to its completion). 203

theorem provers Systems which automatically perform inferences over premises. .. 432

thought experiment An experiment which can be done purely with thought, rather than in a laboratory. .. 532

tit-for-tat strategy A strategy in a game which requires cooperation, whereby a player cooperates unless the other player failed to cooperate on the previous play. 104

top-down Operating in terms of knowledge about a domain, rather than the features present in some input to a process. "Find a sentence" is a top-down instruction. See also **bottom-up** 303

truth One of the truth values which sentences can have, the other main one being falsity, although in some logic there are other values such as "undefined." Truth is the "designated truth value," which means that it is the value that must be maintained from premises to conclusion in valid proofs. 119

truth function A function that maps the truth values of the clauses of a complex sentence onto the truth value of the whole e.g. negation is a truth function that maps a true component sentence P onto its false negation $\neg P$. . 123

truth functional An expression is truth functional if its semantics can be described with a truth function. 44

truth tables A method for specifying the meanings of complex expressions in terms of the truth values of its parts. See also **truth-conditional semantics**. 123

Turing machine An abstract machine which performs computations. 149, 150

Turing test The idea that a system should be deemed intelligent if its performance on some task is indistinguishable from human performance. 528

U

underspecified When the grammar fails to fully determine the meaning of an expression—e.g. the gender of a noun—its analysis is said to be underspecified. 347

ungrammatical The syntactic property of strings of words that are not sentences of the language in question. . . 120

universal machine A Turing machine which can emulate any other Turing machine by encoding it on its tape. 150

utterance An utterance is the event of speaking a sentence or sequence of sentences. Utterances are then particular, concrete events. . . 193, 335

V

validity Validity is a logical property of arguments or proofs. In classical logic, a conclusion is valid if and only if it is true in all interpretations in which the premises are true. In default logic, a conclusion is true if and only if it is true in all *preferred* interpretations of the premises (in a technical sense of "preferred"). . 119

variable A logical variable is a term which is bound by a quantifier and ranges over some set of entities. The quantifier sets a criterion for how many of the entities are relevant; e.g. in the formula $\exists(Fx \wedge Gx)$, the existential quantifier stipulates that at least one entity corresponding to the variable x must have both the properties F and G. .. 120

Venn Diagrams A graphical representation scheme that is similar to **Euler's circles**. 507

verb A syntactic **category**. 224

verb phrase A syntactic **category** representing a **phrase** containing a verb. 124

verification Attempting to prove a hypothesis by finding examples for which the hypothesis is true. See also **falsification**. 41

voicing The production of a musical pitch by exciting the vocal cords. English uses voicing to distinguish the s and z sounds in "sip" and "zip." 19

well-formed Conforming to rules that define possible **form**s. Our **syntactic rules** define well-formedness for our grammar of English. 120

words In a computing context (i.e. the organization of computer data), a word is the next level of organization up from a **bit**. Computers commonly use "8-bit words." In linguistics, a word is the smallest unit of linguistic structure with meaning. 21, 233

world knowledge Knowledge we have about the world. This includes facts, rules, generalizations, and likelihoods of things happening. 372

Z

zombie An organism able to act, but without the same kind of mental life we sense in ourselves. 529

W

Index